A PILLAR OF THE CONSTITUTION

A PILLAR OF
THE CONSTITUTION

THE HOUSE OF LORDS
IN BRITISH POLITICS, 1640 – 1784

EDITED BY
CLYVE JONES

THE HAMBLEDON PRESS
LONDON   AND   RONCEVERTE

Published by The Hambledon Press, 1989

102 Gloucester Avenue, London NW1 8HX (U.K.)

309 Greenbrier Avenue, Ronceverte WV 24970 (U.S.A.)

ISBN 1 85285 007 8

FOR DAVID IN FRIENDSHIP

British Library Cataloguing in Publication Data

A Pillar of the constitution: the House of Lords in
British politics, 1640-1784
1. Great Britain. Parliament. House of Lords, 1640-1784
I. Jones, Clyve
328. 41 '071'09

Library of Congress Cataloging-in-Publication Data

Includes bibliographies and index
1. Great Britain. Parliament. House of Lords — History —
17th century
2. Great Britain. Parliament. House of Lords — History —
18th century
3. Great Britain — Politics and government — 1603-1714
4. Great Britain — Politics and government — 1714-1820
I. Jones, Clyve, 1944-
JN621.P53 1989 328.41'071'09 88-37274

Printed and bound in Great Britain by
The Camelot Press, Southampton

Contents

Preface

The pendulum of historical research is now definitely moving the House of Lords' way. This is as a result not only of a reaction within the study of British history generally, but also of a more specific reaction within the study of parlimentary history. There has recently been a move away, or at least a call for such a move, from research into radical minorities within society to a study of elites, and how such elites wielded the political and social power which was theirs by definition.[1] 'It is now taken for granted', writes F.M.L. Thompson, 'that at least until 1914 the English landed aristocracy was the dominant group in society and politics. Twenty or thirty years ago, however, this was a startling and controversial proposition that flew in the face of the Marxist orthodoxy of the triumph of industrial capitalism and of the liberal orthodoxy of the triumph of individualism and parliamentary democracy'.[2] Within parliamentary history there has been a move from the antics of the radical minorities in the Commons to a study of the peerage and its political functions both at the local level and at Westminster. This latter refocusing of the historical perspective is something of a reaction to the myopic concentration of parliamentary historians in the twentieth century on the lower House.[3] This received an official imprimatur with the establishment in 1951 of *The History of Parliament*. Though it had been planned in the 1930s to include the Lords and in 1951 it was announced that the upper House would form part of the project,[4] the first three volumes published laid the foundations for a concentration on the Commons which the editors claimed had been established as a principle

[1] Such a call has come from, amongst others, Mark Kishlansky ('Desert Island Radicals', *Times Literary Supplement,* 7 Sept. 1984, p. 16), Linda Colley ('The Politics of Eighteenth-Century British History', *Journal of British Studies*, XXV [1986], 372), and Jonathan Clark (*Revolution and Rebellion: State and Society in England in the Seventeenth and Eighteenth Centuries* [Cambridge, 1986], p. 91).

[2] 'F.M.L. Thompson Looks at the Long Run of the English Aristocracy', *London Review of Books*, 19 Feb. 1987, p. 6.

[3] This continues to be the case. John Millar in his 'Charles II and his Parliaments', *Transactions of the Royal Historical Society*, XXXII (1982), 1-23 ignores the Lords during the very decades when modern historiography has most neglected the House.

[4] Review by Herbert Butterfield, *E.H.R.*, LXXX (1965), 802.

as early as 1929.[5] This has remained the guiding principle ever since and there is no sign of the project moving to include the Lords. Thus all the research on the second pillar of the parliamentary triumvirate has received no official backing from Parliament itself.[6]

The nineteenth-century Whiggish notion (perpetuated by Namier in this century)[7] that the Commons was the principal vehicle of constitutional progress, which has so dominated parliamentary historiography, was begun to be challenged by modern work on the upper House before the First World War. The work of C.H. Firth on the Civil War Lords (1910) and of A.S. Turberville on the House from the Restoration to the early nineteenth century (published between 1913 and 1958) are the modern beginnings of a serious study of the upper chamber. The 1920s saw the publication in America by Frances H. Relf of the debates in the Lords in the 1620s, and a tradition of fine editions of primary source material has continued from that country with the work, above all, of Elizabeth Read Foster, who in 1983 produced the definitive work on the procedure and working of the early Stuart Lords.[8] Sadly there has been little published to date on the politics of the House in the seventeenth century as a whole. The historiography of the eighteenth-century House, however, received a much needed fillip in the 1960s by a seminal article by David Large (published in 1963) on the rise of parties between 1783 and 1837,[9] and by a very important chapter on the parties in the Lords by Geoffrey Holmes in his *British Politics in the Age of Anne* published in 1967.[10] It would be no exaggeration to credit the recent expansion of research and publication on the Lords in the period 1660 to 1832 to these two authors, who revealed that not only were there questions of interpretation to be solved but that a much needed narrative and analysis of the workings of the House of Lords was needed. Several authors have responded to the call with Michael McCahill leading the way with several articles and the only book (so far) on the Lords in the

[5] Sir Lewis Namier and J. Brooke, *The House of Commons, 1754-1790* (3 vols., 1964), p. v, see also p. xiii.

[6] For a bibliography of works on the Lords published between 1900 and 1985 see *Peers, Politics and Power: The House of Lords, 1603-1911*. ed. C. Jones and D.L. Jones (1986), pp. xvii-xxix. Full details of works cited below may be found there.

[7] See W.C. Lowe, 'Bishops and Scottish Representative Peers in the House of Lords, 1760-1775', *Journal of British Studies*, XVIII (1978), 86. According to Linda Colley, Namier's 'belief that the House of Commons was uniquely a "microcosmos of the British political nation" explains why the so-called History of Parliament Trust still ignores the House of Lords': 'A Talented Past', *London Review of Books*, 23 April 1987, p. 7.

[8] *The House of Lords, 1603-1649: Structure, Procedure and the Nature of its Business* (Chapel Hill, N.C., 1983).

[9] 'The Decline of "the Party of the Crown" and the Rise of Parties in the House of Lords, 1783-1837', *E.H.R.*, LXXVIII (1963), 669-95.

[10] A Revised Edition was published by Hambledon Press in 1987.

eighteenth century to appear since the work of Turberville.[11] Other work of note has come from G.M. Ditchfield, Clyve Jones, and W.C. Lowe.

Much of the recent work on the Lords has been collected together and republished as *Peers, Politics and Power: The House of Lords, 1603-1911*, edited by C. Jones and D.L. Jones (Hambledon Press, 1986). The idea for the present collection of essays arose while preparing that volume of reprinted articles and has been designed, in part, as a companion volume providing a forum for new research and to fill some of the more obvious gaps, both chronological and thematic, revealed by *Peers, Politics and Power*. The present volume has a shorter time span than the previous one, covering only the last 60 years of the seventeenth and the first two thirds of the eighteenth centuries. The reason for this was strictly practical – most of the new work on the Lords available for publication is on this period. The cut-off date of 1784 is, however, not an arbitrary one. Besides being the date of a major general election, it also represents the beginning of William Pitt the Younger's firm grasp on the administration. The year also saw the beginning of the rapid expansion of the membership of the Lords by Pitt's creation of peers at a rate never seen since the early Stuarts, an expansion which was to alter the character of the peerage and the House of Lords.

The editor would like to thank the authors for their co-operation and Alasdair Hawkyard for compiling the index.

September 1988   C.J.

---

[11] *Order and Equipoise: The Peerage and the House of Lords, 1783-1806* (1978).

List of Contributors

J.S.A. Adamson is a Fellow of Peterhouse, Cambridge.

J.V. Beckett is a Reader in History at the University of Nottingham.

Jeremy Black is a Lecturer in History at the University of Durham.

G.M. Ditchfield is a Lecturer in History at the University of Kent at Canterbury.

Clyve Jones is an Assistant Librarian at the Institute of Historical Research, University of London.

Michael W. McCahill is the Dean of the Faculty at Brooks School, North Andover, Massachusetts.

Andrew Swatland is a teacher in Croydon.

Stephen Taylor, formerly a Fellow of Jesus College, Cambridge, is a Lecturer in History at the University of Reading.

Abbreviations

B.L.	British Library
B.I.H.R.	*Bulletin of the Institute of Historical Research*
Bodl.	Bodleian Library, Oxford
C.J.	*Commons Journal*
Cobbett, *Parl. Hist*	*Cobbett's Parliamentary History of England . . . 1066 to . . . 1803*, ed. W. Cobbett (36 vols., 1806-20)
C.S.P.Dom.	*Calendar of State Papers Domestic*
C.S.P.Ven.	*Calendar of State Papers Venetian*
D.N.B.	*Dictionary of National Biography* (63 vols., 1885-1901)
E.H.R.	*English Historical Review*
G.E.C., *Complete Peerage*	G.E.C[ockayne], *The Complete Peerage* (13 vols., 1910-59)
H.L.R.O.	House of Lords Record Office
H.M.C.	Historical Manuscripts Commission
L.J.	*Lords Journals*
P.R.O.	Public Record Office, London
R.O.	Record Office
Soc.	Society
S.R.O.	Scottish Record Office, Edinburgh
U.L.	University Library

Note: Place of publication is London unless otherwise stated.

Chapter 1

Introduction: The Peerage and the House of Lords in the Seventeenth and Eighteenth Centuries

J.V. Beckett and Clyve Jones

1

Few of those who witnessed the abolition of the House of Lords in 1649 would have been willing to lay heavy odds that it would have a significant role in the British constitution more than three centuries later. On the eve of the Civil War the peers, as a group, were in financial difficulties; and the abolition of the House may have been at least partly inspired by the fact that much of its credibility had been lost with attendance having dwindled to a point at which it was unusual for more than half a dozen peers to be in the chamber.[1] In the years which followed, sequestration of estates appears to have damaged the peers interests even further, but all was far from lost. In 1660 the House was restored – though its revival remained in the balance until the last moment – and the Earl of Clarendon expected that their lordships would 'easily recover that estimation and reverence that is due to your high condition'.[2] In fact, the peers recovered remarkably quickly from the difficult days of the 1640s and 1650s, perhaps because, as recent research has revealed, the depredations of these years were less damaging to the fortunes of the greater royalists than has often been supposed. Politically the peers also bounced back in 1660. The upper House was arguably stronger after 1660 than before 1649, since the abolition of Star Chamber permitted the House to resume its position as the supreme court of appeal.

Throughout the century and a half which followed the Restoration contemporaries saw the Lords as the most important of the two Houses of Parliament, although historians have tended to concentrate attention disproportionately upon the Commons. Perhaps this is because the peers failed to re-establish a claim to arbitrate in financial and taxation matters, but there is little doubt that the House of Lords increased its prestige as the result of annual and longer Parliaments after 1689, while the peers gained a boost to their reputation from the role they took in the 1688

[1] J. Cannon, 'The Isthmus Repaired: The Resurgence of the English Aristocracy, 1660-1760', *Proceedings of the British Academy*, for 1982 LXVIII (1983), 432-4.

[2] Anon., *The Antient Land-Mark Skreen or Bank betwixt the Prince or Supreme Magistrate* (1659); *L. J.*, XI, 238.

revolution and the parliamentary settlement of 1689. By opposing an arbitrary monarch the peers were able to claim they had saved the country from popery and despotism. Even so, while individual peers held, and indeed often dominated high office (the Privy Council in the seventeenth century, the Cabinet in the eighteenth century), as a body the upper House fell prey to party appointments and control, and in the longer term this reduced its effectiveness as an independent chamber. This slide began in Queen Anne's reign and was pressed further by Walpole, until by the middle of the eighteenth century the political independence of the Lords was in some doubt.[3]

The apparent erosion of power needs to be kept in perspective. Peers filled the great offices of state, and gained considerable control over borough seats in elections to the Commons. They continued to exercise power in local government, in the army and the civil service, and through the control they enjoyed over the Church. Even within the upper House they had a significant function to play either in promoting and defending issues of national importance with a bearing on their own localities, or through introducing local legislation. Between 1787 and 1806 peers were the principal petitioners in 15 of the 58 enclosure bills presented from Nottinghamshire.[4] And in the final resort, while it was the owners of the great landed houses which might dominate the Cabinet, and whose growing wealth appears to have put them on a pedestal, quite apart from bringing them promotion within the ranks, the stratification within the peerage was rather more important outside the House than within its walls where the humblest baron's vote counted just as much as the Duke of Newcastle's. Who were these humble barons and worthy dukes?

Membership of the House was limited to the male heads of families who had been granted a peerage within the English (or from 1707 the British) peerages,[5] the 26 Church of England bishops (who were lords of Parliament), and, from the time of the Anglo–Scottish Union in 1707, 16 peers elected as representatives of the Scottish peerage. Occasionally

[3] J.V. Beckett, *The Aristocracy in England, 1660-1914* (Oxford, 1986), pp. 403-35; C. Jones, 'The House of Lords and the Growth of Parliamentary Stability, 1701-1742', in *Britain in the First Age of Party, 1680-1750: Essays Presented to Geoffrey Holmes*, ed. C. Jones (1987), pp. 85-110.

[4] M.W. McCahill, *Order and Equipoise: The Peerage and the House of Lords, 1783-1806* (1978); *idem*, 'Peers, Patronage and the Industrial Revolution, 1760-1800', *Journal of British Studies*, XVI (1976), 84-107; J. Cannon, *Aristocratic Century: The Peerage of Eighteenth-Century England* (Cambridge, 1984), chap. 4.

[5] At the Anglo-Scottish Union in 1707 the English and Scottish peerages were 'frozen' and any creations from that date were in the new British peerage. It is essential to keep this distinction clear for it had important implications for the Scottish peerage (see below pp. 85-6). Contemporaries often failed to make such a distinction referring to all non-Scottish peerages as English. Some modern historians have also fallen into error on this point.

numbers in the House were supplemented by calling up eldest sons of English and British peers in their lifetime – an event which occurred on 18 occasions during the eighteenth century,[6] On the other hand numbers were depleted by the fact that at any given time a number of peerage houses were in minority or headed by a female, while Roman Catholic families were automatically excluded. In the course of the eighteenth century 49 females held peerages in their own right, but wielded little political influence; 60 or more peers were Catholics, a handful were lunatics, and a number of others failed to attend the House through impecunity or ill health. Consequently a simple count of English and British peerages, and an addition of 42 for the bishops and the Scottish peers provides only a rough guide to the number of members of the House, though there is no doubt that it did become more populous as time went by. In 1600 a maximum turnout would have seen less than 100 members in the chamber, but this rose to about 150 after the Restoration, to about 220 before William Pitt expanded the British peerage in the closing decades of the eighteenth century, and to slightly more than 300 by the opening of the nineteenth century. This number was in turn supplemented in the wake of the 1801 Anglo-Irish Union by the admission of 28 Irish representative peers elected for life and four Irish bishops sitting in annual rotation.

2

Any male holding a title within the English, or from 1707 British peerage was automatically entitled to a seat in the upper House (except for Scottish peers with British titles between 1712 and 1782). This privilege was obtained either by letters patent or by the receipt of a writ of summons. In the sixteenth century the legal definition hardened so that writs of summons became inalienable hereditary rights, and by 1603 no one can have entertained any serious doubts about the identity of English peers of the realm. All dukes – the title was usually reserved for royalty until the early seventeenth century – marquesses, earls, viscounts and barons who were the head of their particular family were entitled to a seat in the Lords. Although the eldest sons of dukes, marquesses and earls held courtesy titles – the Earl of Kingston's heir, for example, was known as Viscount Newark – they had no right to a seat in the Lords, although they were permitted to stand for election to the Commons during their father's lifetime (a privilege denied to Scottish peers and their eldest sons after 1707). This was why Lord North sat in the Commons throughout his years as prime minister 1770-82; it was only in 1790, long after his active days as a politician had come to an end, that North succeeded his father, the first Earl of Guilford, and so became

---

[6] Cannon, *Aristocratic Century*, p. 13.

entitled to a seat in the upper House.

In quantative terms the English/British peerage grew substantially during the seventeenth and eighteenth centuries. As a result of Elizabeth I's parsimony with titles, at her death in 1603 there were only 55 male peers of the realm. According to Lawrence Stone she deliberately intended 'to maintain the peerage as a caste for men of ancient lineage',[7] with the result that by 1603 only 18 per cent of peers were in the first or second generation.[8] From the execution of the Duke of Norfolk in 1572, until 1623, there were no English dukes,[9] and well over half the peers in 1603 were barons, still sitting on the lowest rung of the ladder. Under these circumstances it is hardly surprising that James I found himself overwhelmed by a tide of demand for new creations which had been dammed up for the past 20 years. There was undoubtedly an urgent need to admit new blood in order to maintain the close relationship of title to landed wealth, and James I's reputation for liberality with titles in Scotland ensured that he was inundated with requests. Most of the creations and promotions of the early years of his reign were unexceptionable in view of the rise of new families, though the acceptance of favours, which eventually turned into the sale of titles, was a less welcome side to this change of policy. Even so, down to 1615 hardly anyone was admitted to the peerage who lacked social acceptability in terms of birth and wealth,[10] Thereafter the situation began to deteriorate; titles were sold for cash by the Crown, and nominations were given to courtiers as rewards for service. From 81 in 1615 the peerage expanded to 104 in 1625 and to 126 in 1628, largely through 35 earldoms and eight viscounties, as well as the controversial dukedom of Buckingham awarded to the King's favourite, George Villiers. The great sale came to an end in 1630 when Charles I resolved to end this unseemly scramble, but between them the first two Stuarts created a total of 121 peers, which, allowing for 38 extinctions, produced a net gain of 83 titles. Between 1603 and 1642 the peerage had doubled in size.[11]

By the time Charles II was restored to the throne in 1660 there were about 120 English peers. As in 1603, however, there was considerable clamour for promotion, resulting both from the blockage of the previous 20 years, and from the demand for rewards for loyalty to the new King during his years of exile. By 1682 the peerage numbered 159, and this

---

[7] L. Stone, *The Crisis of the Aristocracy* (Oxford, 1965), pp. 97-9.

[8] D. Palliser, *The Age of Elizabeth* (1983), p. 68.

[9] H. Pirie-Gordon and A.H. Doubleday, 'The Ducal Title in the British Isles', in G.E.C., *Complete Peerage*, VIII, 721.

[10] Stone, *Crisis of the Aristocracy*, pp. 100-103.

[11] *Ibid.*, pp. 170, 758. Peerage figures given here and in Clyve Jones's essay below, pp. 79-112, do not always agree. Some of the problems of counting numbers are outlined in Beckett, *Aristocracy in England*, pp. 26-40, 482-95.

figure would have been higher but for a level of extinctions running at nearly 59 per cent.[12] Charles II was particularly profligate with the previously highly exclusive dukedom, largely to find appropriate titles for his many bastard sons. William III created 27 peers, called six sons of existing peers to the House in their father's lifetime, and made 16 promotions. Many of these honours were distributed in two groups, the first during the spring of 1689 and the second in the spring of 1694, and among the recipients were a number of prominent activists in the events of 1688/89 Revolution, various commoners who had served in major ministerial posts, and five of William's foreign servants. The latter, all men of social standing in Holland and Germany, aroused some antipathy among the xenophobic English.[13]

By 1700 the peerage numbered about 170 but it grew only slowly under the Hanoverians to around 180 by 1780.[14] During Queen Anne's reign the most controversial incident was the decision in 1711-12 to elevate 12 men to the peerage to save the ministry of Robert Harley, Earl of Oxford, an action regarded by many as unconstitutional.[15] The arrival of the Hanoverians in 1714 ushered in a period of 60 years reminiscent of the Tudor century. George I created 20 new peers between 1714 and 1718, another monarch rewarding loyal supporters, but thereafter the rate of creation slowed down markedly, particularly under George II, who was reluctant to make any creations at all, and during the first 20 years of his grandson's reign. The result was that although the celebrated Peerage Bill failed,[16] the Hanoverians acted between 1719 and the early 1780s as if it had passed. Despite a significant fall in the extinction rate numbers had changed hardly at all by 1780, but, as the result of a change in government policy after 1784, the peerage expanded to reach 267 by 1800, a rise of more than 40 per cent over the previous two decades.

Perhaps most significant of all is that the peerage could not be described as long-lived. In 1700 38 per cent of the group held peerages which had been in existence less than 20 years, and 82 per cent were of seventeenth century origin. By 1800 only 6.2 per cent of peerages pre-dated 1600. Too much should not be read into this figure, since although it points to the high rate of extinction among peerage families, it does not imply a rapid increase in new blood from trade, industry and the professions; rather, almost all entrants were connected (and usually closely connected) to existing peerage families. In the course of the

[12] Cannon, 'Isthmus Repaired', p. 436.

[13] H. Horwitz, *Parliament, Policy and Politics in the Reign of William III* (Manchester, 1977), p. 311; see also p. 84 below.

[14] Beckett, *Aristocracy in England*, pp. 486-7; Cannon, 'Isthmus Repaired', p. 436.

[15] Anon, *Reflections on a Paper lately Printed, Entitled, A Letter to Sir Miles Wharton, concerning Occasional Peers: Address'd to the Guardian and Examiner* (1713). See also below pp. 91-2, 94.

[16] See chapter 4, below.

eighteenth century just ten per cent of new creations involved men without previous direct peerage connections.[17] George I was extremely careful, making sure that higher titles were effectively reserved for existing peers receiving promotion, and continuing the long-standing policy of admitting newcomers only to the lower titles of viscount and baron. Similar care was exercised by George II, and in the early years of his reign by George III, while even when the peerage was opened up from 1784 the majority of entrants already had close links with the group.

Normally individuals were admitted to the peerage at the lowest level and consequently at any given time the monarch was likely to be receiving requests both for the grant of a peerage and also for promotion within the ranks. However, neither admission nor promotion could be earned in the sense that a man might negotiate a series of hurdles as a result of which he was automatically entitled to some honour. Since the grant was entirely due to royal favour the best that individuals in search of a peerage could hope for was to create the right conditions, and then to hope the Crown would take notice. Even though it was possible to drop hints in the right direction, it must have been galling to some families who found themselves overtaken by an upstart who had gained the ear of the King. This was particularly likely between 1615 and 1630 when hard financial bargaining was the route many men pursued to a peerage. In 1624 John Holles attempted to hide the fact that he was about to buy an earldom by seeking preferment to the Council of War, as 'some excuse unto the world . . . why his Majesty should receive him unto this honour'. A few paid directly into the Treasury, including the Earl of Devonshire (£8,000) and the Earl of Warwick (£10,000) in 1618-19, but most found a more roundabout method of purchase. After 1624 the commonest means of acquiring a peerage was to make a payment to the Duke of Buckingham or his relatives. After Buckingham's death Charles I revived the practice of sale briefly in the 1640s,[18] but thereafter peerages were awarded only to families who satisfied unwritten but important criteria. Of these perhaps the most crucial was patience, since it often took several generations of careful planning to aspire to a title. For the King and ministers keeping families in suspense had the added effect of ensuring political loyalty.

The first and essential qualification for peerage status was land. Without a substantial landed estate no individual could hope for a peerage. Landownership was an essential guarantee of standing within the community, it provided the solid basis which enabled a man to take an independent standing in the community, and it ensured that an individual was able to afford the lifestyle which went with a title. On the

[17] Cannon, *Aristocratic Century*, pp. 15-26.
[18] Stone, *Crisis of the Aristrocracy*, pp. 105-19.

other hand it was never the case that families able to show a particularly large rent roll automatically qualified. Even in 1641 when the peerage had been expanded to take in 121 families, another 30–40 gentry families were at least as rich as many of those at the bottom end of the group.[19] This proportion probably did not change very much through time. Rank was also reflected in wealth. In the early seventeenth century dukes, marquesses and earls were economically, politically and socially superior to viscounts and barons, thereby creating an important rift within the ranks of the peerage. In these circumstances it was normally the case that the higher the rank in the peerage the greater the landed estate, hence the titles bestowed on the Dukes of Bedford and Newcastle in the later seventeenth and early eighteenth centuries.

Land alone was no guarantee of admission and peerages were seldom, if ever, awarded to men without an established family line, often stretching back several generations. This was not an invariable rule. Many of James I's and Charles I's creations were men whose pedigree was thought to be less than perfect, but this was seldom the case in the later seventeenth and eighteenth centuries. Not surprisingly there were those who invented, or at least doctored their pedigrees, a practice against which Joseph Addison wrote in strong terms in 1714. Later in the century the Earl of Chesterfield ridiculed bogus pedigrees by incorporating Adam and Eve de Stanhope in his own.[20] The early Hanoverians were particularly anxious to establish the accuracy of a man's pedigree, even refusing grants to men with long service records in the state who they regarded as unqualified. When Nathaniel Curzon wanted his claim to a dormant peerage to be raised with George III in 1760 he sent along a pedigree drawn by the Somerset Herald.[21]

Land and pedigree were the two major qualifications for the peerage, but it helped to have had a respectable education, and to have married appropriately. Fathers took great care to ensure that their daughters were married into suitable families, and that their sons did not disgrace themselves with the choice of partner they (or their parents) selected. Newcomers to the peerage almost invariably intermarried with the group before they received the call; between 1600 and 1799, 59 per cent of peerage newcomers had married within the higher reaches of the English aristocracy. Political and state service also helped.[22] Seventeenth-century monarchs happily granted titles to their supporters, while the political peerage came of age when Queen Anne created twelve new peers in 1711–12 at the behest of her prime minister, the Earl of Oxford.

---

[19] *Ibid.*, p. 57.
[20] Joseph Addison, *The Spectator*, No. 612, 27 October 1714; *Horace Walpole's Correspondence*, ed. W.S. Lewis (48 vols, New Haven, 1937–83), XX, 181.
[21] *Correspondence of King George III*, ed. Sir John Fortescue (6 vols, 1927), I, 5, 12.
[22] Cannon, *Aristocratic Century*, pp. 80–92.

This particular case created a precedent, and thereafter potential applicants for the peerage were not afraid to couch their requests in party and political terms, pointing to their record of service in the House. Leading ministers usually received preferment. George II's only dukedom went to the existing Duke of Newcastle, a move designed to ensure the continuation of his title and rank despite the fact that he had no direct male heir. Among other leading politicians honoured during George II's reign were Walpole, created Earl of Orford in 1742, and William Pulteney. However, while Walpole was honoured for distinguished service, Pulteney's decision to accept the earldom of Bath, which was seen by many as effectively a gift from Walpole – his political opponent – ruined his prestige.[23] Finally, as good a way as any to ensure rapid elevation was through military service. For his role in the wars against Louis XIV's France in the early eighteenth century, Marlborough received a dukedom, together with a royal estate, a house, and a £5,000 state pension designed to enable him to live up to the position.

As a result of these qualifications for the peerage, the men who sat in the House of Lords were a social group with a recognizable internal stratification. They headed the most powerful landed houses in the state, and enjoyed extensive acres sometimes spread across several counties and including more than one country house. The wealthiest also enjoyed a lifestyle commensurate with their political and social position. Many enjoyed the luxury of a town house where they would spend several months of the year sampling the delights of the London 'season' while attending to parliamentary business. When at home in the country during the summer and early autumn they would look into estate business and engage themselves in their wider social role as the arbiters of local government and the guardians of the community. On the other hand to lump them altogether can also be misleading since the peerage was nothing if not varied.

A clear example of stratification is to be seen in terms of incomes. Lawrence Stone's estimates suggest a mean gross income for the peerage in 1602 of £3,360, or £2,930 net, rising to £6,030 gross and £5,040 net by 1641.[24] Comparative figures of a similar nature are difficult to calculate for later periods, and in any case they tend to hide the peaks and troughs. At the top were the men of wealth with estates scattered over many counties, and with several large mansions and extensive acreages. There were always a handful who stood out from the pack. In 1602 the Earl of Shrewsbury, with an income from land and industrial profits of £7,500, was probably the wealthiest of all the peers, with three others collecting gross rentals of between £5,400 and £7,199; but by 1641 there were 23

---

[23] *D.N.B.*
[24] Stone, *Crisis of the Aristocracy*, pp. 760-2.

peers with incomes from rent of £6,600 or more, the five most subtantial (with £13,000 or more) including the Percys, the Seymours and the earls of Devonshire. By 1683 rental receipts on the Earl of Rutland's estate totalled £14,482, while the Earl of Devonshire enjoyed an annual average income exceeding £17,000. On the Earl of Bedford's extensive estates in Bedfordshire and Buckinghamshire and lucrative properties in London, estate rental income was about £15,000 in 1692, while the Duke of Newcastle's various estates netted about £25,000 annually in the 1690s. By 1710 incomes in excess of £10,000 were regularly found among peers above the rank of baron. The dukes of Newcastle, Bedford, Beaufort, all had had more than £30,000 annually, while the dukes of Ormonde, Somerset and Devonshire, and Lord Brooke, had between £20,000 and £30,000. The Bedfords' rental, from only part of their estates, rose to £37,000 by 1739, and to £51,000 by 1771. The Devonshires' income reached £35,000 by 1764, and the earls of Warwick and Derby were also substantial figures by the middle decades of the eighteenth century. The latter were drawing over £47,000 from 32 different estates by the end of the century.[25]

These were the wealthiest, and beneath them the peers stretched downwards to a group of men with a few hundred acres and a single, not necessarily substantial house; some, indeed, who were almost impecunious. It was unusual for individuals to be elevated to positions higher than that of baron or viscount (though occasionally politicians broke this rule),[26] partly to ensure that no one rose too high without the financial means. Even in the late nineteenth century the three premier ranks tended to be peopled by men who were substantially wealthier than their lesser brethren, while a quarter of the largest landowners were untitled.[27] A few peers, for one reason or another, were not wealthy. At the same time the uniquely English system of primogeniture, which ensured that landed estates descended to the eldest son, and the fact that titles usually descended to the eldest male heir, helped to ensure that the Continental problem of noble poverty had no equivalent in England. Estates were generally held together in the male line with the current 'owner' holding the family title. This did not always ensure money and title matched; the 13th Lord Willoughby of Parham was reckoned to be worth no more than £100 a year in the later seventeenth century, and the 1st Earl of Warrington's decision to accept an earldom in 1690 was taken against family advice that with an income of little more than £2,000 a

---

[25] *Ibid.*; Beckett, *Aristocracy in England*, pp. 288-9; Cannon, *Aristocratic Century*, p. 146.

[26] The most spectacular exceptions were the four men who, in the seventeenth and early eighteenth centuries, became dukes; Buckingham (1623), Albermarle (1660), Leeds (1694) and Marlborough (1702).

[27] Beckett, *Aristocracy in England*, p. 44.

year he was in no position to cultivate the expected lifestyle.[28]

Such examples were not numerous, but at the bottom of the heap there were always a handful of peers whose financial position made them prey to political bribery. Peers received no financial remuneration for attendance at the House, and some undoubtedly preferred the delights of their country estates, particularly as this almost invariably involved less expenditure than spending the parliamentary session living in London. Since peers were entitled in certain circumstances to vote by proxy their political influence could be felt even if health, finance, or general preference, meant they stayed away from the House.[29] Poor lords were a common enough feature throughout the eighteenth century; between 1754 and 1762 the Duke of Newcastle is reputed to have distributed £50,000 to 16 poor lords, partly to ensure their political loyalty as well as to make sure they voted in the Lords.[30]

3

The second group in the House of Lords throughout the period were the 26 bishops of the Anglican Church who were not peers but lords of Parliament, and were the sole spiritual element after the expulsion of the abbots and priors at the Reformation. The two archbishops (Canterbury and York), and the 20 English and four Welsh bishops, all held seats by virtue of their Crown appointment. Although their positions were not

[28] J.V. Beckett and C. Jones, 'Financial Improvidence and Political Independence in the Early Eighteenth Century: George Booth, 2nd Earl of Warrrington', *Bulletin of the John Rylands University Library*, LXV (1982), 8-35; E. Gregg and C. Jones, 'Hanover, Pensions and the "Poor Lords", 1712-13', *Parliamentary History*, 1 (1982), 173-80.

[29] The use of proxy votes in the Lords, whereby a member could leave his vote with a fellow lord to be cast in his absence, was controlled by a series of rules (the standing orders of the House) and customs. These have been usefully summarised in *A Register of Parliamentary Lists 1660-1761*, edited by D. Hayton and C. Jones (University of Leicester Department of History Occasional Publication No. 1, 1979), pp. 9-10. The main ones were that proxies could not be used in any committees (even the Committee of the Whole House); no lord could (after 1626) hold more than two proxies; bishops could only hold those of other bishops and peers those of peers; and where a lord voted in person he was obliged to cast his proxy votes (if they were called for), though this did not always happen. The rules were sometimes changed; in 1689, for example, proxies were restricted in their use in judicial cases, and they were abolished altogether in such cases in 1697. By the end of the seventeenth century it was usual for proxy votes to be cast on the same side of the question as the holder of the proxy voted. There are exceptions to this custom; see *The London Diaries of William Nicolson, Bishop of Carlisle, 1702-1718*, ed. by C. Jones and G. Holmes (Oxford, 1985), pp. 606-7. Friction and political embarrassment often resulted when proxy holders disregarded the views of the lords whose proxy they held (see below p. 139). The practice of proxy voting was abandoned by a standing order of the Lords in 1868, having been last used in 1864: *L.J.*, C, 99; XCVI, 538.

[30] Sir Lewis Namier, *The Structure of Politics at the Accession of George III* (2nd edition, 1957), pp. 221-5.

hereditary, once appointed they were not subject to re-election, although in extreme cases they could be removed from their sees and likewise from the Lords; Thomas Watson of St. David's, for example, was dismissed in 1699 for simony and maladministration, while Francis Atterbury was removed from Rochester in 1723 for treason.[31] For the most part, once installed, a bishop remained a bishop, but age and infirmity often meant that their active role in political or parliamentary affairs could be curtailed. John Hough, Bishop of Worcester 1717-43, and the only bishop not to be promoted during Sir Robert Walpole's tenure of political power, did not attend Parliament for at least the last decade of his life.[32]

The fact that they were virtually irremovable placed the bishops theoretically above political pressure from the current administration, but in practice it was well understood that dissension from the ministry's political line could result in loss of promotion,[33] and translations were used by politicians to reward the favoured in the knowledge that few bishops could resist the lure of a richer and more prestigious see. This did not always work to the material benefit of the man involved, as Benjamin Hoadly found when in 1721 he was moved from one of the poorer Welsh sees to Hereford – his 'being Moved from Bangor is turn'd to a great Mortification', one contemporary wrote, 'for upon inquiry, he finds the Bishoprick he has to be worth less than Bangor, the late Bishop haveing leased out of the Bishoprick an estate of above four hundred pounds a year for one and twenty years to come, which it seems by some accident he had power to do'.[34] Fortunately for Hoadly this proved to be only a temporary setback, since he proceeded to make rapid progress up the ladder of preferment, via Salisbury, to Winchester in 1734. Winchester, together with Durham and London, made up the senior English bishoprics.

Although promotion was dangled like a carrot before politically loyal bishops, this did not necessarily create a pliant bench slavishly providing governments with a solid bloc of votes. There were many cases of individual opposition among the bishops, and not infrequent cases of mass revolt against government policies, particularly those perceived to be of an anti-clerical nature. The early seventeenth-century bishops faced a dichotomy between their position in society as religious leaders and as members of the political elite. The friction which this produced in the parliamentary arena led eventually to their removal from the Lords in

---

[31] Bishops could also be suspended from office, as was Abbot of Canterbury in 1627, for displeasing the King. He was later reprieved.
[32] Jones, 'The House of Lords', p. 94.
[33] See Benson of Gloucester's comments in 1736, in *ibid.*, p. 95.
[34] B.L., Add. MS. 61463, f. 177; Charlotte Clayton to the Duchess of Marlborough, 22 August 1721.

1642.[35] Although they returned with the restoration of the upper House in 1660, the bishops became increasingly the political pawns first of party and then of the Crown.

During the party struggles of Queen Anne's reign the bench was sharply divided, and the bishops were often found in the midst of the political fray.[36] With the change in the nature of the party system in the 1720s when the dominance of Walpole's administration led to the formation of something approaching a one-party state, the political role of the bishops altered. Stephen Taylor shows that they came to regard their position largely as one of support for the King's government, as the upholders of the Anglican supremacy, and only when these two roles deviated did their actions cause discomfort to the administration.[37] As a result, they acquired a reputation – unfairly as it turned out – of passivity towards the administration, and much of the animosity of the 1620s resurfaced in the years of Walpole's supremacy. Bishop Smalbroke, one of the few bishops in regular opposition by the end of Walpole's tenure of power,[38] was berated in 1738 for the 'badness of the morals and principles of the present times', being partly due to the bench of bishops 'who blindfold serve the Ministers views and schemes on every occasion, be they for the good of the public or not, or ever so scandalous'. Smalbroke confessed that 'there was some reason to complain of it', but in fact this was an exaggeration coming only two years after the defeat of the Quakers Tithe Bill largely at the hands of the bishops. Even in 1736, however, the Earl of Egmont had been prepared to suggest a revival of 1642 and the removal of the bishops 'out of the House of Lords'.[39] Others thought translations should be halted in an effort to make the bishops more independent of the administration, although this rather over-rated the role of patronage as a motive determining the bishops' actions.[40]

Much of this adverse criticism reflected the exaggerated idea of the role and numerical strength of the bishops in the Lords, which, as we shall see, also applied to the Scots. This kind of wishful thinking tended to originate among those who believed a cause they supported to have been damaged because of the actions of the bishops or the Scots. Bishop Atterbury provides a good example in his deliberations on the repeal of the Occasional Conformity and Schism Acts in 1718. The bill of repeal was carried by 18, of whom 11 were bishops, on 19 December. On 3 January 1719 Atterbury wrote to Bishop Ottley of St. David's:

[35] Unpublished paper by Esther Cope.
[36] G. Holmes, *British Politics in the Age of Anne* (1967), pp. 396-400.
[37] See below, pp. 137-63.
[38] See below, pp. 143-5, 151.
[39] H.M.C., *Egmont Diary*, II, 482, 270-1.
[40] See below, pp. 140-41; S.J.C. Taylor, 'Church and State in England in the Mid-Eighteenth Century: The Newcastle Years, 1742-1762' (Cambridge Ph.D., 1987), pp. 88-101.

had those 11 Bishops who voted for the Bill, voted against it, it had been thrown out by 4. Or had the Scots Lords (who with the Duke of Argyle were 17) been away, and Lord North been there (who was confined to his Bed by a Feaver) still the Bill had miscarried, though the 11 Bishops had voted for it.[41]

Atterbury was clearly a subscriber to the 'might-have-been' theory of history, but this kind of talk could have done little for the general reputation of the bishops even though it was a crucial religious issue in which they could be and were legitimately involved. Indeed, on the first day of the debate, the issue of repeal was left to be 'entirely taken up by the Bishops, and the Debate at 7 or 8 at night adjourned to the next day, which the Temporal Lords employed to the same cause to as late an hour'.[42]

The bishops of the mid to late eighteenth century have continued to suffer from a bad press for their supposed unquestioning support of the King's government. The bench, however, was by no means a solid ministerial phalanx. Bishops tended to speak only on matters touching the Church, and a surprisingly large number voted, at least occasionally, with the opposition. As the eighteenth century progressed, some bishops tended to follow the fortunes of relations or patrons among the politically active peerage, and from the mid-1760s each political group could look for support from its own episcopal group or bishop. The pattern appears to have changed again in the later 1760s and early 1770s, to one where the bishops offered increased support to ministries as they became more stable, although a small minority of bishops continued to vote with the opposition. On the other hand numerical support by the bishops for the ministry was poor; Lord North was not in the position of Walpole of being able to rely on most of his bishops most of the time.[43]

4

The Anglo-Scottish Union of 1707 threw a new and unpredictable element into the political arena at Westminster with the admission of 16 representative peers from north of the border. Although the union of the two crowns in 1603 had removed the ultimate source of patronage to London, and the more able and affluent members of the Scottish peerage began to drift south, the centre of Scottish parliamentary life remained in Edinburgh; indeed, after the Glorious Revolution the Scottish Parliament took on a new lease of life, and the management problems this posed contributed to the final parliamentary union of 1707.[44] Once

[41] National Library of Wales, Ottley MS, 1704.
[42] *Ibid.*
[43] W.C. Lowe, 'Bishops and the Scottish Representative Peers in the House of Lords, 1760-1775', *Journal of British Studies*, XVIII (1978), 87-97; see below, pp. 190-91, cf. pp. 217-20.
[44] D. Szechi and D. Hayton, 'John Bull's Other Kingdoms: The English Government of Scotland and Ireland', in *Britain in the First Age of Party*, pp. 250, 252-3.

parliamentary power and patronage were removed to Westminster the Scots found themselves entering what must have seemed like an alien political world, but one flowing with milk and honey for the politically ambitious with the determination to claim their share. Scottish peers rushed to be elected as one of 16 representatives allocated to the British House of Lords in the Act of Union. The steady drift south among the Scottish peerage during the seventeenth century, lured by the wealth of London and the social cachet of the Court, developed in the eighteenth century into what has been termed with some accuracy, the political diaspora of the Scottish ruling elite.[45]

There were about 135 Scottish peers in 1700, and in the race for the glittering prizes of patronage, office and money, which it was hoped would result from an elective seat in the Lords, a head start was given to those territorial magnates and clan chiefs who had dominated Scotland's near medieval political system before the Union. These political 'bosses' often had English, and specifically London connections which strengthened their hand in the chancy game of peerage elections in the early days of the Union. These blissful days of political freedom soon passed as the British ministry in London sought, and gained, control of the elections. After 1710 no Scot was elected as one of the 16 representatives unless he had been on the government's list. Even the power of the greatest magnate could not protect one of his clients, a point dramatically underscored by the failure of the Earl of Ilay, the Duke of Argyll's brother, to be re-elected in 1713 after deserting the Oxford ministry. Similarly, following the opposition to Walpole in the Lords during 1733-34 of the *Squadrone Volante*, a group of dissident Scottish Whigs, all its members were omitted from the ministry's list and failed to be re-elected in 1734. However, the government was not totally free to put any peer it wanted onto its list; it was bound by tradition to support where possible the great magnates, previous representative peers, and the candidates of important supporters.[46]

Almost inevitably the Scottish representative peers (together with the 45 M.P.s) were sucked into the British party system and lost all semblance of being the independent representatives of North Britain which the Act of Union had envisaged. In the early years of the eighteenth century the representatives rapidly became pawns, although they retained the capacity to turn and bite the hand that fed them if they feared Scottish interests were at risk. Generally those peers failing to support the ministry risked paying the ultimate price – a return ticket to

[45] K. Robbins, 'Core and Periphery in Modern British History', *Proceedings of the British Academy*, for 1984, LXX (1985), 278-80, 284.

[46] Jones, 'The House of Lords',p. 95; M.W. McCahill, 'The Scottish Peerage and the House of Lords in the Late Eighteenth Century', *Scottish Historical Review*, LI (1972), 180 n.5.

the mass of the Scottish peers who had no access to Westminster. In effect the Union had created a two tiered Scottish peerage; those who were elected to Westminster and those who were not. This duality cut across all other divisions within the Scottish peerage – status, rank, wealth, clientage – and on occasion some of the poorest were elected and some of the most prestigious left out in the cold.[47] In any case the Scottish representatives were generally poorer than the Englishmen they sat next to in the Lords: in 1710 only the Duke of Hamilton, with an income of about £9,000 annually, could boast more than £5,000 (which itself was a figure almost certainly below the average for English peers at that date) while at least seven of the 16 had incomes of £2,000 or less.[48]

From 1710 election as a representative peer depended on an individual's track record, though occasionally a peer with sufficient clout could force himself onto the list despite being not quite to the taste of the ministry.[49] Those excluded from Westminster resented the good fortune enjoyed by their brethren, and in the early years after the Union some of them sought redress by aiming at a British peerage which carried with it a seat in the Lords, just as English peerages before 1707 had done.[50] Both the Duke of Queensberry (in 1707), and the Duke of Hamilton (in 1711) gained British dukedoms, but these were unpopular promotions among the English peers. The venality of the Scots, and fears that the Lords would be swamped by a sea of British creations produced two House of Lords rulings which remained in force for 70 years to the dismay of the Scots. In 1709 Scottish peers with British titles were prohibited from voting for the 16 representatives, and – even more critically – two years later they were prevented from taking what they believed to be their rightful seats in the upper House. English peers with Scottish titles, and Scottish peers with English titles possessed both privileges, but an attempted revolt against these injustices failed in 1712, and the second ruling was reinforced by the 2nd Duke of Dover's case in 1720, which made the lot of the excluded Scots all the harder.[51]

[47] In 1711 Lord Home had to borrow £100 to attend the Lords: see Holmes, *British Politics*, p. 394. Scottish peers not elected accepted the two tier system partly because there was always the chance of their heirs being elected or gaining access to Westminster. Consequently they all (excluding the 16 representatives and the 9 others selected to be of the 25 hereditary peers) strongly opposed the Peerage Bill as it would have cut off this potential opening.
[48] D. Szechi, 'Some Insights on the Scottish M.P.s and Peers Returned in the 1710 Election', *Scottish Historical Review*, LX (1981), 62.
[49] For example, three Jacobites were returned in 1713; see C. Jones, '"The Scheme Lords, the Neccessitous Lords, and the Scots Lords": The Earl of Oxford's Management and the "Party of the Crown" in the House of Lords, 1711-14', in *Party and Management in Parliament, 1660-1784*, ed. C. Jones (Leicester, 1984), p. 132.
[50] The Duke of Argyll was created Earl of Greenwich in the English peerage in 1705 and sat in the Lords by that title after the Union.
[51] See below, pp. 103-4.

In an attempt to pacify the Scots the ministry made a number of offers up to – and including – the 1719 Peerage Bill, to convert the 16 elective peers into 25 hereditary ones.[52] Naturally these schemes were supported by those in line for one of the hereditary peerages, but bitterly opposed by most of those who expected to be excluded. Several attempts after 1719 to reintroduce the Scottish clauses of the bill foundered on resistance from north of the border and on English xenophobia. A small loophole in the Hamilton peerage resolution of 1711 was exploited by Lord Oxford in 1712 when he created his son-in-law, Lord Dupplin, a British peer with the title of Lord Hay. In 1719 Dupplin succeeded his father to the Scottish earldom of Kinnoull but continued to sit in the Lords, without objection, under his British title. Walpole took further advantage of this device in 1722 by creating British peerages for the heirs of the Dukes of Roxburghe and Montrose. The sons continued to sit in the Lords when they eventually succeeded to their dukedoms.[53] However, the loophole was employed sparingly, and the just grievance of the Scots was not rectified until 1782 when the Lords reversed the 1711 resolution and Scots with British titles were freely allowed to sit in the House of Lords. A consequence of this decision was that pressure mounted from the Scots to be awarded British peerages, pressure to which the government responded unenthusiastically.[54]

The second half of the eighteenth century witnessed both a change in attitude to the position of representative peers and in their role in the Lords. Until the 1760s being one of the 16 was much sought after as a passport to patronage. By the reign of George III a seat as a representative had come to be regarded more for the honour it bestowed than as a political duty with consequent rewards. This change of attitude meant that the Scots were no longer well integrated into partisan politics in the upper House, and they grew more independent of the 'party of the Crown' by comparision with their stand earlier in the century.[55] Some ministries, particularly the first Rockingham administration, had considerable trouble with the Scots, who sometimes proved to have diverse interests and an adventurous spirit in politics. By 1784 many of the Scots seem to have stopped thinking that election to the Lords was an honour, preferring to believe that representative peers 'suffer in reputation without gaining in consequence' by such elections. The increased wealth of the peers towards the end of the century, the

[52] See below, pp. 84–7.

[53] G. Holmes, 'The Hamilton Affair of 1711–12: A Crisis in Anglo-Scottish Relations', *E.H.R.* LXXVII (1962), 281.

[54] W.C. Lowe, 'Bishops and Scottish Representative Peers in the House of Lords, 1760–1775', *Journal of British Studies*, XVIII (1978), 102–3.

[55] *Ibid.*, pp. 104–5; McCahill, 'The Scottish Peerage', pp. 195–6; G.M. Ditchfield, 'The Scottish Representative Peers and Parliamentary Politics, 1787–1793', *Scottish Historical Review*, LX (1981), 20, 29.

increased capacity to acquire British peerage (and with them an automatic seat in the Lords), and the dwindling numbers of mere Scottish peers, all help to explain this change in attitude. On the other hand those peers who were elected displayed a spirit of independence which was ironic given that Scots with British titles (after the reversal of the House's ruling in 1782) were less independent in their relations with the ministry of the day than those who were elected.[56]

By the late eighteenth century the ministry were finding it increasingly difficult to control elections for the 16. There had been various abortive attempts at reform of the electoral system during the century, including efforts to escape from ministerial dominance. This campaign for independence grew in the 1770s and at the 1774 election two of the independent representative peers were elected, but with approval from the government in an attempt to weaken the independents' cause.[57] By 1784 12 of the representatives were government candidates, and in the 1790s the number fluctuated between nine and 13. In these years the government's 'henchman', Dundas (later Viscount Melville), was entrusted with the management of Scotland, and he had built up his own interest there. When he ceased to be a minister he used his interest against the new administration in 1806 and 1807 and secured the return of 15 of his friends in the latter election. The Scots had thus ceased to be part of the disintegrating 'party of the Crown', and eventually were subsumed into the new party system in the Lords.[58] In any case, in a House swollen with new British titles and 28 representative peers (and 4 bishops) from Ireland their voice sounded very much more faintly than it had in earlier generations.[59]

[56] Lowe, 'Bishops and Scottish Representative Peers', p. 101; McCahill, 'The Scottish Peerage', pp. 186, 176-7.

[57] Ditchfield, 'The Scottish Representative Peers', pp. 14–15; McCahill, 'The Scottish Peerage', p. 182.

[58] D. Large, 'The Decline of the "Party of the Crown" and the Rise of Parties in the House of Lords, 1783-1837', *E.H.R.*, LXXVIII (1963), 677-80.

[59] One irony of the way in which the Scottish peers were integrated into the Westminster system concerned the titles they used in the Lords. Unless they were one of the 16 representatives they could take a seat at Westminster only if they had an English, or British title in addition to their Scottish title (before 1712 and after 1782), but precedent demanded that they be known in the Lords not by their most prestigious title (of whatever creation, and the one by which they would normally be known to the outside world), but by the title which permitted them access to the Lords. Consequently the Duke of Argyll sat in the Lords from 1705 as the Earl of Greenwich. Although he received the dukedom of Greenwich in the British peerage in 1719, under the terms of the 1712 ruling on Scottish peers he continued to sit in the house under the title Earl of Greenwich. Three other Scottish dukes, Buccleuch, Montrose and Atholl, sat in the Lords as, respectively, the (English) Earl of Doncaster, the (British) Earl Graham and the (English) Baron Strange, which title was converted to an earldom in 1786.

5

In the Peerage Bill debate of 4 March 1719 Lord Stanhope pressed the case for the stabilizing of the membership of the House of Lords in terms of a balanced constitution. 'It was a constant rule in Government,' he avowed, 'to preserve an equal balance and due equilibrium between the several parts of it, that one might not outweigh the other.'[60] This post-Revolutionary view of the tripartite British constitution found almost universal acceptance. The 'founding fathers' of the 1689 settlement, while disposing of an over-mighty King, had established a 'parliamentary monarchy' in which Parliament, made up of King, Lords and Commons, was to remain the essential and abiding feature of government in Britain. In the seventeenth century, rule by one of the elements had been tried and found wanting. Charles I's 'personal rule' of 1629 to 1640 had foundered on the need to call Parliament to provide finance for his Scottish war. Although two parts of the parliamentary triumvirate (Lords and Commons) had won the Civil War against the third (the King), the Lords had been abolished in 1649, and the unicameral experiment with the Commons from 1649 to 1653 failed to re-establish secure government. The various parliamentary experiments of the Lord Protector led to the creation of an 'Other House' of nominated lords, but this tripartite government did not represent the true social and political interests of the English nation. The Restoration Settlement saw not merely the reinstatement of hereditary monarchy but also the return of the old parliamentary order with the Lords revived alongside the Commons. Though the Commons in the 1660s were reluctant to concede to the Lords, it was recognised that the peers and bishops constituted 'the necessary-house above'.[61]

From 1689 the Lords were arguably the most formidable member of the parliamentary triumvirate. Although the 1689 Revolution Settlement and the 1701 Act of Settlement left the monarch with considerable powers, and by the end of the seventeenth century the Commons had laid an unchallengable claim to control the raising of finance, the Lords (representing a resurgent aristocratic section of society) became the dominant partner in the constitution for more than a hundred years. By 1760 the overt supremacy of the Lords had been partially undercut by the Commons, largely as a result of the long premiership of Sir Robert Walpole. Members of the upper House had

---

[60] Brampton Bryan MSS. (Christopher Harley, Brampton Bryan Hall, Herefordshire), bundle 117, folder 'Odds and Ends': F[rancis] P[rideaux] G[wyn] to [Edward Harley *jr*], 5 March 1718/19; see below p. 96.

[61] D. Hirst, 'The Conciliatoriness of the Cavalier Commons Reconsidered', *Parliamentary History*, VI (1987), 224.

however used their wealth and increasing involvement in elections, to acquire a considerable hold over a large proportion of the membership of the Commons, particularly the borough M.P.s. This symbiotic relationship between the two Houses bound the consitution closer together, while blurring the earlier, more sharply defined relations of the parliamentry triumvirate. The young George III missed the mark when he wrote that 'the British constitution [is] a mixture of three forms of Government' – monarch, aristocracy and democracy. The pervasive influence of the aristocracy in the Lords and Commons had produced an oligarchic form of government in partnership with the monarchy. George III was closer to the truth when he stated that 'the King & people may in some degree be looked upon as contending partys, & the Lords as a mediating power to keep the true balance'; but he misunderstood the true basis of the aristocratic hold on government when he lamented that 'the power of the Lords is indeed now much diminished'.[62] Outwardly the House of Lords may have been perceived as a weaker pillar of the constitution than the Commons, but in reality the oligarchic elements in both Houses were the real strength upholding the constitutional temple.[63]

Many of the attacks on the constitution in the later eighteenth century focussed on what was perceived as the power of the King through patronage in creating an oligarchic form of government which threatened the purity of the balanced British constitution of King, Lords and Commons.[64] In practice the idea of such a constitution was largely a myth, and the monarchy had found a willing and equal partner in the aristocracy. The staying power of the British aristocracy was remarkable, and its continued tenacity has ensured that the House of Lords has remained a central pillar of the constitution into the present century.[65]

[62] P.D.G. Thomas, '"Thoughts on the British Constitution" by George III in 1760', *Historical Research*, LX (1987), 362.

[63] The imagery of the constitution being a temple held up by three pillars, or a pair of scales supported on a triangle labelled King, Lords and Commons, was a pervasive one in the eighteenth and early nineteenth centuries. See H.T. Dickinson, *Caricatures and the Constitution, 1760-1832* (Cambridge, 1986), p. 24.

[64] *Ibid.*, p. 29.

[65] 'F.M.L. Thompson Looks at the Long Run of the English Aristocracy', *London Review of Books*, 19 February 1987, pp. 6-7.

Chapter 2

Parliamentary Management, Men-of-Business and the House of Lords, 1640-49*

J.S.A. Adamson

1

Parliament men made their speeches in the two Houses at Westminster. Their decisions were frequently made elsewhere. In informal meetings in Westminster Hall, in the lobbies, the Court of Requests; in the taverns of King Street and near Old Palace Yard; and in the houses of the nobility: there members of both Houses met during the 1640s for consultation and debate on the business of Parliament, deliberations which were possibly no less important in their effect on the course of policy than were the formal, and better documented, proceedings of the House of Lords and the House of Commons. Obtaining the assent of those two Houses – essential to the passage of all bills and ordinances – required on occasions, careful management and coordination. In any Parliament there was the problem of divergent interests, competing factions, rival ideologies. For the members who convened at Westminster in November 1640, each of these elements was present with heightened intensity and concentration; management acquired a corresponding importance in the transaction of parliamentary affairs. Adopted by rival interests on an unprecedented scale during the 1640s, the techniques employed, and the incidence of their employment, transformed not only the conduct of parliamentary business, but profoundly shaped the public perception of what Parliament was, and the interests it served, in the world outside Westminster. This essay is an attempt to illustrate the range of managerial techniques devised during the 1640s, the ends to which they were employed, and the effect that they had on the attitudes to Parliament and its business in the decade of the English Civil War.

2

Charles I's assent to the bill preventing the dissolution of the Long Parliament without its own consent[1] removed the principal constraint on

* I am grateful to Professor the Earl Russell, Miss Sheila Lambert, and Dr. J. S. Morrill for reading and commenting upon an earlier draft of this paper.
[1] 16 Car. I, cap. 7 (10 May 1641).

the open deployment of managerial tactics that had operated in the decades before the Civil War.[2] Hitherto, management of the the major business of the session had been the province of the King and his Council; Parliament was the King's High Court, summoned at his behest, dismissable at his command. Private 'men of business' had of course played a major role in the Commons since at least the reign of Elizabeth.[3] But in so far as they dealt with matters contentious (or at least those so regarded in the eyes of the Queen), they usually acted under the aegis of a Privy Councillor or of a conciliar faction.[4] Where the monarch perceived that management in Parliament was being usurped by 'private interests' or 'factious persons' – as Charles I was wont to do – there were punitive measures at his disposal: arrest of the delinquents; or, in the last resort, dissolution of the Parliament. Arrest of members during Parliament time was a sanction imposed, even against Privy Councillors, by the first two Stuart kings. During the 1621 session, James I had arrested a Privy Councillor, Southampton, and his collaborators in the Commons, Sandys and Selden;[5] two decades later his son had recourse to the same tactic when he tried to arrest another Privy Councillor, Lord Mandeville, and the five members of the Commons who were the allies of Mandeville's faction in the House of Lords[6] (an incident to which contemporaries, with a more precise notion of what constituted an 'M.P.', referred as the attempt on 'the sixe Members').[7] For Charles I in 1641, dissolution of the Parliament was, however, no longer an option that remained open. Deprived of this trump, the King turned to stacking the cards: during the second session of the Parliament, beginning in October 1641, Charles set out to manage the House of Lords (and thereby the Parliament), to stem the tide of reform, and to recoup some of the ground he had lost in the legislative concessions he had made during the spring.[8]

The discovery of the missing correspondence between the King and

[2] A. Fletcher, *The Outbreak of the English Civil War* (1981); Sheila Lambert, 'The Opening of the Long Parliament', *Historical Journal*, XXVII (1984), 265-87.

[3] M.A.R. Graves, 'Thomas Norton the Parliament Man: An Elizabethan M.P., 1559-1581', *Historical Journal*, XXIII (1980), 17-35.

[4] G.R. Elton, *The Parliament of England 1559-1581* (Cambridge, 1986), 104-5, 207-10, 323-9. M.A.R. Graves, 'The Management of the Elizabethan House of Commons: The Council's Men-of-Business', *Parliamentary History*, II (1983), 11-38.

[5] S.R. Gardiner, *History of England from the Accession of James I to the Outbreak of the Civil War* (10 vols, 1901), IV, 133.

[6] B.L., Loan MS. 29/46/16: warrant to the justices of Middlesex for the arrest of the five members, 4 Jan. [1642]. Cf. *A judicious speech made by . . . the Lord Kimbolton in Parliament* (1642).

[7] *An answer or necessary animadversions upon some late impostumate* [sic] *observations* ([3 Aug.] 1642), p. 26 (B.L., E 108/39).

[8] For the first session of the Parliament, see Lambert, 'The Opening of the Long Parliament', pp. 265-87.

Edward Nicholas, Clerk of the Council[9] (and shortly to be a Secretary of State),[10] during the months before and during the second session of the Long Parliament reveals in detail for the first time the management and planning which created, from October 1641, the royalist party in the House of Lords.[11] As early as July, Nicholas had assumed the role of Secretary of State, de facto, linking the King and his entourage in Scotland (during the summer of 1641) with the Queen and with the King's supporters at Westminster. Plans were laid for the forthcoming session; a caucus of royalist peers was mobilised to attend the House.[12]

Never a promising student of Parliaments, even in 1641, Charles was characteristically uncertain as to who his supporters were in the House of Lords. It was left to the Queen, and to her confidant, Lord Dunsmore, to provide the list of peers who were to be approached to form the nucleus of his party in the upper House.[13] Eleven lay peers were sent a 'circular letter' by Nicholas, with an injunction from the King to keep secret the fact they had been approached, requiring their attendance in 'the service of his Majestie' at the start of the second session, scheduled for 20 October 1641. The standard letter, sent to each of these peers, leaves no doubt as to the efficiency with which the royalist counter-attack was being planned.

> My very good Lord, I have receaved commaunds from his Majestie to write to your Lordshipp in his name not to fayle to attend the first day of the next meetinge in Parliament which wilbe the 20th of this moneth. I know your Lordshipp's good affeccon to the service of his Majestie and the publique would prompt you to have bene here att that tyme without any remembrance, but now that your Lordshipp understands his Majestie's desire and expectacon of your presence then, I am confident you wilbe the more dilligent not to fayle it. I am likewise commanded to entreate your Lordshipp not to be knowne that you have receaved any significaccon of his Majestie's pleasure to this effect, least other lords should take excepcon that they have not had the like.

Dated 8 October 1641, this letter was sent by Nicholas, in the King's name, to the principal spokesman for the King's interest in the Lords, the Earl of Bristol,[14] and to ten other royalist peers: the Earls of Bath,

---

[9] P.R.O., SO 3/12 (Signet Office docquet book), f. 72v.

[10] *Ibid.*, f. 177.

[11] Guildford Muniment Room, Surrey R.O., MS. 52/2/19, and MS. 85/5/2 (Bray deposits).

[12] Guildford Muniment Room, MS. 85/5/2/11. Cf. *ibid.*, MS. 52/2/19/9a: Nicholas to the Queen, 19 Aug. 1641.

[13] *Ibid.*, MS. 52/2/19/17: Nicholas to the King, 7 Oct. 1641. For Nicholas's relations with Lord Dunsmore, see Dunsmore's letter to Nicholas of 28 June 1637: P.R.O., S.P. 16/362/62.

[14] For Bristol's role in the House of Lords in 1641 see B.L., Harleian MS. 6424 (diary of John Warner, Bishop of Rochester).

Newcastle, Huntingdon, Devonshire, Cumberland, and Northampton; and Lords Poulett, Cottington and Seymour.[15] All were royalists in the Civil War. All but Cottington (the former Master of the Court of Wards), and the 3rd Earl of Devonshire were later to see service in the royalist cause as military commanders. Organization gave rise to a new sense of confidence among this group of royal supporters. Bristol witnessed to this at the start of session when he warned provocatively that if the Commons failed to introduce legislation for obtaining sufficient supply, the Lords would take the initiative themselves.[16]

Perhaps the most interesting feature of Nicholas's draft, however, is an addendum he scrawled on the page for his own reference: 'I wrote the same day a lettre to the Bishop of London [William Juxon] to write to the same purpose to all bishops which are well affected'.[17] In securing the attendance of those bishops he deemed politically reliable, Bishop Juxon was to have a central role in the management of the royalist party in the Lords – the 'party whip' of the episcopal faction that was loyal to the King. A former Lord Treasurer, Juxon was among the bishops at the centre of the attack on clerical officeholding; in October 1641, he drew up the list of bishops whose attendance was to be required at the forthcoming session; and he also wrote the letters conveying the King's commands.[18] When the king sought, later in that month, to expand the number of episcopal yes-men in the House of Lords,[19] it was Juxon who provided the King with detailed notes on the candidates for vacant sees

[15] Guildford Muniment Room, MS. 85/5/2/11.

[16] *Orders from the High Court of Parliament for the voting of the new bills of subsidies by the Lords House* (1641), sig. A3v.

[17] Guildford Muniment Room, MS 85/5/2/11.

[18] *Ibid.*; Christ Church, Oxford, Muniment Room, Evelyn Collection, Nicholas Letters Box, unfol.: Juxon to Nicholas, 8 Oct. 1641.

[19] The first list of nominees for filling the vacant bishoprics was made by the King and Bishop Juxon before the King's departure for Scotland, almost certainly in August 1641, in response to the threat of impeachment against the 13 bishops for their part in the 1640 Canons (*L.J.*, IV, 340; *The Diary and Correspondence of John Evelyn*, ed. W. Bray and H.B. Wheatley, [4 vols, 1906], IV, 88-90: Nicholas to the King, 19 Sept. 1641 and the King's apostil). While the original list (like most of Juxon's papers) does not appear to survive, its complexion – judging from Nicholas's comments in his letter of 19 September – was strongly Arminian. It was in response to seeing this list that Nicholas suggested to the King the appointment of a number of divines 'of whome there is not the least suspic'on of favouring the Popish partie'. In the list ultimately adopted by the King, the inclusion of such men as Prideaux and Brownrigg was a second thought, an exercise in public relations with an overtly political rationale: that 'your Majestie would gayne not only their votes', but the votes of others who would no longer identify the bishops with a plot 'to connive at Popery' (*Evelyn Correspondence*, IV, pp. 88-90). The political and propagandistic nature of this second series of nominations probably accounts for the reluctance of Dr. Richard Holdsworth – the anti-Laudian Master of Emmanuel for whom Juxon procured the *congés d'élire* in November – to accept the see of Bristol (P.R.O., S.O. 3/12, f. 174; for Holdsworth, see also, Lord North, *A Forest Promiscuous* [1659], part III, p. 217).

which subsequently formed the basis for the appointments.[20] And it was Juxon who procured the Signet Office warrants for filling the vacancies.[21]

The surviving attendance records of the second session of the Parliament reveal that Juxon was not without effect in rallying his episcopal brethren to 'the King's service' in the House of Lords.[22] Until the anti-episcopal riots at the end of December 1641 brought to an end the attendance of this clique in the Lords, Juxon could count on a regular attendance of some 10 to 15 bishops. In a House of Lords in which there was a narrow margin between supporters and opponents of further reform (or, from the King's perspective, further encroachment on his just rights), the marshalling of the bishops in the King's interest was critical. While their ranks remained firm, they augmented the numbers of peers on whose loyalty the King could rely; thus, the combined vote of the bishops and royalist peers narrowly outflanked the group of peers which supported further delimitation of the monarch's powers.[23]

From the perspective of those who wished to press ahead with the reforming legislation which had been introduced in the Commons, it was the bishops – dragooned into attendance at the King's command – who were the King's line of defence against further demands from the Parliament. Remove their votes, and the King's narrow but none the less effective majority in the upper House would be destroyed at the same stroke. It was hardly coincidental that within two weeks of Juxon having written to the 'well affected' bishops, the Commons sent the upper House a resolution to disenfranchise the 13 bishops accused for their part in framing the Canons of 1640.[24] The list of the bishops the Commons sought to deprive of their votes in the upper House corresponds almost exactly with the list of bishops known to have attended the House from

[20] *Evelyn Correspondence*, IV, 96-7: Nicholas to the King, 3 Oct. 1641. Cf. the King's apostil of 12 Oct. to Nicholas letter of 5 Oct., in *ibid.*, IV, 99. For Juxon's advice to the King, see *ibid.*, IV, 113-4: Nicholas to the King, 27 Oct. 1641.

[21] P.R.O., SO 3/12 (Signet Office docquet book), f. 174 (Nov. 1641). Nicholas acted as Juxon's agent in procuring the warrants for the Chancery letters of *congé d'élire*: *ibid.*, and P.R.O., SO 3/12 (Signet Office docquet book), ff. 174v-175.

[22] H.L.R.O., MS. Minutes VIII, unfol. Presence lists were not entered into the formal Journal of the House, during this Parliament, until late in 1643; lists of peers attending were, however, entered daily in the Minute Books (or Scribble Books) from which the Journals were subsequently compiled.

[23] Guildford Muniment Room, MS. 85/5/2/21.

[24] *C.J.*, II, 292. Holles was sent to the Lords concerning the charge against the thirteen bishops, on 22 October. While the Commons wished to proceed with the 'sequestering' of the bishops from the upper House, they nevertheless laid aside the rather more contentious question of what crime the bishops had actually committed in framing the Canons: *C.J.*, II, 295. Impeachment proceedings were initiated against the bishops only on 4 August 1641, not in December 1640: *L.J.*, IV, 340; cf. J.S. Morrill, 'The Religious Context of the English Civil War', *Transactions of the Royal Historical Society*, 5th ser., XXXIV (1984), 166.

the start of the second session in October until the King's attempt to arrest the five members in January 1642 – Juxon's constituency of 'well affected' bishops. Of the total of 15 bishops known to have attended the House of Lords during this period (October–December 1641), 11 were on the list the Commons aimed to exclude at the beginning of the session.[25] Despite the Commons' efforts to attack this group in the Lords from 22 October, Nicholas could write confidently to the Queen on the 26th 'that the Bishops partie is like to ballance the other side'.[26]

Beholden to the King for promotion, the bishops now seemed beholden for their votes. For the principal parliamentary opponent of their right to sit in the Lords, Viscount Saye and Sele, the subservience of the bishops to management in the interest of the King during the autumn of 1641 provided damning evidence against them. As early as May 1641, Saye had argued that the bishops 'have such an absolute dependency upon the King that they sit not here as freemen'.[27] As their pastoral careers depended on the King, they were 'thereby at devotion for their votes'.[28] Lord Brooke raised the same objection when he questioned, in November 1641, 'how fit these Spirituall Lords may be to sit as Law-maker in That Highest Court, by whose fundamentall Orders . . . None ought to have Vote but Free men'.[29] The pastors had become the sheep, led whither the King (and Bishop Juxon) would lead them. It was this realization which prompted moderate, *episcopalian* peers to agree reluctantly to the exclusion of bishops from the House of Lords in the aftermath of the King's attempt to arrest Mandeville and the five members.[30] Management had imbued the entire question of bishops' votes with a distinctly secular, political colour; episcopacy as a system of

[25] The 11 bishops whom the Commons desired to seclude, and who were regular attenders at the House of Lords during the second session, were Walter Curle of Winchester, Godfrey Goodman of Gloucester, Joseph Hall of Exeter, Robert Wright of Coventry and Lichfield, George Coke of Hereford, Matthew Wren of Ely, Robert Skinner of Bristol, John Towers of Peterborough, Morgan Owen of Llandaff, William Piers of Bath and Wells, and John Warner of Rochester. H.L.R.O., MS. Minutes VIII.

[26] Guildford Muniment Room, MS. 85/5/2/21.

[27] *Two speeches of . . . Viscount Saye and Seale* ([27 May] 1641), p. 6 (B.L., E 198/16). This speech, topical again after the exclusion of bishops from the House of Lords early in 1642, was reissued with the spurious claim that it had been delivered in the debate of 26 Jan. 1642: *A speech in Parliament of William Lord Saye and Seale . . . against the supremacy of bishops* (1642), (Cambridge U.L., Syn. 7.64.122/54).

[28] *Ibid.*, p. 7.

[29] Robert, 2nd Lord Brooke, *A Discourse opening the Nature of that Episcopacie* ([Nov.] 1641), p. 37; although published in November, the *Discourse* had been written during the parliamentary recess.

[30] *Two speeches in the House of Lords* [19 Dec. 1642] *for and against accommodation* (1642), pp. 3-4 (B.L., E 84/35). Significantly, it was Saye and Sele who prevailed with the Earl of Pembroke to cast his vote for bishops' exclusion (see Lord Brooke's remarks in *ibid.*, p. 5). For the Earl of Stamford, another episcopalian who was later a parliamentarian, see R[obert] Kirle, *A coppy of a letter writ from Serjeant Major Kirle to a friend in Windsor* (n.d. [1643]), p. 3.

church government became tainted with the secular consequences of the creation of a 'prelatical party' in the House of Lords. Whereas in the first session of the Long Parliament, the King had been seen to agree, with surprising readiness, to the legislation presented from the Houses, now, since the organization of the royalist caucus in the Lords, from October 1641, almost none of the major Commons' bills was passing the hurdle of the upper House. Pym's speech of 27 October alluded to the efficiency of this episcopal caucus in blocking this body of legislation. For '[the bishops] have deprived the subjects of those good Lawes that are already made for them [in the Commons]', and therefore should be deprived of their votes for the future.[31] To many, the bishops had become the contrivers of the impasse between the Commons and the House of Lords.[32]

Throughout the second session, the King guarded this episcopal front-line defence against further encroachment by the Parliament. On hearing that a bill for their exclusion had been presented in the House of Lords, Charles instructed the Earl of Bristol to act as *agent provocateur*, to renew a dispute between the two Houses, thus providing further time to mobilise pro-royalist support against exclusion of the bishops.[33] In early November, when the Queen feared there would be insufficient royalist support among the peers to prevent the exclusion of bishops from the House, she sent an urgent letter to Nicholas, ordering him to summon the Earl of Carnarvon to give his attendance in the Lords – one of a series of initiatives directed towards managing the House.[34]

But if Juxon knew who were the 'well affected' to the King, so too did the Commons. The attempt to deprive the 13 bishops of their votes in the Lords was not only, or even primarily, intended as punishment of these bishops for their part in framing the 1640 Canons. It was intended not merely against a section of the episcopate in Parliament, but against *the* section of the episcopate that attended the House in the King's interest.[35] Three months later, in December, 12 out of the total of 15 bishops attending the House signed a Protestation complaining of the mobs that had 'violently menaced' and intimidated them from appearing in the House of Lords.[36] Just as in October the bishops' role in formulating the Canons of 1640 had provided the pretext for launching an attack on the

[31] *The substance of a conference at a Committee of both Houses in the Painted Chamber* (1641), p. 2.

[32] J.S. Morrill, 'The Attack on the Church of England in the Long Parliament, 1640-1642', in *History, Society and the Churches: Essays in Honour of Owen Chadwick*, ed. D. Beales and G. Best (Cambridge, 1985), pp. 105-24.

[33] Apostil of 28 Oct. 1641 by the King to Nicholas's letter of 21 Oct. 1641: *Evelyn Correspondence*, IV, 110; cf. Nicholas to the King, 12 Nov. 1641: *ibid.*, p. 133.

[34] *Ibid.*, pp. 128-9: the Queen to Nicholas, 8 Nov. 1641.

[35] H.L.R.O., MS. Minutes VIII.

[36] B.L., Stowe MS. 361, f. 98. *Parliamentary or Constitutional History of England* (24 vols, 1751-62), X, 138-9.

13 bishops who were regular attenders in the Lords, so in December the Protestation of the 12 bishops provided the pretext for renewing this attack. Ten out of the 12 bishops who signed the December Protestation had been on the Commons' list of those whose exclusion was desired at the start of the session for their complicity in the Canons of 1640. The attempt to impeach the 12 bishops in December 1641 struck directly at the King's power-base in the Lords. In losing the 12 bishops to the Tower, Charles stood also to lose his means of control of the upper House. It was this dire prospect that provoked Charles to his panic-inspired attempt to arrest Mandeville and the five members.[37] For it was this bi-cameral group which was responsible for managing the bishops' prosecution. Successful prosecution of the bishops had potentially devastating consequences for the efficacy of the King's interest in the Lords. It was the wider implications of the prosecution of the bishops, claimed a speech attributed to Viscount Mandeville, that 'provoked [the bishops'] malice against us [Mandeville and the five members] and was the principall cause of this their plot'.[38] Thus the attempt on the five members and the larger question of the role of the bishops in the King's management of the House of Lords were intimately linked. Breaking that episcopal party meant breaking the power of the royalist faction in the Lords. No bishop, no King's party.

The partisan management of the House of Lords during the autumn of 1641 profoundly affected the fortunes of the episcopate, and powerfully identified the issue of episcopacy with one factional interest within the Parliament.[39] Yet the organization of this coalition of bishops and royalist peers was itself a response to what the King perceived as the high-jacking of the Parliament by a carefully organised factional interest in both Houses. It was the efficiency of the 'faccous party'[40] – the term

[37] Professor Fletcher (*Outbreak*, p. 179) suggests that it was the report 'suddenly current' on 30 December that the Commons were about to impeach the Queen, that precipitated Charles's intervention. Yet this was merely another aspect of the predicament caused by the successful attack on the bishops. The Commons, at most, could draw up articles against the Queen; only the Lords could impeach her. What made the rumours of 30 December so threatening for the King was the knowledge that, with the bishops out of the House, he could no longer be confident of his control of the Lords.

[38] *A judicious speech made by . . . the Lord Kimbolton in Parliament* (1642), [pp., 3-5]. Viscount Mandeville, from 1642 the 2nd Earl of Manchester, sat in Parliament by virtue of his father's barony of Kimbolton.

[39] Montagu MSS. (the Duke of Buccleuch, Boughton House, Northamptonshire), MS. 4, f. 32: William Montagu to the 1st Lord Montagu of Boughton, 16 Dec. [1641]. Significantly, the list of peers who were against bishops' votes in the upper House, compiled by the M.P., John Moore, corresponds almost exactly to the list of future parliamentarians. B.L., Harleian MS. 480 (John Moore's diary), f. 1v.

[40] Guildford Muniment Room, MS. 52/2/19/16: Nicholas to Thomas Webb, 5 Oct. 1641. See also *Evelyn Correspondence*, IV, 93: Nicholas to the King, 27 Sept. 1641: 'I heare there are divers meetings att Chelsey att the Lord Mandevilles house and elsewhere, by Pym and others, to consult what is best to be donne at their next meeting in Parliament'.

Nicholas used to describe the group centred upon Essex, Warwick, Saye and the 5th Earl of Bedford in the Lords, and Pym, Holles, and Strode in the Commons – that provoked the royalist counter-attack in the Lords during the second session. The origins and activities of this group in the first session of the Long Parliament is a subject which lies outside the scope of this essay; what concerns us here is the extent to which the activities of such groups were the result of management and organization – not merely of chance congruities of opinion within the two Houses. By examining, in a series of case studies, the relations between such prominent figures in the Commons as Pym, Strode, Holles and Samuel Browne, and leading members of the House of Lords, one may hope to elucidate the type and extent of their activities, and the place of men-of-business in the fortunes of the nobility at Westminster. Did 'clientage' or matters of political creed and ideology provide the bond between peers and their allies in the Commons? How effective were the Lords as parliamentary managers? Sufficient evidence survives to suggest that careful bi-cameral management was becoming an increasingly established and important feature of politics during the Long Parliament. Both its incidence and the sophistication of its techniques increased with the pressures of war.

3

Explicit evidence of co-ordination between peers and Commons of course rarely survives: not least because much of the organization would have been undertaken verbally, at informal meetings in the Palace of Westminster or elsewhere. In a Parliament whose members were habitually jealous of their privileges and in which 'faction' and 'party' still had deeply opprobrious connotations,[41] evidence of collusion between members could sound the death-knell of a bill. Yet evidence survives to suggest that management and orchestration of parliamentary business was a far more common phenomenon than individual speakers found it politic to admit. The more contentious the measure was likely to be in the Houses, the stronger was the imperative to see its way smoothed by proficient management.

One such matter was the decision, in July 1642, to raise an army, and to grant a commission to the Earl of Essex as commander-in-chief of the Parliament's forces – a decision which seemed to move the Parliament decisively towards the threshold of civil war.[42] A document surviving in the papers of the relatively obscure Welsh polemicist, John Jones of Kellilysday,[43] provides a first-hand account of the bi-cameral

---

[41] M.A. Kishlansky, *The Rise of the New Model Army* (Cambridge, 1979), pp. 16-7.

[42] *L.J.*, V, 204-6; *C.J.*, II, 668-73.

[43] B.L., Add. MS. 33374 (Jones papers). For his somewhat eccentric views on the law during the 1650s, see B.L., Add. MS. 26651, ff. 31v-43v.

management which preceded the adoption of this resolution by the two Houses. Jones had been invited to Northumberland House on the morning of 12 July 1642, to discuss with the Earl of Northumberland and the Earl of Essex the draft of a treatise on the 'rights and prerogatives' due to the King and Parliament. The two peers were clearly interested in finding a polemicist to provide a public justification for the actions which they were about to undertake; Jones, for his part, was after a patron, and apparently willing to cut his ideological cloth to fit his hoped-for benefactor.[44] Instead of the meeting being a private one between himself and the two earls, Jones found that discussion of the contents of his treatise was only part of the agenda for a meeting convened by Essex and Northumberland at which were present leading members of both Houses.[45] To his surprise, Jones found 'there dyd meete there six Earles, one lord and M[aste]r Pymm', who consulted on Jones's draft and discussed amongst themselves the course to be adopted for the momentous business which they had decided to undertake that day.[46] Significantly, while there were seven peers attending the meeting[47] there was only one member of the Commons present – the professional peer's man-of-business, John Pym,[48] whose close links with this dominant group in the Lords enhanced his status and authority within the lower House. The nature of the meeting, and the social relations between its participants, strongly suggests that it was the peers who would be making the decisions; Pym who would be reporting and managing them

[44] B.L., Add. MS 33374, ff. 19v-20.

[45] *Ibid.*, f. 19v.

[46] *Ibid.*, ff. 19v-20. The context of the discussion on Jones's treatise was an attempt by Essex and his associates in the Lords to come up with a further reply to the King's *Answer to the Nineteen Propositions*. It is highly likely that the form of reply earlier adopted by this group, Henry Parker's *Observations* (1642), had been similarly presented to this group of peers for discussion and approval. Parker's *Observations* appeared around ten days before the meeting of 12 July described by Jones; and it was on this day that Parker was formally appointed as Essex's secretary. *The List of the Army raised under the command of his excellency Robert Earl of Essex* (1642), sig. A3 (B.L., E 117/3).

[47] B.L., Add. MS. 33374, ff. 19v-20. Two of the earls are named (Essex and Northumberland), the identities of the remaining five peers may be conjectured as the 5th Earl of Bedford (who was shortly afterwards appointed Essex's Lieutenant-General), Bolingbroke, the Earl of Holland (a friend and close ally of the earl); the one 'lord' is probably either Mandeville, or Viscount Saye. The Earl of Warwick was then with the Fleet in the Downs (*L.J.*, V, 194, 197); Lord Brooke was in Warwickshire – both of whom would otherwise have been likely to have attended.

[48] Kent Archives Office, U269/C287 (Sackville papers): Lord Newburgh to Earl of Bath, 12 August 1642; B.L., Add. MS. 11692 (Bouverie MS.), f. 27: Essex to Pym, 5 Nov. 1642. J.H. Hexter, *The Reign of King Pym* (Cambridge, Mass., 1941). Northumberland MS. (the Duke of Northumberland, Alnwick Castle, Alnwick, Northumberland), Y.III.2(4)7: petition of Robert Scawen to Lord Keeper Coventry [undated, but late 1630s and before Jan. 1640], ff. 29, 39. (I owe this reference to Professor the Earl Russell).

(without reference to whence these resolutions derived) in the lower House.[49]

Having missed prayers and the reading of petitions in the two Houses during the morning, the members attending the meeting at Northumberland House took the brief journey down Whitehall 'to the Parliament house', to effect the resolutions of their cabal.[50] With felicitous speed and efficiency, three momentous resolutions were approved by the Parliament: that Essex be made a general; that an army be raised forthwith; and that a petition be sent to the King to avert a civil war.[51] The members of both Houses resolved to uphold this cause, not in swearing allegiance to Parliament or the liberty of the subject, but in the utterly feudal undertaking that 'they will live and die with the earl of Essex' in this cause.[52]

The groundwork of the morning's legislation had been well laid. Pym yielded place to his social superior, Denzell Holles (the brother of an earl, and Essex's friend and ally), for the honour of presenting the resolutions to the Lords.[53] There the legislation was approved with a promptness which testified eloquently to managerial skill which lay behind its presentation. An impressed John Jones noted in his account of the day's proceedings that it was 'wythin three houres after [the end of the meeting at Northumberland House that] the Earle of Essex was made a Generall'.[54] Although the resolutions formally started their life in the Commons, the House of Lords was passing legislation which its leading members had already approved. In a lower House which was none the wiser, Pym appeared as the decisive leader, the *pater patriae*, steady and authoritative in the moment of crisis. To the Commons, here was 'King Pym';[55] but his king-makers were members of the House of Lords.

4

It was in the nature of such arrangements that peers should strive to leave the independence of the privilege-conscious House of Commons apparently unviolated. It hardly availed an M.P., when moving a

[49] For an example of such arrangements at the time of the army plot, see Kent Archives Office, U951/C261/31 (Knatchbull MS.): Sir Norton Knatchbull to his wife [May, 1641].

[50] B.L., Add. MS. 33374, f. 20.

[51] *C.J.*, II, 668-9; *L.J.*, V, 204-6. It is likely that it was in connection with this petition that Northumberland and Essex were interested in Jones's definitions of the just 'rights and prerogatives' of the King and Parliament: B.L., Add. MS. 33374, ff. 19v-20.

[52] *C.J.*, II, 668-9; *L.J.*, V, 206, 208.

[53] H.L.R.O., M.P. 19/8/1642, f. 180. *L.J.*, V, 205-6.

[54] B.L., Add. MS. 33374, f. 20.

[55] For the use of this term during mid-1641 see Guildford Muniment Room, MS. 52/2/19/16: Nicholas to Thomas Webb, 5 Oct. 1641.

question in the Commons, to announce that he had been put up to making his speech at the request of a member of the Lords. Sponsors of legislation in which they had a vested interest took pains to cover their tracks. When the Lords Commissioners of the Great Seal wanted all royalist compositions to pass the Seal in 1645 – thus vastly increasing their income from Chancery fees – the apparently disinterested Bulstrode Whitelocke was 'ingaged' to move the motion in the Commons. Only the survial of Whitelocke's 'Annals' provides any clue as to the real source, and motivation, of this bill.[56] Even so, peers could not entirely avoid committing such arrangements to paper, and a chance survival amongst the papers of the Speaker of the Commons, William Lenthall, illustrates how a piece of Commons business could appear to be 'spontaneous' – as the Commons' resolution to appoint Essex as Lord General had seemed – while being carefully orchestrated beforehand by a peer.

In February 1644, Viscount Saye, as Master of the Court of Wards, needed a clerk for his Court, as the previous incumbent, Hugh Awdeley, had been sequestered from office for royalism.[57] He briefed a series of M.P.s, including Speaker Lenthall, all of whom were factional allies of long standing in the lower House. Saye first instructed the Devon burgess, William Strode (who, like Pym, had been one of the 'five members' of 1642), to move a petition in the House. Then John Goodwyn, chairman of the Commons' Committee for Petitions and burgess of Haslemere, was presented with a copy of the document which Strode had been primed to speak to in the debate.[58] Saye had already drafted the text of what was to be a 'Commons' order' for the appointment of a clerk, and had left it with Goodwyn, who was to speak first in the debate.[59] Saye then wrote to Lenthall, detailing the arrangements so far and instructing him on his role.

> I pray you call for a petition and an order annexed wch is in M[aster] Goodwins hand and let it be read this morneing That I may sitt [in the Court of Wards] one day while this terme lasts. Master Stroud, one of the

[56] B.L., Add. MS. 37344 (Whitelocke's Annals), f. 18v.

[57] For Awdeley, B.L., Egerton MS. 2978 (misc. State Papers), f. 76. For his later career see Bedfordshire R.O., Harvey MS., HY 922 (Hugh Awdeley corr.). I owe this last reference to Dr. Wilfrid Prest.

[58] For Goodwyn, see John Rylands University Library, Manchester, Eng. MS. 302 (Pink papers), f. 208; B.L., Add. MS. 27990 (Sir John Percivall papers), f. 38v. For his relations with the Earl of Pembroke, see Randolph Caldecott (Pembroke's secretary) to Michael Oldisworth, 13 March 1647: H.L.R.O., M.P. 13/3/1647, f. 34. For his activities on the Committee for Petitions, see P.R.O., S.P. 28/252/1, f. 367v; Bodl., MS. Tanner 59, f. 703: Scots commissioners to Lenthall, 2 Feb. 1647. Goodwyn's activities in 1647 in connection with Saye's parliamentary negotiations for a new constitutional settlement are discussed in J.S.A. Adamson, 'The English Nobility and the Projected Settlement of 1647', *Historical Journal*, XXX (1987), 598.

[59] Bodl., MS. Tanner 62, f. 555: Saye to Lenthall, 10 Feb. 1644.

Committee, will informe the house that their is all iustice in this that is desired by your very affeconate frend.[60]

If peers such as Viscount Saye were prepared to expend such care in the pre-arrangement of speakers in the Commons to secure the employment of a clerk, it is likely that he was no less careful in matters of national importance, such as the reception in the Commons of a bill from the Lords to create a central executive committee for Parliament,[61] for which Strode also appeared as a prominent advocate[62] – a matter to which we will return.

Profoundly affecting the relationship between the two Houses and their members during the 1640s was the massive expansion of the role of joint-committees of Lords and Commons during the years of civil war. Formal contacts between peers and members of the lower House before the 1640s had been confined almost exclusively to the procedure of the conference – a device for consultation between the Houses which had become increasingly formal and precedent-bound since the latter part of James's reign.[63] In contrast to the formality of conferences the numerous executive committees that proliferated from the time of the Recess Committee of 1641 – the Committee for Advance of Money, the Committee of Both Kingdoms, the Committee for Compounding, the Derby House Committee, among a forest of others – provided points of contact between members of both Houses which were relatively informal, regular, and private. They provided opportunities for members of each House to become familiar with their colleagues in the other, and to establish relationships of collaboration and cooperation which, in scale, had no parallel in earlier Parliaments. In the case of the Saye's orchestration of proceedings in the lower House over of the Clerkship of the Wards in 1644, both the M.P. Saye chose to move the appointment (William Strode), and the eventual recipient of the office (Miles Corbet),[64] were members of a joint-committee which Saye regularly attended and over which he exercised, at this time, almost

---

[60] *Ibid.*

[61] B.L., Harleian MS. 166 (D'Ewes's diary), f. 7; *L.J.*, VI, 430; W. Notestein, 'The Establishment of the Committee of Both Kingdoms', *American Historical Review*, XVII (1911-12), 482-6.

[62] The letter to Lenthall, in which Strode's advocacy of the clerk is referred to, is almost exactly contemporaneous with the debates on the Committee of Both Kingdoms bills. 'Master Goodwyn's' co-operation in the matter of the clerkship of the Wards did not go unrewarded. With his brother, Robert Goodwyn (burgess for East Grinstead), John Goodwyn was granted the custody of William Savile's lands, then in wardship to the Crown, when the former grantee was sequestered as a delinquent in arms: P.R.O., WARDS 9/556 (Entry Book of Orders), p. 776.

[63] The best discussion of conferences is E.R. Foster, *The House of Lords, 1603-1649* (Chapel Hill, 1983), pp. 126-33.

[64] P.R.O., S.P. 19/1 (Committee for Advance of Money order book), p. 21; S.P. 19/4, pp. 192-3. Corbet was sworn Clerk of the Wards on 23 May 1644: P.R.O., WARDS 9/556 (Wards decree book), p. 643.

despotic control – the Committee for Advance of Money.[65]

Committees provided regular occasions for meetings between members of the two Houses, which in many cases consolidated and developed earlier relations of friendship or acquaintance. In the case of Strode, his acquaintance with Saye dated back at least to the 1620s, when both men had been friends of the puritan divine, John Preston.[66] During 1643 and 1644, this Lords-Commons duo worked in tandem to promote the proceedings against Archbishop Laud; and Saye's pre-arranged staging of the Commons' proceedings revealed in his letter of February 1644 is all the more interesting for the fact that they are contemporaneous with Saye's and Strode's efforts in the two Houses to establish a 'Committee of Both Kingdoms'. This was to be a powerful executive committee comprised of members of both Houses, with a delegation of Scots; and the principal motive for the proposal was to provide a check on the military authority of Parliament's commander-in-chief, the Earl of Essex. For to the managers of this bill, Essex was the all too eirenic and dilatory generalissimo of the army; the legislation usurped his supremacy of command by making the committee responsible for the overall management of the war.

The architect of this contentious bill was Viscount Saye, the peer who had first introduced the legislation in the House of Lords.[67] It was being debated in the Commons in the same week that Strode had spoken at Saye's instruction about the Court of Wards;[68] and when the bill was finally returned to the Lords with the Commons' approval, it was Strode who carried the legislation to the upper House.[69] It seems no less likely that the precise and careful management that underlay Strode's intervention concerning the Wards was present a few days later when he negotiated Saye's bill for the Committee of Both Kingdoms through the obstructions of the lower House.[70]

[65] P.R.O., S.P. 19/2, pp. 54, 57, 89, 134, 167, 259; S.P. 19/90 (Cttee for Adv. of Money corr.), f. 89; *C.J.*, III, 330-1; H.L.R.O., M.P. 6/12/1643, f. 127.

[66] P.R.O., PROB 11/154, f. 102v (I owe my knowedge of this reference to Dr. Nicholas Tyacke); I. Morgan, *Prince Charles's Puritan Chaplain* (1957), p. 72.

[67] *Mercurius Aulicus*, 7th week (11-17 Feb. 1643/4), p. 828 (B.L., E 35/27). S.R. Gardiner, *The History of the Great Civil War 1640-1649* (4 vols, 1901), I, 305. Gardiner, unwilling to credit the peers with anything so decisive as this bill, conjectured that Saye had to be 'persuaded . . . to move it', and suggested that the bill was passed when 'the Lords were in an inattentive mood'.

[68] Bodl., MS. Tanner 62, f. 555.

[69] H.L.R.O., M.P. 16/2/1644, ff. 181-2; *L.J.*, VI, 429.

[70] B.L., Harleian MS. 166 (D'Ewes's diary), f. 7; Add. MS. 18779 (Walter Yonge's diary), ff. 56v-57. The Commons found the House of Lords' bill too radical, and a second, compromise measure was suggested by St. John on the basis of a draft by John Crewe (also an M.P. associated with Saye's parliamentary interest). Saye's bill was not finally adopted by the Commons until May 1644. *C.J.*, III, 504. Valerie Pearl, 'Oliver St. John and the "Middle Group" in the Long Parliament: August 1643-May 1644', *E.H.R.* LXXXI (1966), 490 ff. Gardiner, *History of the Great Civil War*, I, 343.

The relations that peers cultivated with allies in the Commons such as Pym and Strode were thus central to their capacity to influence the course of policy. Allies in the Commons acquired, in return, enhanced status in their own House through their affinity with a 'great lord', and a correspondingly important voice in the counsels which determined what that policy was to be.[71] In the factional battles at Westminster during the Civil War, attacking a rival peer's ally in the Commons was a vicarious attack on the peer himself. The attack, in 1645, on the Earl of Essex's principal ally in the Commons, Denzell Holles (another of the 'five members' of 1642), was clearly planned as part of a broader assault on the earl's influence within the Parliament as a whole.[72] And as in the examples of Strode's collaboration with Saye, it highlights the central importance of members of the House of Lords in determining the outcome of what looks at first sight to be a purely Commons affair.[73]

As in the 1644 attack on Essex – implicit in the establishment of the Committee of Both Kingdoms – it was Saye who managed the activities of the earl's opponents at Westminster. Using information supplied by the turn-coat royalist, Lord Savile,[74] Saye sought to destroy Holles's credit and standing in the Commons by exposing him as a fifth-columnist, a traitor who had been supplying the royalist Council at Oxford with a steady stream of information on parliamentary affairs.[75] Saye induced Savile to present written accusations against Holles, and once again the presentation of the matter in the Commons was preceded by careful management from the Lords. Saye met with Lord Wharton and their confidant in the Commons, the Solicitor-General, Oliver St.

[71] For the influence exerted by a Commons member such as William Pierrepont, for example, see B.L., Add. MS. 63057 (Burnet's historical notes, 2 vols), I, 174-5. Alnwick Castle, Northumberland MS. O. I. 2 (f): Northumberland to Hugh Potter, 24 June 1645.

[72] The extent of Essex's parliamentary interest during the period is analysed in detail in J.S.A. Adamson, *The Nobility and the English Civil War* (Oxford University Press, forthcoming).

[73] Thus it appeared to the diarist D'Ewes whose perception of parliamentary affairs is consistently skewed, not only by his general ignorance of the inner counsels of the leading members of the Commons, but by his almost total ignorance of the inner counsels of the Lords. When he did come into the circle of the Earl of Denbigh in 1644 (a relatively minor figure within the House of Lords), he records the occasion with sycophantic delight. B.L., Harleian MS. 483 (D'Ewes's Latin diary), ff. 109v, 111, 114v, 117.

[74] Bodl., MS. Dep. c. 167 (Nalson papers xiv), f. 372: Committee of Compounding report on Lord Savile, 1646.

[75] The background to these events is discussed in Valerie Pearl, 'London Puritans and Scotch Fifth-Columnists: a Mid-Seventeeth Century Phenomenon', in *Studies in London History presented to Philip Jones*, ed. A.E.J. Hollaender and W. Kellaway (1969), pp. 318ff. Saye's correspondence with Savile had been authorised by the Committee of Both Kingdoms, and was conducted in consultation with his confidants, Lord Wharton and Oliver St. John. H.L.R.O., M.P. June-July 1645, f. 244.

John,[76] whereupon his aristocratic clique resolved 'to advise Mr. *Gurdon* [a member of the Commons] to make the House acquainted with it'.[77]

The appearance of the M.P., John Gurdon, at this point emphasises the new-found importance of committee men in management during the Long Parliament. Like Strode, Gurdon was a member of Saye's clique that ran the Committee for Advance of Money;[78] Holles, the victim of Gurdon's attack in 1645, later spoke of him as the shameless lackey of his masters in the Lords.[79] And at Saye's prompting, Savile sent his written accusations against Holles to Gurdon for presentation in the Commons.[80] The political significance of these carefully staged manoeuvres went far beyond questions of Holles's wrongdoing in corresponding with Oxford. The attack on Holles, as Whitelocke perceptively observed, was part of a larger design to discredit 'Essex's party' in the Commons.[81] A committee was established under the chairmanship of Samuel Browne,[82] but despite Browne's overt sympathy with Saye and hostility to Holles, the charges fizzled out for lack of sufficient evidence. Although this little drama was played out on the floor of the Commons, its real protagonists were Saye and Essex. Saye orchestrated the presentation of charges against Holles as a means of destroying Essex's power base in the Commons (and thereby weakening his position in the Lords).[83] Essex was the real object of attack. Gurdon's role in the Savile affair was a carefully arranged sub-plot in a larger aristocratic feud.[84] Though none of the diarists except Whitelocke noticed, it was two members of the House of Lords who had set up in advance what otherwise looked to be an internal Commons dispute.

The initiative reveals the extent to which disputes within the Commons were becoming, during the mid-1640s, an extension of

[76] For St. John's associations with Saye and Wharton, see *Mercurius Aulicus*, 7th week (11-17 Feb. 1643/4), p. 828 (B.L., E. 35/27); Pearl, 'Oliver St. John', pp. 490ff; and for the survival of these relations into the late 1640s, *Vox Militaris* no. 5 (14-21 Nov. 1648), p. 35 (E 473/8). For his earlier service with the 4th Earl of Bedford, Alnwick Castle, Northumberland MS. Y. III. 2(4)7, f. 39.

[77] [Viscount Saye and Sele], *Vindiciae Veritatis* (1654), p. 140 (original emphasis).

[78] P.R.O., S.P. 19/2. Like Strode's, Gurdon's acquaintance with Saye predated the Long Parliament: he had been a member of the Providence Island Company. P.R.O. (Kew), C.O. 124/2 (Prov. Island Co. minutes), ff. 60v, 109v. Gurdon's brother-in-law, the M.P. Roger Hill, was also a member of the Committee: B.L., Add. MS. 46500 (Hill corr.), f. 29.

[79] *The Memoirs of Lord Holles* (1699), pp. 137-8.

[80] Bodl. MS. Dep. c. 166 (Nalson papers), nos. 60, 65.

[81] The phrase is Whitelocke's: B.L., Add. MS. 37343 (Whitelocke's Annals), f. 405.

[82] Browne's relations with this aristocratic faction are discussed below, pp. 38-9.

[83] [Viscount Saye], *Vindiciae Veritatis*, pp. 138-140.

[84] The Savile affair is discussed in P. Crawford, *Denzil Holles, 1598-1680: A Study of his Political Career* (1979), pp. 114-9, although Gurdon's role in sponsoring the charges in the Commons is not noticed.

factional conflicts within the House of Lords. In this respect, there were strong similarities between these developments and the manner in which, during the 1620s, disputes within the House of Lords itself had reflected, and been an extension of, factional divisions within the Privy Council. Men-of-business such as Pym, Strode and Gurdon linked the political and factional networks of the nobility with the day to day management of business in the House of Commons. Gurdon's part in the aristocratic attack on the Essex-Holles interest in the Commons, for instance, was by no means a one-off occurrence. As a member of the Commons' finance committees, Gurdon was regularly employed by Saye to pursue a particularly unsubtle policy of allowing or disallowing parliamentary grants and pensions along overtly factional lines. While such payments to allies of Gurdon's masters in the Lords were promptly approved,[85] claims for arrears and compensation from opponents of this group in the upper House were consistently delayed and frustrated.[86] The promptness with which the pension of Saye's ally, the Earl of Nottingham, was despatched was in striking contrast to the Sisyphean pace at which the unimpeachable claims of Lord Willoughby, Essex's confederate in the Lords, dawdled through the accounts committees.[87] Essex's collaborators in the Commons watched this development of tactical patronage with frustrated and ineffectual indignation. Holles recalled of some of Saye's clients in the Commons, and of John Gurdon in particular, that they:

> were so impudent as some of them would not stick to give it for a reason, openly in the House, why they would not grant their desires, that they took notice how they [the peers] gave their Votes: Mr. *Gurdon* is the Man I have heard say so several times.[88]

In July 1646, Gurdon and Sir Henry Mildmay – Saye-Northumberland allies from Advance of Money and Revenue Committee respectively – inspected the Lords' Journal, presumably with a view to examining the lists of dissents, which for many major votes were as good as division

---

[85] For the cases of the Earls of Nottingham and Stamford, see below, pp. 43-4.

[86] *The Memoirs of Lord Holles*, pp. 137-8. For Gurdon's relations with Saye, [Saye], *Vindiciae Veritatis*, p. 138; Bodl. MS. Tanner 62, f. 552: Saye to Lenthall, 10 Feb. 1644; P.R.O., S.P. 16/515, f. 340.

[87] P.R.O., S.P. 28/252/1 (Cttee Acc. Order Bk), f. 327v (7 Nov. 1646); H.L.R.O., M.P. 5/3/1647, f. 48; *L.J.*, IX, 58. B.L., Egerton MS. 1048 (Parliamentary papers), f. 49r-v. For a similar case involving one of Essex's allies in the Commons, see that of Sir John Clotworthy: P.R.O., S.P. 28/252/1 (Cttee Acc. Day Bk), ff. 128v, 359, 363v, 372v, 375, 367, 389-391v; S.P. 28/255 (Cttee Acc. corr.), unf.: Clotworthy to John Glover and John Stephens (members of the committee), 8 Jan. 1645.

[88] *Memoirs of Lord Holles* (1699), pp. 137-8.

lists.[89] Instances of opposition by Essex's faction to the initiatives of the Saye-Northumberland group in the Lords were used, by the latter group's men-of-business in the Commons, as prima facie reasons 'why they would not grant their desires'.

If Gurdon's involvement with the peers may, perhaps, be dismissed as the deferential obedience of a second-rank back-bencher, what then do we make of the role of Samuel Browne, a Lincoln's Inn lawyer who enjoyed a status in the Commons during the later 1640s analagous to that of Pym and Hampden in the years 1640-1643 – a man whom Whitelocke described as being, with St. John and the younger Sir Henry Vane, one of the 'grandees of that party'.[90]

5

The political career of Samuel Browne reveals the extent to which aristocratic men-of-business became the agents not only of the individual peer who was their patron, but also of a coordinated series of aristocratic interests within the Parliament. Dr. Pearl has suggested a general (and coincidental) affinity between the policies adopted in the Commons by the circle associated with such men as St. John and Browne and the political views of Lord Saye and Sele.[91] But this affinity has been regarded as one of general ideology rather than an alliance directed to specific action and underpinned by relations of patronage and management.[92] Browne's rise to prominence in the Long Parliament with the 'middle group' has normally been explained, at least in part, by his kinship with Oliver St. John, his first-cousin.[93] In fact, Browne – who came from a Northamptonshire clerical family – was only remotely related to the St. Johns of Bletsoe and the famous Solicitor-General.[94] Far

[89] *C.J.*, IV, 621. The Committee of Revenue provided another weapon for these factional skirmishes. Factional overtones are clearly evident in the markedly different treatment the Committee meted out to peers with similar financial obligations to the Crown. Northumberland was excused his obligations to pay fee-farm rents due to the Crown; Manchester was hounded by the Committee with peremptory demands that he pay his outstanding rents into the Exchequer forthwith. H.L.R.O., Willcocks MS. (Manchester papers) 2/2/584: Cttee of Rev. to Manchester, 23 April 1646; Alnwick Castle, Northumberland MS., O. I. 2(f): Northumberland to Potter, [April-May] 1646.

[90] B.L., Add. MS. 37344 (Whitelocke's Annals), f. 20v.

[91] Valerie Pearl, '"Royal Independents" in the English Civil War', *Transactions of the Royal Historical Society*, 5th series, XVIII (1968), 82-3.

[92] D. Underdown, *Pride's Purge: Politics in the Puritan Revolution* (Oxford, 1971), pp. 63-4.

[93] *D.N.B.* ('Samuel Browne'). P. Zagorin, *The Court and the Country* (1969), p. 142, D. Underdown, 'Party Management in the Recruiter Elections, 1645-8', *E.H.R.*, LXXXIII (1968), 239.

[94] F.A. Page-Turner, 'The Browne Family of Arlesey', *Publications of the Bedfordshire Historical Record Soc.*, II (1914), 137-55.

from being an independent and unattached leader within the House, he was intimately tied, by employment and political inclination, with the fortunes of the aristocratic clique associated with the Earl of Northumberland and Viscount Saye in the House of Lords.

His career, like that of John Pym, followed the familiar pattern of service in the employ of peers whose politics was closely in sympathy with his own. Before his election to Parliament, Browne had been Northumberland's attorney in the Court of Commons Pleas,[95] in receipt of a regular retainer.[96] Northumberland seems to have been responsible for his election at Dartmouth – for the enfranchisement of which the earl had expended considerable sums of money. During the 1640s, he remained on friendly terms with his old employer,[97] and by 1646 he had moved to the service of Salisbury (probably recommended by Northumberland, the earl's son-in-law).[98] Browne took over the stewardship of Salisbury's Middlesex estates[99] and used his influence as chairman of the House of Commons' Accounts Committee to keep discreetly from public view the remarkable patronage empire that his master, Salisbury, and his allies in the Lords, were building up within the Civil War Exchequer.[100] He was, like Pym, a professional peer's man-of-business. Did that make him, then, merely a 'client'; or did his prosperous career in aristocratic employment also have an ideological element?

For Samuel Browne, as for most M.P.s associated with interests in the Lords, it was both patronage *and* ideology which bonded him to the Saye-Northumberland interest in the Lords – an interest to which his master, Salisbury, was also a committed adherent. He shared the anti-clericalism of his aristocratic associates, working closely with the managers of Archbishop Laud's trial. There he delivered a devastating attack on the evils that resulted from permitting clerical influence in the

---

[95] Kent Archives Office, De L'Isle MS., U 1475/A 98 (stray from the Alnwick archive).

[96] *Ibid.*, U 1475/A 99.

[97] For collaborations between Browne and the Earl of Northumberland on the Committee of Both Kingdoms, see, *C.S.P. Dom.*, 1644, pp. 145, 155, 218, 268. Browne similarly co-operated with the earl on the Sequestrations Committee to protect the estate of the widow of Sir Nicholas Byron. *L.J.*, IX, 493.

[98] Hatfield MSS. (the Marquess of Salisbury, Hatfield House, Hertfordshire), Box L/6. At Lincoln's Inn many of Salisbury's legal agents were already among his friends: after the election of the Salisbury client, John Harington, Browne assisted this parliamentary novice in the writing of his speeches. *The Records of the Honourable Society of Lincoln's Inn: Admissions* (2 vols, 1896), 28 Oct. 1616. Underdown, *Pride's Purge*, p. 20.

[99] Hatfield MSS., A. 41, ff. 19-20. Cf. Box L/6; A. 161/2; A 44/1, f. 4.

[100] P.R.O., S.P. 28/252/1 (Cttee Acc. Order Bk), f. 345. *C.J.*, V, 239. On the Exchequer influence of this group, particularly the Earls of Pembroke and Salisbury, see J.S.A. Adamson, 'The Peerage in Politics, 1645-9' (Cambridge Ph.D., 1986), chapter 1.

King's counsels.[101] In March 1646, after the Saye-Northumberland faction had thrown out a proposal from the City in favour of a clericalist, High Presbyterian church, Saye, Northumberland, Salisbury and their allies went to a meeting of Common Council to present in person their disapproval of the City's actions. It was Browne who acted as spokesman for the Commons (at the request of this group in the Lords), at this formal admonishment of the City Fathers for their lobbying on behalf of Essex and the High Presbyterian cause.[102]

As the margins between the rival factions in the Lords narrowed during the years 1645-6,[103] the collusion of such committed and influential supporters became ever more crucial to ensure the desired outcome to business in the upper House. Careful management was imperative. The Earl of Essex held regular Sunday afternoon meetings at Essex House in the Strand – occasions which provided opportunities for consultation with his stalwart allies in the Commons such as Holles and Sir Philip Stapleton, and for lobbying the support of wavering souls from both Houses.[104] Amongst the Lords, proxies were solicited; attendances sought.[105] As the battle for votes intensified, the peers' allies in the Commons – seldom far from the scene of these aristocratic manoeuvres – were enlisted to deploy their influence in the interests of their Lords. At stake was both the settlement of the church and the secular government of the post-war kingdom. In the Lords there were divisions between the advocates of an Erastian Presbyterian church – which tolerated some Independent congregations – to be established in a state where the King's powers were stringently defined (a group centred on Northumberland, Salisbury and Saye and Sele); and a second, rival faction, organised around the Earl of Essex and Lord Willoughby. This group, in collusion with the Scots Commissioners, sought a High Presbyterian, clericalist church on the Scots model; and a secular government in which their were few real checks upon the monarch's powers – particularly in relation to the controversial question of the

---

[101] Worcester College, Oxford, Clarke MS. LXXI (transcript of Laud's trial), unf., entries for 11 Sept. 1644. This speech, which has hitherto been thought lost (see *D.N.B.*, 'Samuel Browne'), contains a detailed exposition of Browne's attitudes to the relations between the church and the civil power. For D'Ewes's impressions of Browne, B.L., Harleian, MS. 483 (D. Ewes's Latin diary), ff. 109, 113v.

[102] H.L.R.O., M.P. 11/3/1646, f. 145-6. Bodl. MS. Tanner 60, f. 554 r-v.

[103] The margin between the factions in divisions in the House of Lords from 1645-7 was seldom more than three or four votes in a House which could command an attendance of almost 30 peers. The division lists are set out in Adamson, 'The Peerage in Politics', Appendix B.

[104] B.L., Add. MS. 37344, ff. 29, 31v-2.

[105] Dr. Williams's Library, MS. 24.50 (Thomas Juxon's diary), ff. 44r-v; Sir Simonds D'Ewes, *The Journals of all the Parliaments during the reign of Queen Elizabeth* (1682), p. 7.

King's power over the militia.[106]

The narrower was the margin between these competing factions in the House of Lords, the greater was the necessity for managers in the Lords to use all the means at their disposal – including enlisting the support of their allies (such as Browne) in the Commons – to consolidate and augment their factional support in the upper House. In this quest for votes, even the relatively simple matter of a request for a reduction in a county's assessment became embroiled in the carefully managed factional politics of Westminster.

In mid-June 1646, a group of Gloucestershire M.P.s sought to exempt the county from the weekly assessment of £200 paid towards the upkeep of the Bristol garrison. Significantly, even though they were members of the Commons, their first recourse was not to their own House, but, through his steward, to a local landholder who was also a member of the House of Lords. Richard Dowdeswell, steward to the 2nd Earl of Middlesex, was approached by the delegation of Gloucestershire M.P.s to try to have the assessment removed. Middlesex's financial interests were closely involved, as Dowdeswell pointed out to his master, 'Considering what a greate estate your Lordship hath in that County'.[107] It was at this point that the entire matter became involved in the Earl of Essex's attempts to manage the House of Lords. Middlesex had hitherto been an intermittent supporter of the Saye-Northumberland group; by gratifying the Earl of Middlesex (and the Gloucestershire M.P.s who were his suitors), Essex hoped to maintain Middlesex's errant vote within his own fold.

Without prompting from Middlesex, Essex and Lord Willoughby of Parham took the opportunity to promote the financial interests of the peer whom they hoped to secure as an ally. The matter was referred to a Lords' committee with a quorum of two, who turned out to be none other than Essex and his henchman, Lord Willoughby. 'Soe the Earle of Essex and the Lord Willowby of Parram heard the busines fully', Dowdeswell reported, 'and Comannded mee to draw it in to a Case, wch I did yesterday'. Dowdeswell presented it to Lord Willoughby, 'who promised the assessment would be removed'.[108]

Essex's adversaries in the Lords were not, however, to be so simply out-manoeuvred. Discerning that politics lay behind Essex's sudden

---

[106] Adamson. 'The Peerage in Politics', pp. 116-149. When, in May, Holles and Lewis re-opened the attack on lay commissioners in the Commons, it was Browne who salvaged a remnant of Erastian control over ecclesiastical jurisdiction with his compromise expedient of a centralised parliamentary committee for appeals. *C.J.*, IV, 552-3. *L.J.*, VIII, 355, 358.

[107] Kent Archives Office, Sackville MSS. (Cranfield papers), U 269/C 250 (unsorted estate corr.), unf.: Richard Dowdeswell to the Earl of Middlesex, 17 June 1646.

[108] *Ibid.*, U 269/C 250, unf.

interest in Gloucestershire assessments, the Northumberland group sought an alternate means of ingratiating themselves with the wavering Middlesex. Essex and Willoughby effectively controlled proceedings in the Lords' committee; but his opponents could still work effectively in the Commons. On 15 June, Salisbury sent his own steward to present Middlesex's agent with an alternate, and rival, source of patronage.

> Mr. Samuell Browne on Monday last sawe mee in the Court of requests [Dowdeswell informed Middlesex,] and of himself came up to mee and pulled me by the cloake and told me these words, Trouble noe Lords [namely, Essex and Willoughby] to bee yo[u]r Sollicitor, you shallbe heard when ever you come and have Iustice done you, and of that rest assured.[109]

Dowdeswell, a peer's agent at Westminster, was not slow to appreciate that the reason for Browne's sollicitude was that Browne, also a peer's man-of-business at Westminster, was acting on behalf of the Northumberland group. 'And I am not insensible of the hand whence this comes', he wrote to Middlesex, 'nor never wilbee whiles I live'.[110] The patronage Browne received from Northumberland and Salisbury reinforced his allegiance to their faction in the House of Lords; he was prepared to work as a member of the Commons to consolidate the aristocratic interest with which his master was associated in the upper House, by winning the Earl of Middlesex's vote to their cause. But patronage was only part of that bond. Upon the efficacy of such bi-cameral management depended not only such relatively minor matters as the assessment of Gloucestershire, but also such fundamental questions as the form of the church settlement (which was then being modified in Parliament), and the content of the peace terms (which were about to be offered to the King). Samuel Browne was in a technical sense the Earl of Salisbury's client – a man in receipt of an annual fee; but at the heart of that relationship lay not the reciprocal benefits of patronage, but a common series of objectives as to the settlement of church and state. Patronage witnessed to this common bond; it did not substitute for it.

Or so it was amongst the principled. For those who sought, by management, to minimize the unpredictability of Parliaments had to contend with the fact that, in a division, the votes of the venal and the disinterested counted alike with those of the zealous and the committed. As Walpole and the Duke of Newcastle were to rediscover, votes could be brought, and waverers attracted to a particular group by the promise of fiscal reward. In this, the Long Parliament was no exception.

In such financial matters, more than any other, the support of men-of-business in the Commons was often critical for the outcome of business in the House of Lords. Two days before a crucial division in the Lords on

---

[109] *Ibid.* For Browne, Hatfield MSS. A. 161/2, 148/17; Box L/6.
[110] Kent Archives Office, U 269/C 250, unf.: 17 June 1646.

8 May 1646, in which Essex seemed likely to defeat the Commons' vote to remove the King from the custody of Essex's allies, the Scots, Saye's friend and client, Richard Knightley,[111] moved the Commons to consider the unfortunate financial plight of the Earl of Stamford.[112] Stamford, a moderate and a trimmer, was seen as a likely addition to the Saye-Northumberland group's numbers in the Lords. With remarkable coincidence this call upon the Commons' charity came on the same day the House heard the news of the King's flight to the Scots: a decisive vote in the Lords was forthcoming in which Stamford's vote would be essential if the Saye-Northumberland group were to retain control of the House. On the motion of Saye's ally, Knightley, it was on this day that the House voted an allowance of £1,500 a year to compensate Stamford for his losses in the parliamentary cause.

Stamford's fortunes and misfortunes in the payment of this pension reveal the overtly political nature of the grant. The initial payment was to be made immediately on the revenues of Goldsmiths' Hall, with annual payments of £1,500.[113] While Stamford supported Saye and Northumberland in the divisions of May 1646,[114] all went well. However, by the beginning of June 1646 he had, like the Earl of Middlesex, transferred his allegiance to Essex's group. His shift in allegiance had immediate consequences for the payment of his pension. For Lord Saye and for Knightley, Stamford had proved to be a bad investment. For Stamford, his change of allegiance had also killed the goose that laid the £1,500 egg: although the first instalment of Stamford's annuity was forthcoming from Goldsmiths' Hall, after he transferred his allegiance to Essex's faction in the Lords the payments promptly stopped.[115] Stamford had to wait for the more beneficent days of the Rump to claim his arrears.[116] As the efforts of such aristocratic allies as Samuel Browne, John Gurdon, and Richard Knightley illustrate, the Commons could be used by peers as part of their attempts to manage the House of Lords. Cooperation from their men-of-business in the Commons was essential in rewarding political allies in the Lords and consolidating their support.

Another such political pensioner was Charles Howard, 3rd Earl of Nottingham, a consistent fellow-traveller with Saye's political group.

---

[111] [Robert Chestlin] *Persecutio undecima. The churches eleventh persecution* ([1648], 1681 edn), p. 28. H.L.R.O., Braye MS. 2, f. 44.

[112] *C.J.*, IV, 536-7 (6 May 1646).

[113] *Ibid.*

[114] Adamson, 'The Peerage in Politics', Appendix B, tables 7 and 8.

[115] P.R.O. (Kew), A.O. 1/361/15 (Audit Office decl. acc.: forfeits) mem. 12, dorse.

[116] He was, according to Lord Lisle, the first peer to take the Engagement after the execution of the King; and one suspects that it was more than republican zeal that moved him to declare his support so early for the new régime. Kent Archives Office, De l'Isle MS., U 1475/C83/26: Lisle to Leicester, 21 Feb. 1650.

Indeed, Nottingham's support had been decisive in thwarting Essex's High Presbyterian campaign of March 1646, and in establishing an Erastian church settlement as desired by the peers of the Saye-Northumberland group. Within a week of supporting this faction in these divisions in the House of Lords,[117] Nottingham was awarded a pension of £500 per annum, to be drawn on the revenues of the Sequestration Committee.[118] In practice, however, almost all the annual instalments were paid by the Committees of Revenue and for Advance of Money – both bodies controlled by the Saye-Northumberland group.[119] Northumberland himself was the beneficiary of the Haberdashers' Hall Committee's largest grant of largesse, £10,000;[120] and it is hardly surprising that one of the specific demands of the Earl of Essex's allies in the City was for the abolition of this highly politicized 'Committee for Advance of Money at Haberdashers' Hall'.[121]

In such a sophisticated political structure, consultation between Lords and Commons became a matter of course: not only at such early morning conferences as that described by Jones at Northumberland House in July 1642, but also – when business required it – during the parliamentary sessions. Saye and Nathaniel Fiennes used to 'compare Notes' in the Court of Requests while the Houses were sitting.[122] Ushers and clerks were used to convey messages from waiting M.P.s to members of the upper House, requesting meetings or seeking instructions on how to proceed in the lower House. Compromising missives, such as that sent by the M.P. Arthur Annesley to Lord Hunsdon (endorsed 'In the lobby waighting your lo[rdsh]ps commands'), provide glimpses of the workings of a political system which we have only begun to reconstruct.[123] The 'archive' for this side of parliamentary proceedings was of its nature ephemeral and frequently compromising. Such letters are remarkable not so much for their rarity, but for the fact they have survived at all.

[117] H.L.R.O., M.P. 11/3/1646, f. 146.
[118] *C.J.*, IV, 488.
[119] Folger Library, Washington D.C., MS. X. d. 35 (Cttee Rev. warr.); P.R.O., E 407/8/167, f. 17; E 407/8/168, f. 17; E 404/235 (Cttee Rev. warr.), unf.; P.R.O. (Kew), A.O. 1/361/15 (Audit Office, decl. acc.); H.L.R.O., M.P. 19/1/1648, f. 22.
[120] P.R.O. (Kew), A.O. 1/361/15 (Audit Office, decl. acc.), mem. 11, dorse: 9 Jan 1647.
[121] Corporation of London R.O., Common Council Journal 40, f. 180v.
[122] *Mercurius Pragmaticus*, no. 6 (19–26 Oct. 1647), p. 44 (B.L., E 411/23).
[123] H.L.R.O., M.P. 31/8/1648, f. 144: Annesley to Lord Hunsdon, 8 Sept. 1648. For Hunsdon's later intervention at Annesley's behest see: Bedfordshire R.O., Lucas MS. (Earls of Kent papers), L 29/90: Lord Hunsdon to [Bulstrode] Whitelocke, 18 Oct. 1648.

6

Such connections between groups of peers and their corresponding allies in the Commons were fundamental to parliamentary management during the decade of the Long Parliament – in coordinating legislation, in granting pensions, in attacking a rival's supporters in the lower House. Patron-client relations continued to be an important element in social and political relationships formed at Westminster; but in the context of parliamentary management, these were subsumed within a larger network of relations – amongst which common ideological objectives baulked large – that linked members of the Commons with factions within the House of Lords. Contemporaries described such networks within the Parliament as 'interests' – a concept which, though normally associated with a particular peer ('Lord Saye's interest in Parliament', 'my Lord of Pembroke's interest'), referred simultaneously to that peer's allies within the House of Lords *and* to his collaborators in the Commons. Thus, when Thomas Coke referred to Lord Saye's 'interest in the houses',[124] he meant not only the particular allies and clients that were associated with Saye personally, but also those peers and *their* allies and clients in the Commons – men such as Salisbury's steward, Samuel Browne – who could be presumed to be willing to pursue the same course. Browne's attitude in relation to the Gloucestershire rating petition, recounted above, highlights the place of a peer's man-of-business in the Commons within the larger context of an aristocratic interest: although he was the client of the Earl of Salisbury, his actions were on behalf of the larger entity of the Saye-Northumberland interest in the Parliament. This was a broader, less precisely defined series of relationships between members of both Houses, embracing men such as William Strode and Oliver St. John who were, so far as is known, not 'clients' at all, but men motivated by common aspirations as to how the Civil War should be fought and as to the ends for which peace should be made.

Likewise, Denzell Holles was the dominant figure in what Whitelocke called 'Essex's party' in the lower House,[125] notwithstanding there was, strictly speaking, no patron-client relationship between him and the earl. Indeed, there is no evidence that peers ever attempted to demand the adherence (or the votes) of M.P.s who were their servants and stewards. M.P.s such as Walter Kyrle (burgess for Leominster and steward of Essex's Herefordshire estates)[126] or Hugh Potter (burgess for Plympton

---

[124] Bodl. MS. Dep. c. 170 (Nalson papers), f. 193.
[125] B.L., Add. MS. 37343, f. 405.
[126] Devereux Papers (the Marquess of Bath, Longleat House, Wiltshire), IV, f. 266. B.L., Add. MS. 11047 (Scudamore papers), f. 141.

and steward of the Earl of Northumberland's northern lands),[127] were both relatively minor figures in Parliament – of more use to their masters gathering rents in the provinces than gathering votes at Westminster. Far more important as potential allies of peers were those members of the Commons who were figures of standing and repute within their own House. It is hardly surprising that of the five members that Charles I tried to arrest in 1642 – not least for the fact that they were men of standing and influence in the lower House – four out of the five were closely identified with aristocratic interests during the 1640s. Pym, Hampden and Holles were closely associated with the Earl of Essex;[128] William Strode with Viscount Saye and Sele;[129] and even Sir Arthur Hesilrige (like another dominant figure in the Commons, Oliver Cromwell),[130] was always on the fringes of the Saye-Northumberland interest in the House of Commons.[131]

In this sense, the sophisticated aristocratic 'interests' of the 1640s – and their role in the management of parliamentary affairs – had no parallel in earlier Parliaments.[132] In the Parliaments of the 1620s, as Professor Russell has argued, the relations between a peer and his client in the Commons were essentially personal: they conferred reciprocal benefits and obligations, but they did not impose a duty upon the client to take a particular 'line' in the Commons, except where the patron's personal interests were at stake.[133] Congruities in voting between individual peers and their clients in the Commons certainly occurred; though there seems

[127] Alnwick Castle, Northumberland MS O.I.2(f): Hugh Potter correspondence. P.R.O., S.P. 21/27, f. 29v.
[128] For Pym and Holles, above, pp. 30-1. For Hampden's associations with the Earl of Essex: J.H. Hexter, *The Reign of King Pym* (Cambridge, Mass., 1941), pp. 93-4, 115-6; though Hexter regards Essex as Hampden's stooge, a view for which there is only a small amount of highly questionable evidence in favour, and much against. (The sources cited by Hexter to substantiate his view of Hampden's relations with the Earl are a report in the *C.S.P. Ven.,* and a 'rumour spread at Oxford', reported in *Mercurius Aulicus.* Neither source is unimpeachable. Cf. Hexter, p. 115n.)
[129] Above, pp. 32-5.
[130] Adamson, 'The English Nobility and the Projected Settlement of 1647', pp. 585-600.
[131] Hesilrige was a major supporter of the Saye-Northumberland group's religious legislation in 1647: *C.J.,* V, 333, 348; during the 1650s he was perhaps the most forceful apologist for a restoration of the House of Lords: *Diary of Thomas Burton, Esq. . . . from 1656 to 1659,* ed. J. Towill Rutt (4 vols, 1828), IV, 77-78. For his own stature within the Parliament as a dispenser of patronage, Northamptonshire R. O., Isham Letters 252: John Corneye to Sir John Isham, 11 Jan. 1647; and B.L., Add. MS. 27990 (Sir John Percivall's notes), f. 44.
[132] I am grateful to Professor M.A.R. Graves for a discussion on this point.
[133] C.S.R. Russell, 'The Parliamentary Career of John Pym, 1621-9', in *The English Commonwealth, 1547-1640: Essays in Politics and Society Presented to Joel Hurstfield,* ed. P. Clark, A.G.R. Smith, and N.R.N. Tyacke (Leicester, 1979), pp. 149-52; idem, *Parliaments and English Politics 1621-1629* (Oxford, 1979), pp. 9-18.

little evidence that such congruities were the result of regular management, much less the result of a bond between the individual member of the Commons and a *group* of peers in the upper House. Yet it was precisely this type of relationship which developed between like-minded groups in the two Houses of Parliament during the Civil War. Founded on common objectives, promoted by the daily contacts in committees of the two Houses, and reinforced by patronage, the aristocratic 'interest' in the 1640s was a far more complex phenomenon than the patron-client nexus; and recent attempts to overstate the role of clients, or to see them as tame lackeys of the Lords, have been justly censured.[134] Important as patronage and clientage were within parliamentary interests, they were by no means a prerequisite either for identification with a particular factional grouping, or for collaboration within it. Cummulatively, these networks of relations, directed towards a common perception of how the post-war settlement should stand, constituted a whole which was infinitely greater than the sum of its individual parts.

This extension of aristocratic faction to include a substantial number of members of the Commons was perhaps inevitable in a Parliament in which the major conflict was not one of Lords *versus* Commons, but a contest between two or more rival, bi-cameral factions, competing for dominance in the post-war settlement. The fact that they sought profoundly differing versions of what that settlement ultimately should be gave an ideological aspect to the workings of patronage and clientage networks: there was no antithesis between 'faction' and 'matters of principle'.[135] The organization of factions, the granting of pensions, the Sunday meetings at Essex House, the private and informal conferences in the Court of Requests:[136] each served to further the establishment of the constitutional and religious principles that rival groups sought to have enshrined in the post-war settlement. That both factions should have recourse to pressure groups within, and outside, Parliament was neither a new nor a surprising development in English politics: most aspects had been anticipated in the political manoeuvres of 1641-2. From the King's mobilisation of a royalist party in the House of Lords in 1641 to the factional pensioners of the mid-1640s, what was remarkable about the

---

[134] D. Hirst, 'Unanimity in the Commons, Aristocratic Intrigues, and the Origins of the English Civil War', *Journal of Modern History*, L (1978), 62-3, 66-8, Cf. C. Hill's review of the following work in *Journal of Ecclesiastical History*, XXXVIII (1978), 476; and J.C.D. Clark, *Revolution and Rebellion: State and Society in England During the 17th and 18th Centuries* (Cambridge, 1986), p. 155.

[135] Cf. the remarks in J.P. Somerville's outstanding study, *Politics and Ideology in England, 1603-1640* (1986), p. 3.

[136] For reported examples, see *Mercurius Pragmaticus*, no. 6 (19-26 Oct. 1647), p. 44 (B.L., E 411/23); and Denzell Holles, *A grave and learned speech. Or an apology delivered* ([20 July] 1647), p. 6 (B.L., E 399/14).

managerial practices of the 1640s was their sophistication in planning and execution. Clearly evident in the tactics of each of the Westminster 'interests', management transformed the conduct of politics, emphasising the adversarial aspects of parliamentary business.

What was new, however, was neither management in itself, nor the presence of ideological and factionial conflict within the Parliament; it was the scale on which such techniques of management were adopted, and the consistency with which they were deployed which was unprecedented. In turn, these developments fostered a perception of the Long Parliament, in the world outside Westminster, as a body riven by faction and motivated by self-interest.[137] The committee system, so important for providing points of contact in the organization of aristocratic interests, was a particular target of attack. 'For no Committee was so soon made', recalled one ejected M.P., '[than] it was immediately converted to serve the revenge, envie, avarice, or other corrupt humours and passions of the Authors'.[138] Confused and confusing as these interests were for the observer unfamiliar with the labyrinthine complexity of parliamentary alignments, it was hardly surprising that the journalists of the news-book trade, and the majority of pamphleteers, oversimplified and schematised in an attempt to give an apparent coherence to the bewildering intricacy of parliamentary politics. 'Presbyterians' and 'Independents' provided improvised terms with which to describe the workings of these two dominant bi-cameral interests.

One of the most striking features of the political vocabulary of the 1640s was the manner in which these terms 'Presbyterian' and 'Independent' – originally ecclesiological distinctions – came to be applied to the configurations of secular, parliamentary factions.[139] However imprecisely such terms as 'Presbyterian' and 'Independent' were used, their absorption into the political vocabulary registered a profound change in the manner in which parliamentary politics was perceived. In the briefer sessions of the Elizabethan and early Stuart Parliaments, the principal and obvious division in Parliament, in terms of organization and procedure, was the hierarchical division between Lords and Commons. By the mid-1640s, the most apparent divisions relating to parliamentary organization and procedure were the vertical,

[137] Giles Grene, *A declaration in vindication of the honour of Parliament, and of the Committee of the Navy and Customes* (1647), sig. A2.
[138] G. S., *A letter from an ejected Member of the House of Commons to Sir John Evelyn* ([16 Aug.] 1648), p. 10.
[139] The application of such terms to parliamentary politics became increasingly common from 1646 onwards, when the principal basis for the association was the correspondence between the political interest of the Earl of Essex and its support for *iure divino* Presbyterianism, and the opposition to this campaign mounted by the Saye-Northumberland interest in the Lords and their allies in the House of Commons.

bi-cameral divisions of 'interests' – groups of like-minded members in the Lords and Commons acting in concert to advance common ends. It was to these groupings within the two Houses that contemporaries applied the shorthand of 'Presbyterians' and 'Independents' – most famously in Clement Walker's *Anarchia Anglicana* of 1648.[140]

The bi-cameral structure of the Parliament obviously remained the central influence on procedure; but increasingly it was by-passed by the development of powerful joint-committees of both Houses (the Committee of Both Kingdoms, the Derby House Committee and the Committee of Revenue for example), and by private organization of parliamentary interests. Such interests had one common object: to minimize the extent to which the individual Houses acted as independent arbiters of legislation. Of course, the most efficient management and the employment of the most able men-of-business could never definitively guarantee the outcome of a bill; but for those who adopted such methods, it could greatly increase the chances of achieving the desired result. Almost invevitably, this development provoked the charge that the two Houses were no longer a 'free Parliament'. Just as in 1641 the King's management of what Nicholas termed 'the Bishops partie'[141] in the Lords was denounced by Pym as being 'altogether aberated from free Parliamentary proceedings',[142] the same charge emerged in the remonstrances of the army in the late 1640s – now used against those who had been amongst the 'honest party' of 1640-42. Those who formerly acted for the public good are now

> awed or over-born by a prevailing party of men of other private Interests crept in, and that neither we, nor any other can reasonably expect Right, Freedom, or Safety (as private men), or to have things acted in Parliament for public good, while the same parties continue there in the same Power, to abuse the Name and Authority of Parliament, to serve and prosecute their private Interests and passions.[143]

This accusation was a persistent theme in the army's public declaratrions and remonstrances of 1647-8.[144] And to this extent the army's propaganda provides a running commentary on the increasing importance of bi-cameral management – of the tactics of rival coalitions of Lords and Commons – throughout the late 1640s. One of the

[140] [C. Walker], *Anarchia Anglicana: or, the history of Independency* (1648), part I, pp. 1-13, *et passim*.
[141] Guildford Muniment Room, MS. 85/5/2/21.
[142] *A worthy speech made by Master Pym to the Lords* (1641[2]), p. 5. The speech was delivered on 31 Dec. 1641.
[143] *An Humble Remonstrance from His Excellency* (25 June 1647). The remonstrance is dated at St. Albans, 23 June.
[144] M.A. Kishlansky, 'Ideology and Politics in the Parliamentary Armies, 1645-8', in *Reactions to the English Civil War, 1642-1649*, ed. J.S. Morrill (1982), pp. 163-83.

justifications the army claimed for its purge of the Parliament in 1648 was that the independence of the Commons had been usurped by effective dominance from the House of Lords. The army's *Remonstrance* of November 1648 reproved the supine lower House: 'the Lords, in every thing relating the treaty' with the King 'going before you, and haling you after'.[145] Commons clients and men-of-business of members of the Lords formed an obvious target, in December 1648, when the army set about reforming the membership of the lower House.

The role of the peers in parliamentary management suggests that the House of Lords was not seen during the 1640s as a declining or secondary element in the legislative processes of Westminster. The personalities and actions of peers and their men-of-business affected decisively the course of politics during the turbulent decade of civil war. Management of parliamentary business by peers played an increasingly important role in determining the outcome of proceedings, not only within the House of Lords, but within the Commons as well – a circumstance which contributed to the perception of the Parliament as self-interested and corrupt, and made the peers so 'dangerous'[146] to the committed radicals of 1649. In determining the course of parliamentary policy, the resolutions taken in the houses of the nobility, in the Court of Requests, and in the lobbies of Westminster, could be as equally important as the prolix debates of the Houses. During those years of civil war the future seemed fraught with uncertainty. In Parliament, at least, the Lords left little to chance.

---

[145] The *Remonstrance* is printed in *The Parliamentary or Constitutional History of England*, XVIII, 170.

[146] *C.J.*, VI, 132. The Commons' resolution to dispense with the House of Lords termed the House 'useless and dangerous'. Cf. *The Moderate*, no. 30 (30 Jan–6 Feb. 1649), sig. hh[v].

Chapter 3

The Role of Privy Councillors in the House of Lords, 1660-1681

Andrew Swatland

1

During the early modern period monarchs usually had far tighter control over the House of Lords than over the House of Commons. This was especially true in the reign of Charles II when the development during the 1670s of a substantial opposition party meant that the Court found it increasingly difficult to exert much influence over the Commons. In contrast, there were fewer occasions when Charles II and his ministers lost control over the upper House. Historians have ascribed Charles II's authority over the Lords to several factors. These include the extensive use of royal patronage. Many peers held Court posts and offices in the administration.[1] A significant proportion of the House, 48 per cent in 1680, possessed peerages which were rewards for loyal service to Charles II and his father during the years after 1642.[2] The 26 prelates, disparagingly referred to by their critics as the 'deadweight' because of their propensity to vote as the government desired, owed their seats directly to Charles II.[3] Therefore, it is argued, a majority of peers usually supported royal policies in the House of Lords in this period.

Historians have however neglected the central role played by those lords who were members of the Privy Council in the management of the House during the reign. Privy Councillors canvassed votes, secured proxies from absentees, urged potential government supporters to attend frequently, chaired committees where much of the business of the House was conducted and represented the House of Lords at conferences with the House of Commons. Through such activities they significantly enhanced the King's grip on the House of Lords. Precisely how they managed the chamber will be investigated later. First other questions need to be considered: to what extent did they participate in the

---

[1] E.S. De Beer, 'The House of Lords in the Parliament of 1680', *B.I.H.R.*, XX (1943-5), 23.
[2] *Ibid.*
[3] A.C. Swatland, 'The House of Lords in the reign of Charles II, 1660-1681', (Birmingham Ph.D. thesis, 1985), pp. 18, 23-4; K.H.D. Haley, *The First Earl of Shaftesbury* (Oxford, 1968), p. 523.

legislative and judicial activities of the House of Lords; what were the main developments in management techniques during the reign; how effective were Privy Councillors in managing the Lords for the King? But before these and other questions can be considered it is necessary to examine the composition and responsibilities of the group of councillors sitting in the chamber.

2

On the basis of the number of Privy Councillors sitting in the Lords the potential for management was considerable. Between 1660 and 1681, when Charles dissolved his last Parliament, no less than 64, or 24 per cent of the 262 peers eligible to sit in the House were Privy Councillors.[4] The figure for the numerically larger House of Commons was about two per cent. Not only was there a numerical preponderance of Privy Councillors with which to strengthen the King's authority in the Lords, but among these men were the principal ministers of the realm. During Charles II's reign the influential offices of Lord Treasurer, Lord Chancellor, Lord Privy Seal and Lord Chamberlain were always enjoyed by noblemen. These were the officials who were intimately involved in the formulation and implementation of royal policy and therefore were in a position to convey the King's views on a particular issue to other members of the Lords.

Also of benefit to the Crown was the regular attendance of a majority of Privy Councillors. Like the bishops, members of the King's Council were expected to attend the House of Lords and serve his interests there. Of all the lords, Privy Councillors were normally the most diligent in their attendance.[5] In the spring session of 1675 twenty-nine Privy Councillors sat in the House, and 18 attended on 40 or more of the 49 sittings. Of the 26 Privy Councillors who attended in the autumn session, 19 were present at 16 or more of the 21 sittings.[6] This high rate of attendance is typical of the other sessions during the reign. Because of their assiduous attendance Privy Councillors were in a strong position to influence proceedings in the chamber.

But successfully to influence proceedings in the House extensive parliamentary and administrative experience and expertise were required. Obviously unfamiliarity with procedure and precedents could impede the progress of legislation in Parliament.[7] Privy Councillors

   [4] Swatland, 'House of Lords', pp. 351-6; P.R.O., PC2: Privy Council Registers, LIV-LXIX (1660-1681).
   [5] Attendance lists for the House are given for each sitting in the Journals, but they are not always entirely reliable.
   [6] Swatland, 'House of Lords', p. 31.
   [7] *Ibid.*, p. 62.

were among the most experienced and competent members of the House. No less than 40 had acquired parliamentary experience by sitting in the House of Commons.[8] Fifteen had sat in the Lords before its abolition in 1649, and were thus in a position to advise their less experienced colleagues on matters of procedure.[9] Lord Robartes (Lord Privy Seal 1661-73), having first sat in the Short Parliament of 1640, had built up an extensive arsenal of precedents and procedure.[10] In 1661 he was able to advise the House about the significance of a tied vote, arguing from a sixteenth-century precedent.[11]

The presence of Lord Robartes and his ministerial colleagues assisted in the smooth functioning of the House in another important respect. Most ministers were experienced and competent administrators and several, like Lords Ashley (later Shaftesbury), Anglesey, Robartes and Manchester harnessed this expertise to the routine business of the House. Anglesey brought his considerable knowledge of the law, trade and religion to the Lords when he frequently chaired committees discussing bills of a legal, economic and religious nature.[12] The Earl of Sandwich, an expert on foreign trade and president of the Privy Council's Committee for Trade and Plantations, played a leading role in the revision of the 1671 Foreign Commodities Bill in a committee appointed by the House.[13] Other Privy Councillors had acquired administrative experience via Court posts or officers in the localities; many were Lord Lieutenants.[14] Moreover, as advisers to the King and by attending sessions of the Privy Council and its attendant committees, they obtained a detailed understanding of the workings of government. Clearly such experience made Privy Councillors well qualified to help bear the legislative and judicial workload of the House of Lords.

But before we can examine in more detail their role in the routine business of the House it is necessary to outline their governmental responsibilities within Parliament. There is no evidence that Charles II laid down strict guidelines on how Privy Councillors were supposed to act in the House of Lords. However, by studying their actions there it is possible to gain an insight into what he expected from members of his Council. Ministers, in particular, provided the King with a communications conduit between the Court and the Lords. They kept their master informed of proceedings in the chamber. During the heated

---

[8] *Ibid.*, pp. 351-6.

[9] *Ibid.*

[10] Lord Robartes kept a parliamentary notebook in which he entered precedents and information on procedure (B.L., Harleian MS. 2243).

[11] *L.J.*, XI, 288.

[12] Swatland, 'House of Lords', p. 77.

[13] F.R. Harris, *The Life of Edward Montagu, First Earl of Sandwich* (2 vols., 1912), II, 224-31.

[14] Thirty-two Privy Councillors were Lords Lieutenant during the years 1660-81.

debates on the impeachment of the Earl of Clarendon in November 1667 Privy Councillors reported to the King on developments in the affair, providing him with the names of lords who opposed imprisoning the former Lord Chancellor.[15] They also transmitted royal messages to the House. The Lord Chamberlain, the Earl of Manchester, delivered Charles II's message on 13 July 1663 which asserted that 'several matters of fact' in Lord Bristol's attempted impeachment of Clarendon, were 'untrue' and were regarded by his majesty as 'a Libel against his Person and Government'.[16] Largely by making his views known to the House most lords rallied to Clarendon's defence and the impeachment failed.[17] Later, on 19 June 1678 when the House was debating a controversial bill for disbanding forces raised to fight France, Lord Treasurer Danby 'by the King's command' informed their lordships of 'the state of affairs abroad and the necessity of a longer time for their disbanding the army'.[18] The Lords accordingly complied with the King's desire and amended the bill.

Such royal messages were infrequent, limited to one or two a session; but Privy Councillors did not sit idly on their benches in the chamber for they regularly served the King's interests in the legislative process. They introduced government bills into the House; promoted and defended such measures on the floor of House and at committees. At times they were required to amend or oppose legislation which encroached upon the King's prerogative powers, or which was contrary to known royal policies. Usually this meant speaking for the Court in important debates, chairing committees and voting in divisions. These duties, we shall see, intimately involved them in the day to day functioning of the House. Indeed, nowhere was their presence more marked than in the legislative process.

It is sometimes forgotten by historians that the prime responsibility of Parliament in the seventeenth century was the enactment of legislation. Charles II's House of Lords devoted more time to legislation than to any other business. Although as the supreme court the House was also concerned with judicial cases, these occupied far less of the Lords' time. Between 1660 and 1681 over 900 bills were read in the upper House, which was almost twice the total number of judicial and privilege cases received by their lordships.[19] The majority of legislation (two-thirds) considered by the Lords consisted of private bills.[20] These originated

[15] B.L., Egerton MS. 2539, f. 140: Sir John Nicholas to Sir Edward Nicholas, 14 Nov. 1667.

[16] *L.J.*, XI, 559.

[17] See Haley, *Shaftesbury*, pp. 168–9.

[18] H.L.R.O., Manuscript Minutes, XX: 19 June 1678.

[19] Swatland, 'House of Lords', p. 51.

[20] *Ibid.*, p. 55.

mainly from private individuals, local communities and business interests. Public bills on the other hand, which concerned the nation as a whole as well as sections of it, and unlike private bills were not subject to the payment of fees to the officers of the House, comprised only one third of all legislation. Of these only a minority originated with the King and his ministers, or concerned royal policies.[21] Despite the relatively small number of bills which affected the government, Privy Councillors assumed a prominent role in the consideration of all types of legislation in the House of Lords.

Although approximately a quarter of the chamber consisted of Privy Councillors, as in other periods of history only a minority of these took a leading part in the business of the House at any one time.[22] Because of the scarcity of reports of debates it is only possible to identify these 'men of business' by reference to the frequency a lord chaired a committee, or represented the House at a conference.[23] These men are named in the Journals and in the committee minute books. From these sources it is evident that the principal men of business were Lords Anglesey, Bridgwater, Ashley, Manchester, Robartes and Essex.[24] The Earl of Anglesey managed more conferences than any other peer. The Earl of Bridgwater was so active as a committee chairman that it is likely that his seat on the Privy Council in 1667 was recognition of his usefulness to both the Court and the House of Lords. His chairmanship of 119 'select committees' was only bettered by the Earl of Dorset who chaired 170.[25]

Why were these and other industrious Privy Councillors so active in the House of Lords? Like the majority of lords, they regarded it as their duty to the King and the country to involve themselves in the business of the House.[26] They believed it was their responsibility to redress national and local grievances. Thus, many were willing to serve on committees. The Earl of Bridgwater enjoyed attending Parliament and serving on committees. He wrote that 'it doth agree so much with my nature and disposition, that I cannot find in my heart to forbeare it . . .'[27] Clearly the extensive parliamentary and administrative experience of Privy Councillors made them the obvious men to chair committees. A high

---

[21] *Ibid.*, p. 56.

[22] See M.W. McCahill, *Order and Equipoise: The Peerage and the House of Lords, 1783-1806* (1978), p. 128.

[23] One cannot use the lists of committee members in the Lords Journals as a guide to activity since appointments did not correspond to the actual attendance at committee meetings (Swatland, 'House of Lords', pp. 73-4).

[24] See the Appendix for a list of committee chairmen.

[25] R.W. Davis, 'Committee and other Procedures in the House of Lords, 1660-1685', *Huntington Library Quarterly*, XLV (1982), 32.

[26] Swatland, 'House of Lords', p. 29.

[27] Hertfordshire R.O., AH 1064 (Ashridge Collection): Bridgwater to John Halsey, 4 Oct. 1661.

proportion of them were thus appointed by their fellow lords.[28] It is no coincidence that Bridgwater, who had a thorough grounding in religious matters, was nominated to the chair of almost every committee dealing with religious legislation during the 1660s and 1670s. Moreover, the Earl of Manchester was regularly appointed by the House to chair the Committee of the Whole House because of his extensive experience in that capacity before 1649.[29]

The chairmanship of this large committee was virtually monopolised by Privy Councillors. In fact they chaired the committee on more than 90 per cent of the bills and other matters debated there during the reign, and most major public bills were considered by the Committee of the Whole.[30] It was composed of every lord present in the chamber and unlike in formal debates which were presided over by the Lord Chancellor, any lord could speak as often as he wished on the same subject. Therefore the most articulate councillors, like Lords Danby, Anglesey and Finch in the 1670s could dominate proceedings. No doubt the appointment of a Privy Councillor as chairman was an advantage for the Court, for he directed proceedings, interjected with his own views and formally reported on the committee's progress to the House.[31]

Privy Councillors did not, however, monopolise the chair of 'select committees' to the same extent.[32] They still played a prominent role though, presiding over approximately half of all such committees between 1660 and 1680.[33] It is likely that the proportion of Privy Councillors chairing select committees would have been higher but for the fact that, unlike Committees of the Whole, these met either early in the morning or after three o'clock in the afternoon when the House was not generally sitting. Often at these times those Privy Councillors who held government offices had their own administrative duties to perform. From the Committee Minutes it is evident that the chairman had considerable influence over the operation of his committee. He was responsible for ensuring that each bill was carefully scrutinised, paragraph by paragraph, for advising other members on technical points and when the parties concerned in a private bill could not agree, he

---

[28] Swatland, 'House of Lords', pp. 69, 75.

[29] E.R. Foster, *The House of Lords, 1603-1649: Structure, Procedure and the Nature of its Business* (Chapel Hill, N.C., 1983), p. 271, n.267. Manchester had also directed proceedings when he had acted as speaker early in the Convention Parliament.

[30] Swatland, 'House of Lords', p. 67.

[31] *Ibid.*, pp. 66-70. During Committees of the Whole the Lord Chancellor vacated the woolsack and sat at his place at the top of the earls' bench, thus enabling him to speak like any other member.

[32] 'Select committee' was not a contemporary term. It is used in this essay to distinguish between the Committee of the Whole and committees of fewer lords appointed by the House and meeting in specific committee rooms.

[33] See below Appendix, pp. 75-7.

endeavoured to effect a compromise.[34]

Also as ordinary committee members Privy Councillors served the House by drafting bills and writing amendments.[35] Not only did Anglesey pen preambles, provisos and amendments during his twenty years in the House, but he also drafted bills such as that for distinguishing Protestant Dissenters from Popish recusants in 1680.[36] Lord Ashley, Chancellor of the Exchequer, also played a significant role in drafting and revising legislation. In April 1662 he prepared amendments for a customs bill.[37] Later in March 1673, when he was Earl of Shaftesbury and Lord Chancellor, he assisted in the amendment of the Test Bill so that it was more acceptable to the Duke of York and the Court.[38]

But the diligence of such men did not stop here. Private bills, which would not normally pass either House without powerful sponsors in Parliament, often received assistance from Privy Councillors. Interested parties frequently applied to these lords as the most influential and experienced members of the chamber to steer a particular bill through the House.[39] In March 1664 Bishop Henchman (London) noted in his diary that the Marquess of Dorchester introduced on behalf of the Heralds a bill for registering the marriage and descents of the nobility and gentry.[40] Later Sir Robert Paston, both sponsor and interested party in the controversial Yarmouth Fishing Bill obtained the support of Lord Lindsey, the Lord Great Chamberlain, when the bill was at its committee stage in the Lords. On 20 February 1665 both men dined with most of the committee members, and when the committee met at 3 p.m. Paston's Bill passed unanimously without any amendments. It is impossible to know the extent to which this hospitality influenced the members of the committee, especially as Charles II had 'sent for my Ld of Dorset who was chairman & my noble friend, and bad him from him tell those Lds that were against mee That he would never breake up the Parlament till mine act were past'.[41]

Government bills were likewise promoted by Privy Councillors in the House. Baron Ashley presented a fee-farm rents bill to the House on 15 March 1670. The measure enjoyed the King's approbation. Later Ashley was nominated to chair the committee considering the bill, thereby

---

[34] Swatland, 'House of Lords', pp. 74, 76.

[35] Most bills were drafted by lawyers (Foster, *House of Lords*, p. 191).

[36] H.L.R.O., Committee Minutes II, 387; III, 377; Manuscript Minutes XIV: 19 Jan. and 6 Feb. 1667.

[37] *Ibid.*, Committee Minutes I, 244.

[38] *Ibid.*, III, 29, 31; Manuscript Minutes XVII: 15, 18, 19 March 1673.

[39] Sessions were generally short and there was always a multitude of bills in both Houses (Swatland, 'House of Lords', pp. 13, 18).

[40] Bodl., Rawlinson MS. A 130: Bishop Henchman's Parliamentary Journal (1664-7), p. 9.

[41] B.L., Add. MS. 27447, f. 338: Sir Robert Paston to his wife, 21 Feb. 1665.

enabling him to influence proceedings on it.[42] Another important government bill, the 1675 Non-resisting Test Bill, was introduced into the chamber by Lord Lindsey. In the subsequent protracted debates and at divisions of the House it was defended by the overwhelming majority of Privy Councillors, despite persistent opposition to it from 'Country' peers.[43] These and further examples of Privy Councillors promoting government measures in the chamber confirm the leading role played by these men in the legislative business of the upper House.

They were also prominent in conferences with the House of Commons. On average two-thirds of the members of committees appointed by the House of Lords to manage conferences consisted of Privy Councillors.[44] Conferences, which involved a committee from each House meeting in the Painted Chamber, were used to forward business that required the agreement of both Houses, in particular legislation which was objected to or altered by one chamber against the wishes of the other. Conference managers, who were nominated by their respective Houses, often delivered papers, or communicated verbally the reasons for their House's position on a specific issue. For instance, Lord Chancellor Finch succinctly outlined the Lords' position on a money bill in April 1677. A contemporary reported that 'he used all his elegance and rhetoric to represent the eminent danger of the kingdom at this time and how defenceless the want of this bill would make it and in what great hazard the bill was (in) by the Commons denying to the Lords their just rights'.[45] Sometimes, such as in the dispute over Skinner's suit in 1668, a heated exchange of views occurred with the representatives of each House putting forward arguments and propositions.[46] It was normally a minister who reported at length to the House of Lords on the course and outcome of each conference.

Besides managing and reporting conferences Privy Councillors involved themselves in judicial cases. As the highest court the Lords received appeals from a variety of courts, most notably from the Chancery.[47] It also determined writs of error from the Common Law courts. Between 1660 and 1681 over 300 judicial petitions and writs of

[42] H.L.R.O., Manuscript Minutes XVI: 18 March 1670; Committee Minutes II, 318; Main Papers, vol. 11 March-2 April 1670, 31 March 1670: minute sheet from the committee.

[43] Haley, *Shaftesbury*, pp. 374-80; A. Browning, *Thomas Osborne, Earl of Danby* (Glasgow, 3 vols. 1944-51), III, 122-5.

[44] The Journals of the House of Lords list those lords appointed to manage conferences.

[45] B.L., Add. MS. 29571, f. 388: Christopher Hatton to Lord Hatton, 19 April 1677.

[46] H.L.R.O., Committee for Privileges Minutes II, 55 (8 May 1668); *L.J.*, XII, 496-500, 508-12; XIII, 509-10.

[47] For a consideration of the Lords' judicial functions see Chapter 3 of Swatland, 'House of Lords'.

error were presented to the House and its Committee for Petitions.[48] Generally the Lords' handling of cases was efficient and impartial.[49] Despite short sessions, the House was able to reach a decision in approximately 50 per cent of all error and Chancery appeals.[50]

One reason for this success was that a number of peers were well-versed in the law. Among the most experienced were Privy Councillors. Thirty-five peers had received a legal training and of these 12 were Privy Councillors.[51] Five, Lords Anglesey, Clifford, Clarendon, Finch and Holles, had qualified as barristers, and two more, Shaftesbury and Dorchester, were benchers in Gray's Inn.[52] Others had acquired legal knowledge before 1649, or as the reign progressed, simply by hearing legal cases in the House, like Lord Bridgwater.[53]

Most legal cases concerned private suits and were thus usually of very little interest to the majority of lords. Therefore, it is unlikely that Privy Councillors were normally as prominent in judicial matters as in legislative ones. This conclusion seems to be borne out by the fact that they rarely chaired the Committee for Petitions, where petitions were examined before the suit was heard on the floor of the House. Of the six Privy Councillors to occupy the chair between 1661 and 1677 none chaired it on more than four occasions. In fact, the Earl of Dorset, never a Privy Councillor, chaired 63 per cent of meetings.[54]

It is impossible to determine how active Privy Councillors were in judicial proceedings in the chamber itself because of the almost total absence of surviving accounts of legal debates. However, there is evidence to show that they were involved in promoting petitions. The Duke of Albemarle was canvassed to bring in a petition in June 1663 and Lord Halifax was asked to present to their lordships Stoughton's petition in April 1679.[55] Earlier in January 1674 the Earl of Brecknock (Duke of Ormond in the Irish peerage), the Lord Steward, spoke in support of a petition introduced by Lord Westmorland on behalf of the Earl of Shrewsbury against the Duke of Buckingham, which accused him of murder and adultery.[56]

[48] *Ibid.*, p. 94.
[49] *Ibid.*, pp. 115-30.
[50] *Ibid.*, pp. 130-1.
[51] *Ibid.*, pp. 349-56.
[52] *Ibid.*, p. 112.
[53] Henry E. Huntington Library, San Marino, California, Ellesmere MS. 8431: Danby to Bridgwater, 18 March 1681.
[54] H.L.R.O., Committee for Petitions Minutes III (1660-94); Swatland, 'House of Lords', p. 118. There is no evidence to explain why Dorset was not appointed to the Privy Council.
[55] Lismore MS. (the Duke of Devonshire, Chatsworth, Derbyshire) 33/62: Richard Graham to the Earl of Cork, 27 June 1663; B.L., Althorp Papers, Halifax Correspondence, C/9: Algernon Sidney to Halifax, 13 April 1679.
[56] B.L., M/636, Verney Papers (microfilm copy), reel 27: Sir Ralph Verney to Edmund Verney, 8 Jan. 1674.

Highly controversial cases and those of a wider political significance certainly attracted considerable interest among Privy Councillors. Of course these represented a very small minority of cases considered by the House. One such case from the mid 1660s, which concerned Lord Robartes, the Lord Privy Seal, and his son, witnessed long and bitter debates in the House.[57] The sensitive issue of the Lords' powers over Chancery occupied the Lords for several days and in the course of their debates Lord Ashley, a close colleage of Lord Robartes, objected to the fact that two peers had entered a protest with reasons appended to it in the Journal following a decisive vote, because it 'seemed to condemne what the house had ordered as unjust'.[58] Other legal cases which also concerned Privy Councillors included the impeachment and trial of Viscount Stafford in 1680, the famous case of *Skinner* v. *The East India Company*, which led to a dispute with the Commons over whether the Lords could exercise an original jurisdiction, and three appeals to the House in 1675, which occasioned another bicameral dispute over the Lords' rights to determine appeals from Chancery.[59]

One must not exaggerate the impact which Privy Councillors had on the functioning of the House of Lords. Certainly many played an important role in the chamber, but not all did. In any period of history certain Privy Councillors are more interested in parliamentary business than others. If we take the chairmanship of committees and the management of conferences as a guide to a peer's prominence in the business of the House, then about one third of Privy Councillors were relatively inactive; chairing three or less committees and managing no more than three conferences.[60]

Other lords who were not Privy Councillors were also influential and hardworking members of the House. The Earl of Dorset, probably because of his proven ability and willingness to serve the House, chaired more 'select committees' than any other lord. He also presided over the vast majority of meetings of the Committee for Petitions.[61] Other active committee chairmen included the Duke of Richmond and Lords Bolingbroke and Lucas.[62] Many peers were involved in sponsoring and promoting bills. Lord Mohun, who had estates in Cornwall, brought in a bill on 18 April 1664 for erecting a parish church at Falmouth. He had been asked to do so by the inhabitants of the town because he was the

---

[57] National Library of Wales, Wynn Papers, 2371: Hugh Moris to Maurice Wynn, 4 April 1663; 2372: Henry Bodvel to Maurice Wynn, 5 April 1663; Bodl., Rawlinson MS. A 130, pp. 16, 23, 25, 27-8, 30, 49, 50-2.

[58] Bodl., Rawlinson MS. A 130, p. 52.

[59] Swatland, 'House of Lords', pp. 98-105, 129, 324-34.

[60] See below Appendix.

[61] Swatland, 'House of Lords', pp. 77-8, 118.

[62] *Ibid*.

local landowner.[63] Before becoming a Privy Councillor in 1678, the Earl of Ailesbury was frequently approached by interested parties to advance their bills in the chamber.[64] Several peers regularly represented the House at conferences. Lord Lucas (1660-1671) and Lord Colepeper (1673-1681) were appointed to manage 31 and 24 conferences respectively. But it was not normally such men who managed the House for the Court; the delicate work of political management was done by Privy Councillors.

3

Charles II's reign witnessed major developments in the way Privy Councillors influenced proceedings in the House of Lords. During the ministry of the Earl of Danby (1673-9) management techniques became more sophisticated and widespread. Concerted efforts were made to influence attendance; the proxies of absentee lords were assiduously collected; Court peers were kept informed of royal policies in the chamber and lists of potential supporters were compiled prior to key votes.

Before the ascendancy of the Earl of Danby ministerial attempts to manage the upper House were sporadic and superficial. This was the case during the Earl of Clarendon's ministry (1660-7). The Lord Chancellor himself occasionally used the age-old tactic of speaking to peers whom he thought could be persuaded to vote with the government. He persuaded the Duke of York and seven bishops to support the royal line on the Ministers' Bill in February 1662.[65] Sometimes known government adherents were asked to be present when a controversial measure was about to be considered in Parliament. Aware that the bishops were intending to introduce the Five Mile Bill into the Oxford Parliament, Clarendon urged Lord Burlington to attend.[66] From the surviving evidence it appears that neither Clarendon nor other Privy Councillors made strenuous efforts to manipulate proxies. The Earl of Anglesey solicited proxies during the acrimonious debates on the Irish Cattle Bill in November 1666.[67] Other peers who were not English Privy Councillors, like Lord Conway and the Irish peer Lord Orrery,

---

[63] Bodl., Rawlinson MS. A 130, p. 9.

[64] Wiltshire R.O., 1300 (Ailesbury Papers), 552: Countess of Rutland to Ailesbury, n.d. [c.1666]; 553, Lady Abergavenny to Ailesbury, [c.1666]; 655, Lady Cholmondeley to Ailsbury, [c.1667].

[65] *The Rawdon Papers*, ed. E. Berwick (1819), p. 137.

[66] B.L., Althorp Papers, Burlington Correspondence, B/4: Clarendon to Burlington, 18 July 1665; R. Hutton, *The Restoration: A Political and Religious History of England and Wales, 1658-1667* (Oxford, 1985), p. 235.

[67] Bodl., Carte MS. 47, f. 136: Anglesey to Ormond, 13 Nov. 1666.

obtained proxies for the government during the mid 1660s.[68] Such managerial activities were on a far smaller scale than those used under Danby. During the years from Clarendon's fall to Danby's ministry attempts at management were still piecemeal. Occasionally Lord Arlington, Secretary of State, reminded peers to send in their proxies.[69] The main reason for the limited nature of parliamentary management was that neither the King nor his ministers saw any necessity in regularly organising members of the upper House. On most occasions the majority of peers supported royal policy.[70] There was as yet no consistent opposition group in the chamber.[71]

From the spring of 1675 ministerial attempts at managing the House became more conspicuous and thorough. During the 1674 session an extremely vocal group of opposition peers had appeared in the chamber. This group, referred to by contemporaries as the 'Country party', had emerged in the midst of the current widespread belief that the Court actively favoured Popery, and sought the establishment of Catholicism and arbitrary government at the expense of Englishmen's liberties, property rights and, most importantly, the Protestant religion.[72] The heir presumptive was a recent convert to Catholicism and in 1673 had married a Catholic princess. Charles II, having no legitimate children of his own, would almost certainly be succeeded by a Catholic. The King's foreign policy was decidedly pro-French and it was only in 1674 that the war against the Dutch had ended: a war in which England had been allied with 'absolutist' France. Country peers advocated tough laws against Papists, including the Duke of York, a Protestant foreign policy and religious toleration for Protestant nonconformists.[73] Thus, shortly before Parliament assembled in 1675, Danby had every reason to be concerned about the management of the Lords.

Notwithstanding this threat posed to the government's authority in the Lords, the actual policies pursued by the Lord Treasurer made effective parliamentary management necessary. Danby's principal aim was always to reduce the Crown's debts. Largely because of the widespread belief that the Court was inclined towards Popery Danby had failed to obtain financial assistance from the Commons in 1673 and 1674. Indeed his own religious policies were distasteful to conservative Anglican gentry in the lower House; for he had approved the 1673 bill to

---

[68] Bodl., Carte MS. 35, f. 126: Conway to Ormond, 13 Nov. 1666; B.L., Add. MS. 37206, f. 149: Orrery to Ormond, 8 March 1664.

[69] P.R.O., S.P. 29/267, f. 54: Lord Frescheville to Williamson, 29 Oct. 1669; B.L., Add. MS. 29571, f. 190: Christopher Hatton to Lord Arlington, 10 Feb. 1673.

[70] There were exceptions such as during the proceedings on Clarendon's impeachment in 1667 (see below pp. 68-9).

[71] Swatland, 'House of Lords', pp. 231-9.

[72] For a detailed analysis of the 'Country Party' see *ibid.*, pp. 239-73.

[73] *Ibid.*, pp. 250-60.

relieve Protestant Dissenters and voted for the Comprehension Bill of the following year.[74] Prior to 1675 Danby was viewed by these men as seeking to alter the Restoration Church Settlement – a settlement which rigidly Anglican members regarded as inviolable.[75] To improve his chances of obtaining supplies from the Commons, Danby decided to adopt policies, which he hoped would demonstrate to the religiously conservative country gentry who dominated the chamber, the government's commitment to the Church of England.

Since the 1674 session many of the government's traditional supporters, like Lords Dorset, Bridgwater, Ailesbury and Brecknock had joined the opposition.[76] This fact prompted Danby to turn to the conservative Anglican peers and bishops for assistance. They comprised slightly over half the House in 1675. But, because of the Declaration of Indulgence, the Duke of York's marriage and conversion and the King's continued sympathy for Nonconformists, these men were deeply perturbed by the threat from Papists and Puritans to the established Church.[77] To conciliate staunch Anglicans in both Houses the Court adopted a rigidly Anglican religious policy and an anti-French foreign policy. The penal laws were ordered to be vigorously enforced against all Nonconformists in early February 1675. On 15 April Lord Lindsey introduced a bill to impose tough restrictions on Puritans and Catholics. This Non-resisting Test Bill was intended to give Cavalier-Anglicans a monopoly of offices in church and state.[78] Though the bill failed to pass the Lords because of a protracted privilege dispute with the Commons, it did help to achieve Danby's most immediate aim. Anglican and former Royalist peers rallied to support the Lord Treasurer in the House, particularly in debates on the Test, giving the Court a numerical superiority there.[79] Most of these lords remained the Court's staunchest adherents for the remainder of the reign. I have argued elsewhere that they comprised a 'Court party' – a party united by its support for Danby's policies and fairly consistent in its voting habits.[80] Much of the responsibility for this development lay with the Lord Treasurer and, in particular, the methods he adopted to manage the Court party in the House of Lords.

Danby was the first minister to resort to whipping in the Lords on a significant scale. Just as for the Commons, he compiled lists of probable Court supporters before the Houses assembled in April 1675.[81] Later, he

[74] *Ibid.*, p. 290.
[75] *Ibid.*, pp. 288-9.
[76] *Ibid.*, p. 290.
[77] *Ibid.*, p. 292.
[78] Haley, *Shaftesbury*, p. 380.
[79] Swatland, 'House of Lords', p. 294.
[80] *Ibid.*, pp. 287-8, 295-306.
[81] *C.S.P.Ven.*, 1660-75, XXXVIII, 381; B.L., Add. MS. 28091, ff. 161, 175, 177: lists on the Test Bill.

estimated how many votes the Court could muster if the opposition were to force a division on the legality of the 14 month prorogation when Parliament assembled on 15 January 1677.[82] To bolster the numbers of Court supporters Danby tried to ensure that those peers who attended infrequently were asked to be present at the beginning of a parliamentary session. At least six such peers were sent letters asking them to attend on 15 February.[83] Such letters did hasten peers to Westminster and swell the ranks of the government's adherents. For instance, 66 Court peers attended on 15 February 1677, as compared with only 38 Country peers.[84]

Another feature of Danby's management was his exploitation of proxies. Several weeks before every session from 1675 to 1678 the two Secretaries of State wrote to likely absentees desiring them to sign and return proxy forms. Usually they were asked not to fill in the name of the recipient, enabling Danby to nominate proctors of his own choice.[85] The Earl of Suffolk was instructed to sign a blank proxy form in October 1675, which was assigned to Danby's associate Lord Maynard.[86] From 1675 to 1678 the Lord Treasurer obtained on average between ten and 15 proxy votes from absentees each session.[87] Some lords of course, sent their proxies to Danby and his colleagues without any prompting.[88] As a result of such diligence and Danby's management, for the six sessions from 1675 to 1678 the Court controlled on average 78 per cent of the proxies entered in the clerk's book.[89] All these were held by loyal Court peers and bishops. Indeed during this period 52 per cent of all proxies were in the hands of Privy Councillors alone.[90] On several occasions this superiority in proxy votes enabled the Court to win divisions in the House. The most notable was on 20 November 1675 when the Court, despite being outnumbered in the chamber by its opponents, held 16 proxies, thereby enabling it to defeat the motion that the King should be addressed to dissolve Parliament by 50 votes to 48.[91]

The Lord Treasurer also ensured that those Court lords who attended

---

[82] Swatland, 'House of Lords', pp. 306-7.
[83] *Ibid.*, p. 307.
[84] *Ibid.*, p. 298.
[85] *Ibid.*, p. 308.
[86] *C.S.P.Dom.*, 1675-6, p. 343.
[87] H.L.R.O., Proxy Books V and VI.
[88] Swatland, 'House of Lords', p. 308.
[89] *Ibid.*
[90] H.L.R.O., Proxy Books V and VI.
[91] *Ibid.*, VI: proxies entered between 21 Sept. and 20 Nov. 1675; B.L., Add. MS. 35865, f. 224: list of peers voting on whether to address the King to dissolve Parliament, 20 Nov. 1675. For further information on divisions in the House of Lords see R.W. Davis, 'Recorded Divisions in the House of Lords, 1661-1680', *Parliamentary History*, I (1983), 167-71, and A.C. Swatland, 'Further Recorded Divisions in the House of Lords, 1660-1681', *ibid.*, III (1984), 179-82.

were kept informed about the King's business in Parliament. He regularly held secret meetings to coordinate tactics in either chamber before and during a session. These were generally only attended by a few senior ministers who were closely involved in parliamentary mangement. The details of parliamentary management were not usually discussed at meetings of the Privy Council. By Charles II's reign the Privy Council was no longer the forum where government policy was finally decided; rather this occurred in a small cabinet council, known variously as the Secret Committee, the Committee for Foreign Affairs or the Committee of Intelligence. Meetings were attended by the King's inner ring of advisers, who in the main were also Privy Councillors. In this committee Lords Danby, Finch, Guilford (Lauderdale) and Brecknock met several times about the preparations for the 1677 session.[92] Earlier, on 19 April 1675, Danby, Anglesey and Finch had met to discuss the objections made by Country peers to the oath in the Test Bill.[93] There is also evidence to show that sometimes, when major pieces of legislation were being considered in the Lords, Danby provided Court peers with sheets of paper containing arguments to be used in debates. Several copies of such sheets have survived relating to his own Bill of Attainder of April 1679.[94]

The effect of Danby's parliamentary management is clearly seen in the consistent behaviour of Court lords in votes in the House. From 28 divisions and protests between 1675 and 1681 58 Court peers, who voted at least twice, had an average consistency rate of 81 per cent.[95] Privy Councillors rarely voted contrary to the King's wishes. On five key issues between 1675 and 1678 almost 80 per cent of them consistently voted with the Court.[96] Whereas 20 Privy Councillors opposed the Country party's design in December 1678 to commit Danby to the Tower following his impeachment by the Commons, only four, Bridgwater, Essex, Newport and Strafford, who were never firm Court adherents in the 1670s, voted with the opposition.[97] This consistency among the majority of Privy Councillors was in stark contrast with the period before Danby's ministry, when factions of the King's Council

[92] *C.S.P.Dom.*, 1676-7, p. 480.

[93] B.L., Add. MS. 40860, f. 86: Anglesey's diary entry for 19 April 1675.

[94] Swatland, 'House of Lords', p. 309.

[95] These divisions and protests are discussed at length in Swatland, 'House of Lords', pp. 382-400.

[96] The five lists were: opinion on Danby's Test Bill (spring 1675); whether to address the King to dissolve Parliament (20 Nov. 1675); whether the test about transubstantiation should be added to the oaths of allegiance and supremacy in the Test Bill (15 Nov. 1678); whether to adhere to their amendments in the Disbanding Bill (26 Dec. 1678); and whether to commit Danby to the Tower of London (27 Dec. 1678). See *ibid.*, pp. 384, 386, 388-9, 390, 398-400.

[97] *Ibid.*, pp. 398-400.

openly disagreed with each other in the House of Lords.

The Earl of Danby and his close associates were not the only peers to manage the Lords during the 1670s. Similar managerial ploys were adopted by the Earl of Shaftesbury and the other leaders of the Country party. They wrote to absentees asking them to attend or send in their proxies.[98] They too held private meetings for the discussion of tactics to be employed in the upper House.[99] Also they tried to win support for their policies outside Parliament, and thereby, influence the views of members inside. Their speeches, protests and political pamphlets were printed and disseminated in London and the provinces.[100] This management helped to give the Country party considerable unity in the House. Country peers were even more party consistent in their voting habits than their Court counterparts. For the 43 Country lords who are recorded as voting twice or more during the period 1675–81 there was a consistency rate of 95 per cent between divisions. Thirty-four opposed the Court in all their recorded votes.[101]

4

It would not be appropriate to conclude this essay without considering how effective Privy Councillors were in managing the House of Lords. One area of royal policy where their influence was pronounced was religion. Through his minsters the King was able to persuade the Lords to accept or revise religious legislation in the early 1660s. He was frequently able to accomplish this because the House was almost evenly split between those who wanted a narrow Anglican Church settlement, and when this had been accomplished in 1662, to preserve the religious status quo; and those, including Charles II, many of his Privy Councillors and Presbyterian peers, who preferred a more comprehensive church and later wished to modify the 1662 Church Settlement.[102] By exerting pressure on the Lords, Charles II was able to tip the balance of opinion in his favour. A good example of this concerns the 1662 bill to confirm the Ministers' Act of 1660. The Commons had so extensively altered the measure that the amendments would have led to the ejection of Presbyterian ministers from their livings and the establishment of a narrow Anglican ministry, which the King was eager to avoid. The Lords were evenly divided in their attitude towards the Bill when it came up to them in January 1662; a point which was underlined

---

[98] *Ibid.*, p. 265.
[99] *Ibid.*, p. 266.
[100] *Ibid.*, p. 268.
[101] *Ibid.*, p. 264.
[102] See *ibid.*, pp. 177–211 for a discussion of the religious composition of the House and the peers' role in the Church Settlement.

by a tie vote on 29 January.[103] Later the Lord Chancellor obtained the support of seven bishops, the Duke of York and the Catholics. Together with the Presbyterians, they persuaded the House to discard the Commons' amendments, thus confirming the 1660 Act without change.[104]

Other religious bills which members of the Privy Council were instrumental in persuading the peers to accept or amend according to royal wishes, included the 1663 Bill of Ecclesiastical Affairs, the 1670 Conventicle Bill and the Comprehension Bill of 1674.[105] The extent of ministerial influence on such legislation in the House of Lords should not be exaggerated. For the King's ministers to have made their views felt in the chamber there had to be a sizeable body of receptive and sympathetic peers. Indeed, as the King's attempts to revise the Bill of Uniformity show, the votes of several bishops, Catholics and of 25 to 40 Presbyterians were of the utmost importance.[106] Their votes, together with those of leading Privy Councillors like Lords Clarendon, Brecknock and the Duke of York, ensured that the House accepted the King's dispensing proviso in March 1662.[107] This proviso, introduced by Clarendon, would have enabled Charles, had it not been rejected by the Commons, to use his royal prerogative to establish a broader church than was originally envisaged by the bill's narrowly Anglican sponsors.

In the field of financial legislation Privy Councillors successfully applied pressure on the House of Lords. The peers received with suspicion a poll bill on 8 March 1678 because it infringed their highly esteemed privilege of taxing themselves.[108] Only members of the Commons were to be tax commissioners. With deteriorating finances Charles II was intent on the peers passing the measure quickly and without amendment. His views were communicated via Privy Councillors to members of the Court party and on 12 March the bill passed unamended, thereby avoiding a potentially damaging dispute with the House of Commons.[109] The Commons did not accept that the Lords had the right to alter financial bills. Earlier, in April 1677, the

---

[103] *L.J.*, XI, 373.

[104] *Rawdon Papers*, p. 137. The term 'Presbyterian' is used here to denote peers who favoured a broad Church of England, which would include most Presbyterian and moderate Independent ministers and toleration for those peaceable Dissenters who would not conform to such a church. These peers also wanted to strip the church of 'Popish' practices and ceremonies. See *Reliquiae Baxterianae*, ed. M. Sylvester (1696), p. 278.

[105] Swatland, 'House of Lords', pp. 210-1, 213-9.

[106] *Ibid.*, pp. 202, 204-7.

[107] B.L., Add. MS. 22919, f. 203: Sir William Morrice to Sir George Downing, 21 March 1662; H.M.C., *Rawdon-Hastings MSS.*, IV, 129.

[108] H.M.C., *Ormonde MSS.*, IV, 413.

[109] *Ibid.*, p. 414.

Lords had agreed to pass a supply bill unamended because the Lord Chancellor and Lord Treasurer had spoken forcefully to members of the House.[110]

Also, on many occasions Privy Councillors vigorously defended the King's prerogative powers when these seemed jeopardised by the actions of either chamber. Lords Clarendon, Butler, Berkeley, Anglesey and the Duke of York were against the word 'nuisance' in the 1666 bill to prohibit the import of Irish cattle. In common law the word debarred the use of the royal dispensing power. However, along with the other opponents of the bill they persuaded the House to substitute for 'nuisance' a milder phrase which did not inhibit the use of the dispensing power. Thus Charles could greatly dilute the effect of the statute.[111] When the King's power to prorogue Parliament for more than a year was questioned by opposition peers on 15 February 1677 several Privy Councillors upheld the King's right in the lengthy debate.[112] The Earl of Anglesey and Lord Finch argued that his authority to prorogue was not restricted by medieval statutes, but was unlimited.[113] Perhaps the most famous occasion when Privy Councillors rallied to the aid of the royal prerogative occurred on 15 November 1680 when the King's right to name his successor was challenged by the Exclusion Bill. Twelve of the 17 Privy Councillors present at the division voted with Court to reject the bill after its first reading.[114]

However, especially during the 1660s there were several occasions when neither the King nor his ministers could persuade a majority of peers to comply with royal policies. On 12 November 1667 the former Lord Chancellor was impeached by the Commons for treason. The King vigorously backed Clarendon's impeachment, hoping the Lords would commit him to the Tower to await his trial. Charles's aim was to use Clarendon as a scapegoat for his government's mishandling of the Second Anglo-Dutch War. The Duke of Buckingham had persuaded him that Clarendon's impeachment would conciliate the Commons and induce it to consider requests for money.[115] Charles made his views clear to the peers, speaking to many individually. Several Privy Councillors,

---

[110] Swatland, 'House of Lords', pp. 160-1.

[111] *L.J.*, XII, 86; B.L., Althorp Papers, Burlington Correspondence B/3: Robert Boyle to Lord Burlington, 24 Oct. 1665; Bodl., Carte MS. 35, f. 30: Conway to Ormond, 14 Jan. 1667; 47, f. 130: Anglesey to Ormond, 13 Nov. 1666; f. 138: same to same, 15 Jan. 1667.

[112] Bodl., Carte MS. 79, ff. 31-43: Lord Wharton's notes on the debate (15-16 Feb. 1677).

[113] *Ibid.*, f. 31; *Lord Nottingham's Chancery Cases*, ed. D.E.C. Yale (Seldon Soc., 2 vols., 1954, 1961), II, 982-8.

[114] Swatland, 'House of Lords', pp. 313-6, 398-400.

[115] C. Roberts, 'The Impeachment of the Earl of Clarendon', *Cambridge Historical Journal*, XIII (1957), 10-2.

notably Buckingham and Albemarle, exerted their influence too.[116] Yet, with the exception of 28 peers who signed a protest on 20 November and possibly a few others who did not, the vast majority refused to imprison Clarendon.[117] Most of these lords refused to obey the King because they believed that commitment on a general charge of treason would establish a precedent for the indiscriminate imprisonment of innocent lords, without specific written charges being produced by the Commons.[118] The peers' personal safety was regarded as more important than the short-term expediency of Charles II. Other instances of when Privy Councillors could not persuade the Lords to act as the King desired include the passing of the Earl of Derby's Estate Bill (1662), which threatened the basis of the Restoration land settlement, the disputes with the Commons over Skinner's case (1668-70), the Foreign Commodities Bill (1671), and the Lords' refusal to ratify the Declaration of Indulgence in March 1673.[119]

It would be unfair to lay all the blame for these failures at the feet of Privy Councillors. Sometimes, as with the Declaration of Indulgence, the King was out of step with the views of most peers. The peers' reaction to the Declaration was determined by their profound fear of Popery and their distrust of royal intentions.[120] On other occasions, such as during the protracted dispute with the Commons over their original jurisdiction in Skinner's case, the House of Lords placed the defence of its privileges before the King's interests. Charles wanted the Lords to surrender this privilege so that the disruption of normal parliamentary business, and in particular financial bills, would cease.[121]

The very nature of the King's style of government split the Privy Council. Often between 1660 and 1675 conciliar divisions weakened the government's ability to manage the House of Lords. During the 1660s the Council was divided between former Royalists and former Parliamentarians. At his Restoration Charles had appointed a mixed Privy Council representative of the diversity of religious and political opinion that existed within the ruling elite. Between May 1660 and May 1661 24 English peers were members of the Privy Council.[122] Of these, 11 were ex-Parliamentarians – having either fought for Parliament during the Civil War or supported the subsequent regimes during the

---

[116] Swatland, 'House of Lords', pp. 162-3.

[117] *Ibid.*, p. 163.

[118] *Ibid.*, pp. 163-4.

[119] *Ibid.*, pp. 162, 164-5, 169-70, 278-80; Harris, *Earl of Sandwich*, II 333-7.

[120] Swatland, 'House of Lords', pp. 169-70.

[121] *Ibid.*, pp. 164-5.

[122] P.R.O., PC2/LIV, ff. 24, 28, 35, 57, 95; LV, f. 1.

Interregnum – and 12 were former Civil War Royalists.[123] Most of the former held a variety of Puritan views. Like the King, they wanted Presbyterian ministers included in a broad Church of England, and toleration for those whose scruples made them unable to conform.[124] The more hardline Anglican-Royalist members favoured an exclusively Anglican Church and the prosecution of Nonconformists.[125] Contemporaries reported bitter wranglings between Privy Councillors at Council meetings. In September 1662 there were great disputes as to whether Presbyterian ministers should be continued in their livings as the King had promised in his Declaration of Breda, or whether the Act of Uniformity should be vigorously enforced.[126] Later this disunity manifested itself in the Lords in February 1663, when rigidly Anglican Privy Councillors opposed the King's bill to dispense ministers from the provisions of the Act of Uniformity. Presbyterian members like Lords Robartes, Manchester and Anglesey vigorously promoted the measure. However, on this occasion the opponents of the Bill were unable to prevent it from being committed to a Committee of the Whole House, though they were able to draw out proceedings on the measure in a sub-committee in March.[127]

As the decade progressed several Privy Councillors built up followings of like-minded peers at Court and in Parliament. Leaders of rival factions included the Dukes of Buckingham, Albemarle and York and Lords Arlington, Clarendon and Brecknock. Broadly speaking their intentions were to undermine their rivals and to influence royal policy.[128] Charles II's approach to politics encouraged factions to flourish. Even his advisers frequently had difficulty in determining his actual views on a specific issue, for he tended to disguise his thoughts with dissimulation. It is no wonder that the policies of his ministers were sometimes at variance with one another and that ministers sought to impose their own policies on the King.

Therefore it is not surprising that Privy Councillors were often in

[123] The former Parliamentarians were Albemarle, Anglesey, Ashley, Carlisle, Holles, Leicester, Manchester, Northumberland, Robartes, Sandwich and Saye and Sele. The ex-Royalists were Berkshire, Brecknock, Clarendon, Colepeper, Cornwallis, Dorchester, Lindsey, Norwich, St. Albans, Seymour, Somerset and Wentworth. I have not included the Earl of Southampton among the latter peers, since he lived in retirement on his estate and took no active part in the Civil War. Also his religious views were closer to the Presbyterian lords than to the Anglican-Royalists. See Swatland, 'House of Lords', p. 186.

[124] *Ibid.*, pp. 359-60, 364-6.

[125] *Ibid.*, pp. 190-1, 359-60, 372-3.

[126] Bodl., Carte MS. 32, f. 3: O'Neale to Ormond, 2 Sept. 1662.

[127] Haley, *Shaftesbury*, pp. 164-6; H.L.R.O., Committee Minutes I, 295, 298.

[128] Swatland, 'House of Lords', pp. 232-6, 283-5; P. Seaward, 'Court and Parliament: The Making of Government Policy, 1661-1665' (Oxford D.Phil. thesis, 1986), pp. 75-98.

disagreement over business in the House of Lords. Royal control over the House invariably suffered as they pursued conflicting policies. They were deeply divided over whether to agree with Charles and commit Clarendon in November 1667. At least seven, including Buckingham, Arlington, Albemarle and Bath supported the King, but the majority were of the opposite opinion.[129] Had most Privy Councillors supported the impeachment of Clarendon it is possible that the outcome of the key votes in the House would have been very different. Divisions among Privy Councillors had been decisive in 1666 during the proceedings on the Irish Cattle Bill: an issue which had almost evenly split the House of Lords. Charles was anxious for the House to reject the Bill, since by proposing to prohibit the import of Irish cattle into England, it would also curtail the customs duties from trade with Ireland. At least seven Privy Councillors shared views similar to the King's, but the majority did not.[130] They believed the importation of cheap cattle was responsible for a drop in prices for their own cattle, which in turn depressed rents. A few, like Ashley and Buckingham, promoted the measure as a means of discrediting the Earl of Brecknock, the Lord Lieutenant of Ireland, who through intermediaries endeavoured to defeat it. The votes and proxies of these Privy Councillors proved decisive. The bill passed the House by 63 votes to 47, which included many proxy votes, on 23 November. Had at least ten Privy Councillors, holding between them eight proxies, not voted for the bill it would almost certainly have failed to pass.[131]

During the ministry of the Earl of Danby such divisions among Privy Councillors were rare.[132] In part this was because the Privy Council itself was more homogeneous. In February 1679 only six of the 32 noble members had Parliamentarian or Presbyterian antecedents.[133] As ex-Parliamentarians died Charles replaced them with more compliant

[129] *L.J.*, XII, 141.

[130] The seven Privy Councillors who opposed the bill were Archbishop Sheldon, Lords Clarendon, Anglesey, Butler, Brecknock, Berkeley of Berkeley and the Duke of York (Bodl., Carte MS. 34, f. 413: Southwell to Ormond, 31 Oct. 1665; 35, f. 30: Conway to Ormond, 14 Jan. 1667; 47, f. 130: Anglesey to Ormond, 13 Nov. 1666; f. 138: same to same, 15 Jan. 1667; *L.J.*.., XII, 86).

[131] These peers were Southampton, Buckingham, Ashley, Robartes, Carlisle, Berkshire, Dorchester, Manchester, Arlington and Northumberland (Bodl., Carte MS. 217, ff. 352-3: Anglesey to Ormond, 10 Nov. 1666; 35, f. 126: Conway to Ormond, 13 Nov. 1666; Nottingham U.L., (Portland Collection, Cavendish MS.) PW1/190: Northumberland to Newcastle, 14 Nov. 1666; H.L.R.O., Proxy Book V: proxies entered after 18 Sept. 1666).

[132] There were differences of opinion on whether to prorogue or dissolve the Cavalier Parliament, but apart from the vote on 22 November 1675, they did not manifest themselves in the Lords (B.L., Stowe MS. 207, ff. 60-1: Harbard to Essex, 16 Jan. 1675; 212, f. 193: same to same, 15 June 1677).

[133] The six were Lords Robartes, Anglesey, Carlisle, Fauconberg, Maynard and Salisbury (P.R.O., PC2/LXVII, f. 2; LXVIII, f. 3).

Anglican-Royalists, who generally supported Danby's policies. Several prominent Privy Councillors who sided with opposition members in the House – nobably Buckingham, Shaftesbury, Holles and Halifax – were removed from the Council board. Also from 1675 the government pursued far more consistent policies than previously. Danby's vigorous defence of the Church of England, his enforcement of the laws against Dissenters and his anti-French foreign policy appealed to the vast majority of Privy Councillors.[134] These policies, in conjunction with his systematic management of the Lords, ensured that from 1675 the King's grip upon the House was more secure than it had been at any time earlier in the reign.

Danby's efforts at management were made considerably easier because the vast majority of bishops voted with the Court party after 1675. Charles II and his ministers had always believed it was essential for the 24 bishops and two archbishops to regularly attend, because at times their votes were vital in determining the outcome of a division in the chamber.[135] From 1661 to 1681 the Archbishops of Canterbury – generally Privy Councillors – wrote systematically to the bishops shortly before each session, reminding them of their duties in Parliament. As a result of this policy over half the bishops attended every session and others sent their proxies. When business involving the church was anticipated an attendance of two-thirds was not unusual.[136]

Until the orthodox Anglican policies of the Earl of Danby, the bishops did not consistently adhere to royal policy in the House of Lords. On several occasions Archbishop Sheldon had urged his colleagues to attend and defend the Church of England against government policies. In December 1662 the bishops were told to be present when Parliament met on 18 February because the Act of Uniformity was threatened by the King's Declaration of Indulgence: a measure which Charles wanted Parliament to approve.[137] Ten years later Sheldon instructed the prelates to repair to Westminster and, if necessary, cast their votes against the Second Declaration of Indulgence.[138]

The other development which reinforced ministerial control over the Lords during the 1670s was the personal presence of Charles II at debates in the House. From March 1670 the King had begun attending debates informally, generally sitting in a chair by the fireplace.[139] He attended

---

[134] Swatland, 'House of Lords', pp. 295–302.

[135] *Ibid.*, p. 19.

[136] *Ibid.*, p. 24.

[137] Bodl., Tanner MS. 48, f. 69: Frewen to Sheldon, 6 Dec. 1662; *The Correspondence of John Cosin, Bishop of Durham*, ed. G. Ornsby, (Surtees Soc., LII, LV, 1868–70), LV, 101.

[138] B.L., Harleian MS. 7377, f. 39: Sheldon to the Bishop of Bangor, 28 Dec. 1672; f. 42: same to Henchman, 6 Feb. 1673.

[139] For the reasons why Charles II began attending debates in the House see Swatland, 'House of Lords', pp. 154–6.

very assiduously. He was present for 51 of the 59 sittings of the Second Exclusion Parliament of October 1680 to January 1681.[140] He did not speak openly in debates, but he did make his opinions clear by talking quietly to peers individually. As with Danby's Test Bill and the Exclusion Bill, he often canvassed votes in the House. His presence prevented Country peers from misrepresenting his views on a particular subject. On 28 November 1678 the House debated an address from the Commons for the expulsion of the Queen from Whitehall. Country peers claimed she was implicated in the plot to kill her husband. The Lords, however, overwhelmingly rejected the address because 'the king carried himself most worthily, shewing a detestation of what some thought might be acceptable to him . . .'[141]

When the vast majority of Privy Councillors supported the policies of Charles II their management of the House of Lords was generally effective. Thus, with the exception of the demise of the 1675 Test Bill, which failed to pass the Lords because their lordships eventually channelled all their energies into a privilege dispute with the Commons, from 1675 to 1681 the King did not suffer a single major defeat in the upper House. Prior to this date divisions between Privy Councillors had contributed to the King failing to get his way in at least six major issues in the House.[142]

The fall of the Earl of Danby in March 1679 did not result in any noticeable reduction in the King's authority in the chamber. There is less evidence of widespread management of the House by leading ministers. Lords Finch, Brecknock and Bath conveyed the King's views to Court peers and solicited votes.[143] During the Christmas recess on 31 December 1680 Lord Chancellor Finch and the Earl of Radnor (formerly Lord Robartes) met to discuss legislation pending before the Lords.[144] The King himself continued to attend zealously and exert influence on peers.[145] But proxies were not managed in the same way. Following the royal assent to the Second Test Bill on 30 November 1678, proxies were limited to those lords who had actually attended and subscribed to the oaths and the declaration against Catholicism in the Act. Occasionally

[140] *L.J.*, XIII, 610-742.

[141] H.M.C., *Ormonde MSS.*, p. 723.

[142] These issues concerned the Earl of Derby's Estate Bill (1662), the Irish Cattle Bill (1666-7), the impeachment of Clarendon (1667), *Skinner* v. *the East India Company* (1668-70), the Foreign Commodities Bill (1671) and the Declaration of Indulgence (1673).

[143] B.L., Add. MS. 28049, f. 20: Bath to Danby, 1 April 1679; Bodl., Carte MS. 79, f. 164 (proceedings of the Oxford Parliament, 21-22 March 1681); H.M.C., *Ormonde MSS*, p. 724; Devonshire Collection (Duke of Devonshire, Chatsworth) G/2: Ailesbury to Devonshire, 6 Nov. 1680.

[144] Leicestershire R.O., (Finch Papers) P.P. 65: brief notes of speeches by Lord Chancellor Finch and Lord President Radnor, 31 December 1680.

[145] B.L., Add. MS. 28049, f. 20: Bath to Danby, 1 April 1679; Haley, *Shaftesbury*, p. 601.

peers who were ill were urged to attend, if only to take the oaths and make a proxy.[146] By 1679 there was perhaps less need systematically to manage the House. As a result of Danby's policies a substantial and permanent party of 40 to 60 Court supporters existed in the Lords, which almost guaranteed the Court a majority in divisions in the House.[147] Also the issues surrounding the Popish Plot and Exclusion Crisis not only ensured that these peers attended in good numbers, but that they rallied behind the King when his prerogatives and policies were threatened by opposition members.[148]

5

For the reign as a whole members of the Privy Council made a considerable contribution to the management of the House of Lords. Only a small number, usually leading ministers, were involved in the types of political management outlined above. Many more though played a central role in the routine proceedings of the House; promoting legislation, chairing committees and representing the House at conferences. Here they represented the interests of the King, their fellow members, the political nation and of private individuals. Of course Privy Councillors were not alone in performing these tasks. Many ordinary members actively participated in the functioning of the House. However, without a large number of Privy Councillors actively involving themselves in the business of the House, it is unlikely that the Lords would have been able to deal with the volume of legislation it did. Over 900 bills were read there during the 23 parliamentary sessions of the reign. It is even more certain that without their presence during the 1670s, when an organised opposition emerged in both Houses of Parliament, Charles II would have found the Lords extremely difficult to control.

[146] H.L.R.O., Proxy Book VI, 30 Nov. 1678; B.L., Add. MS. 29556, f. 124: Finch to Hatton, 13 March 1679.
[147] Swatland, 'House of Lords', pp. 294, 310.
[148] *Ibid.*, pp. 312–17.

Appendix

Privy Councillors sitting in the House of Lords, 1660-1681

KEY
1. Period of appointment to Charles II's Privy Council.
2. Member of the House of Commons before elevation to the Lords.
3. *Religious views*

P:	Presbyterians. These peers conformed to the Church of England, but favoured broadening it to include Presbyterian ministers. Most also wanted toleration for peaceable Protestant Dissenters.
P?:	Probable Presbyterians.
A:	Rigid Anglicans. These peers advocated the exclusion of Presbyterian clergymen from the Church of England and the enforcement of the penal laws against Nonconformists.
C:	Catholic peers.
C?:	Probable Catholics.
P/A, A/C:	Religious views changed significantly during the reign: Presbyterian to Anglican; Anglican to Catholic.

4. *Political persuasions, 1675-1681*

Ct:	Member of the 'Court Party'.
Cy:	Member of the 'Country Party'.
Cy/Ct, Ct/Cy:	Changed party allegiance.

5. Number of Committees of the Whole House chaired between 1660 and 1680.
6. Number of 'select committees' chaired between 1660 and 1680. Only lords who chaired committees on three or more separate bills are listed.
7. Number of occasions a lord managed a conference.

SOURCES
A.C. Swatland, 'The House of Lords in the Reign of Charles II, 1660-1681' (Birmingham Ph.D thesis, 1985), pp. 67, 77-8, 349-400; P.R.O., PC2 (Privy Council Registers, 1660-1681), LIV-LXIX; *L.J.*, XI-XIII; H.L.R.O., Committee Minutes, 1661-1680; *The Complete Peerage,* ed. G.E. Cokayne (2nd edn., 13 vols, 1910-59).

Lords	1	2	3	4	5	6	7
E. Ailesbury	1678-1679, 1681-1685	MP	A	Ct	3	57	25
D. Albemarle (1st)	1660-1670	MP	P	—	—	—	—
D. Albemarle (2nd)	1675-1685	MP	A	Ct	—	—	—

Lords	1	2	3	4	5	6	7
E. Anglesey	1660–1685	MP	P	Ct	8	77	144
E. Arlington	1662–1685	MP	P/A	Ct	—	—	2
E. Bath	1663–1685	—	A	Ct	—	—	2
L. Berkeley of Berkeley	1678–1679	—	P?	Ct	—	7	27
L. Berkeley of Stratton	1663–1678	MP	A	Ct	—	3	—
E. Berkshire	1660–1669	MP	C	—	—	—	—
E. Brecknock	1660–1685	—	P/A	Ct	2	5	22
(D. Ormond in the Irish peerage)							
E. Bridgwater	1667–1685	—	A	Cy	37	119	117
D. Buckingham	1662–1674	—	P	Cy	1	11	25
L. Butler	1666–1679, 1680	MP	A	Ct	—	—	4
E. Carlisle	1660–1679	MP	P	Cy/Ct	—	6	21
E. Chesterfield	1680–1685	—	P?	Cy/Ct	—	—	—
E. Clarendon (1st)	1660–1667	MP	P/A	—	—	—	29
E. Clarendon (2nd)	1679, 1680-5	MP	A	Cy/Ct	1	8	18
L. Clifford	1666–1673	MP	C	—	1	—	—
L. Colepeper	1660	MP	A	—	—	—	—
V. Conway	1681–1683	—	A	Ct	—	—	—
L. Cornwallis	1660–1662	MP	A	—	—	—	—
E. Craven	1666–1679, 1681–1685	—	P	Ct	—	—	2
D. Cumberland	1662–1682	—	—	Ct	—	—	—
E. Danby	1672–1679	MP	A	Ct	—	—	—
M. Dorchester	1660–1679	MP	C?	Ct	—	4	—
E. Essex	1672–1681	—	P	Cy	7	33	58
V. Fauconberg	1672–1685	—	P	Cy	—	—	23
L. Finch	1673–1682	MP	A	Ct	—	—	31
(E. Nottingham 1681)							
D. Gloucester	1660	—	—	—	—	—	1
E. Guilford	1661–1682	—	A	Ct	—	—	—
(D. Lauderdale in the Scottish peerage)							
V. Halifax (Earl 1679)	1672–1676, 1679–1685	MP	P	Cy/Ct	2	3	46
L. Hatton	1662–1670	MP	P?	—	—	—	—
L. Holles	1660–1676, 1679	MP	P	Cy	—	—	49
E. Leicester	1660–1677	MP	P	Cy	—	—	—
E. Lindsey (2nd)	1660–1666	MP	A	—	—	—	—
E. Lindsey (3rd)	1666–1679, 1682–1685	MP	A	Ct	—	—	1
E. Manchester	1660–1671	MP	P	—	18	16	63
L. Maynard	1672–1679	—	A	Ct	—	—	—
D. Monmouth	1670–1685	—	P?	Ct/Cy	—	—	4
D. Newcastle	1670–1685	MP	A	Ct	—	—	—
V. Newport	1668–1679	MP	P	Cy/Ct	1	—	11
E. Northampton	1673–1679	MP	A	Ct	2	41	25
E. Northumberland	1660–1668	MP	P	—	—	—	3
E. Norwich	1660–1663	MP	A	—	—	—	—

Lords	1	2	3	4	5	6	7
E. Oxford	1670–1679,						
	1681–1685	—	—	Ct	—	—	6
E. Peterborough	1674–1679	—	A	Ct	—	—	—
E. Portland	1662–1663	MP	A	—	—	26	20
L. Robartes	1660–1685	—	P	Cy/Ct	8	41	56
(E. Radnor 1679)							
E. St. Albans	1660–1679	MP	C	Ct	—	—	—
E. Salisbury	1679–1681	MP	P	Cy	—	—	8
E. Sandwich	1660–1672	MP	A	—	—	—	10
V. Saye and Sele	1660–1662	—	P	—	—	—	—
L. Seymour	1660–1664	MP	A	—	—	—	1
E. Shaftesbury	1660–1674,						
(L. Ashley to 1672)	1679	MP	P	Cy	2	42	113
D. Somerset	1660	MP	A	—	—	—	1
E. Southampton	1660–1667	—	P	—	—	—	30
E. Strafford	1674–1679	—	P	Ct/Cy	—	—	—
E. Sunderland	1674–1681	—	—	Ct/Cy	—	—	1
L. Vaughan	1661–1679	MP	A	Ct	—	—	—
L. Wentworth	1660–1665	MP	A	—	—	—	—
M. Winchester	1679–1685	MP	P	Cy	—	—	19
M. Worcester	1672–1685	MP	A	Ct	—	—	4
D. York	1660–1679	—	A/C	Ct	—	—	—

Bishops

Henry Compton	1676–1685	—	—	Ct	—	5	9
(London)							
Nathaniel Crew	1676–1685	—	—	Ct	—	—	3
(Durham)							
Humphrey Henchman	1663–1675	—	—	Ct	—	—	7
(London)							
George Morley	1675–1679	—	—	Ct	—	—	5
(Winchester)							
Gilbert Sheldon	1663–1677	—	—	Ct	—	—	7
(Canterbury)							
William Sancroft	1678–1685	—	—	—	—	—	—
(Canterbury)							

Totals	70	40	A:26	Ct:31	93	504	1053
			P:20	Cy:9			
			C:3	Cy/Ct:6			
			P/A:3	Ct/Cy:3			
			A/C:1				
			A?:1				
			P?:3				

Chapter 4

'Venice Preserv'd; or A Plot Discovered': The Political and Social Context of the Peerage Bill of 1719[*]

Clyve Jones

1

It was Disraeli who first coined the term 'Venetian oligarchy' for the aristocratic control of eighteenth-century British government.[1] His view was based on an analogy with the Venetian republic where it was difficult for an outsider to penetrate the closed mercantile aristocracy once the *Libro d'oro* had been compiled in the thirteenth century. This 'Golden Book' listed all the major families in Venice and it was only from their ranks that the republic's ruling elite could be chosen. Despite Disraeli's perceptive label the myth has survived that Hanoverian society was ruled, in contrast to Venice, by an open elite continually replenished by recruits from other classes. Recent writings on the British aristocracy have, however, successfully challenged this myth. The British peerage was essentially more exclusive than many of its contemporary continental counterparts.[2] It is clear that in Britain there was in operation a de facto 'Golden Book' of the upper stratum of society from which the ruling elite was chosen, with very few outsiders breaking into this circle without the passport of some family connexion with the peerage.

Given the operating of this 'unofficial' closed ruling class, it is strange that more attention has not been paid by historians to the attempt in 1719

[*]References to the Additional Georgian Archives and the Stuart Papers in the Royal Archives, Windsor Castle, are made by the gracious permission of Her Majesty the Queen. I should like to thank the late Lady Ravensdale, the Earl of Dalhousie, the Earl of Haddington, Lord Eliot and Mr. Christopher Harley for allowing me to consult and quote from their papers. Earlier drafts of this essay were read by John Beckett, Eveline Cruickshanks, David Hayton, Carole Rawcliffe, Stephen Taylor and Graham Townend. I should like to thank them all for saving me from many errors and for the references they supplied.

[1] In *Sybil*, chapter 3.
[2] For the most recent work see L. and Jeanne C. Fawtier Stone, *An Open Elite? England, 1540-1880* (Oxford, 1984); J. Cannon, *Aristocratic Century: The Peerage of Eighteenth-Century England* (Cambridge, 1984); J.V. Beckett, *The Aristocracy in England, 1660-1914* (Oxford, 1986). The terms 'aristocracy' and 'peerage' are not synonymous. For the problems surrounding definition and nomenclature see J.V. Beckett, 'The English Aristocracy', *Parliamentary History*, V (1986), 133-42. This paper is concerned only with the narrower and readily definable category of the peerage.

to create an official 'Golden Book' for the British peerage by means of the Peerage Bill. This would have restricted the Crown's prerogative over the creation of peerages (princes of the royal blood exempted), so that after the initial creation of six more titles and the replacement of the 16 elected Scottish representative peers by 25 hereditary ones, future creations would have been limited to the number of extinctions within the peerage (an existing Scottish peerage replacing vacancies within the 25 hereditary titles). Thus a closed number of 209 peers would have forever remained at the head of British society and political life.[3]

This unjustified neglect of the Peerage Bill may be attributed to the simple fact that it failed, and history tends to favour the successful. It is also true that the size and composition of the British peerage for some 60 years after 1719 was to remain just the same as if the bill had become law. None the less, the whole episode reveals much, not only about the politics of early Hanoverian Britain, but also about contemporary attitudes to the social position of the peerage. It is the contention of this essay that, though there were strong ascertainable political motives behind the bill, there were also pressing social reasons for its introduction, and that paradoxically it was these very same social reasons that brought about its defeat.

2

The standard modern interpretation of the Peerage Bill, and one that has found its way into the textbooks,[4] is that of Basil Williams, first published in 1932 in his biography of the 1st Earl Stanhope and based on the earlier work of E.R. Turner published in 1913.[5] Not surprisingly, Williams credits Stanhope with the authorship of the bill, claiming that the earl had neither forgotten nor forgiven the Earl of Oxford's abuse of the Crown's prerogative to create 12 peers in 1711-12 in order to secure control of the Lords.[6] In this interpretation Stanhope conceived the bill as part of an overall package of reform which he and the prime minister, the Earl of Sunderland, were endeavouring to push through Parliament in 1718-19. This included the repeal of the Occasional Conformity and Schism Acts and an attempt to reform the universities and repeal the

---

[3] In 1719 the English and British peerage stood at 178 members (see below Table A, p. 90). To this would have been added the six new peers and the 25 Scottish hereditary members of the Lords.

[4] See, e.g., W.A. Speck, *Stability and Strife: England, 1714-60* (1977), pp. 195-6.

[5] *Stanhope: A Study in Eighteenth-Century War and Diplomacy* (Oxford, 1932), pp. 403-18; E.R. Turner, 'The Peerage Bill of 1719', *E.H.R.*, XXVIII (1913), 243-59. See also, A.N. Newman, *The Stanhopes of Chevening* (1969), pp. 77-9, 82-4.

[6] Williams, *Stanhope*, p. 384.

Septennial Act.[7] According to Williams the real political reason for the Peerage Bill was the Whig Schism, which had begun in April 1717.

Tensions between the leading members of the Whig party, which had become apparent shortly after the Hanoverian succession and were not held in check by any effective opposition from the emasculated Tory party, had broken to the surface when Townshend and Walpole left the ministry in April 1717, taking four other Cabinet members with them into opposition. More significantly, they also took a large section of the Whig party in the Lords, though Sunderland and Stanhope, with the help of George I, wooed some peers back to the government over the summer recess. This schism in the ruling party coincided with a quarrel between the King and the Prince of Wales. Thus Sunderland and Stanhope found themselves opposed in Parliament by the schismatic Whigs, the friends of the Prince of Wales, and by the Tories. Opposition Whigs and Tories, however, proved unable to sustain their concerted co-operation beyond the summer of 1717.[8] Yet the government faced a potentially critical situation in the Lords should some unifying bond be found, and the following months were to show that certain areas – notably religion, foreign policy and the military – were capable of temporarily supplying such bonds.[9] Hence Sunderland and Stanhope came to fear a loss of power or the succession of the Prince, both of which would have placed them in an untenable position politically and might even have endangered their liberty or their lives. This predicament, according to Williams, was not only the occasion of but the reason for the Peerage Bill. The bill was designed to curtail the royal prerogative so that any future King or ministry would not be able to dislodge Sunderland and Stanhope and their followers from their position of dominance in the Lords.

There is certainly some truth in Williams's interpretation, and the idea that Sunderland and Stanhope needed the bill to safeguard themselves from future 'persecutions' by the Prince of Wales was current at the time. Even 'An Excellent New Ballad' in circulation by June 1719 was explicit on this point:

> He [Sunderland] told them you know the King has a son,
> who should he succeed, we're surely undone,

[7] See G. Townend, 'Trials and Visitations', *Times Higher Educational Supplement*, 11 April 1986, p. 15 (on reform of the universities); and *idem*, 'Religious Radicalism and Conservatism in the Whig Party under George I: The Repeal of the Occasional Conformity and Schism Acts', *Parliamentary History*, VII (1988), 24–44.

[8] C. Jones, 'The Impeachment of the Earl of Oxford and the Whig Schism of 1717: Four New Lists', *B.I.H.R.*, LV (1982), 66–87.

[9] Townend, 'Religious Radicalism'; J. Black, 'Parliament and the Political and Diplomatic Crisis of 1717-18', *Parliamentary History*, III (1984), 77–101.

But the Game had been ours, had we made thirty one . . .[10]

The heir to the throne clearly did oppose the bill, though his party in the Lords, led by Lord Lumley, his Master of the Horse, were all for it, while the Prince's followers in the Commons were to join with Walpole to vote against it, and the night the bill was defeated on 8 December 1719 there was a 'great appearance' at Leicester House, the home of the Prince. The Prince not only did not wish to succeed to a reduced prerogative, but is reported by his wife as fearing an attack upon him should the bill succeed, 'perhaps so far as to exclude him the crown'. Such a reaction may have been tinged with panic, but it was shared by the Princess of Wales who considered 'that Oxford's 12 Lords are nothing in comparison of 32 [*sic*] lords made by an Act and perhaps for the destruction of everything'.[11] Indeed both the Prince and Princess were active in the spring and autumn of 1719 lobbying M.P.s against the bill.[12]

There were, however, more immediate political reasons for the introduction of the bill which lay in the uncertain majority the ministry had in the House of Lords. The votes over the annual Mutiny Bill in February 1718 had, for example, produced majorities as low as 11, whereas in the previous year the lowest majorities on the Mutiny Bill had been more than double that figure. In March 1718 the Forfeited Estates Bill was carried by majorities of only six and seven. Bonet, the Prussian ambassador, noted that the 1717-18 session had produced the lowest government majorities of the reign.[13] Sunderland's answer was a Cabinet reshuffle followed by a distribution of honours amongst peers

[10] Quai d'Orsay, Archives Etrangères, Correspondance Politique, Angleterre, 335: Detouches to Dubois, 14 Dec. 1719 (I owe this reference to Eveline Cruickshanks); Bodl., MS. Rawlinson D.440, ff. 93-4: 'An Excellent New Ballad', endorsed 'June A. 1719. Given me [Thomas Hearne] by my worthy friend Mr. Edward Prideaux Gwyn' (I owe this reference to David Hayton).

[11] Royal Archives, Windsor Castle, Additional Georgian Archives [hereafter cited as R.A., Add.] 28/49: [Princess Caroline of Wales] to [Mrs. Charlotte Clayton], [?March 1719]. The number would have been 31: i.e. 25 Scottish hereditary and six new British peerages. For the 'appearance' see B.L., Loan 29/67: Edward Harley *jr.* to Abigail Harley, 17 Dec. 1719; for the Prince's supporters in the Lords see Cheshire R.O., DCH/X/8 (Cholmondeley MSS.): N[ewburgh] to Cholmondeley, 5 March [1719]. The present author intends to publish an edition of these Newburgh letters.

[12] R.A., Add. 28/49, 51, 54, 56: [Princess Caroline] to [Mrs. Clayton], [?March, ?late Nov., ?8 Dec. 1719]; *Annals and Correspondence of the Viscounts and the First and Second Earls of Stair*, ed. J.M. Graham (2 vols., 1875), II, 104-5.

[13] Black, 'Parliament and the . . . Crisis of 1717-18,' p. 86. There had been rumours earlier in February 1718 that among changes envisaged was the creation of *six* new peers: Lord Chief Justice King, Sir Joseph Jekyll, Hugh Boscowen, Sir Richard Child, and the two Irish peers Lords Molesworth and Midleton (Henry E. Huntington Library, San Marino, California, LO 8325 [Loudoun papers]: [Sir David Dalrymple] to [Loudoun], 11 Feb. 1718). The only new peerage created between April 1717 and March 1719 was Lord Lucas, eldest son of the Duke of Kent.

and M.P.s, and an ecclesiastical policy which, he hoped, would win over more of the bishops to the government's side.[14] He was also fortunate that the naval success in the Mediterranean at Cape Passaro in the summer of 1718 silenced many of the ministry's critics. The government's majority in November 1718 on the Address, which included congratulations on the recent naval triumph, rose to 33 in the Lords. All was not well, however, and low majorities continued in the upper House. So much opposition was aroused by certain aspects of the repeal of the Occasional Conformity and Schism Acts that Sunderland was forced to drop the clause which would have abrogated the Test Act. Clearly the ministry needed to secure a firmer majority in the Lords if it was to survive and carry its controversial reform programme, and in the winter of 1718-19 this majority had to be secured as quickly as possible. This is the context in which the timing of the Peerage Bill needs to be seen, and this context would seem to support much in the Williams interpretation.

However, new material has recently come to light, showing that Sunderland (and not Stanhope) was probably the originator of the bill and that its genesis can be traced back beyond the Whig Schism and the immediate political context. Furthermore, despite the fact that the two chief ministers hoped that the new peers would remain loyal to them as well as give them a majority in the Lords, as the 12 peers created by Lord Oxford had remained loyal to him,[15] the fact that Oxford had lost power shows the inherently shaky logic in the reasoning of the two ministers – at least if Williams's interpretation of their motives is correct. A new monarch determined to establish a new ministry could reasonably expect to win over the House of Lords in time once its members saw which way the wind blew.[16] As Walpole was later to show, patronage (which could only flow from the King) was a powerful weapon in influencing some men's political stance. The two chief ministers, particularly Sunderland, were politicians of experience and clearly there lay behind their espousal of the Peerage Bill more than the crude expectation of creating a quick majority which would keep them in power come what may.

[14] Townend, 'Religious Radicalism'.

[15] So reported Friedrich Wilhelm von der Schulenburg, who attended George I in England: Hesse Staatsarchiv Darmstat, Gräflich Görtzisches Archiv, F23, 153/6: Schulenburg to Görtz, 5 May 1719. I owe this reference to Graham Townend.

[16] Contemporaries commented on this possibility, particularly in reference to the new Scottish hereditary peers (West Sussex R.O., Goodwood MSS. 1168: Robert Munro to [Gordon], 3 March 1718/19). Even the Duke of Somerset hinted at this when introducing the motion on the condition of the peerage into the Lords on 28 Feb. 1719, see Brampton Bryan MSS. (Christopher Harley, Brampton Bryan Hall, Herefordshire), Bundle 117, folder 'Odds and Ends': E[dward] P[rideaux] G[wyn] to [Edward Harely jr], 28 Feb. 1718/19. The present author and Stephen Taylor plan to publish an edition of this valuable correspondence.

3

One major area of political contention behind the introduction of the Peerage Bill which has not been explored by historians is that of the continuing problem of the Scottish representatives at Westminster, both in the Lords and the Commons. Very soon after the Anglo-Scottish Union came into effect in 1707, the Scots became disillusioned with their lot. Their agitation and the intermittent disruption they caused in government was one of the causes behind the Earl of Oxford's *coup de théâtre* during the Christmas recess of 1711, when between 28 December and 1 January 1712 – five days that shook the political establishment – he persuaded Queen Anne to create 12 new peers to re-establish a majority in the Lords for the administration's peace policy.[17] These creations caused dismay on constitutional grounds, even among one or two of Oxford's own Cabinet. The Whigs never forgave Oxford, and this act formed part of the party's demonology for the last four years of Anne's reign. When Oxford was impeached in 1715 this abuse of royal power, as the Whigs saw it, formed one of the main articles of the impeachment. Again and again in the debates and correspondence over the Peerage Bill reference was made to this act of Tory infamy.[18]

Oxford had revealed in a conversation with the Earl of Dartmouth that one reason for the 12 creations was to teach the 'extravagant' Scottish representative peers a lesson by letting 'them see they were not so much wanted as they imagined'.[19] After the result of the Hamilton peerage case in December 1711, in which the House of Lords refused to allow Scottish peers given post-1707 British peerages to sit by right of that peerage, the Scottish representative peers had organised a boycott of the upper House which, from their point of view, was less than successful, but which did cause Oxford moments of disquiet. One strategy aired to tempt the Scots back into supporting the administration

[17] For details of the crisis which precipitated this act, see C. Jones, 'The Division that Never Was: New Evidence on the Aborted Vote in the Lords on 8 December 1711 on "No Peace Without Spain"', *Parliamentary History*, II (1983), 191-202; G.S. Holmes, 'The Hamilton Affair of 1711-12: A Crisis in Anglo-Scottish Relations', *E.H.R.*, LXXVII (1962), 257-82; *The London Diaries of William Nicolson, Bishop of Carlisle, 1702-18*, ed. C. Jones and G. Holmes (Oxford, 1985), pp. 569-70, 575-6.

[18] See G. Burnet, *History of His Own Time* (6 vols., Oxford, 1833), VI, 94-5; *The Diary of Sir David Hamilton, 1709-14*, ed. P. Roberts (Oxford, 1975), pp. 35-7. In 1760 George III lamenting the diminution of the power of the Lords put most of the blame on 'Queen Anne's creating twelve new Lords on some particular debate in 1712 that it might be carry'd to her mind', P.D.G. Thomas, '"Thoughts on the British Constitution" by George III in 1760', *Historical Research*, LX (1987), 362. Even in 1798 the Duke of Bedford's condemnation of Pitt's peerage creations contained a reference to Lord Oxford (Cobbett, *Parl. Hist.*, XXXIII, 1315).

[19] Burnet, *History*, VI, 95.

was the offer of a new system of representation, whereby the 16 elected representative peers were to be replaced by 25 or 30 hereditary peers, the other Scottish peers being permitted to offer themselves for election to the Commons.[20] This came to nothing, but the same idea (except for the question of eligibility in Commons' elections) was to form part of the Peerage Bill. Of the 11 resolutions relating to the peerage which passed the Lords on 3 March 1719, the first six were concerned with establishing 25 hereditary Scottish seats in the upper House. Indeed on 28 February 1719 Argyll seconded Somerset's motion on the state of the peerage with 'a long speech, setting forth the great discontent among the peerage of Scotland, that since the union there had been made near forty new peers of England [*sic*], which quite altered the proportion of the 16 to the old number at the time of making'.[21]

When the Scots, both Commoners and peers, entered the promised land of post-Union Britain, they found not only an alien political system to which they had to accommodate themselves, but a political gravy train in which they were determined to travel. It must be remembered that on average Scots (including the peerage) were much poorer than their English counterparts.[22] Consequently they soon acquired a reputation in English eyes for greed, political malleability and mendacity. This reputation was greatly exaggerated by English xenophobia, but it had sufficient ground to affect English political and social attitudes. Oxford himself had found that the Scottish peers had 'now come to expect a reward for every vote they gave'.[23] The Hamilton case had foundered upon the English peers' fear of being swamped by Scottish peers with new British titles. This fear had also been tinged with contempt for the members of an inferior peerage. Thus the Hamilton case effectively closed off an avenue of patronage to which the Scots had looked for political reward – an avenue which cost the government nothing in financial terms and which, to judge from the number of references in contemporary correspondence, satisfied a need among the

[20] Holmes, 'Hamilton Affair', pp. 273-4; C. Jones, '"The Scheme Lords, the Neccessitous Lords, and the Scots Lords": The Earl of Oxford's Management and the "Party of the Crown" in the House of Lords, 1711-14', in *Party and Management in Parliament, 1660-1784* (Leicester, 1984), pp. 133, 149 n. 85; S.R.O., GD45/14/352/13-15 (Dalhousie papers): [Balmerino] to [Maule], 24, 26, 31 Jan. 1712; Mellerstain Letters (the Earl of Haddington, Mellerstain, Berwickshire), V: [Baillie of Jerviswood] to [Montrose], 19 Jan. 1712; S.R.O., GD220/5/268/4 (Montrose papers): [same] to [same], 19 Jan. 1712. This is the first reference I have found to the number of 25 hereditary peers designed to replace the 16 elected peers.
[21] *L.J.*, XXI, 89. The preamble to the bill also concentrates on the rectification of the Scottish peerage's position. For Argyll's speech see Cheshire R.O., DCH/X/8: N[ewburgh] to [Cholmondeley], 3 March [1719].
[22] See D. Szechi, 'Some Insights on the Scots Peers and M.P.s Returned in the 1710 General Election', *Scottish Historical Review*, LX (1981), 61-75.
[23] Burnet, *History*, VI, 95.

Scots for social advancement.[24] Though the Scottish boycott of the Lords early in 1712 failed and they returned to the administration's fold, various slaps in the face[25] left a feeling of 'second-class citizenship' among the Scottish peerage. Their discontent continued and periodically agitation broke out. In 1716, for example, there were negotiations between the ministry and the Scottish peers at the time of the Septennial Bill in which the Scots hoped to replace the 16 representative peers by 25 hereditary ones. These negotiations foundered partly because of divisions amongst the Scots and partly because the Scots wanted the removal of the bar to their being granted British peerages, and this latter may have frightened the ministry.[26] In 1719 the Peerage Bill was clearly seen by Sunderland and Stanhope as an answer to these discontents amongst the Scottish peers.

However, besides the difficulties the ministry encountered in the Lords, Sunderland and Stanhope also faced problems over their majority in the Commons. Sunderland's solution was again a Scottish one. If he could gain the backing of both the 16 peers and the 45 Scottish M.P.s the ministry's position in Parliament would ease. The Scottish parliamentary representatives at this time were largely divided into two factions: the members of the *Squadrone* led by, among others, the Duke of Roxburghe, who was Secretary of State for Scotland, and the followers of the Duke of Argyll and his brother, the Earl of Ilay.[27] Argyll had been in opposition to the ministry since his dismissal from the Prince of Wales's household upon the King's insistence in 1716. After the Whig Schism in 1717, however, he had become dissillusioned with the dissident Whigs, particularly Walpole. In November 1718 Sunderland opened negotiations with a group of *Squadrone* peers and Argyll. The Scots in general were to be won over by the inclusion in the Peerage Bill of the 25 hereditary seats, while Argyll was to be offered a position in the ministry (and eventually a British dukedom). In return Argyll was to carry his considerable interest in the Commons, and his own vote along with that of his brother and possibly four followers in the Lords, into the

---

[24] See, e.g., H.M.C., *Polwarth MSS.*, II, 315, 326, 342, 444.

[25] See, e.g., the Queensberry case, in C. Jones, 'Godolphin, the Whig Junto, and the Scots', *Scottish Historical Review*, LVIII (1979), 759-71.

[26] Huntington Lib., LO 7634: Stair to [Loudoun], Paris, [22 April]/3 May 1716, [15]/26 May 1716; S.R.O. GD135/145/84, 82 (Stair papers): [?Charles Cathcart] to Stair, 4, 16, 28 April [1716]; GD135/141/7 (unfoliated): [?Robethon] to Stair, 14, 27, 9/20 April, 7/18 May 1716. On 15 Nov. 1715, 33 Scottish peers had petitioned George I complaining of the disablement of Scots with British peerages from sitting in the Lords (S.R.O., GD220/6/1773/14).

[27] *House of Commons, 1715-54*, ed. R. Sedgwick (2 vols., 1970), I, 159, shows that of the 45 Scottish M.P.s elected in 1715, 38 were Whigs and seven Tories.

ministerial fold.[28] Argyll broke with the Prince of Wales in December 1718 and signalled his move to the ministry by voting, along with his brother, for the committing of the bill to repeal the Occasional Conformity and Schism Acts.[29] The Campbell interest in the Commons also followed suit by voting for the repeal.[30]

Thus the Scottish connexion *was* a major factor which persuaded the ministry to include a Peerage Bill in their reform programme. Unfortunately the ministers had to contend with the remainder of the Scottish peers, who were not to be included in the 25. The problem of these excluded peers had been foreseen by the ministry in the earlier negotiations of 1716,[31] but their neglect in 1719 led to their organised opposition which contributed to the final wrecking of the bill.[32]

4

While the 'Scottish dimension' has been largely overlooked by previous historians, the 'social dimension' has been almost totally ignored. The Hamilton case had revealed fears amongst the English peers of a diminution in the social position of the British peerage by an influx of Scots largely unable to maintain the dignity and social status required of a peer. Such concerns with status were genuine, and were not only held by many individual peers but by the peerage collectively.[33] Indeed, in 1701

---

[28] For Argyll see P.W.J. Riley, *The English Ministers and Scotland, 1707-1727* (1964), pp. 264, 268; and for his interest see J.S. Shaw, *The Management of Scottish Society, 1707-1764* (Edinburgh, 1983), pp. 46-7.

[29] B.L., Add. MS. 47028, ff. 264-5. Fourteen of the 16 representative peers voted for the bill.

[30] Cobbett, *Parl. Hist.*, VII, 585-8.

[31] Twenty-five was considered to be, perhaps, too small a number, see S.R.O., GD135/141/7: [?Robethon] to Stair, 14, 17, 9/20 April, 7/18 May 1716.

[32] The force of the petitions sent to Parliament by the excluded Scottish peers is difficult to measure; they did have some effect, but of those entitled to petition only 32% (32 out of 101) did so, 30% were unasked, and 39% either voted for the Peerage Bill on 3 March 1719 or refused to sign a petition (B.L., Loan 29/163/10). Earl Cowper, the main opponent of the bill in the Lords thought, however, that the consent of the Scottish peerage was crucial to the bill's success, for their opposition he believed 'would raise a rebellion in Scotland, by which the King and Parliament will destroy the basis upon which the title of King of Scotland and the Union is founded' (R.A., Add. 28/52: [Princess Caroline] to [Mrs. Clayton], expressing Cowper's views given to the Prince of Wales).

[33] See J.V. Beckett and C. Jones, 'Financial Improvidence and Political Independence in the Early Eighteenth Century: George Booth, 2nd Earl of Warrington (1675-1758)', *Bulletin of the John Rylands University Library*, LXV (1982), 8-35; E. Gregg and C. Jones, 'Hanover, Pensions and "Poor Lords", 1712-13', *Parliamentary History*, I (1982), 173-80. Lord Newburgh during the Dover case in Jan. 1720 expressed a fear that a successful case would 'break a barrier that will let in an inundation of Scots into our house' (Cheshire R.O., DCH/X/8: to Cholmondeley, 12 Jan. [1720]).

Viscount Longueville had proposed unsuccessfully in the Lords that minimum financial qualifications should be imposed for newly created peers: £3,000 for a baron, £4,000 for a viscount, and so on. In December 1719 Jonathan Swift was of a similar opinion that 'Titles should fall with Estates'.[34] Few of the Scottish peers would have been able to meet such qualifications, and some English peers also would have failed, including Lords Hunsdon and Willoughby of Parham, who were in a condition of virtual beggary.[35]

There were many gentlemen who were the financial equals of peers, and not a few, like Sir Michael Warton – 'the richest man for to be a gentleman only that was in all England' with a reputed £15,000 a year – who were their betters. Warton was unusual in the fact that he was offered a peerage by Oxford in 1711 and turned it down.[36] Probably a more typical member of the wealthy gentry was Richard Norton, a Hampshire gentleman of £4,000 a year, who wrote to Oxford in January 1712 asking for a peerage. He failed to get one, and is to be found writing in the same vein to Lord Cowper in 1717.[37] It was this kind of lobbying that the Peerage Bill was designed to curtail.

Not only was there much uneasiness within the peerage and within government about the increasing size of the peerage, but there was concern too about the increased demand for peerages, and about the circumstances of some of those who had recently been elevated. A few contemporaries certainly expressed the feeling that there had indeed been too many creations in the recent past: Oxford's 'creation of the Jury of Peers in the late Reign', wrote one opponent of the bill, 'may have one good effect, even when it do's not pass, which is it may curb the Crown, and hinder that *vast Glut* of Creations which has overflow'd us like a Torrent since the Revolution'.[38] The Scots had been successfully blocked from acquiring British peerages by the outcome of the Hamilton case in 1711, but barely ten days later Oxford's 'dozen' had been ennobled, some of whom, such as Samuel Masham, were considered to be of dubious lineage and financial standing. Social acceptability and sufficient wealth to maintain a peerage were increasingly coming to be the sine qua non for a seat in the Lords. With the 'financial revolution' of the 1690s, and the fortunes that had been made since the Glorious Revolution from the profits of war, there were many men of the new 'moneyed interest'

---

[34] B.L., Add. MS. 30000E, f. 211; *The Correspondence of Jonathan Swift*, ed. H. Williams (5 vols., Oxford, 1963-5), II, 331: to C. Ford, 8 Dec. 1719.

[35] Holmes, *British Politics*, pp. 393-4; Gregg and Jones, 'Hanover, Pensions and the "Poor Lords"', pp. 175-9.

[36] Holmes, *British Politics*, p. 394; H.M.C., *Portland MSS.*, V, 133.

[37] H.M.C., *Portland MSS.*, V, 136; Hertfordshire R.O., D/EP F55 (Panshanger papers), ff. 159-60, 161-2: Norton to [Cowper], 30 June, 20 Aug. 1717.

[38] Christ Church, Oxford, Wake MS. 21, f. 107: W. Wotton to [Wake], 7 March 1718/19. My italics.

with little or no pedigree and little or no land to their name. The social elite nursed growing fears towards these men of money as contenders for peerages:

> for God knowes the peerage in these days are strangely degenerated [wrote Lord Ailesbury in the mid-1690s], and I had rather trust a poor honest cobbler than a great part of my brethren. And the peerage also is become so cheap and despicable by such unwarrantable promotion and in such numbers besides, that I insert what I have publicly declared that if I had no succession, and that it was in my power to do it, I would resign up my title and live as a single gentleman . . .

Robert Benson, created Lord Bingley in 1713, was one of the men of this type to acquire a peerage before the time of the Peerage Bill. A man of wealth who became Chancellor of the Exchequer under Lord Oxford, he was the son of a York attorney who, though he left him an estate reputedly worth £1,500 a year, was described as a 'man of mean extraction'. 'I am intirely of your mind about Benson [wrote Lord Berkeley of Stratton]. Every year the house [of Lords] receives some great blow, that I am perswaded (setting aside my being a member of it), it is the interest of the publick to have its *dignity* kept up.' There were genuine fears that these swallows did indeed herald a summer; and in February 1719 there was a rumour circulating concerning the new peers to be promoted by the Peerage Bill. The five named individuals were Lord Chief Justice King, a self-made lawyer whose father had been a grocer and salter; the M.P. Nicholas Lechmere, from a legal family; the M.P. Hugh Boscawen, the government's manager in Cornwall, with an estate of £3,000 a year; Sir Gilbert Heathcote, a vintner who was governor of the Bank of England; and the wealthy Sir Richard Child, M.P., with an estate of over £10,000, who had bought his Irish viscountcy of Castlemaine in 1715 from the King's mistress, the future Duchess of Kendal.[39] This situation of fear and rumour was to be exploited by Sunderland and Stanhope in the debates on the bill in early March 1719. That this political ploy was a success is shown by the extensive cross-party support the bill received in the upper House.

How much truth was there behind these fears: was Venice really in peril by the time of the Peerage Bill? The figures produced by the ministry in the spring of 1719 (see Table A) appeared to confirm

---

[39] *Memoirs of Thomas, Earl of Ailesbury* (2 vols., 1890), I, 304; *The Wentworth Papers, 1705-1739*, ed. J.J. Cartwright (1883), pp. 133, 347 (my italics); Brampton Bryan MSS. 177: G[wyn] to [Harley], 28 Feb. 1718/9; G.E.C., *Complete Peerage*, II, 177; VII, 275, 504; Sedgwick, *House of Commons*, I, 476, 549; II, 123. It is significant that Boscawen, Lechmere and King acquired peerages in 1720, 1721 and 1725 respectively. See also above note 13 for a rumour that some of them were in line for a peerage in February 1718.

Table A
The Increase in the English (from 1707, British) Peerage, 1603-1718

Reigns	Total numbers at end of reign	Numbers created	Numbers extinct	Numbers added	% increase on previous reign	Average annual rate of creation	Average annual rate of addition
Elizabeth I	59						
James I	104	62	17	45	76.3%	2.81	2.04
Charles I (to 1649)	142[1]	59	21	38	36.5%	2.45	1.58
Charles II	153	64	53	11	7.7%[2]	2.56	0.44
James II	153	8	8	0	0	2.00	0
William III	162	30	21	9	5.9%	2.30	0.69
Anne	168	30	24	6	3.7%	2.30	0.46
George I (to 1718)	178	20	10	10	5.9%	4.44	2.22
Total		273	154	119		2.86	1.02

The Increase in the Peerage, 1689-1718

1689-1718		80	55	25	16.3%	2.75	0.86

[1] By 1658 the number of peerages had shrunk to 119 due to extinctions during the Interregnum, see J.V. Beckett, *The Aristocracy in England, 1660-1914* (Oxford, 1986), p. 486.
[2] Taking the 1658 figure of 119 the increase to 1685 is 9.2%.

Source: A List of the Peers existing at the Time of King James *the First* . . . (see note 40).

contemporary impressions.[40]

There had been, according to these official figures, 273 creations since 1603, but because of 154 extinctions of titles in the same period the overall increase in the size of the peerage had been 119. This, however, meant a threefold increase in the period 1603 to 1718 from 59 to 178. Furthermore, since 1689, 80 titles had been granted as against 55 extinctions, so that the increase over this shorter period was 25. This was more than double the rate of increase over the previous 30 years (1660–89), when, despite 72 creations, the heavy rate of extinctions (61) resulted in only 11 extra peers being added to the membership of the Lords. The early Stuart period had, however, seen an increase of 83. Could there have been some residual fear among the peerage harking back to the indiscriminate creations of James I's reign? George I, like his predecessor of a century earlier, was inaugurating a new, foreign dynasty, and like James I (and William III) brought numbers of his fellow-countrymen in his train.

It was however probably the increase in the peerage since the 1688 Revolution which most influenced the attitude of the Lords in 1719. The percentage increase in the period 1689 to 1718 over the peerage as it stood at the end of James II's reign was 16.3. This represented an annual addition to the peerage of nearly one a year (0.86), with creations running on average at 2.75 a year. But the rate of creations had grown faster since 1714; in fact it had nearly doubled from 2.30 under Anne to 4.44 a year under George I. This figure is perhaps a little distorted by the Coronation creations in October 1714, when George I thanked those who had stood by the Hanoverian settlement. Six new peers were created in that month – the largest single creation since before the Revolution with the exception of Oxford's 'dozen'.[41] None the less George I did create a further 14 peers up to the end of 1718, nearly half the total created by Anne in 12 years. The peerage was certainly expanding at a rate which began to worry members of the House of Lords.

But what of the social background from which these new creations

---

[40] Published in *A List of the Peers existing at the time of King* James *the First His Accession to the Crown, and of those who have since been advanced to the Peerage by Claim of antient Right, by Writ or by Patent; as also of the several Peers Extinct in His and the succeding Reigns.* A copy can be found in P.R.O., S.P. 35/19/72, based on a manuscript copy with notes and computations not published (*ibid.*, 35/19/71). This table is not totally accurate (see note 53 below). The following discussion is based on this table, supplemented by G.E.C., *Complete Peerage* and A.S. Turberville, *The House of Lords in the XVIIIth Century* (Oxford, 1927), pp. 501-13: Appendix A, List of Peerage Creations, 1702-83.

[41] The figures in this analysis are of new creations of peerages and do not take into account elevations in rank within the peerage which have no effect on the numbers sitting in the Lords. At his coronation William III created 11 titles of whom seven were already peers; Anne created no coronation titles; George I created 14 of whom eight already had peerages. See G.E.C., *Complete Peerage*, II, Appendix F.

Table B

The Social, Occupational and National Background of Peers Created between 1689 and 1718

Dates	Royal	Called to Lords in father's barony	Other eldest sons created peers	Other sons created peers	Brothers created peers	Nephews created peers[1]	Mother was daughter of peer[2]	Other relation of a peer
1689–1702	2[3]	6	0	2	0	2	2	1
1702–1714	1	4	2	3	0	0	0	1
1714–1718	1	4	0	1	2	2	0	1
Total	4	14	2	6	2	4	2	3

	Scottish peer	Eldest son of Scottish peer	Irish peer	Bt	Kt	Son of Kt	M.P.	Foreigner	Naval or Army officer	Other[4]
1689–1702	1	0	3	3	1	4	15	5	2	1
1702–1714	3	1	2	3	2	5	26	0	0	2
1714–1718	0	0	6	4	1	0	17	0	2	1
Total	4	1	11	10	4	9	58	5	4	4

[1] Nephews in male line.
[2] Only connexion with the peerage was through mother.
[3] One, Princess Anne's son, the Duke of Gloucester, died while still a minor.
[4] That is, not an Irish peer at the time of creation, not related to a peer, a baronet, or a knight.

Source: G.E.C., *Complete Peerage.*

came? Table B tabulates the social, occupational and national origins of all the peers created between 1689 and 1718.[42] An analysis of these creations shows that 33 out of 79 (41.7 per cent) had close family ties to a peer. Indeed 16 (20.2 per cent) were themselves the eldest sons of peers who had been called to the Lords in one of their fathers' peerages, or had been created a peer, and would eventually succeed their fathers. Consequently they represented no permanent expansion of the membership of the upper House.

Of those creations tabulated in the lower half of Table B, few, including the Scots and the Irish, could claim a social background distinguished enough to impress the English peerage. As we have seen Scots had always been viewed with suspicion, and, when in 1707 the Union opened the door for the Scots to the English political and social elite with the possibility of their acquiring British titles and hereditary seats in the House of Lords, the English peers reacted quickly. This antipathy to the Scots was not merely based on a fear of being swamped politically by new British creations, but also of being swamped socially. With one or two exceptions (such as the Duke of Hamilton with extensive interests in Lancashire), the Scots were unable financially to support a peerage in an English context (the most notable example was the Earl of Home, who had to borrow £100 in 1711 to enable him to attend the Lords).[43] This was also true, to some extent, of the Irish peerage, though many more Irish titles were held by Englishmen than were Scottish titles. None the less Irish titles were regarded as 'second-class' peerages, and in the eighteenth century increasingly became viewed as 'consolation prizes' for Englishmen.[44] In the 30 years prior to 1719, the Scottish and Irish peers represented 20.2 per cent of those to whom English or British peerages were given.

Lower down the social scale still, baronets, knights and sons of knights represented some 29 per cent of the creations in the period 1689 to 1718. Some knights and even some of the baronets were from fairly lowly backgrounds. The most notable case was probably Lord Haversham, who had himself been created a baronet in 1673, but came from a London merchant family involved with Oliver Cromwell.

Many of the persons discussed in the above categories were also M.P.s at the time of their elevation to the peerage or had previously sat in the Commons; this applied even to some of the Irish and (before 1707)

---

[42] Table B is constructed from information in G.E.C., *Complete Peerage*, which produces slightly different totals for the creations of each of the three reigns (1689-1718) from those tabulated in the official government figures published in 1719 (see Table A): 28 under William III; 31 under Anne; 20 under George I.

[43] Holmes, *British Politics*, p. 394. See Jones 'Scheme Lords', p. 165 for the government's handouts to Home.

[44] See below, p. 108, and note 103.

Scottish peers. The high proportion of new peers (73.4 per cent) who had sat in the lower House reflected two facts: first, that it was common, and became increasingly so in the eighteenth century, for the eldest son of a peer to serve a kind of political apprenticeship as an M.P.;[45] and secondly that a peerage was increasingly regarded as a reward for political effort and (sometimes) distinction.[46] It was to be argued in the debates on the Peerage Bill that too many wealthy M.P.s were being sucked into the Lords to the detriment of the lower House.

If we leave aside this particular fear of the concentration of wealth in the upper House and the English peers' snobbish and xenophobic dislike of the Scots and Irish (and the Dutch and Germans raised to the peerage by William III), it seems that few, probably less than 10 per cent, of the peerages created between 1689 and 1718 represented *parvenu* wealth and low social status.[47] Was this nevertheless a substantial enough element to convince the peerage that their Venetian-style oligarchy was in peril? Probably so, when one considers that the English lords *did* look down on the other peerages and that recent trends in the rate of expansion of the size of the House of Lords were perceived by some to be alarming. Even Walpole in his attack on the Peerage Bill conceded that the peers were 'much concerned in the Preservation of their Dignities', and Lord Newburgh believed the bill 'will be a great addition to the value of the peerage'.[48] There were probably enough examples of men of lowly social status but political expertise being rewarded, and enough examples of titles being bought,[49] to frighten the older peerage families into closing ranks against a future influx of 'undesirables'.

[45]   See J. Cannon, 'The Isthmus Repaired: The Resurgence of the English Aristocracy, 1660-1760', *Proceedings of the British Academy*, for 1982, LXVIII (1983), 447.

[46]   See M.W. McCahill, 'Peerage Creations and the Changing Character of the British Nobility, 1750-1850', *E.H.R.*, XCVI (1981), 259-84.

[47]   Perhaps the most notable examples were Lords Bingley (see above, p. 89), Haversham (above, p. 93), and Masham (above, p. 88). There was also some comment when Robert Harley was created Earl of Oxford that 'his estate is not large enough'. Fifty years earlier it had been valued at £1,500 p.a. (B.W. Hill, *Robert Harley, Speaker, Secretary of State and Premier Minister* [New Haven and London, 1988], p. 1). This attitude could only have reinforced the hostility towards the creations of 1711-12.

[48]   Walpole in *The Thoughts of a Member of the Lower House*, p. 10; see also Turner, 'Peerage Bill', p. 235; Cheshire R.O., DCH/X/8: [Newburgh] to Cholmondeley, 5 March [1719]. Walpole went on to argue that this concern over the preservation of dignity was so strong that it would prevent the peerage provoking the Crown into creating too many peers so that the Bill was unnecessary.

[49]   In the recent past both Lords Barnard and Romney had bought their peerages. See *The House of Commons, 1660-1690*, ed. B.D. Henning (3 vols., 1983), III, 622; Sedgwick, *House of Commons*, II, 243. The most notorious case happened at the time of the Peerage Bill when in April 1719 Chandos received his dukedom after bribing the King's mistress, the Duchess of Kendal. Romney gained his barony by a similar route. Selling peerages was not new. There had been much agitation amongst the older families in the early seventeenth century when James I sold peerages on a large scale.

5

The Duke of Somerset, known as the 'proud duke', introduced the motion on the condition of the peerage into the Lords on 28 February 1719. He concluded with the plea that it was necessary to preserve 'the dignity of that house, and thought limiting the number of those that were to sitt there was one way towards it'. Three days later, on 3 March, the first full day of debate on Somerset's motion, Sunderland began for the ministry with a long 'historical deduction' on the condition of the Scottish peerage, and then 'toke notice of the great increase of the English peerage in the late Reigns . . . [and] talk'd a good deal of limiting the number'. Sunderland's main adversary in the debate, Lord Cowper, while opposing the idea of a legal curb on the Crown's prerogative in creating peers, significantly accepted the necessity of some limitation. He thought that there had indeed 'been in some reigns an abuse or at least an excessive use of the prerogative', and a voluntary limitation was necessary to preserve the dignity of the Lords. It was the ministers' responsibility, not that of the law, to screen the King 'from the importunities of those who might press for honours, when they did not deserve them' and to recommend only those 'whose transcendent merits called for them, and whose choice the whole world would approve'.[50] Thus it is clear that the opposition to both the ministry in general and the bill in particular shared the government's basic premise upon which the campaign for the bill was founded – the preservation of the exclusiveness of the peerage. With the sole exception of Lord Oxford (on 28 February and 2 March) all the other peers and bishops who spoke, of whom many were not friends to the ministry, agreed that the number of peers should be 'restrained', if necessary by legal means.[51]

On the following day, 4 March, the English peerage (as opposed to the Scottish) was specifically debated. Lord Carlisle proposed limiting the peerage to its present number plus six,[52] and that subsequent creations should only be made to replace extinctions. This was seconded by the

[50] Cowper continued to hold that discreet restraint by the Crown to limit creations to those who deserved them was best, but by September 1719 he had come to believe that things had gone so far 'that I am afraid discretion and publick good, without a legal restriction, will never hinder the abuse from proceeding further' (Christ Church, Oxford, Wake MS. 21, f. 162D: Cowper to [Wake], 20 Sept. 1719).

[51] Brampton Bryan MSS. 117: G[wyn] to [Harley], 28 Feb., 4 March 1719; Cobbett, *Parl. Hist.*, VII, 589–92.

[52] No evidence has been found to indicate why the number six was chosen. As early as Feb. 1718 there had been rumours of six new creations (see note 13 above), and this is the earliest instance of that number. Clearly the ministry could not create many more while at the same time denouncing Oxford's 'dozen'. Together with the nine new Scottish seats, they may have felt that six were enough to ensure a majority.

Duke of Kingston. Then Stanhope rose to 'third' the motion with the strongest expression hitherto of what might be termed the 'protectionist' argument in favour of limitation. The peerage, he calculated, had been increased since 1603 by 120,[53] but he thought that in order to maintain the balance between the several parts of the government the present number was the 'proper standard for the future'. In the past the increasing wealth and power of the Commons, by means of the increase in trade, had led to the most considerable of them being created peers. This had 'from time to time (he thought) contributed towards supporting the dignity of that house [the Lords]', but recent creations had led more commoners to think of obtaining peerages. It was becoming increasingly difficult for the Crown to withstand this demand for honours. A limitation would strengthen the honour and independency of the peerage, and would also confer equal advantage on the Commons; for to maintain the balance between the two Houses it was necessary to have men of wealth and power in the lower House.[54] Too many in the Lords would swing the balance in favour of the upper House.[55]

Though not expressly stated, the tone of Stanhope's speech hints at the peerage's fear of leaving the door of the Lords open for men of recently acquired wealth. This was probably a deliberate appeal to the Country and Tory ethos of those within the House of Lords who might otherwise have been expected to oppose the bill as a Whig measure designed to prevent any possible future Tory ministry creating peers (which in part it was). The government judged the climate of opinion correctly, for despite the future Tory M.P. Edward Prideaux Gwyn's forecast that the Tories in the Lords would oppose the bill,[56] on the whole they did not.[57]

Country opinion had long opposed the 'new moneyed interest' created by the 'financial revolution'. Country opinion also disliked newcomers into the social elite, and was later to show its dislike of those

---

[53] 273 creations, 154 extinctions, net gain 119 (see Table A). These figures were official government ones published and delivered to the Lords on 5 March (see Cobbett, *Parl. Hist.*, VII, 593). Many lists were drawn up at this time and they mostly fail to agree on the figures (see Beckett, *Aristocracy in England*, p. 482), but this does not detract from the point Stanhope made of the overall increasing size of the peerage.

[54] This argument was shortly to appear in public in the pamphlets *Six Questions, Stated and Answered* and *The Old Whig* published on 19 March (see Turner 'Peerage Bill', p. 252).

[55] Brampton Bryan MSS. 117: G[wyn] to [Harley], 5 March 1718/19.

[56] *Ibid.*: same to [same], 28 Feb. 1718/19.

[57] Tory M.P.s, however, were a different matter. Both Sunderland and James Craggs drew up calculations of support and opposition (see below, pp. 99-100) and agreed that 162 Tory M.P.s were against the bill, with only three doubtful and the case of Sunderland only four in favour (see Sedgwick, *House of Commons*, I, 84-5). For the general Tory support of the bill in the Lords see Cheshire R.O., DCH/X/8: N[ewburgh] to [Cholmondeley], 3 March [1719].

peers from new families who helped to run the Lords for Walpole.[58] If Stanhope's ploy was to harness this sentiment he was successful, for there was to be little open hostility to the bill in the upper House. Even the ministry's most consistent opponent over the bill, Lord Cowper, had by the debate on 4 March sunk most of his qualms about legal limitation and only quibbled over the precise number of new peers who were to be chosen directly by the King. The Duke of Kingston had suggested that all six should be freely nominated by George I without pressure from the administration, something that seemed unlikely to be agreed to by Sunderland and Stanhope if they were to ensure the continuing loyalty of the new peers to the ministry. Fourteen other lords spoke to the debate that day, of whom at least six were Tory opponents of the government yet 'not one had opposed this Resolution of restraining the number'.[59] Even Townshend, leader of the schismatic Whigs in the Lords, declared he was not against limiting the peerage, only against doing it in an unjust manner.[60]

Only one formal division was recorded in the Lords on any aspect of the enquiry into the condition of the peerage or the subsequent bill, either during the bill's first appearance in the House (March–April 1719) or on its reappearance in the autumn (November 1719). This division on 3 March in the Committee of the Whole House was on the resolution that the 16 elected Scottish peers be replaced by 25 hereditary peers. The resolution was carried by 86 to 30.[61] The minority was probably largely composed of Tories and may have been prompted by the still prevalent fear of too many Scots in the Lords. Some bishops may have opposed the idea, fearing that an equal number of (Presbyterian) Scots and bishops in the House would be bad for the Church of England.[62] All other decisions of the House on the bill were carried with little or no opposition,[63] and certainly no one was prepared to force a formal vote. This strongly underlines the almost unanimous cross-party support the bill received in

[58] See e.g., Royal Archives, Stuart Papers 102/68: Orrery to [the Pretender], [28 Jan. 1727]; *ibid.*, 238/319: Cockburn to [Edgar], 7 Dec. 1741.

[59] Brampton Bryan MSS. 117: G[wyn] to [Harley], 5 March 1718/19.

[60] Cobbett, *Parl. Hist.*, VII, 501. A position shared by the Tory Earl of Nottingham. Townshend even encouraged the Scots to speak in favour of the bill (Cheshire R.O., DCH/X/8: N[ewburgh] to [Cholmondeley], 3 March [1719]).

[61] H.L.R.O., MS. Minutes, 11 Nov. 1718–1 Oct. 1719.

[62] Christ Church, Wake MS. 8, f. 94: Humphrey Prideaux to Wake, 11 March 1719. There were important Tories with the majority on this vote including Trevor, Harcourt and Buckingham (Cheshire R.O., DCH/X/8: N[ewburgh] to [Cholmondeley], 3 March [1719]).

[63] Gwyn had hinted at this lack of opposition as early as 7 March, see Brampton Bryan MSS. 117: to [Harley], 7 March 1718/19. Cowper tried to divide the House further after the initial vote, but failed because the Tories were in favour of the 'English' provisions of the bill, and all subsequent decisions were 'unanimous' (Cheshire R.O., DCH/X/8: N[ewburgh] to [Cholmondeley], 3 March [1719]).

the Lords, only Cowper and Nottingham maintaining any form of active opposition. Even the Prince of Wales's active opposition could not prevent his faction in the Lords strongly supporting the bill.[64] The ministry's appeal to the social exclusiveness of the peerage had paid off.

6

The standard interpretation of the Peerage Bill as propounded by Basil Williams praises the ministry's choice of the Duke of Somerset to propose the initial resolution on the state of the peerage on 28 February 1719, since 'his advocacy gave the proceedings the appearance of being a spontaneous move of the peerage in defence of its own rights'.[65] This has the clear implication that the 'plot' behind the bill was only discovered by the world at large on that day, the ministry alone knowing in advance what was proposed. This is untrue, for the earliest reference so far found, that the ministry was considering such a move, dates from late December 1718. Ministers had been in negotiation with some of the Scots, most notably Argyll, Montrose, Roxburghe and Stair, in November over the 25 hereditary peerages.[66] Both Sunderland and Stanhope appear to have been involved, though the lead came from the former.[67] By late December the negotiations had reached a satisfactory stage and Sunderland was able to promise the Scots that the ministry would use 'their power to settle *the* pe[er]age'.[68] A driving force in these preliminaries was the desire of the Duke of Argyll for a British dukedom. He had been granted an English earldom in 1705, which guaranteed him a permanent seat in the Lords after the Union, but he believed that his support for the Union in 1707 deserved a higher reward,[69] a feeling no doubt exacerbated by the elevation to British dukedoms of both Queensberry and Hamilton. The negotiations and subsequent manoeuvrings, which started with his reconciliation with the ministers in the winter of 1718 and culminated in his appointment as Lord Steward in February 1719, the month the Peerage Bill was unveiled, clearly indicate that Argyll's support was crucial to the bill. A fact confirmed in April 1719 when, despite the bill's lack of parliamentary progress, Argyll

[64] See above, note 11.

[65] Williams, *Stanhope*, p. 405.

[66] S.R.O., GD135/141/13A/51: Montrose to Stair, 19 Nov. 1718; H.M.C., *Polwarth MSS.*, II, 72-3, 75.

[67] Schulenburg in his correspondence, 121/6 (see note 15 above) indicates that Sunderland was the driving force behind the bill. I owe this reference to Derek Mackay and Edward Gregg.

[68] Huntington Lib., LO 8326, 8328, 8331: [Sir David Dalrymple] to [Loudoun], 22, 27, 30 Dec. 1718 (my italics). In two of these letters (8328, 8331) it is worth noting that the reference is to 'the peerage' not to 'our peerage', i.e. the Scottish peers.

[69] H.M.C., *Mar and Kellie MSS.*, p. 368.

was raised to a British dukedom.[70]

Throughout January and February 1719 the ministry was working out the details of the bill, which was indeed kept a close secret from the public until a few days before Somerset introduced his motion in the Lords on 28 February. Edward Prideaux Gwyn informed Edward Harley *jr* on the 25th that such a bill would be brought into the upper House a few days later. He correctly outlined the main details, thus proving that the bill had been largely settled and that Somerset's call for a consideration of the state of the peerage was a sham. Though the ministry had played their cards closely, some leak had caused the loss of the element of surprise. Gwyn also forecast accurately the long-term future of the bill: 'the advantage accruing by this Bill to the Lords is so apparent that it will certainly pass with ease through their house, but if the Commons consent they must surely be very forgetful of themselves'.[71] The Commons were indeed to prove the crucial element in the equation, as Sunderland had clearly realized quite early on.

Around the 28 February, James Craggs, one of the Secretaries of State, compiled a forecast of support of and opposition to the bill within the Commons, at the same time drawing up a canvassing list for use in the ministry's campaign in the lower House.[72] The initial forecast was not encouraging, with only 194 M.P.s thought to favour the bill and 233 thought to oppose it (of whom, significantly, some 71 were Whigs). There were also 126 M.P.s whose views and intentions were doubtful (of whom all but three were Whigs). Thus at the very beginning the ministry found that around 23 per cent of the Commons were undecided on a question in which the ministry was already in a substantial minority. Some time in mid-March, while the Peerage Bill was proceeding

[70] Argyll was out of favour with the Prince of Wales by Dec. 1717 (Huntington Lib., LO 8328: [Dalrymple] to [Loudoun], 27 Dec. 1718). Montrose reported an intention to introduce a clause in committee which would have allowed Argyll to sit by right of his Scottish dukedom: 'if it Carried [it] would be new and unprecedented . . . [and] would be a feather in his cap and show his interest in the house'. Montrose organised against it and the clause was not introduced (S.R.O., GD220/5/828/25: [Montrose] to Mungo Graham, 21 March 1719). For Argyll's importance in the ministerial negotiations preceeding the bill see G.M. Townend, 'The Political Career of Charles Spencer, Third Earl of Sunderland, 1695-1722' (Edinburgh, Ph.D., 1984), pp. 260-1. Even after becoming a British duke Argyll was not affected by the 1711 ruling of the Lords; he continued to sit by virtue of his 1705 English title of Earl of Greenwich.

[71] Brampton Bryan MSS. 177: G[wyn] to [Harley], 25 Feb. 1719.

[72] B.L., Stowe MS. 247, ff. 184-91, 193-200. The canvassing list has 125 M.P.s on it, each one allocated one or two (and a few cases three) M.P.s or peers (and in Nicholas Lechmere's case, the King himself) to persuade them to vote for the bill. Twenty-six peers are listed. Most were responsible for one M.P., but several were given more, most notably Sunderland (14), Cadogan (13), Stanhope (11), Argyll (6), and Roxburghe, Montrose and Newcastle (4 each). The list included two Tory peers: Carnarvon (later Chandos), and Coventry.

smoothly through its various stages in the Lords (apart from the petitions against it from various groups of Scottish peers),[73] Sunderland drew up a second forecast for the Commons.[74] He detected that the position had somewhat improved, and that 211 M.P.s were now for the bill with 223 (including 61 Whigs) against. There were still, however, 121 doubtfuls (some 22 per cent of the House). Clearly things did not look good for the ministry in the Commons at the time that the committee stage for the bill was completed in the Lords.

Despite a small shift in support for the bill in the weeks between the two forecasts, the trend was not rapid enough for the ministry to be sure of reaching a majority in the time remaining. The problem was the large proportion of the doubtfuls, most of whom were Whigs (118 out of 121 in Sunderland's forecast). The ministry was clearly worried, as it was right to be, for most of these doubtfuls eventually voted against the bill in December 1719.[75]

The question of converting minority support in the Commons into a majority was made more difficult for the ministry by the 'paper war' which broke out on 14 March, when Sir Richard Steele launched the opposition attack on the bill with *The Plebeian*, thus opening the gates to a flood of pamphlets issued both by the ministry and opposition.[76] The arguments pro and con were widely rehearsed for public consumption, and the 'plot' by the ministry to 'subvert' the constitution was one of the main planks of the opposition's programme, brilliantly expounded by Walpole, amongst others.[77] It is significant that much of the ministry's propaganda rested on the social and political benefits to be derived by the peerage from the bill, an argument thinly disguised for wider public consumption.

By early April 1719, however, despite the bill's rapid progress through the Lords, the ministry was clearly nervous and felt that it was losing the public argument. On 9 April the third reading of the bill was ordered for the 14th; on that day, with 520 M.P.s rumoured to be still in London and the Commons planning a call of the House, Stanhope

---

[73] For a glimpse of the activity behind the petitions of the Scottish peerage opposition to the bill, see H.M.C., *Portland MSS.*, V, 578-82. It is significant in the light of the social dimension of the bill that opposition to some of the 16 representative peers becoming part of the 25 hereditary peers was that some had no lands in Scotland and some had poor estates (*ibid.*, pp. 580-1: Eglinton to [Dundonald], 19 March 1718/19).

[74] B.L., Add. MS. 61465, ff. 188-93 (formerly Blenheim Palace MSS. D.II.9, 10).

[75] See Sedgwick, *House of Commons*, I, 29, 84-5. By 14 March Newburgh was convinced that the bill would not pass the Commons (Cheshire R.O., DCH/X/8: to [Cholmondeley], [14 March 1719]).

[76] Steele was answered on 19 March by Addison in the first number of *The Old Whig*, see P. Smithers, *The Life of Joseph Addison* (Oxford, 2nd edn., 1968), pp. 448-9.

[77] For a summary of the 'war' and the gist of the most important pamphlets see Williams, *Stanhope*, pp. 406-8; E.R. Turner, 'Peerage Bill', pp. 243-59.

informed the Lords that the third reading would be postponed for two weeks. Everyone knew that in effect the bill was being abandoned, for Parliament was prorogued only four days later and all incomplete legislation was lost. The opposition had successfully dished the bill. Bolingbroke was astonished at the ministry's 'unaccountable management' which had led it 'to open the session with such an attempt and not to have told noses better'.[78] Sunderland, however, was not a man to give up easily.

We do not know when Sunderland and Stanhope actively started to plan the return of the Peerage Bill in the next session of Parliament. Perhaps it had always been their intention, ever since they realized that the bill would not pass the Commons in the spring of 1719. The standard interpretation, that the ministry sprang the bill upon an unsuspecting Parliament on the third day of the new session on 25 November 1719, does not stand up to close examination. Negotiations clearly went on within the ministry, and hints began to emerge in correspondence as early as June 1719, when the Duke of Chandos reported that he had heard from Sunderland himself that the bill would be reintroduced.[79] This proves that Sunderland had taken the decision before he went to Hanover at the end of August.[80] He accompanied Stanhope largely to overcome the influence of Bernstorff, one of George I's German advisers, who was known to be opposed to the Peerage Bill.[81] The English ministers reported back to their colleagues in Britain on the progress of their discussions with the King. As early as 21 September, Sunderland informed John Aislabie, Chancellor of the Exchequer, that George had resolved to have the bill reintroduced,[82] and in October Sunderland

[78] Quoted in H.T. Dickinson, *Bolingbroke* (1970), p. 149; Cheshire R.O., DCH/X/8: N[ewburgh] to Cholmondeley, 14 April [1719]; B.L., Loan 29/96: Oxford to Lord Harley, 14 April 1719. It is only fair to say that until quite late some thought the bill would pass, but that 'it will be a hard run match' as Montrose put it on 2 April, when he estimated the ministry's Commons' majority at about 20 (S.R.O., GD220/5/829/1, 2: to Mungo Graham, 2, 7 April 1719). For the estimate of the number of M.P.s in London, see Herefordshire R.O., A81/IV/Francis Brydges correspondence, 1712-19: William to Francis Brydges, 14 April 1719.

[79] Huntington Lib., ST 57/16 (Stowe papers), p. 188: Chandos to Harcourt, 12 June 1719. The source of this news is described as Lord S., but an earlier letter identifies this as Sunderland. As early as April 1719 there were reports that the bill would be brought in next session (B.L., Loan 29/163/Misc. 79: Ruglen to –?–, 14 April, 5 May 1719).

[80] See Townend, 'Political Career of . . . Sunderland', pp. 264-7.

[81] See below, Appendix, where the attitude of the King to the bill is discussed.

[82] Leeds City Archives, Vyner MSS., catalogue item 5709: Sunderland to Aislabie, 21 Sept. 1719 (letter now lost). I owe this reference to Graham Townend. On 26 September Robethon, another of the King's German advisers, wrote to Polwarth, ambassador in Copenhagen, who was anxious for a British peerage, that Sunderland would bring in the bill in the next session (H.M.C., *Polwarth MSS.*, II, 326; see also p. 383).

confirmed this and outlined his plans to the Duke of Newcastle.[83]

News of the possible revival of the bill was not, however, confined to closed government circles. In September and October Archbishop Wake was questioning Cowper over tactics should the bill reappear in the winter session. As early as 5 September Cowper had heard that the bill would be brought in 'with some alteration that would make it more palatable to the House of Commons'.[84] By the end of October the Duke of Roxburghe, acting on behalf of Sunderland, was organizing the proxies of the Scottish peers.[85] Thus the cat was out of the bag north of the border long before Parliament met. Indeed the Duke of Montrose had been in Hanover in the autumn keeping up the pressure on the ministry for the bill.[86]

Parliament's reassembly on 23 November 1719 had been preceded by a pre-sessional meeting on the previous evening, where no doubt the government's forces were briefed on the bill.[87] The bill was introduced on 25 November by the Duke of Somerset and received its first reading. Within five days it had completed all its stages in the Lords and was sent to the Commons. The ministry was confident it would not face the same opposition it had done in the spring; indeed as early as October Craggs was hoping for a successful session of Parliament, and to this effect it was reported that Sunderland had done 'all humanly speaking that can be done to gain the tories, soe far as to promise [to] dissolve the parliament and take tory measures'. The Tories, however, were not to be so easily won: 'they answered, that He had deceiv'd them too often to be beliv'd upon that head, which would make them wear the livery of Peers'. Sunderland was perhaps also hoping to rely on the ministry's foreign policy successes and the proposed repeal of the Septennial Act, which might be seen as a sort of quid pro quo to the Commons for supporting a

---

[83] B.L., Add. MS. 32686, f. 149: Sunderland to Newcastle, 22 Oct. 1719, n.s.

[84] Christ Church, Wake MS. 21, f. 154: Cowper to [Wake], 5 Sept. 1719; see also Hertfordshire R.O., D/EP F62, ff. 99-100, 103-4: Wake to Cowper, 7 Sept., 20 Oct. 1719.

[85] P.R.O., S.P. 43/60, f. 199: Roxburghe to Stanhope, 30 Oct. 1719 (I owe this reference to Graham Townend); Huntington Lib., LO 9059: Roxburghe to Loudoun, 29 Oct. 1719.

[86] Montrose was predicting the bill's reintroduction by early October (S.R.O., GD220/5/1938/9: to Polwarth, 6 Oct. 1719, n.s.). For his activities in Hanover, see *ibid.*, 11: 3 Nov. 1719; 220/5/830/7-8: [Montrose] to [Graham], 2 Nov., 18 Oct. 1719.

[87] The only evidence for the meeting is Christ Church, Wake MS. 8, f. 156: Sunderland to [Wake], 23 Nov. 1719. No list is known to survive of those who were summoned or attended. For a discussion of the development of more effective management of the Lords, see C. Jones, 'The House of Lords and the Growth of Parliamentary Stability, 1701-1742', in *Britain in the First Age of Party, 1680-1750: Essays Presented to Geoffrey Holmes*, ed. C. Jones (1987), pp. 96-101.

bill to perpetuate the status quo in the Lords.[88] The ministry had, however, reckoned without Walpole, who had found the perfect opportunity for harrassing the government. It seems inconceivable, after his brilliant performance in the 'paper war' against the bill, that he could have done anything else. His claim that he based his telling attack on the bill in December on a chance remark overheard concerning the social pretentions of an M.P. for his children and grandchildren belies the case he had earlier put forward in his pamphlets. Nevertheless, his attack was grounded upon social as well as political factors. He appealed to the ambitions felt by most M.P.s for the betterment of either themselves or their families, by asking if they would 'consent to the shutting the door upon [their] family ever coming into the House of Lords'.[89] This speech, possibly the most forceful of his career, sealed the fate of the bill, and speaker after speaker rose in the Commons to support him. The bill was rejected in a full house after a ten hour debate by 269 votes to 177 on 8 December 1719.[90]

As in the spring, the whole question of the Scottish peerage was intimately linked with the autumn reintroduction of the Peerage Bill. The rectification of its anomalous position remained one of the chief aims of the ministry. On 24 November the second Duke of Dover (the Scottish third Duke of Queensberry, who that day came of age) asked the Lords that he be sent a writ of summons as a holder of a British title, notwithstanding the decision of the House over the Hamilton case in 1711. The writ had been debated on 10 December and on the 18th the Lords read Dover's petition. The case dragged on into the new year, and was heard on the 12 and 14 January 1720, but after the failure of the Peerage Bill the outcome was inevitable. On 14 January Dover's right to sit as a British peer was rejected and the Hamilton ruling was reaffirmed. As with the earlier case the divisions over Dover's claim ran across party lines, with Sunderland himself opposing the duke's right to sit except by

---

[88] Eliot MSS. (Lord Eliot, Port Eliot, St. Germans, Cornwall), Bundle 'Secretary Craggs. File 1': Craggs to [Sir John Norris], 23 Oct. 1719; R.A., Add. 28/54: [Princess Caroline] to [Mrs. Clayton], [? 27 Nov. 1719]; cf. *ibid.*, 28/56: [same] to [same], [? 18 Dec. 1719]. See also H.M.C., *Polwarth MSS.*, II, 403, for the ministry's efforts to win over M.P.s in late November. For the proposed repeal of the Septennial Act see Williams, *Stanhope*, pp. 410–14.

[89] H.M.C., *14th Report*, Appendix IX (Onslow MSS.), 459. All the best pamphlets of the spring 'paper war' were reprinted in the autumn (Cheshire R.O., DCH/X/8: N[ewburgh] to [Cholmondeley], 10 Dec. [1719]).

[90] Cobbett, *Parl. Hist.*, VII, 609–27; Cheshire R.O., DCH/X/8: N[ewburgh] to Cholmondeley, 8 Dec. [1719].

a special act of Parliament.[91] Anti-Scottish feeling still ran high in the Lords, and, although they were prepared to tolerate a limited expansion of a further nine Scottish peers within the terms of the Peerage Bill, as in 1711 they could not stomach the prospect of an open-ended commitment allowing any Scots with British titles a place in the Lords.

The Scottish representative peers, having come so close to establishing hereditary seats in the Lords, were unwilling to let things lie; indeed on 22 January 1720 Stanhope promised Lord Polwarth that the ministry would try to reintroduce the Peerage Bill in the next session, 'at least what relates to Scotland'.[92] Over the next two decades the Scots continued to agitate for a Scottish Peerage Bill. They came closest to success in 1721-22 when they had ministerial backing, but again they foundered on the rocks of English social resentment and political fear. Montrose thought the bill would be successful, for some who had formerly opposed it now saw how much it would be in their interest. On the other hand, however, the Scots themselves were divided, for, as well as the strong resentment of those Scottish peers who would deliberately have been left out in the cold by such a bill, there was the added factor of opposition from Argyll and his brother Ilay. Significantly the latter, in contrast to his position in 1719, thought that the bill ought not to come in without the consent of all the Scottish peers.[93] Such a bill was inevitably doomed, for a British House of Lords so dominated by English peers would never consent to grant the Scottish clauses of the 1719 Peerage Bill without the quid pro quo of closing off their own peerage to newcomers.

[91] Brampton Bryan MSS., Bundle 102: G[wyn] to [Harley], 14 Jan. 1719/20. At first Dover was determined to bring in a bill, but eventually decided against it (S.R.O., GD220/5/831/5, 6, 8: Montrose to Graham, 23, 26 Jan., 2 Feb. 1720). Lord Newburgh described the division on 14 January as 'mix'd whiggs and torys, courtiers and antecourtiers', and he considered the making of a peer by an act of Parliament as 'quite new and extraordinary' and if successful that it would lead to 'an inundation of Scots into our house' (Cheshire R.O., DCH/X/8: N[ewburgh] to [Cholmondeley], 12, 14 Jan. [1720]).

[92] H.M.C., *Polwarth*, II, 444. There was even a rumour in the autumn of 1720 that Walpole would ensure the passage of the Peerage Bill and the repeal of the Septennial Act as part of an 'undertaking' to bring all the previous factions together (H.M.C., *Portland MSS.*, VII, 281-2).

[93] S.R.O., GD220/5/836/2: Montrose to Graham, 5 Sept. 1721; GD 248/562/69a/61 (Seafield papers): [Pitsligo] to Deskford, 30 Dec. 1721; H.M.C., *Polwarth MSS.*, III, 30, 33, 37; H.M.C., *Mar and Kellie MSS.*, pp. 522-3; S.R.O., GD124/15/1224/4 (Mar and Kellie papers): Ilay to Lord Grange, 27 Feb. [1722]. For details of the opposition campaign against the proposed bill see S.R.O., GD45/14/390 (Dalhousie papers): letters to H. Maule, 1721-22, especially no. 27: Pitsligo to Maule, 8 Oct. 1721, where peerages are considered property. There had also been a rumour of 'a Scotch Peerage bill' in March 1721 (B.L., Loan 29/67: [Edward Harley *jr*] to Abigail Harley, 12 March 1720/21).

7

The Peerage Bill had formed a central plank of the Sunderland ministry's ambitious programme of reform, a programme that was only partly successful. The Occasional Conformity and Schism Acts were indeed repealed in early 1719, but the reform of the universities, the Peerage Bill, and the repeal of the Septennial Act all failed. The latter indeed barely left the drawing-board, being abandoned early upon the suggestion of the Duke of Newcastle. The repeal was probably designed to lengthen the life of the current Parliament as well as providing a possible pay-off for the Commons' support of the Peerage Bill.[94] If both the repeal of the Septennial Act and the Peerage Bill had succeeded they would undoubtedly have led to a more oligarchic form of government which would have grown stronger at the expense of the royal prerogative. The idea of curtailing the prerogative, even in the specific respect of the creation of peerages, was no new thing. Lord Wharton at the time of the 1688-9 Revolution had aired this suggestion.[95] There is a feel about the Sunderland ministry's overall direction of policy that it was out to strengthen Parliament's hold on affairs at the expense of other similar institutions – but at the same time ensuring that Parliament represented the status quo and was firmly under ministerial control.

The representative institutions of the Church of England, the Convocations of Canterbury and York, were suppressed in 1717; and in Ireland Convocation did not meet after 1713. The Declaratory Act of 1720 saw the British Parliament finally settle the question of legal appeals to the Irish or British House of Lords in favour of Westminister over Dublin. Even further out on the fringes of power the Cornish Parliament of Tinners was not allowed to meet under George I. Everywhere a Westminster-based oligarchy was being strengthened at the cost of representative institutions on the periphery.[96] The wings of the ministry's far-ranging reforms had, however, been clipped; and the Peerage Bill – potentially the most oligarchic reform of all – had been

---

[94] Williams, *Stanhope*, pp. 411-13.

[95] The proposals are in Bodl., MS. Carte 81, f. 766; see Lois G. Schwoerer, *The Declaration of Rights, 1689* (Baltimore, 1981), p. 238.

[96] See J.C.D. Clark, *Revolution and Rebellion* (Cambridge, 1986), pp. 129-30; Eveline Cruickshanks, 'The Convocation of the Stannaries of Cornwall: The Parliament of Tinners, 1703-1752', *Parliaments, Estates and Representation*, VI (1986). The Declaratory Act further circumscribed the legislative powers of the Dublin Parliament, see Isolde Victory, 'The Making of the Declaratory Act, 1720' (forthcoming). I am grateful to Dr. Victory for allowing me to read a draft of her essay. In the crisis over the South Sea Company there were rumours of a move to further strengthen the oligarchic hold of Parliament by a Scottish Peerage bill 'and Another [bill] to Prolong the Parliament' (B.L., Loan 29/67: [Edward] to Abigail Harley, 12 March 1720/21).

defeated. How far did this failure effect the growth of oligarchy in the remaining years of the eighteenth century? How different was the development of the peerage without the constraints of the Peerage Bill from what it might have been if the limitations on creations had become law? The short answer is not at all.

Table C gives the numbers of creations and of extinctions in the British peerage by decades from the demise of the Peerage Bill until the end of the eighteenth century. The rapid rise in the number of additions to the peerage between 1714 and 1718 was at an annual rate of 2.22 (see above Table A, p. 90), faster than the annual increase under the early Stuarts. Converted into an equivalent figure for a ten year period this annual rate gives 22 additions in ten years. Table C shows that this rate of addition was not reached again until the 1780s (which saw the mass creations of the Younger Pitt in 1784),[97] and was not exceeded until the 1790s. If the terms of the Peerage Bill *had* come into effect (i.e. only six brand new creations plus others to compensate pro rata for the number of extinctions), again not until the 1780s would the legal limitations have had to be called into effect.

Two reasons for this state of affairs are clear: first, the high rate of extinctions continued until the end of the century and, until the 1780s, more than balanced creations; and secondly, successive monarchs, especially George II,[98] were reluctant to over-dilute the peerage. Further, there was a move in the century towards special remainders upon the creations of peerages by which the title could pass to a cadet branch. By this method peerages were more likely to survive the rigours of inheritance by primogeniture.[99]

George II's reluctance is illustrated by the case of the four peerages created between June 1733 and January 1734. These aroused contemporary comment, and were only accepted by the King himself because Walpole wished to strengthen the ministerial leadership in the Lords in the wake of the Excise crisis.[100] Three of these four creations (Hervey, Hardwicke and Talbot) were brought into the Lords because of their political and parliamentary talents. They underlined a possible problem which could have vexed later ministries had the Peerage Bill actually been made law. If extinctions were few, how could an administration inject new talent into its ranks in the upper House? This

---

[97] For these see Gerda C. Richards, 'The Creations of Peers Recommended by the Younger Pitt', *American Historical Review*, XXXIV (1928-9), 47-54.

[98] See *Lord Hervey and His Friends, 1726-38*, ed. the Earl of Ilchester (1950), p. 200.

[99] See Cannon, 'The Isthmus Repaired', p. 437. This should not be exaggerated, for according to Cannon 'during the reign of George I nearly half the peerages granted included special remainders': not a large number. Special remainders were not infrequent before George I.

[100] See Jones, 'The House of Lords and the Growth of Parliamentary Stability', p. 90.

Table C
British Peerages Created 1719 to 1799[1]

Date	Number of creations	Number of extinctions[2]	Increase in the size of the peerage	Percentage increase of total peerage[3]
1719-29	11	11	0	0
1730-39	4	13	−9	−5
1740-49	16	16	0	0
1750-59	7	18	−11	−6.2
1760-69	27	13	+14	+7.8
1770-79	12	15	−3	−1.7
1780-89	32	11	+21	+11.7
1790-99	42	11	+31	+17.4
Total	151	108[4]	+43	+24.1

[1] The English, Scottish and British peerages taken together.

[2] The figures in this column include the extinction of Scottish titles which did not entitle the holder to a seat in the Lords (unless one of the 16 representative peers). Therefore the figures (and percentages) for the increase of the size of the British (and English) peerage should be larger (see below, note 4).

[3] Percentages of the base figure of 178 peerages in 1718 (see above, Table A).

[4] Thirty-nine Scottish peerages became extinct between 1719 and 1799 (see Beckett, *Aristocracy in England*, p. 488); thus the number of extinctions in the British peerage was 69, giving a total increase of 81. This represented a 45.5% increase in the British peerage between 1719 and 1799.

Source: G.E.C., *Complete Peerage*.

difficulty was clearly foreseen by contemporaries: 'The Lords degenerate by Luxury Idleness etc. and the Crown is always forced to govern by new Men', wrote Swift, who regarded this as the 'one invincible obvious Argument' against the bill.[101] Indeed the impression is that in the Lords the bulk of the work done was performed by peers of the first generation. In fact, however, the actual rate of extinctions in the eighteenth century was sufficiently high for any ministry to have coped with this problem had it arisen.

Part of the necessary social safety-valve for aspiring families who looked for a peerage as a confirmation of their rising status (the very point at the centre of Walpole's attack on the bill in December 1719) was provided in the later eighteenth century by expanding the Irish peerage to meet demand. Table D shows that the rate of growth of Irish titles was four times that of the British peerage between 1719 and 1799. Increasingly the Irish peerage was used either as a 'consolation prize' or as a 'probationary' title for the Englishmen who aspired to a British title, but were considered unsuitable or unready for one.[102] Up to the time of the Peerage Bill few Irish titles had been given to Englishmen who had no connexion (particularly in land) with Ireland. This was less and less the case after 1719. Irish titles also had the added bonus for a ministry of honouring a politician while keeping him a member of the British House of Commons, and therefore not denuding the lower House of talent.[103] None the less, Irish peerages were considered as second class by the English,[104] an attitude that was keenly felt by the Irish.[105]

8

Recent work, particularly by John Cannon and John Beckett, on recruitment to the British peerage in the eighteenth century has shown that virtually no one who was entirely unconnected with the peerage,

[101] *Correspondence of Jonathan Swift*, II, 331: to Charles Ford, 8 Dec. 1719. This argument was touched on by Steele in his *A Letter to the Earl of O——d, concerning the Bill of Peerage* (1719).

[102] See Cannon, *Aristocratic Century*, p. 16, but cf. pp. 28-31.

[103] A notable example was Sir Richard Child, a man with an estate of £10,000 a year, whom the government were concerned in 1716 might be given a peerage. They wished him to remain in the Commons, and in 1718 he acquired an Irish viscountancy, and in 1731 an Irish earldom. Sedgwick, *House of Commons*, I, 549. See also Beckett, *Aristocracy in England*, p. 110.

[104] In one case Irish lords were coupled with mere squires in the search for a suitable constituency. See *The Art of Politicks, in Imitation of Horace's Art of Poetry* (London, 1731), p. 43. I am grateful to David Hayton for this reference.

[105] See Lord Egmont's disgust in 1733 at the Prince of Orange's wedding when Irish peers were not allowed to precede English peers of a lower rank: B.L., Add. MS. 46984, Appendix II, [f. 141]: 2 Nov. [1733]. See also H.M.C., *Egmont Diary*, II, 43, 59, but cf. III, 138.

Table D
Irish Peerages Created 1719 to 1799[1]

Date	Number of creations	Number of extinctions	Increase in size of peerage		Percentage increase of peerage	
1719-29	18	6	+12	(118)[2]	+11.3[3]	
1730-39	7	8	−1	(117)	−0.9	−0.8[4]
1740-49	8	4	+4	(121)	+3.7	+3.4
1750-59	19	7	+12	(133)	+11.3	+9.9
1760-69	28	12	+16	(149)	+15.1	+12.1
1770-79	27	9	+18	(167)	+16.9	+12.1
1780-89	29	10	+19	(186)	+17.9	+11.4
1790-99	32	6	+26	(212)	+24.5	+13.9
Total	168	62	+106		+100	

[1] It is difficult to calculate exactly the number of Irish peerages extant in 1719. *Liber Munerum Publicorum Hiberniae*, ed. R. Lascelles (2 vols., 1824-30), I, part 1, p. 50, lists 91 titles in 1714; 12 were created in 1715 giving a total of 103. On the other hand the *Liber* gives the number in 1760 as 133 (p. 51), and working backwards to 1719 using the figures in the third column of this table (based on a tabulation of G.E.C., *Complete Peerage*) gives 106. This figure has been used as the base figure for the percentage increase.

[2] Figures in brackets are the total number of the peerage at the end of each decade.

[3] The first figure in this column represents the percentage increase each decade on the 1719 base figure of 106.

[4] The second figure in this column represents the percentage increase each decade over the previous decade's total (i.e. a percentage of the previous decade's total as given in brackets; see note 2 above).

and therefore of an unsuitable social background, achieved a title.[106] This situation had been hinted at as early as 1963 by F.M.L. Thompson, who divided the English landed elite in to two groups: the higher – essentially the peerage; and the lower – the gentry.[107] Despite differences of interpretation in recent work, it seems that there was much social mobility upwards into the lower elite, but little into the peerage.[108] Thus, while Disraeli's comparison with a 'Venetian oligarchy' certainly held good for the peerage, it probably did not apply lower down the social scale. The paucity of peerage creations for most of the eighteenth century can largely be laid at the door of the Hanoverian monarchs who were reluctant to expand the size of the Lords. The peerage was not so much a closed elite as a 'non-opened' one circumscribed by a political decision. Thus the spirit, if not the letter, of the Peerage Bill survived both Walpole's oratory and the vote of the House of Commons in December 1719; and, indeed, it lived on to influence British politics for the rest of the eighteenth century. Even after the Lords had witnessed an unprecedented expansion of its membership in the late eighteenth and early nineteenth centuries,[109] the constitutional crisis over the Reform Bill in 1831-32 revealed a government anxious to prevent as far as possible a permanent enlargement of the upper House if it indeed proved necessary for the King to create peers to force the bill through Parliament. 'The truth is', wrote Lord Holland,[110]

> if we should resort to the measure of increasing our vote in the Lords . . . I conclude we shall take some pains to render such honours as little of a permanent increase to the House of Lords as possible and that a large proportion of any new votes we may obtain will be either of Elder sons called up by write [*sic*] or professional Men without ambition.

Later, despite admitting that 'the number of urgent and of reasonable

---

[106] Cannon, *Aristocratic Century*, pp. 1-37; Beckett, *Aristocracy in England*, pp. 91-131.

[107] In his *English Landed Society in the Nineteenth Century*.

[108] For the most recent assessment of the contending interpretations, which finds that the English landed elite as a whole was open, see D. Spring and E. Spring, 'Social Mobility and the English Landed Elite', *Canadian Journal of History*, XXI (1986), 333-51.

[109] M.W. McCahill, 'Peerage Creations and the Changing Character of the British Nobility, 1750-1850', *E.H.R.*, XCVI (1981), 259-84. For George III's idea in 1760 that 'it were therefore much to be wished that the number of Peers were limited; for if the power of the Lords should be anihilated, Despotism would instantly follow the loss of liberty' for the Lords acted 'as a mediating power to keep the true balance' between the King and the people, see Thomas, '"Thoughts on the British Constitution"', p. 362.

[110] Herefordshire R.O., J56/IV/16 (Cornwall papers): Holland to [Sir George Cornwall], 12 Sept. [1831], 28 March 1832. Cornwall had applied for the revival of the barony of Fanhope which had been in his family but had become extinct in 1443. He wrote that he was 'under the Impression that it may be found necessary to create Peers chosen perhaps from Commons not of much Mark, and not members of Parliament' (*ibid.*: [Cornwall] to [?Lord Palmerston], n.d., draft).

claims [to peerages] are very great', Holland still concluded that the government must avoid 'too great a permanent increase of the House of Lords [and that] the calling up of Eldest Sons and the claims of Childless persons are supposed by many to be preferable'.

Appendix

The King and the Peerage Bill

One of the intriguing paradoxes of the Peerage Bill is the attitude of the King: he was clearly prepared to allow the bill to proceed, yet it severely curtailed his prerogative. The problem is the lack of direct evidence and the conflicting nature of the circumstantial evidence. The case for believing George I supported the bill is largely based on the fact that it was introduced, that on 3 March 1719 the King sent a message to the Lords via Stanhope that he would waive his prerogative rather than obstruct the bill, that in September and October 1719 Sunderland reported from Hanover that the King was resolved to revive it,[111] and that at the time of its first introduction in March 1719 the King was listed by James Craggs on his canvassing list with the task of lobbying Nicholas Lechmere.[112] Why would the King so support a reduction in his prerogative? First, it clearly damaged the future position of the Prince of Wales making is more difficult for the Prince to impose a ministry against the wishes of the House of Lords. George was also much under the influence of Sunderland and Stanhope and perhaps did not fully understand the implications of the bill. His latest biographer considers him to have been the captive of his ministers,[113] an enslavement made worse by his personal dislike of Townshend and Walpole. In the summer

[111] Cheshire R.O., DCH/X/8: N[ewburgh] to [Cholmondeley], 3 March [1719]; Leeds City Archives, Vyner Catalogue, item 5709: Sunderland to Aislabie, 21 Sept. 1719; B.L., Add. MS. 32686, f. 149: Sunderland to Newcastle, 22 Oct. 1719, n.s. (see Williams, *Stanhope*, p. 410).

[112] B.L., Stowe MS. 247, ff. 193–200; see above p. 99. The King was also involved in encouraging the Earl of Cholmondeley, the Treasurer of the Household, to attend the autumn session or to deposit his proxy (Cheshire R.O., DCH/X/8: N[ewburgh] to [Cholmondeley], 30 Oct., 21 Nov. [1719]).

[113] Ragnhild Hatton, *George I: King and Elector* (1978), p. 244.

of 1717, shortly after the Whig Schism, the King was reported to have been prepared to employ Tories rather than have the brothers-in-law back on their terms.[114] However, by 1718 George may have secretly approached Walpole to sound him out.[115]

There are some indications that George I disliked the Peerage Bill. James Craggs thought that most of the Germans at the British Court were against the bill precisely because it limited the King's prerogative.[116] They may well have hoped to become peers themselves on the lines that William III's Dutch favourites did in the 1690s. Bernstorff certainly gave out that the King opposed the bill, and may have leaked this information to Lord Oxford for use in the debates in the Lords.[117] The Princess of Wales also reported that Sunderland had returned from an interview with the King 'under an uncertainty what to do', concluding that the bill would either fail or be dropped. She further reported that George was troubled and 'that He cant forgive himself'.[118]

In the absence of any clear evidence the King's biographer concluded that he was probably not in favour of the bill but went along with it to keep his ministers content and to further the Whig programme of toleration and university reform which he supported.[119]

A last word may be left to 'An Excellent New Ballad' which contains the lines:

> . . . up Sunderland rose,
> And said the King values not which way it goes, . . .
> Then God bless the King and may he long live,
> tho he loo[?]s not, 'tis true, his money to give,
> Yet he cares not a fig for his Prerogative . . .[120]

[114] Schulenburg correspondence (see note 15, above).

[115] Hatton, *George I*, p. 245.

[116] *Stair Annals*, II, 104. See also J.M. Beattie, *The English Court in the Reign of George I* (Cambridge, 1967), p. 235 note.

[117] *Stair Annals*, II, 405; Linda Colley, *In Defiance of Oligarchy: The Tory Party, 1714-1760* (Cambridge, 1982), p. 190.

[118] R.A., Add. 28/50, 51a: [Princess Caroline] to [Mrs. Clayton], [? March 1719].

[119] Hatton, *George I*, p. 244.

[120] Bodl., MS. Rawlinson D.400, ff. 93-4.

Chapter 5

*The House of Lords and British Foreign Policy, 1720-48**

Jeremy Black

'As it is of the utmost consequence that the consideration of the Preliminaries in the House of Lords should be opened and supported by Peers of the most independent and respectable characters and abilities, I cannot address myself with more propriety than to your Lordship in hoping that you will undertake to move or support an address, which, agreeably to the usual forms, will accompany that deliberation. Should your Lordship do me the honour to wish for any information from me on this important subject, I should have the greatest satisfaction in communicating to your Lordship without reserve everything which is within my knowledge.'

Lord Grantham, Foreign Secretary, to Earl of Harrington, 1783[1]

This essay will address itself to two problems. In the first and shorter section the impact of the House of Lords on the formulation and conduct of British foreign policy will be discussed. The section will concentrate on the years 1720-48, but will also range more widely chronologically. The second section will consider the problem of the quality of the Lords' debates on foreign policy. Neither topic has been discussed hitherto, and there are significant problems in tackling both problems. However, it is necessary to redress the current habit of discussing the parliamentary handling of foreign policy simply in terms of the Commons.

It is easy to understand how this habit developed. The perspective was one shared by many contemporaries. Discussing diplomatic negotiations in 1701, Count Tallard, who had been French Ambassador since 1698, wrote of '. . . Les Communes (car il n'est question que d'elles) . . .'[2] Foreigners commenting on parliamentary activity tended

* I am grateful to Eveline Cruickshanks for commenting on an earlier draft of this essay. I should like to express my gratitude for assistance given by the British Academy, the British Council, Professor Michel Fleury, The German Academic Exchange Scheme, the Staff Travel and Research Fund of Durham University, the Twenty-Seven Foundation and the Warden and Fellows of Merton College Oxford. Unless otherwise stated all dates are in Old Style.

[1] Bedfordshire R.O., Lucas papers, 30/14/363/1: Grantham to Harrington, 12 Feb. 1783, n.s. I would like to thank Lady Lucas for permission to quote from this collection.

[2] Archives du Ministère des Rélations Exterieures, Correspondance Politique, Angleterre [hereinafter AE. CP. Ang.] 191, f.135: Tallard to Louis XIV, 5 Apr. 1701, n.s.

to share Tallard's sense of priorities. Furthermore, significant parliamentary debates over foreign affairs were held generally in the Commons. There are few signs that managing the Lords in the field of foreign policy presented as much of a problem as dealing with the Commons. A comparison between the Commons and the Lords over the Spanish depredations and Dunkirk issues in 1729 and 1730 is instructive in this respect. Possibly the greater sensitivity of the Commons to commercial issues, the representation of London in the House and the opportunities that this permitted for the use of petitions and addresses as devices to link parliamentary and extra-parliamentary views explain the contrast in the former case, but in 1730 there was no doubt that the centre of the political storm over Dunkirk was located in the Commons, when there was no obvious reason why it should not have been in the other House.

There is no doubt of the influence of Parliament as a whole in the conduct of foreign policy. Despite claims that the ministry was certain of parliamentary support, because of the widespread distribution of places and pensions, it has been recently suggested that Parliament's independence should not be underestimated and that parliamentary views on foreign policy were held to be of great importance. The recent tendency to refocus the traditional view of the sovereignty of the King in Parliament by stressing the independence of royal action in the field of diplomacy, means that it would be mistaken to claim that Britian followed a parliamentary foreign policy in the sense of one based simply on a consideration of what Parliament would accept.[3] However, the constitutional and political roles of Parliament in the conduct of foreign policy were significant. The principal legal right, that of voting the funds necessary for the military forces, British and foreign, that were expected to give substance to foreign policy, would have been emasculated had the 'Country' strategy, advocated with varying degrees of plausibility by Tories and opposition Whigs, of dispensing with a standing army and limiting treaty commitments, been carried out. The following of a contrary policy, albeit with significant variations, by successive Court Whig ministries ensured that Parliament had to be approached frequently with requests for financial assistance. This fiscal role was restricted to the Commons, and, in that constitutional or legal sense, the Commons possessed a formal authority in the field of foreign policy significantly greater than that of the Lords. Much of the parliamentary discussion on the subject of foreign policy in the second quarter of the century took place during Commons debates on fiscal measures

[3] J.M. Black, 'Foreign Policy in the Age of Walpole', in *Britain in the Age of Walpole*, ed. J.M. Black (1984), pp. 163-6; J.M. Black, *British Foreign Policy in the Age of Walpole* (Edinburgh, 1985), pp. 75-92.

designed to ensure an adequate military strength for the furtherance of this policy.

However the role of Parliament was not restricted to its constitutional prerogatives. As with much in the eighteenth-century British political system, the 'constitution', itself no immutable or clear entity, was related to a flexible and changing set of political practices and conventions that affected the parliamentary discussion of foreign policy. Parliament represented the best forum for the public presentation of government policy and this in an age when European states, whether 'absolutist' or in possession of important agencies of representative government, were increasingly concerned to achieve a good public defence of policy, not least in the field of foreign policy.[4] Thus the process by which in the Wars of the League of Augsburg and Spanish Succession between 1689 and 1713 Parliament acquired a position of greater importance in the discussion of foreign policy reflected not so much a gaining of the initiative in the face of royal and ministerial opposition as a development that served different interests at the same time that it caused episodic political difficulties. The eliciting of parliamentary support for public definitions of policy was associated with the organisation of a system of public finance that increased the capabilities of British foreign policy. This was in political terms more significant than the weakening of the royal prerogative discerned by Mark Thomson, and calls into question Graham Gibbs's suggestion that 'the advent of a parliamentary foreign policy added an element of instability, as well as inflexibility, to a system which already appeared in European eyes to be chronically unstable'.[5]

The wider political role of Parliament in the discussion of foreign affairs persisted after 1713. Foreign policy continued to be a contentious issue in domestic political debate with the Whig attack on the Peace of Utrecht and the political tensions created after 1714 by the Hanoverian commitments of George I. It is possible that ministers felt a continued need for public parliamentary support both because of this domestic debate and because these commitments entailed novel international confrontations that did not match traditional suppositions of British conduct. No attempt was made to limit Parliament's position in the discussion of foreign policy. Politicians were aware of the great importance attached in Europe to parliamentary developments and the consequent need to control them. British envoys were instructed to

[4] J.F. Klaits, *Printed Propaganda under Louis XIV: Absolute Monarchy and Public Opinion* (Princeton, 1976).

[5] M.A. Thomson, 'Parliament and Foreign Policy, 1689-1714', in *William III and Louis XIV*, ed. R. Hatton and J.S. Bromley (Liverpool, 1968), pp. 135-6; G.C. Gibbs, 'The Revolution in Foreign Policy', in *Britain after the Glorious Revolution 1689-1714*, ed. G. Holmes (1969), p. 75.

publicise ministerial accounts of parliamentary events.[6] The mutual benefits that parliamentary consultation brought were expressed by two pamphlets in 1730,

> As to the right of making peace and war, the same is allowed and granted to be part of the King's high prerogative, though we find that the wisest of our monarchs have very rarely entered into any war without the approbation and consent of their parliaments: for who can give better and more wholesome advice and counsel in such arduous affairs?
>
> Though the making of peace is acknowledged to be within the prerogative of the Crown, yet it will most certainly be brought before you for your approbation; which ministers always esteeem to be some kind of security to them.[7]

These were reasonable statements of the case, though they excluded, for obvious reasons of propriety and political partianship, any mention of the financial benefits that could arise from seeking 'wholesome advice and counsel'. A fuller statement was made by a leading London ministerial paper, the *Daily Courant*, in its issue of 1 October 1734,

> In the military part of the domestic indeed, and in both the branches of our foreign policy or government, which regulates our leagues and treaties, our wars or peace with other states, the King has a greater latitude; for, as they are almost all of them individual points or cases, which admit of very few, or no invariable general rules, and do also require the utmost dispatch, and the greatest secrecy, he is therein invested with the entire power of determining both what shall be done, and who shall execute those determinations; subject nevertheless to the regulation of the legislature as to the expense which the public shall furnish towards those transactions; and by which subjection it usually becomes necessary to the Crown to consult their inclinations, in a general manner at least, in most of the momentous undertakings of that sort.

Both Houses of Parliament participated in this wider political role. As it was a role that lacked formal institutional expressions, there is and was a considerable subjective element involved both in the judgement of its general impact and in the specific allocation of responsibility to the individual chambers. An examination of the reports of foreign envoys reveals that diplomats varied in the attention they paid to the two Houses, and the same was the case with British commentators. Allowance has to be made for the nature of the sources. The foreign commentator who has attracted most attention was the French Minister

[6] J.M. Black, 'British Foreign Policy and the War of the Austrian Succession, 1740–48: A Research Priority', *Canadian Journal of History*, XXI (1986), 323-5; P.R.O., S.P. 90/22, 82/45, 84/299, 95/50, 80/71: Townshend to Du Bourgay, 22 Feb. 1726, Townshend to Cyril Wich, 20 Feb. 1728, Townshend to William Finch, 20 Feb. 1728, Townshend to Diescau, 20 Feb. 1728, Harrington to Thomas Robinson, 28 Jan. 1731.

[7] M. Gordon, *The True Crisis*, p. 7; Anon., *The Remembrancer: Caleb's Sensible Exhortation*, p. 4.

Plenipotentiary from 1731 to 1736, Chavigny. Chavigny's principal political contacts were the Tory group led by Sir William Wyndham, whose principal expert on foreign policy was Lord Bolingbroke. As Bolingbroke was not allowed to take his seat in the Lords and as the principal critics of ministerial foreign policy in that chamber during the period were either opposition Whigs or Tories who were not close to Bolingbroke, it is not surprising that Chavigny's reports concentrated on the Commons where he could show his allies in action. Similarly the principal parliamentary diaries for the period, those of Sir Edward Knatchbull and Viscount Perceval, were both kept by members of the Commons.

Nevertheless, without suggesting that the Lords were necessarily the crucial chamber, it is fair to point out that some commentators did pay a lot of attention to it. Just as senior ministers were concerned with its management, so they expected that both chambers should be used to support their policies with public gestures. When in November 1725 Viscount Townshend, the Secretary of State then with George I in Hanover, pressed his London colleague the Duke of Newcastle on his wish that Parliament should be brought to a public declaration of support for the recently-negotiated Treaty of Hanover, he wrote that it would

> when approved by both Houses, discourage our enemies, and let our friends see that we are in earnest, and that they may depend upon their engagements with us, provided the resolutions of the Parliament are followed with the fitting out a strong fleet, without which I can assure you (according to the notion at present universally entertained of us abroad) all the parliament can say will make very little impression in our favour.[8]

Similarly in 1729 Townshend stressed the role of both chambers when he wrote to the British envoy in Paris, Stephen Poyntz, that the French first minister, Cardinal Fleury, was

> mistaken if he thinks that the Parliament is influenced by money, to be thus unanimous in the supporting his majesty in all he has done. This zeal proceeds from the chief men in both houses being convinced that the measures his majesty has hitherto taken are right; but these persons, though they have heartily concurred in what has been done hitherto, are under the greatest anxiety, at the uncertain state of our affairs; and will not be kept much longer in suspense.[9]

To a certain extent such references were doubtless conventional, but it is also possible to point to the fact that the debates in the Lords were reported at length in manuscript newsletters,[10] and that the protests

---

[8] P.R.O., S.P. 43/8, ff. 80-1, 122: Townshend to Newcastle, 27 Nov. 1725, n.s.

[9] W. Coxe, *Memoirs of the Life and Administration of Sir Robert Walpole* (3 vols., 1798), II, 639.

[10] For example the 1730 Perceval newsletters, B.L., Add. MS. 27981.

made by opposition peers were printed in the newspapers or newsletters and regularly forwarded by foreign diplomats. The printing of Lords' protests was common. The opposition in the Lords was heavily outnumbered by the ministry, but the privilege of registering protests enabled it to publicise its opinions. These protests were not on the whole available to London readers, but they were widely disseminated in the provinces. They and the list of signatories, an item of great political importance indicating prestigious and numerous support for opposition arguments, were regularly printed by William Wye in his newsletter, which had, judged by the contents of the provincial press, become by the mid-1730s, the most influential newsletter. Thus, *Wye's Letter* of 7 March 1734 provided a summary of the debate the previous day in the Lords on the election of Scottish peers to Parliament, in which the speakers were named. Two days later *Wye's Letter* printed the protest registered at the end of the debate and the signatories. These reports were regularly printed in the provincial press. Protests carried in *Wye's Letter* for 21 and 28 March 1734 were printed in the *Newcastle Courant* of 30 March and 6 April 1734.

Certain foreign diplomats sought to develop links with peers. Reichenbach, the Prussian Resident in London from 1726 to 1730, developed links with one of the leading Tories in the Lords, the Earl of Strafford. Thomas Wentworth, 1st Earl of Strafford was one of the most influential Tories of the 1720s and 1730s and an active speaker in the Lords. Possibly because of his Jacobite intrigues, or due to a dearth of material devoted to him, his influence has not been brought out in works dealing with the Tories of the period, such as that of Linda Colley. However there is no doubt that he was of considerable influence. An anonymous memorandum in the French archives, written in 1728, referred to him as having the greatest authority among the Tories. Five years later the Prussian visitor Baron Pöllnitz described him as Walpole's greatest opponent in the Lords. The Earl of Essex said of Strafford in 1728, 'he should love him very well if he would not be the occasion of so many debates in the House of Lords.'[11] Strafford was the parliamentarian most cited by Reichenbach, but foreign links were no new development for the peer who had intrigued with Spain in the mid-1720s.[12] It was from Strafford that Reichenbach sought information on British politics and the ministry's interception of his correspondence revealed that through Reichenbach the opposition had both sought

[11] Linda Colley, *In Defiance of Oligarchy: The Tory Party, 1714-60* (Cambridge, 1982); J.M. Black, 'Giving Life to the Honest Part of the City: The Opposition woo the City in 1721', *Historical Research*, LX (1987), 116-7; AE. CP. Ang. 364, f. 394: Anon. memorandum, 31 Dec. 1728, n.s.; C. Pöllnitz, *Lettres et Memoires* (5th ed., Frankfurt, 1738, 5 vols, in 3 books), III, letter 54; B.L., Add. MS. 62558 (Mrs. Caesar's Diary), f. 23.

[12] Royal Archives, Windsor Castle, Stuart Papers, 96/94: 'James III' to Strafford, 23 Aug. 1726, n.s.

information on Anglo–Prussian negotiations and urged the Prussians to be stubborn in order to gain concessions.[13] In a similar fashion Count Philip Kinsky, the Austrian Envoy Extraordinary from 1728 to 1736, displayed support for the opposition Whigs and maintained links with peers in that group, such as the Earls of Chesterfield and Stair.[14]

A connection with individual peers did not entail necessarily a belief in the crucial political significance of the Lords. The cosmopolitan nature of many of the peers, the personal diplomatic experience of a significant number of individual peers, such as Carteret, Chesterfield, Stair and Strafford, and their presence in London helped to ensure that it was relatively easy for diplomats to acquire aristocratic friendships, some of which, such as Kinsky's with the Duke of Norfolk, were of no obvious political significance. The interest displayed by commentators in all types of political crisis ensured that, irrespective of views of its innate political importance, insofar as these are possible to isolate, the Commons received more attention, for it presented problems of management that the Lords did not. A defeat in the Commons, such as that when the ministry failed to block Sandy's Place Bill in March 1730, led to excitement among the diplomatic community,[15] even though it was known that the secure ministerial position in the Lords would help them to surmount the crisis.[16] However, if the Lords received less attention in general that did not mean that they were of no significance. Rather, it is the case that the impression they made on foreign diplomats depended on the particular political conjuncture and the specific connections of individual diplomats. If, in general, the debates in the Lords on foreign policy attracted relatively little interest in the late 1720s, this reflected in part the weakness of the opposition in that period. This situation changed in the 1730s, as defections of prominent politicians with considerable diplomatic experience, Carteret in 1730 and Chesterfield in 1733, led to the more effective presentation of opposition arguments, particularly of opposition Whig views, in the Lords. In contrast to the late 1720s the strength of the opposition in the debates over the Convention of the Pardo in 1739 led to a lot of attention, which can be seen most clearly in the forwarding of copies of the Lords protests. Earl Waldegrave, then envoy in Paris, was certain of the interrelationship of the diplomatic negotiations with Spain and the parliamentary

[13] Hull U.L., Hotham papers, 3/3: Reichenbach to Grumbkow, 17 Mar., 14, 18 Apr. 1730, n.s.

[14] Norfolk R.O., Bradfer–Lawrence papers: Townshend to Horatio Walpole, 14 Oct. 1728; AE. CP. Ang. 385, ff. 194, 285: Chavigny to Chauvelin, 16, 28 Apr. 1734, n.s.

[15] Waldegrave papers (Earl Waldegrave, Chewton Hall, Chewton Mendip, Somerset): George Tilson to 1st Earl Waldegrave, 24 Mar. 1730; Horatio Walpole to Waldegrave, 24 Mar. 1730; P.R.O., S.P. 84/307, f. 47: Charles Holzendorf to Tilson, 7 Mar. 1730, n.s.

[16] Hull U.L., Hotham papers 3/3: Grumbkow to Reichenbach, 14 Mar. 1730, n.s.

situation, including that in the Lords. In June 1739 he informed Benjamin Keene, his counterpart in Madrid, that the latter's reports, 'I fear will bring our friends at home under great difficulties . . . the warmth which has been expressed in the House of Lords upon the past delay of the payment of the ninety five thousand pounds, will I doubt leave no room for future management in case this last dispatch arrives before the Parliament be up.'[17]

The situation altered again in 1742 with the entry into office of Lord Carteret. Prior to 1742 both Secretaries of State had also been in the Lords, a situation that had lasted since Carteret was appointed for the first time in March 1721, replacing James Craggs. Carteret's promotion, in place of Harrington in 1742, and the fall of Walpole shifted the central focus of parliamentary control over foreign policy from the Commons to the Lords. Walpole had had no formal competence in the field of foreign policy, but, after the fall of Townshend in 1730, he had been the most powerful minister in this field, despite Newcastle's challenge to his authority in the late 1730s.[18] This position was occupied by Carteret from 1742 until November 1744 and then by Newcastle until the Seven Years War. This helped to ensure that the crucial statements of ministerial policy were made in the Lords. To a certain extent Carteret displayed less interest in having foreign policy explained in the Commons than Walpole had done. Carteret was aware of the value of parliamentary support for British foreign policy. In May 1743 he wrote to Newcastle from The Hague attributing the 'happy change in this Country since I was here in October last' primarily to parliamentary developments.

> They have a good opinion of the stability of our affairs in England, which they had not when I was here last, but the great majority which His Majesty had in Parliament all the last session had an excellent effect here, and the more because it was not expected: this they have frankly owned to me.[19]

However, neither Carteret's policies nor the manner in which he presented them helped the ministry's parliamentary position. Though an active speaker in the Lords, Carteret's policy was one that could not be defined as parliamentary in the sense of stemming from an awareness of the domestic political constraints upon policy. In 1743 Henry Fox noted 'the Coffee House joke is that Lord C. was looking over the map and by some accident the ink fell down and blotted out England, since which he

---

[17] B.L., Add. MS. 32801, f. 59: Waldegrave to Keene, 22 June 1739, n.s.

[18] J.M. Black, 'An "Ignoramus in European affairs?"', *British Journal for Eighteenth-Century Studies*, VI (1983), 65–75.

[19] P.R.O., S.P. 43/31: Carteret to Newcastle, 19 May 1743, n.s.; 82/64, f. 220: Carteret to James Cope, 7 Dec. 1742.

has never thought of it'.[20] To a certain extent the struggle between Carteret and his ministerial colleagues, led by Henry Pelham and his brother Newcastle, revolved directly around the issue of the extent to which domestic pressures, as expressed in Parliament and by the constitutional and political role of Parliament, should affect policy. Carteret's general neglect of Parliament as a constraining element demonstrated the extent to which the seventeenth-century constitutional struggle to have policy presented in Parliament did not necessarily lead to political influence.

Carteret's position in the Lords, and the fact that many of the politicians who had been opposed to the terms on which former 'Patriots', such as Carteret, had joined the ministry in 1742 were peers and attacked the government in the Lords, helped to ensure that the debates in the chamber received a lot of attention. Significant debates were anticipated and reported by foreign diplomats,[21] domestic observers,[22] and newspapers and magazines, both British and foreign. Press reports were regarded as sufficiently important to lead to attempts to influence their content. In 1744 Horatio Walpole complained about the way in which British parliamentary news was being published in the Amsterdam press, and specifically regretted the publication of a translation of the Lords Protest about the subsidies paid for Hanoverian troops.[23] In the same year Lord Chancellor Hardwicke, acting apparently on his own initiative, attempted without success to use the press in order to restrain the reporting of parliamentary news, a move that stemmed from his anger at frequent inaccurate reporting of debates in the Lords.[24]

Much attention was devoted to what Carteret said, and, in general, the Lords was treated by commentators not as a likely source of political difficulties for the ministry, but as an opportunity to gain an insight into ministerial thinking. Thus, in February 1744, the Bavarian minister, Count Haszlang, sent details of the very strong Lords protest over the Hanoverians, but added that it would have no consequences other than that of raising tension, because the ministry was certain to gain its point thanks to its secure majority. A week later Haslang devoted attention to

[20] B.L., Add. MS. 51417: Henry Fox to Stephen Fox, 17 Aug. 1743; AE. CP. Ang. 415, f. 334, Bussy to Amelot, 2 Oct. 1743, n.s.; AE. Mémoires et Documents, Ang. 8, f. 263: anon. French memorandum, 7 Dec. 1743, n.s.

[21] For example, Staatsarchiv, Marburg, Bestand 4, England, 240, 241: Alt to William VII, 11 Jan. 1743, n.s.; Alt to Frederick I, 24 Dec. 1743, n.s.

[22] Bodl., MS. Eng. Hist. d. 103, f. 45: William King to Orrery, 5 Dec. 1743.

[23] Buckinghamshire R.O., Trevor papers, vol. 37: Walpole to Robert Trevor, 28 Feb. 1744.

[24] B.L., Add. MS. 35587, ff. 263-4, 268-9: Thomas Harris to Hardwicke, 12, 14, 28 July 1744; A.Z. to the *Gazette*, 27 July 1744.

what Carteret had said in a parliamentary speech lasting for over two hours.[25]

In some respects the years of Carteret's ministry represent a highpoint of attention devoted to foreign policy debates in the Lords. This possibly owed something to the sense of emotional tension produced by the abandonment of the Patriot policy by those, such as Carteret, who had joined the ministry. It also owed much to Britain's entry into a major war, the first since the War of the Spanish Succession. During the confrontation with Spain and the subsequent War of the Quadruple Alliance with her, which began in 1718, issues of foreign policy had been overshadowed by the contentious domestic legislative programme of the ministry, while the success of the war had helped to still criticism.[26] Neither of these factors pertained during the War of the Austrian Succession (1740-8). Carteret's fall was followed by a less tense parliamentary atmosphere in the discussion of foreign policy. The reconstitution of the ministry brought several prominent opposition peers, including Bedford, Chesterfield, Gower and Sandwich into office. The direct payment of Hanoverian troops was ended. George II was forced to be more cautious in his unpopular plans for action against Prussia. These changes helped to ensure a different agenda of parliamentary discussions, one in which dissension over foreign policy became less politically significant. This remained the case for the rest of the decade, with the prime locus of conflict between peers over foreign policy being that of the Council, not of the Lords: Newcastle against his colleagues in 1747, Newcastle against Bedford and Sandwich from 1749 to 1751.

That the political significance of debates in the Lords over foreign policy varied in accordance with diplomatic and domestic changes is hardly surprising. The same situation pertained with regard to the Commons. In assessing the impact of the Lords, as of the Commons, it is necessary to dispense with any idea that the power of Parliament, and therefore its significance, lay essentially in its ability to block moves and can be measured by its willingness to act thus. Such an analysis is both misleading in general and leads to a failure to treat the Lords adequately. The general thrust of revisionist work on early-modern representative assemblies has been to stress cooperative rather than combative aspects of their existence. This is particularly appropriate in the case of the eighteenth-century British Parliament, an institution that devoted much of its time to private legislation, such as the right to salmon fishing on the

---

[25] Bayerisches Hauptstaatsarchiv, Munich, Gesandtschaft London, 211: Haszlang to Seinsheim, 4, 11 Feb. 1744.

[26] Deutsches Zentralarchiv, Merseburg, Rep. XI (England), Vol. 41: Bonet to Frederick William I, 4, 18, 22 Mar. 1718, n.s.; J.M. Black, 'Parliament and the Political and Diplomatic Crisis of 1717-18', *Parliamentary History*, III (1984), 77-101.

Spey which exercised the Lords in 1728, and whose cooperation was central to the system of public finance that gave Britain its power. The representative system, as influenced both before and after elections, threw up parliamentarians, whether M.P.s, bishops or Scottish peers, who were prepared to accept the existing distribution of political power. From at least this point of view Britain was politically stable. When combined with the limited amount of contentious leglislation proposed by ministries after the Sunderland/Stanhope ministry had become swept up on the South Sea Bubble, it is not surprising both that Parliament was reasonably cooperative on the essentials of government policy, and that foreign policy, a controversial branch of activity made more so and more volatile by the kaleidoscopic nature of international relations, was a significant topic of debate. However, precisely because of the limited nature of Parliament's constitutional power in this field, its political impact was necessarily indirect. The King had the right of making peace and war, signing treaties, appointing, dismissing and paying diplomats, giving them instructions and receiving their reports. These rights did not exist in the face of parliamentary demands to share them: there were no such demands, as royal prerogative rights in the field of foreign policy were generally acceptable.

The limited nature of direct parliamentary power in the field of foreign policy ensures that the best way to appreciate the impact of parliamentary discussion is to look not at the unsuccessful attempts by opposition parliamentarians to block measures that were within their constitutional competence, such as subsidy treaties, but rather at the general discussion of foreign policy. This directly relates to a neglected topic, the quality of parliamentary debates on foreign policy. Comments on this issue are scanty. Without explaining the basis for his statement, J.R. Jones has claimed that 'wilful misrepresentation of facts, sensationalism and pandering to popular prejudices, partisanship and appeals to xenophobia characterised most parliamentary debates.'[27] Referring to the response to the Quadruple Alliance in 1718, Graham Gibbs stated, 'The debates in parliament added little to the existing public discussion except heat'.[28] It is of course difficult to evaluate the quality of eighteenth-century debates. Conventions of behaviour and speech, standards of argument and proof were different. Furthermore, the nature of the surviving evidence is scanty. Parliament took steps to

[27] The principal topic of political debate in this field related to the relationship between royal rights as King and obligations as Elector. This constituted a new area for debate over the prerogative, one that was defined only after a lot of disagreement. The terms of the Act of Settlement proved very ambiguous and unhelpful in practice.

[28] J.R. Jones, *Britain and the World, 1649-1815* (1980), pp. 13-185; G.C. Gibbs, 'Parliament and the Treaty of Quadruple Alliance', in *William III and Louis XIV*, ed. Hatton and Bromley, p. 301.

restrict spectators and to prevent press coverage. The implementation of the regulations governing the latter was intermittent and this affected the amount of material available in the press. In March 1739, the *York Courant* informed its readers, 'The Publisher of the Lords Protests relating to the Convention (which were designed to be inserted this day) being taken up 'tis hoped the reader will excuse the omission of them, the printer of this paper having no inclination for a London journey at this snowy season of the year.' A week later the paper reported, 'We hear that a strict inquiry is making after the persons, who furnish the coffee houses with written "Minutes of the Proceedings of Parliament", in order to their being apprehended'.[29] On the other hand, in the summer of 1740, the *Newcastle Journal* printed in full the Duke of Argyll's speech on the state of the nation delivered in the Lords on 15 April 1740. The publication of this significant opposition speech was defended by the paper. It is instructive that it felt obliged to defend itself but it also felt free to print,

> As the following speech has not only been printed singly and distributed into a multitude of hands, but has also been offered to the publick in several newspapers, it is thought proper by many impartial persons that our readers ought not to be deprived of satisfying their curiosity with the perusal of it. We hope therefore that our inserting it in the place of our geography, for this week, cannot be construed to our disadvantage, as favouring any particular interest or party. Let the speech and sentiments which it contains, recommend or commend themselves; we do neither, but leave both to the judgment of the public; and shall, as soon as we can obtain it, offer in like manner the reply to it, according to that impartiality which we have taken upon us to maintain it.

The magazines evaded restriction by printing what they claimed were the proceedings of imaginary assemblies, the Senate of Lilliput in the *Gentleman's Magazine*. Some newspapers resorted to the methods of the magazines in order to report parliamentary news. During the 1742 recess the most innovative of the Bristol newspapers, the *Oracle: or, Bristol Weekly Miscellany* printed, under a Bristol byline, the text of a Lords' Protest, with an introductory note, 'We hear some persons of great distinction, who have an absolute right to speak their minds freely on any point that shall come before them, have in an authentick manner protested against a late senatorial proceeding, for the following reasons'.[30]

Nevertheless, the publication of parliamentary reports was not free of hindrance. In December 1742 the vociferous opposition weekly the

[29] *York Courant*, 13, 20 Mar. 1739.
[30] *Newcastle Journal*, 7, 14 June 1740; *Oracle*, 5 June 1742; J.M. Black, 'Parliamentary Reporting in the Early Eighteenth Century. An Abortive Attempt to Influence the Magazines in 1744', *Parliaments, Estates and Representation*, VII (1987), 61-9.

Westminster Journal noted, 'My last paper has produced a very strong representation against the liberty I have taken of inserting any proceedings of the worthy society of INDEPENDENT SCALD-MISERABLE-MASONS, but more especially against the impropriety of publishing any speeches made to that august body'. The publication of recent debates in book form led to the imprisonment of the printer. The most significant action against press reporting of parliamentary debates did not occur as as result of ministerial pressure. Parliament appointed printers to produce items such as the Addresses, and in 1747 these printers, angry at what they regarded as an illegal infringement of their privileges instigated action by the Lords against the printing of Jacobite treason trials conducted by the Lords. The printers of the *Gentlemen's* and *London Magazines*, the principal publishers of parliamentary debates, whose significance had grown with the decline of the manuscript newsletters, were brought before the Lords and released only on condition that they did not repeat the offence. Action was taken against the *Ipswich Journal*. The effect of these moves was to induce caution into the provincial press, end parliamentary reporting in the *Gentleman's Magazine* and end the attribution of speeches to individual members in the *London Magazine*.[31]

It was not simply the restrictions on press reporting that limit the surviving sources. Moves to restrict entry, such as those taken at the Lords at the beginning of 1740, had their effect. Most existing records are limited, the result of individual effort made in an institution that did not encourage such action and reflecting personal interests. The records for many debates, particularly those in the 1730s, do not distinguish between speakers, but simply group together all opposition and ministerial arguments. Debates that are known to have lasted several hours have left recorded speeches that would have taken little time to deliver. The situation is exacerbated by the limited survival of private papers for many of the peers who were politically active. This probably owed much to concern about committing material to paper, a concern that may have stemmed from anxiety deriving from Jacobite intrigues or the skill of the government's postal interception system. Sometime between Townshend's resignation in 1730 and his death in 1738, he wrote to Samuel Buckley, the writer of the *Gazette*,

> I never write anything, but what I desire the ministry may see. There is no great skill nor dexterity in opening of letters, but such is the fate of this administration that they have managed this affair in such a manner as to loose all the advantage of it. Sir Robert having complained to a friend when he was

---

[31] *Westminster Journal*, 11 Dec. 1742; B.L., Egerton MS. 1712, f. 212: William Bentinck to his mother, the Dowager Duchess of Portland, 21 Mar. 1741, n.s.; G.A. Cranfield, *The Development of the Provincial Newspaper 1700-1760* (Oxford, 1962), pp. 163-5.

last in these parts, that they had lost all the intelligence they used to get by the Post-Office which was owning plainly that people were grown wiser than to write anything of consequence by the Post.[32]

It is also known that papers were destroyed. This was sometimes carried out by those who participated in a correspondence, often responding to injunctions to burn letters.[33] In addition, papers were destroyed frequently following death or fall from office, for the prospect of impeachment was still a present one. After the death of Frederick, Prince of Wales, in 1751 his papers were burned. When William Pulteney, who had become Earl of Bath in 1742, died in 1764 his brother, General Pulteney, destroyed all his papers, thus preventing Bath's chaplain Dr. Douglas from writing his biography. This was particularly disastrous because, according to Henry Fox, he had kept significant records,

> Lord Bath is wonderfull angry at the disgrace of his friends, complains of the perfidy of the Pelhams, says he kept a journal of all that passed between the Duke of Newcastle and him in the spring 1741/2 and swears by G— he will print it. He is capable of such a thing and as to the Journal I am assured he has kept one these 10 years, setting down each night the days conversation.[34]

For whatever reason there are no significant private papers for several senior politicians including Carteret and Harrington, while others, such as Townshend, have left only patchy remnants of their correspondence. This is particularly serious in that it leaves unclear the significance of parliamentary discussions of foreign policy to the senior participants, what specific issues their speeches were intended to address and how they saw their speeches. Little also survives by way of drafts of speeches, a gap highlighted by the value of the few that survive.[35]

Aside from the scanty nature of the sources, there is also the problem of bias in those that survive. It is likely that many sources, particularly the press, simplified the arguments in order to present two clear-cut positions, and deliberately stressed rhetorical stances (the 'sensationalism' noted by Jones) at the expense of cautious discussion, and the use of evidence. It has been argued that 'by definition both formally and informally, the legislative approach to foreign affairs is

[32] Bodl., MS. Eng. Lett. c. 144, f. 267: Townshend to Buckley, 16 Sept. [?]; J.M. Black, 'A Diplomat Visits Parliament: An Unprinted Account of the Army Estimates Debate of 1733', *Parliamentary History*, V (1986), 101–6.

[33] Waldegrave papers: Newcastle to Waldegrave, 20 Oct. 1735; B.L., Add. MS. 47012B, f. 13: Sarah, Duchess of Marlborough to Mrs. Southwell, 5 Sept. 1736.

[34] *The Yale Edition of Horace Walpole's Correspondence*, ed. W.S. Lewis (48 vols., New Haven, 1937–83), XX, 239; *Select Works of John Douglas*, ed. W. Macdonald (Salisbury, 1820), p. 56; B.L., Add. MS. 51417, f. 132: Henry to Stephen Fox, 27 Dec. 1744.

[35] P.R.O., S.P. 36/21, f. 217: notes in Newcastle's hand, probably of parliamentary speech, undated [1730].

more partisan and less intellectual than the executive approach'.[36] This is possibly the case, but it does not preclude intelligent discussion of foreign policy by a legislative assembly. Accusations of political bias were also made by contemporaries. In the letter that he sought to insert in the press in 1744 Hardwicke suggested that the magazines were particularly inaccurate,

> The unjustifiable liberty, which has for some time been taken by the compilers of the magazines, of publishing for the most part without the least authority, and in direct contradiction to the resolutions of both Houses of Parliament, what they are pleased to style accounts of the debates and proceedings there, is at last grown to so scandalous an excess, as to call aloud for a remedy. To go no further back, then the last London Magazine, (though I by no means intend to exclude his worthy rival of St. John's Gate,[37]) the performances which its authors have thought fit to give the Public, under the names of three honourable persons, are so far from bearing the least mark of authenticity, that I have been assured by some who were present in the House during the whole debate, and took notes of the principal heads of it, there is not a single expression or turn of thought, which those gentlemen really used, and many things ascribed to them, which they would be ashamed to own. This is a licence taken with an assembly of the highest authority in the Kingdom, which the lowest court of judicature would punish with severity. That such dull and impudent forgeries should be published every month uncensured, is indeed so incredible, that it is not to be wondered, if people at a distance from London are so generally imposed upon by them, and mistake the forced declamations of miserable garreteers, for the masterly eloquence of the greatest men in the nation.[38]

Given the difficulty of establishing what was said in the Lords and of assessing its relevance to contemporaries, it might be suggested that it is futile to judge the quality of the speeches. However, the neglect of this issue also reflects the historiographical difficulty confronting this problem. Most British political historians lack the detailed knowledge of British foreign policy and international relations that would enable them to assess the degree of knowledge and the sophistication of analysis displayed by speakers. Furthermore, most diplomatic historians lack the necessary knowledge of domestic history, and, in particular, of parliamentary practices. More serious is the relative neglect of the issue by these historians. There is a tendency to present foreign policy in a monolithic interpretation in which the actors are the 'British', 'French' *et al.*, and to either ignore or simplify the diplomatic consequences of

---

[36] J.N. Rosenau, 'Private Preference and Political Responsibilities: The Relative Potency of Individual and Role Variables in the Behaviour of U.S. Senators', in *Quantitative International Politics: Insights and Evidence*, ed. J.D. Singer (New York, 1968), p. 49.

[37] *Gentleman's Magazine.*

[38] B.L., Add. MS. 35587, f. 269: A.Z. to the *Gazette*, 27 July 1744.

domestic pressures. In contrast to the ordered series of diplomatic papers, the material for assessing domestic pressures is diffuse, fragmentary and difficult to judge.

Another inevitable problem is the subjectivity implicit in any assessment of quality. Nevertheless, it is important to consider the problem. One of the more impressive features of parliamentary debates was the knowledge of international relations displayed by some parliamentarians. Expert opinion could be presented in Parliament. Both chambers contained several diplomats or former diplomats, and some of these contributed their knowledge to the debates. Not all who had been diplomats revealed the same knowledge or made an equal contribution. Harrington did not take a role in the Lords comparable to that of Carteret or of his colleague as Secretary of State, Newcastle, who lacked any experience of foreign diplomacy. Viscount Cobham, who had spent six months in Vienna in 1714–15 as Envoy Extraordinary, did not make an impression comparable to that of Chesterfield. However, to take the example of Cobham, his letter explaining the resignation of his commission which he sent to Newcastle in December 1743, reveals that his opposition to Hanoverian commitments was not derived from ignorance or xenophobia. He wrote of

> the extreme difficulty and hazard of supporting the Queen of Hungary by an English Army in upper Germany, or of attacking France in her almost impenetrable Barrier of Alsace, Lorraine, or the Netherlands, without the concurrence of the Dutch upon the foot of the last war. The first of these cases existed last year, and the last in the natural course of events must be the question for the ensuing campaign . . . I cannot say, as things are circumstanced, that it is fit for this country to engage in making conquests on the Continent, I mean upon France, for I know no other ground where our army can set their feet but on her territories, unless they will avowedly remain in a state of inaction. Things appearing to me in this light, I must give my opinion against all measures which naturally lead us to take so dangerous a step unsupported as we seem to be at present . . . I have already felt severe marks of His Majesty's displeasure for differing in opinion with his ministers in Parliament.[39]

Cobham's assessment was a reasoned one, based on a grasp of Britain's military and diplomatic position, and it was to be vindicated by the campaign of 1744 when it became rapidly apparent that talk of a successful invasion of eastern France was misplaced. In light of such arguments it is instructive to consider the most recent comment on the parliamentary debates over Hanover in the early 1740s, Graham Gibbs's conclusion that opposition 'arguments were at best grossly over-

---

[39] *Ibid.*, f. 205: Cobham to Newcastle, 9 Dec. 1743.

simplified and exaggerated, and at times totally misplaced'.[40] Much of
the parliamentary language on the subject was certainly aggressive, the
Hanoverian issue being used to discuss fundamental questions of
constitutional propriety and dynastic legitimacy. In January 1744 the
Earl of Sandwich urged the Lords to heed the general national opposition
he discerned to Hanover.

> It may be hoped that these sentiments will be adopted, and these resolutions
> formed by every man who hears, what is echoed through the nation, that the
> British have been considered as subordinate to their own mercenaries;
> mercenaries whose service was never rated at so high a price before, and who
> never deserved even the petty price at which their lives used to be valued; that
> foreign slaves were exalted above the freemen of Great Britain, even by the
> King of Great Britain, and that on all occasions, on which one nation could be
> preferred to the other, the preference was given to the darling Hanoverians.

Rhetoric in modern representative assemblies is not incompatible with
an intelligent assessment of the situation, though the former commands
more attention often, and there is no reason to believe that the situation
was different in the early eighteenth century. One interesting aspect of
the parliamentary furore over Hanover, is that some opposition peers
claimed that their views corresponded with those of the public and were
therefore more worth stating. In January 1744 the Duke of Marlborough
told the Lords,

> It is not possible to mention Hanover, or its inhabitants, in any public place,
> without putting the whole house into a flame, and hearing on every hand
> expressions of resentment, threats of revenge, or clamours of detestation.
> Hanover is now become a name which cannot be mentioned without
> provoking a rage and malignity, and interrupting the discourse by a
> digression of abhorrence.[41]

Such alarmist generalisations were scarcely novel. In November 1739
the Earl of Winchilsea gave his view of British foreign policy over the
previous two decades.

> tame submissions to pacific negotations, which have, as was long since
> foretold, at last ended in an open and declared war; and that at a season,
> which, if we consider the present situation of affairs in Europe, we must
> allow to be the most unlucky for this nation, of any we could have chosen,
> ever since Spain began to insult and plunder, and we to negotiate and
> submit.[42]

---

[40] G.C. Gibbs, 'English Attitudes towards Hanover and the Hanoverian Succession in
the First Half of the Eighteenth Century', in *England und Hannover*, ed. A.N. Birke and
K. Kluxen (Munich, 1986), p. 44.
[41] Cobbett, *Parl. Hist.*, XIII, 562, 564–5.
[42] *Ibid.*, XI, 64.

Alarmist sentiments were not expressed by opposition speakers only. In December 1743 Lord Raymond told the Lords that the opposition were 'the favourers of France, and the betrayers of the great cause of universal liberty'.[43] In judging opposition rhetoric it is necessary to consider the particular problems opposition peers faced. As the Tory Earl of Lichfield told the Lords in December 1743, 'as this House has not of late years been let into any secrets relating to our foreign transactions . . . we can judge from nothing but public appearances'.[44] It is not therefore surprising that, as Hardwicke pointed out, opposition speakers offered little proof in support of their arguments.[45] Furthermore criticism of the role of the monarch had to be indirect, helping to ensure that the Hanoverian issue was treated both as a very significant matter and in a very general way. The opposition were also appealing to a wider public, most obviously in their protests. This public was that of the British public nation, European powers and posterity. The Lords' protest over the Hanoverian troops ending the great debate on 9 December 1743, stated that

> the willingness of the States General . . . or any other power in Europe, to enter into a closer conjunction with us, at this critical time, must chiefly depend upon the idea they shall conceive of the state of this nation at home, especially with regard to the greater or lesser degree of union and harmony, which shall appear to subsist between His Majesty and his people . . . as our votes have, we hope, proved us to the present age, our names in the books may transmit us to posterity Englishmen.[46]

In appealing to such an audience it was possibly felt best, either by the speakers or by the reporters whose accounts we are substantially dependent upon, to adopt a broad and rhetorical approach. Furthermore, it is possible that the euphoria of public speaking, the conceit of conviction and the sense that once in opposition there was no harm in embarrassing the government as much as possible, all combined to encourage a strident style and aggressive approach. However, as suggested above, such a style was not incompatible with the discussion of affairs in an intelligent fashion. The Duke of Newcastle offered the Lords in November 1739 an interesting assessment of the French system of government,

> . . . notwithstanding the great age of the present prime minister of that Kingdom, notwithstanding his present peaceable disposition we cannot entirely trust to it; we know he can alter that disposition, when he finds it proper or necessary so to do; we know the animosity that has so long

---

[43] *Ibid.*, XIII, 305.
[44] *Ibid.*, p. 379.
[45] *Ibid.*, p. 344.
[46] *Ibid.*, pp. 382–3.

subsisted between that nation and this: we know the regard the people of France have for the royal family of Spain; and therefore the prime minister of that Kingdom, notwithstanding the arbitrary form of their government, may, like the ministers in other countries, be forced to chime in with the general inclinations, perhaps the general whim, of his countrymen. Many things may induce the French to alter their present measures, and as their king is absolute master within his dominions, the effects of that alteration may, and probably will be instantaneous.[47]

Part of the problem in discussing foreign affairs was the nature of the international system. Dynasticism provided the principal theme and idiom of the system, and the monarchical control of foreign policy in most states kept it secretive. In the volatile, indeed kaleidoscopic, international system of the early eighteenth century it was difficult to assess let alone predict the policies of other states. Dramatic reversals of policy, such as the French attack on Austria in 1741 or the Prussian abandonment of France the following year, and surprise attacks, such as the Bourbon and Sardinian attacks on Austria in 1733, and the Prussian invasion of Silesia in 1740, produced an atmosphere of uncertainty in which rumour flourished and conspiracy was believed in, because sometimes true. In such a situation it was necessary to judge the policies of actions, often contradictory or ambivalent and difficult to establish. As a result it was simpler to discuss policy in terms of history and to assess intentions in the same terms. The plans of France could, it was argued, be gauged by considering her past policy, an analysis aided by the belief that for each state there was an obvious natural interest dictating a particular course of policy.[48] Parliamentarians who discussed international relations in such a fashion were simply sharing in the common terminology and analytical methods of the day, devices used by statesmen as much as journalists.

Furthermore, the strong historical bent of parliamentary discussion, the frequent reference to past events in British foreign policy, accorded with the general fashion in which international relations were discussed. Just as early seventeenth-century discussions of foreign policy were greatly influenced by the recent experience of sustained conflict with Spain, so discussion after 1713 took place in the shadow of the struggle with France, the Wars of the League of Augsburg (1688-1697) and the Spanish Succession (1702-13). This experience has been crucial not only because of its role in British foreign policy, but also because of its significance in domestic history, not solely political, but also social, economic and fiscal, the war having represented a major burden in all spheres. Many British politicians of the subsequent decades, had served

---

[47] *Ibid.*, XI, 29.
[48] J.M. Black, 'The Theory of the Balance of Power in the First Half of the Eighteenth Century: A Note on Sources', *Review of International Studies*, IX (1983), 55-61.

in these wars, either as diplomats or generals. The future George II displayed great bravery at Oudenarde in 1708. James, Earl Stanhope fought in Spain, where he was captured, while his two brothers were killed in the Spanish war. The Duke of Argyll, the Earl of Stair and Earl Cadogan had all been Marlborough's generals. Party politics had played a major role in the conduct of war. The Peace of Utrecht, negotiated by the Tories in 1713, was both at the time and subsequently a central topic of political debate, defended by Tories, such as Strafford and Trevor in 1718, and by opposition Whigs wooing Tory support, such as Argyll in 1740, and vilified by Whigs, such as Peterborough in 1730.

The frequent discussion of past events, such as Utrecht, the Quadruple Alliance of 1718 and the Alliance of Hanover of 1725, in Parliament reflected in part the limited amount of information available concerning current diplomacy. However, it was also a function of a political society where legitimacy derived essentially from past events, and the nature of the response to them. This was crucial in a country where the succession had been and was contested. Thus the response to the Glorious Revolution and the Hanoverian Succession, both events located concretely in the recent past, defined or could be held to define dynastic loyalty and political affinity. The categories might be rejected by some, for example Tories seeking to avoid the imputation of Jacobitism, but this forced them to define their own view of the past and challenge the arguments advanced by others. Foreign policy played a central role in the debate, because it could be used to defend or criticise particular dynastic choices, and because dynasticism served as a common theme linking constitutional and international affairs. As historians have increasingly stressed the role of successive monarchs in British foreign policy, it is easier to grasp the importance of recent history in the contemporary public discussion of this policy.

The public discussion of policy, in Parliament as much as in the press, was intended to illiuminate diplomacy in terms that could be readily understood, and there was frequently the obvious wish to transform it into ammunition for use in political debate. It was precisely because diplomacy was not separated from such debate but was an integral part of it, that historians, particularly diplomatic historians obsessed with an image of diplomacy as separable from and ideally separated from domestic politics, find frequently the nature of the public debate over foreign policy irritating. However, if it is accepted that no such separation is possible in this period, and that the idea of such a partition is in many senses the fantasy of late-nineteenth-century diplomatic historians, then it is apparent that the terms on which the debates of the period should be judged have to be altered to take note of their political, indeed parliamentary, context. To suggest that parliamentary discussion of foreign policy was designed to serve a political purpose does not imply that it was without standards or quality. Precisely because of the contentious nature of the subject and the particular experience and knowledge of individual speakers, debate tended to be more informed. For example, though the Lords debate of the Treaty of Seville in early 1730 only lasted one day and though it was a contentious issue in a highly-charged session, the debate was of a high quality and well-informed.

> The Lords of Strafford, Bathurst and Gower objected that it was a manifest violation of the Quadruple Alliance by stipulating Spanish instead of Swiss troops, that the lives of the present possessors might be in danger from them and that the King of Spain might perhaps be for keeping these countries for himself, and not to give them up to Don Carlos, that a Spanish garrison in Leghorn would be a further security in the hands of Spain for the good behaviour of England, and would make our trade to Italy lie at their mercy.
>
> The Court said it was not a violation, only an immaterial alteration, the substance and design being preserved, which was the securing of the successions to Don Carlos; that if the Emperor was sincere as to those successions going to Don Carlos he could not object to it; and that our trade to Italy would be as secure as it is now . . .
>
> My Lord Gower said that the Quadruple Alliance stipulated the introduction of Swiss troops only to secure the successions to Don Carlos but also to preserve the feodalite of the Empire against any violation, and that in the Letters Expectative for securing the eventual succession to those countrys the Emperor says he grants those Letters upon consideration . . . of the Quadruple Alliance and that in cases of any deviation from it he says *nec velle nec posse teneri*.
>
> Lord Abingdon said he took every alteration of a Treaty without the consent of all the contracting parties to be a violation of that treaty . . . The Duke of Newcastle said that the Queen of Spain finding that the Swiss had not been introduced though 10 or 12 years had passed since the stipulation for introducing them, feared they never would be introduced, and therefore insisted upon the alteration to Spanish troops.[49]

Apart from the fact that this account, only recently discovered, is far fuller than that in William Cobbett's *Parliamentary History*,[50] it is also apparent that the debate was very well informed. There is no reason to believe that a similar disparity between published accounts and actual debates would be perceived, if more accounts of the latter could be found. Hopefully progress will be made in this direction, although as very few collections that are known to exist remain inaccessible or unexamined, it is likely that progress will be limited. Nevertheless, the surviving evidence suggests that in the field of foreign policy the Lords were a vital force in this period. They did not get the diplomatic papers they wanted and this clearly affected the scope and quality of debates. In

[49] Northumberland R.O., 650/c/18/1 (Delaval MSS.): Anon. to MyLord, 8 Mar. 1729 [1730].
[50] Cobbett, *Parl. Hist.*, VIII, 773-4.

the Lords debate of March 1734 over a royal message seeking the means to augment forces during the recess, Carteret complained that the House had been given no information, and asserted, 'it cannot be expected that I, or any other lord who has not had the honour to be admitted into that secret, should speak so fully to the present question as we might otherwise have done . . . I cannot speak properly to it, in any other way than as relates to our constitution'. Chesterfield also complained that the House had been kept in ignorance. A protest in George I's last Parliament, that of 1717, noted,

> The Papers hitherto laid before the House in order to the consideration of his Majesty's Speech, are such only as concerned the accession of the States-General to the treaty to Hanover, and the letters and memorials since the arrival of the British fleet on the coast of Spain in America; but none of the negotiations or measures (which we suppose to have been many) that have been carried on between the Courts of Great Britain and Vienna, and the Northern powers, which his Majesty's speech and the Resolution also may have relation to, have as yet been communicated to this House: but all those measures, and many others unknown (as we believe to this House) are in our opinions, intended to be approved and justified by this Resolution; to which therefore we cannot concur, no more than if it had declared the measures honourable, just, and necessary.[51]

In addition the Lords had to exercise care to ensure that important business was brought before the House. In April 1726 Strafford complained that George I had sent a message to the Commons the previous month asking for funds to increase the number of sailors in the fleet, and thereby give additional strength to British foreign policy, and that the message had not been communicated to the Lords. The debate sparked off by Strafford's complaint provided a fine display of the view of some of the peers concerning the prerogatives of their house. It also clearly touched a nerve in many peers, for the division preceding the protest was 59-31, a substantially better opposition vote than their last protest, in February 1726, when the division had also been lost, but by 94-15. It is of course the case that a protest did not necessarily represent the strength of opposition sentiment. The extent to which opposition peers who disliked the terms of a protest chose not to sign it is unclear. An interesting suggestion of opposition disunity over a protest can be found in the report of the Saxon envoy on the Army Commissions protest in 1734. De Löss claimed that the strident tone of the protest had angered a lot of the opposition.[52]

In April 1726 Strafford told the Lords that they were 'the grand standing council of the sovereign; the hereditary guardians of the

---

[51] *Ibid.*, IX, 522, 532; VIII, 543.
[52] *Ibid.*, VIII, 511; Hauptstaatsarchiv, Dresden, Geheimes Kabinett, Gesandschaften, 638: De Löss to Augustus III, 5 Mar. 1734, n.s.

liberties and properties of the people, and next the king, the principal part of the legislature, and who therefore have a right to be consulted in all matters of public concern'. He was supported by the opposition Whig Lord Lechmere, who argued 'that it must be for the service of the crown, upon all occasions, to have the advice of both Houses of Parliament,' and 'that it was the undoubted, and inherent right of the House of Peers, to alter and amend all Money-Bills which came from the Commons', a view that was contrary to accepted conventions. Lechmere also claimed 'that, according to ancient usage, all demands of supply should come from the throne in the House of Peers' and, according to the account in Cobbett, Lechmere corroborated all his assertions, 'by several precedents upon record, which, at his desire, were ordered to be read'. Typically, Cobbett's source did not provide any details, so that a speedy reading of the account suggests that it was restricted to fine sentiments, when it is clear that detailed and informed arguments were advanced.[53]

It is clear from such debates that the Lords were an active and vigilant house. To suggest this is not to imply that the House dominated the politics of the period, however much many of its individual members did. As Chesterfield pointed out in the House in December 1740, 'Kings are generally for consulting with such as are of their own choosing, and these are often such as have no dignity, privilege or right by their birth'.[54] Furthermore, although there were important and too-often overlooked disputes over their extent, there is no doubt that the prerogatives of the Lords were limited vis-à-vis those of the Commons. In 1758 Lord Chancellor Hardwicke suggested that there would not be any debate in the Lords over the issue of a subsidy to Prussia, 'As this will be a message of supply, Your Grace knows better than anybody that the return of the House of Lords can only consist of assurances of support',[55] a view that contradicted that advanced by Lechmere in 1726.

Accepting that the political and constitutional role of Parliament was limited, something certain parliamentary historians find difficult to accept or examine, and that this was particularly the case with foreign policy, and that the Lords were no longer the dominant House, it was nevertheless the case that they were still of considerable importance. Clearly this varied depending on political circumstances. In 1711-14, because Harley had such small or non-existent majorities in the Lords, the crucial parliamentary debates on foreign policy, the 'No Peace without Spain' motion, the so-called desertion of the allies, the attitude of the Dutch, and the motion to expel the Pretender from Lorraine, occurred in the Lords. The Whigs forced the debates on Harley because of their strength in the Lords. Walpolean management, being both more

[53] Cobbett, *Parl. Hist.*, VIII, 518-19.
[54] *Ibid.*, XI, 732.
[55] B.L., Add. MS. 32879, ff. 27-8: Hardwicke to Newcastle, 2 Apr. 1758, n.s.

effective and less necessary in the Lords than in the Commons, led to a different situation two decades later. The most dangerous rise in opposition activity in the Lords during the Walpole ministry occurred in 1733. However, the seriousness of the crisis was swiftly lessened, when the ministry's victory in the election of Scottish representative peers in 1734 destroyed the opposition group of Scottish peers which had, the previous year, risen to half the Scottish representation. A consideration of the Lords' handling of issues of foreign policy reveals their constitutional limitations, but it also suggests their political importance and the quality and range of their debates on the subject. To assess the latter it is crucially important to realise the nature of the sources and the role that such debates played in the political conflicts of the period. Foreign policy may be an unfashionable topic for historians today, but it was of central importance in the eighteenth century. To a certain extent the same was true of the Lords. It is important for historians to ponder the observation of the Tory Lord Bathurst, who told the House in 1726 'that the appellation of Parliament being given to the Commons separately from the Lords, was entirely unprecedented'.[56]

---

[56] Cobbett, *Parl. Hist.*, VIII, 519.

Chapter 6

The Bishops at Westminster in the Mid-Eighteenth Century *

Stephen Taylor

1

Bishops of the early modern era were more than diocesan administrators and governors of the clergy and were not expected to be resident solely in their dioceses. The episcopal character also embraced the roles of lord of Parliament, statesman, and spiritual adviser to the royal family, all of which required occasional attendance in London. By the mid–eighteenth century the burden of the latter two was declining. After the Hanoverian succession no bishop appears to have been the personal spiritual confidant of the sovereign, as were James Montagu for James I and John Sharp for Queen Anne; Queen Caroline's circle of theologians had more of the character of an esoteric discussion group. But the bishops continued to hold important positions in the royal household, which required their presence at Court for at least part of the year, most notably those of Dean of the Chapel Royal,[1] Clerk of the Closet,[2] and Lord High Almoner.[3] A more demanding office was that of preceptor to the Prince of Wales, held by Thomas Hayter, Bishop of Norwich, in 1751-2, and after his resignation by John Thomas, Bishop of Peterborough. The duties of such bishops could be onerous: Archbishop Herring once complained that his 'Court attendance is almost without intermission'.[4]

Since the Reformation bishops had also filled fewer and fewer posts in government. John Robinson was the last ecclesiastic to be promoted to high political office. Appointed Lord Privy Seal in 1711, Robinson was

* I would like to thank Professor D.E.D. Beales, Dr. L.J. Colley, Mr. C. Jones and Dr. J.P. Parry for their comments on an earlier version of this paper. I am indebted to Her Majesty the Queen for allowing me to cite the Stuart Papers.

[1] Edmund Gibson, 1721-48; Thomas Sherlock, 1748-61; Thomas Hayter, 1761-2; Richard Osbaldeston, 1762-4; Richard Terrick, 1764-77.

[2] Henry Egerton, 1735-46; Joseph Butler, 1746-50; John Gilbert, 1750-7; John Thomas, 1757-81.

[3] Lancelot Blackburne, 1723-43; Thomas Sherlock, 1743-8; Matthew Hutton, 1748-57; John Gilbert, 1757-8; Robert Drummond, 1758-76.

[4] Nottingham U.L., PWV/121/99 (Portland MSS.): Thomas Herring to William Herring, 30 Nov. 1752.

later one of the plenipotentiaries at the Utrecht peace negotiations, and he retained his seat in the cabinet even after his resignation as Lord Privy Seal in 1713.[5] But some bishops were still expected to be active in civil politics. This was particularly true of the Archbishops of Canterbury, who were Privy Councillors. In 1737 Archbishop Potter attended a cabinet meeting about the Prince of Wales's offer to be chief mourner at his mother's funeral, and minutes for August 1738 suggest that he was involved in discussions about policy towards Spain.[6] During George II's visits to Hanover the archbishops were always made members of the regency council, when their regular attendance was expected, and not merely for formal business.[7] Other bishops were also consulted about public affairs. Thomas Sherlock was asked by the Duke of Newcastle for his opinion on numerous occasions. A number of replies have survived, most notably about the ministerial crises in 1742 and 1743 and about foreign affairs in 1749.[8] It is not clear whether Newcastle was genuinely seeking advice, or merely the opinion of a relatively detached friend. But it was rumoured that Sherlock was responsible for the suggestion to dissolve Parliament a year early in 1747, a decision which threw the electoral preparations of Leicester House into confusion.[9]

In contrast, the burden of parliamentary attendance had increased considerably since annual sessions had become the rule in the reign of William III. Their length and the difficulties of travel meant that the bishop of a remote see, who was in London while Parliament was sitting, found it difficult to spend more than three or four months in his diocese each year. But the presence of a lord in Parliament was still regarded as an obligation, and contemporaries did not make any allowance for the increased demands placed on the bishops in the eighteenth century. Indeed particular stress was laid upon regular attendance. As the Earl of Bath told the Abbé Salier, Zachary Pearce was making little progress in his biblical studies, 'being obliged to attend all Winter, and every day in

---

[5] G. Holmes, *British Politics in the Age of Anne* (1967), p. 387.

[6] B.L., Add. MS. 35586, f. 48: notes on cabinet meeting, 9 Dec. 1737; Nottingham U.L., Ne.C. 100b (Newcastle of Clumber MSS.): cabinet meetings for 7 and 8 Aug. 1738.

[7] B.L., Add. MS. 35598, ff. 314, 358: Herring to Hardwicke, 12 Dec. 1747, 6 Oct. 1748; *Memoirs of a Royal Chaplain, 1729-63. The Correspondence of Edmund Pyle, D.D., Chaplain in Ordinary to George II, with Samuel Kerrich, D.D., Vicar of Dersingham, Rector of Wolferton, and Rector of West Newton*, ed. A. Hartshorne (1905), p. 236.

[8] B.L., Add. MS. 32699, ff. 191-2: Sherlock to Newcastle, 25 Apr. 1742; 32701, ff. 95-6: Sherlock to Newcastle, 4 Sept, 1743; 32719, ff. 203-4: Sherlock to Newcastle, 1 Oct. 1749; cf., 32869, ff. 183-4: Newcastle to Sherlock, 27 Nov. 1756.

[9] *Memoirs of a Royal Chaplain*, p. 127: Pyle to Kerrich, 17 Oct. 1747; *The House of Commons, 1715-54*, ed. Romney Sedgwick (2 vols., 1970), I, 57. Pyle claimed that the promotion of Sherlock's nephew, Jonathan Fountayne, to the deanery of York was his reward for this suggestion.

the House of Lords'.[10] Bad health and old age were excuses for non-attendance, otherwise special pleading was thought necessary to avoid creating a misleading impression.[11] Even at the height of the '45 rebellion, it required not only the entreaties of the local gentry but also the approval of the ministry to convince Archbishop Herring that he was of more use in Yorkshire than in the House of Lords.[12] The privilege of proctorial representation mitigated the burden of personal attendance to some extent. The value of proxies, however, was limited. They could not be used in committees, and they transferred from the donor control over his vote. Thus, Bishop Fleming was greatly embarrassed when he discovered from 'the Publick Prints' that his proxy had been cast against the ministry by Bishop Smalbroke during the debate on the Convention on 1 March 1739.[13] None the less, in common with temporal lords, bishops, especially those from more distant dioceses who often left London before the end of a session, made frequent use of proxies.[14]

Problems of age and health, and the demands of diocesan administration, all contributed to reduce episcopal attendance in the House of Lords. As Appendix 1 (below pp. 157-8) shows, bishops were absent more frequently as they grew older. But in general there is little doubt that the episcopate took seriously its duty to attend Parliament. During the 1740s and 1750s an average of eight bishops were

[10] Westminster Abbey Library and Muniment Room, WAM 64684 (Pearce Papers): Bath to Pearce, 11 Oct. 1749.

[11] B.L., Add. MS. 35587, f. 14: Bishop Hough to Hardwicke, 16 Jan. 1742; 32707, ff. 411-12: Bishop Peploe to Newcastle, 14 July 1746; 32709, f. 158: Bishop Gooch to Newcastle, 2 Nov. 1746; 35590, ff. 196-7, 217-18: Bishop Lavington to Hardwicke, 4 Nov., 18 Dec. 1748.

[12] B.L., Add. MS. 35598, f. 84: Herring to Hardwicke, n.d. (recd. 4 Oct. 1745); f. 86: Hardwicke to Herring, 5 Oct. 1745; ff. 88, 91: Herring to Hardwicke, 6, 9 Oct. 1745.

[13] Fleming was writing to Walpole to ask a favour, and he may merely have been trying to excuse himself. However, this is the only recorded occasion on which he opposed the ministry, and the following session he deposited his proxy with Bishop Butler instead of Smalbroke. Cambridge U.L., Cholmondeley (Houghton) Papers, correspondence, 2867: Bishop Fleming to Walpole, 15 May 1739; *An Authentick List of the House of Peers; as they Voted For and Against the Convention* (1739); H.L.R.O., Proxy Books, 1738-9. For Fleming's voting record see C. Jones, '"That Busy Senseless Place": An Analysis of Government and Opposition Lords in Walpole's House of Lords', *Parliamentary History* (forthcoming), and Appendix 2 below, pp. 159-63. It is not certain whether or not it was believed to be possible in mid-century for a member of the House to determine how his proxy was cast. On the third reading of the Schism Bill in 1714 Wake cast Nicolson's proxy for the bill in opposition to his own vote. On the other hand, in 1743 Gibson withdrew his proxy from Nicholas Claggett in the belief that Claggett was intending to vote for the Gin Bill, which Gibson opposed. The infrequency of cases of 'counter' voting would, however, suggest that it was customary for a proxy to be cast on the same side as the holder's vote. *The London Diaries of William Nicolson, Bishop of Carlisle, 1702-18*, ed. C. Jones and G. Holmes (Oxford, 1985), pp. 606-7; Cobbett, *Parl. Hist.*, XII, 1301.

[14] H.L.R.O., Proxy Books, 1742-62.

present in the House of Lords each day.[15] Individual patterns varied greatly. Frederick Cornwallis, Richard Trevor and Matthew Hutton all discharged their responsibilities with exemplary diligence, whereas Thomas Secker and James Beauclerk were present only occasionally. At first sight the bishops may not appear to have been as diligent as contemporary theory expected. In fact their record was better than that of the peers. They represented just under 13.5 per cent of the membership of the House, but provided nearly 18.5 per cent of those who attended. The bishops were, however, a largely silent presence. It was rare for them to speak during debates not related to religion and the church; Sherlock and Maddox were occasional exceptions.[16] Their silence was often commented upon and was attributed by Bishop Newton to their lack of training in oratory since the suppression of Convocation.[17] Moreover, during these two decades bishops rarely acted as chairmen of committees of the House.[18]

The silent presence of the episcopate attracted criticism from opposition politicians. The Earl of Shelburne commented on the bishops' habit of 'waking . . . just before they vote', but their silence in debates merely confirmed the belief that they were ministerial lackeys.[19] It was reported that when, in 1743, the bishops divided against the second reading of the Spirituous Liquors Bill, the Earl of Chesterfield, 'seeing them come towards him, said, he doubted if he had not mistaken the side, not having had the honour of their company for many years'.[20] In a House which numbered about 195 in mid-century the 26 bishops were indeed a significant group, and through the manipulation of their creation and translation the ministry apparently had the means to control

---

[15] This figure and those which follow have been calculated from the attendance lists for the 22 sessions between 1742 and 1762 printed in *L.J.*, XXVI-XXX. Occasionally it is possible to prove an error in these lists and they should not be regarded as conclusive evidence that any member was or was not present on a certain day, but they provide a reliable guide to general patterns.

[16] B.L., Add. MS. 6043, ff. 83-4, 118, 137: 'Reports of the debates in the House of Lords from 1735 to 1745 by Dr. Secker, whilst Bishop of Oxford'; H. Walpole, *Memoirs of King George II*, ed. J. Brooke (3 vols., New Haven, 1985), I, 80-1.

[17] 'The Life of Dr. Thomas Newton', in *The Lives of Dr. Edward Pocock, the Celebrated Orientalist, by Dr. Twells; of Dr. Zachary Pearce, Bishop of Rochester, and of Dr. Thomas Newton, Bishop of Bristol, by themselves; and of the Rev. Philip Skelton, by Mr. Burdy* (2 vols., 1816), II, 186; F. Kilvert, *A Selection from Unpublished Papers of the Right Reverend William Warburton, D.D. Late Lord Bishop of Glocester* (1841), pp. 341-2.

[18] Only one bishop (Drummond of St. Asaph) was chairman of a committee on three or more occasions in any one session. J.C. Sainty, *The Origin of the Office of Chairman of Committees in the House of Lords* (H.L.R.O. Memorandum No. 52, 1974), pp. 23-6.

[19] *Correspondence of William Pitt, Earl of Chatham*, ed. W.S. Taylor and J.H. Pringle (4 vols., 1838-40), IV, 328: Shelburne to Chatham, 27 Feb. 1744.

[20] Cobbett, *Parl. Hist.*, XII, 1368.

'a solid phalanx of votes'.[21] Opposition politicians claimed that ministers used the promise of advancement to richer and more prestigious sees as a bribe with which to corrupt the bench. Consequently a bill to prevent the translation of bishops was brought into the House of Commons in 1731 with the avowed intention of lessening their dependence on the ministry.[22] Half a century later the same belief informed the ideas of Richard Watson. His proposals to make the revenue and patronage of bishoprics more equal were intended to increase episcopal independence in the House of Lords. They were framed not so much as a plan of ecclesiastical reform, but more as part of the political campaign for economical reform.[23] Critics of the political subservience of the episcopate were confirmed in their opinion by the bishops' involvement in electioneering. Many of them were careful to exercise what influence they possessed discreetly, perhaps more discreetly than most peers, but the 'disagreeable *Submissions*' that Isaac Maddox had to make before the House of Commons following his intervention against Sir Watkin Williams Wynn in Denbighshire in 1741 reflected on the whole bench.[24]

This opposition critique is commonly restated by historians, who portray eighteenth-century bishops as a source of 'dependable pro-ministerial voting fodder in the House of Lords'.[25] Together with the household officers and the Scottish representative peers the bishops formed the core of the 'party of the Crown' in the Lords, giving their support to the ministry of the day.[26] Striking confirmation of the subservience of the episcopate was provided by its behaviour during the

---

[21] N. Sykes, *Church and State in England in the Eighteenth Century* (Cambridge, 1934), p. 50.

[22] *C.J.*, XX, 660; N. Sykes, *Edmund Gibson, Bishop of London, 1669-1748. A Study in Politics and Religion in the Eighteenth Century* (1926), pp. 149-50; Linda Colley, *In Defiance of Oligarchy. The Tory Party, 1714-60* (Cambridge, 1982), p. 106.

[23] R. Watson, 'A Letter to his Grace the Archbishop of Canterbury, printed in 1784', in *Sermons on Public Occasions, and Tracts on Religious Subjects* (Cambridge, 1788), pp. 399-405; T.J. Brain, 'Some Aspects of the Life and Work of Richard Watson, Bishop of Llandaff, 1737-1816' (Wales, Aberwystwyth, Ph.D., 1982), p. 160.

[24] B.L., Add. MS. 5831, f. 165. Herring, in contrast, was active in supporting ministerial candidates during the 1747 elections in York and Nottinghamshire, but was rather more circumspect in his behaviour. Thus, he candidly explained to the opposition candidates, the sitting members, at York, 'that, speaking personally, I had nothing to do with Elections, but whatever influence my Authority could be supposed to carry with it, in a sort of secret operation, that would be directed to the service of his Majesty and the present Administration'. B.L., Add. MS. 35598, ff. 238-9: Herring to Hardwicke, 15 Apr. 1747. See also *ibid.*, ff. 242-4, 246-8, 250-1, 252-3, 254-7: same to same, 20 May, 17, 20, 22, 26 June 1747; 32711, ff. 369-70: Herring to Newcastle, 15 June 1747.

[25] R. Porter, *English Society in the Eighteenth Century* (Harmondsworth, 1982), p. 77; Sykes, *Church and State*, pp. 63-5; A.S. Turberville, *The House of Lords in the XVIIIth Century* (Oxford, 1927), pp. 422-3.

[26] D. Large, 'The Decline of the "Party of the Crown" and the Rise of Parties in the House of Lords, 1783-1837', *E.H.R.*, LXXVIII (1963), 669-95.

debates on the South Sea Company in 1733. On 24 May the ministry lost one motion on a tied vote, but in the crucial division on 2 June they defeated a motion to censure the company's directors by 75 against 70. On both occasions 25 episcopal votes were cast, 24 in person or by proxy for the ministry.[27] This view has been applied in particular to the years of the Whig supremacy; above all, to the middle decades of the century, the years 1742-62, when the Duke of Newcastle acquired almost unchallenged control over the Crown's ecclesiastical patronage and used it to turn the episcopate into 'one of the most solid blocks of support for successive administrations'.[28] The argument may thus be divided into two parts. First, the behaviour of the bishops in the House of Lords demonstrates their subservience to the ministry. Second, the ministry's control over the episcopal creations and translations was the means by which their support was secured. I argue elsewhere that it is far from clear that the bishops' votes were gained by the deliberate exploitation of the patronage at ministers' disposal.[29] The remainder of this essay will focus on the former point. Three themes will be discussed in more detail, concentrating in particular on the years 1742-62: firstly, the voting patterns of the bishops; secondly, their attitudes towards the ministry and the Crown; and, finally, their role as representatives and guardians of the church and clergy.

2

The evidence of the 1733 session and the comments of the ministry's opponents provide, at best, a partial account of the bishops' political behaviour in the mid-eighteenth century. In a period when divisions were rare in the House of Lords, only 74 occurred in the 22 sessions between 1742 and 1762,[30] and fewer division lists survive, the emphasis placed by contemporaries on the duty of attendance suggests that it may provide some measure of political participation. Yet the figures hardly suggest that the bishops believed it to be peculiarly their duty to attend and support the administration. In general they were indeed more diligent than the peers, but on those days when 95 or more lords were present, presumably the days of greatest political importance, they provided just under 14 per cent of the attendance of a House in which

[27] Sykes, *Church and State*, pp. 50-1; Turberville, *House of Lords*, pp. 204-5; J.H. Plumb, *Sir Robert Walpole* (2 vols., 1956-60), II, 276.

[28] J.B. Owen, *The Eighteenth Century, 1714-1815* (1974), p. 153; J.H. Plumb, *England in the Eighteenth Century* (Harmondsworth, 1950), p. 43; Sykes, *Church and State*, pp. 49-51; H.T. Dickinson, *Walpole and the Whig Supremacy* (1973), pp. 79-80.

[29] S.J.C. Taylor, 'Church and State in England in the Mid-Eighteenth Century: The Newcastle Years, 1742-1762' (Cambridge Ph.D., 1987), pp. 88-101.

[30] J.C. Sainty and D. Dewar, *Divisions in the House of Lords: An Analytical List, 1685-1857* (H.L.R.O. Occasional Publications, No. 2, 1976).

they formed about 13.5 per cent of the membership. Moreover, it was not uncommon to find bishops voting against the ministry. Occasionally, and invariably on questions touching the church and religion, the episcopate found itself united in opposition. This happened twice in the 1740s, on the Spirituous Liquors Bill of 1743 and the Bill for Disarming the Highlands in 1748, occasions which will be discussed later in this essay; and three times in the 1730s: twice in 1734, on the Bill to prevent stockjobbing and a proposal that the House should sit on Easter eve, and over the Quakers Tithe Bill of 1736.[31] More frequently individual bishops found themselves opposed to the administration.

Even in the South Sea Company divisions of 1733 one bishop, Reynolds of Lincoln, voted against the majority of his brethren. In the later 1730s and early 1740s he became a persistent critic of the ministry's foreign and war policies.[32] At the same time Bishops Benson and Secker also began to vote against the Court. According to the Duchess of Marlborough they first opposed the ministry on 19 February 1739, in two votes on the affairs of the South Sea Company. Thereafter they continued to support the opposition to the Walpole administration, mostly over the conduct of the war and on country issues, such as place and pension bills, which Secker believed were necessary to reduce 'the over great Dependency of the Commons on the Crown'.[33] Benson later referred to Carteret, Bath and Sandys as men 'of whom when out of place I had a good opinion', and he and Secker were for some years afterwards tainted by participation in a 'formed opposition'.[34] Richard Smalbroke, Bishop of Lichfield, and Henry Egerton, Bishop of Hereford, were also occasionally found among the ministry's opponents, and presumably these were the five bishops whom Secker mentioned as having voted for the Pension Bill on 26 March 1742.[35] They did not, however, form a coherent group. Benson and Secker, who

[31] Royal Archives, Windsor Castle, Stuart Papers, 169/186: Nathaniel Mist to James Edgar, 24 [Apr.] 1734; 170/26: same to same, 1 May 1734; S.J.C. Taylor, 'Sir Robert Walpole, the Church of England and the Quakers Tithe Bill of 1736', *Historical Journal*, XXVIII (1985), 51-77.

[32] Cobbett, *Parl. Hist.*, IX, 115-16. For his opposition in the 1730s and 1740s see B.L., Add. MS. 33002, ff. 407-8: pre-sessional forecast, 1740-1; 6043, ff. 31, 35, 42, and *passim*; *An Authentick List . . . For and Against the Convention*.

[33] B.L., Add. MS. 6043, f. 87 and *passim*; Lambeth Palace Library, MS. 2598 ('The Autobiography of Archbishop Secker'), ff. 26, 28-9, 32 (transcript of Professor Norman Sykes); Yale University, Beinecke Library, Osborn Collection, Stair Box no. 37: Duchess of Marlborough to Lord Stair, 20 Feb. 1739 (a microfilm of this correspondence is in B.L., M/687).

[34] B.L., Add. MS. 39311, f. 149: Benson to Berkeley, 23 Apr. 1743; 32721, f. 418: Hardwicke to Newcastle, 20 July 1750; 32722, f. 233: Newcastle to Pelham, 23 Aug. 1750.

[35] Lambeth Palace Lib., MS. 2598, ff. 31-2. For Smalbroke and Egerton, see B.L., Add. MS. 6043, f. 42 and *passim*.

were brothers-in-law, often acted together,[36] but their opposition to the ministry was no more than intermittent. They supported it 'much oftener than otherwise: and sometimes, when other Bishops as Lichfield, Hereford and Lincoln, voted against it'.[37] Thus, they opposed the motion of 13 February 1741 for the removal of Walpole, whereas Reynolds and Smalbroke not only supported it, but entered their protests against its rejection.[38] Reynolds was the most consistent opponent of the Walpole ministry on the bench, yet even he was still to be found advocating a compromise during the debates on the 1740 Pension Bill, a measure which Benson and Secker supported.[39] Moreover, the two latter remained consistent in their attitudes for some months after Walpole's fall. Secker voted for the Place Bill on 6 April 1742, Benson for the Indemnity Bill on 25 May, and both abstained on the motion approving the sending of British troops to Flanders on 1 February 1743, an occasion on which they were joined by their mutual friend Joseph Butler.[40] Butler, however, had supported the ministry in the late 1730s and early 1740s, despite admitting to Secker that he thought 'the ministers were both wicked men and wicked ministers'.[41] But by this time they felt that their opposition lacked purpose. As Benson explained to George Berkeley, 'it was measures and not ministers I desired to see changed. As I have now little hope of seeing the former, I have less concern about the latter'.[42]

Secker and Benson may have returned to the ministerial fold, even if only *faute de mieux*, but sporadic opposition from the episcopal bench continued in the 1740s and 1750s, although the infrequency of divisions and the paucity of reports of debates make it difficult precisely to define its extent.[43] Two bishops at least occasionally voted against the ministry during these years, Isaac Maddox and Thomas Hayter. Maddox opposed

---

[36] But not invariably. On 19 January 1741 Secker supported the ministry on a procedural motion, whereas Benson had joined Smalbroke, Egerton and Reynolds in opposition. On 10 February 1741 Secker opposed and Benson supported the ministry on another tactical motion for a call of the House. B.L., Add. MS. 6043, f. 69.

[37] Lambeth Palace Lib., MS. 2598, f. 26.

[38] B.L., Add. MS. 6043, f. 85; *L.J.*, XXV, 597. Egerton also supported the ministry on this occasion; see *A True and Exact List of the Lords Spiritual and Temporal who Voted For and Against the Address to Remove a Certain Great Man* (1741). Thus also Secker and Benson consistently supported motions on the employment of Hanoverian troops, although not without reservations. Benson felt that 'if it was right in regard to our Foreign affairs, [it] was certainly very impolitic in regard to our Domestic ones'. B.L., Add. MS. 39311, f. 49: Benson to Berkeley, 23 Apr. 1743; 6043, ff. 90, 155.

[39] B.L., Add. MS. 6043, ff. 138-9.

[40] *Ibid.*, ff. 118, 130, 155; Lambeth Palace Lib., MS. 2598, ff. 31-2.

[41] Lambeth Palace Lib., MS. 2598, f. 30.

[42] B.L., Add. MS. 39311, f. 149: Benson to Berkeley, 23 Apr. 1743.

[43] The evidence of contemporary management and division lists, drawn on in the following analysis, is tabulated below, pp. 159-63.

the Buckingham Assizes Bill, on which Bishop Willes of Bath and Wells abstained, and led the attack on the Orphans of London Relief Bill in 1748; made an 'extraordinary Speech' against the proposed limitations on the power of the regent during the debate on the Regency Bill in 1751; and supported the attempts, generally regarded as a prelude to repeal, to postpone the operation of the 1753 Marriage Act.[44] Hayter voted against the Militia Bill of 1756 and was consistently listed as an opponent of the ministry in the management lists for the debates on the Habeas Corpus Bill of 1758.[45] Both these bills, however, split all party groups. Maddox and Hayter, moreover, both supported the Duke of Bedford's motion to lay before the House papers relating to the cabinet council's investigations of allegations of Jacobitism against Andrew Stone, Sub-Governor to the Prince of Wales and Newcastle's onetime secretary, William Murray, the Solicitor-General, and James Johnson, Bishop of Gloucester.[46] Hayter's opposition can be traced to his resentment at the ministry following the row over the Prince of Wales's education, which had resulted in his resignation as preceptor.[47] The reasons behind Maddox's dissatisfaction are less clear, especially as he had the reputation of a staunch ministerialist following his behaviour during the 1741 elections and his parliamentary interventions in the 1730s. It is possible, however, that his political connections were with Walpole and that he lost sympathy with the ministry after 1742; he was one of only nine lords in a full House to support the attempt inspired by Walpole, now Earl of Orford, to overturn the judgment of Lord Chancellor Hardwicke in the case of *Le Neve* v. *Norris* in 1744.[48] Moreover, even the constant attendance at Court demanded of an Archbishop of Canterbury did not prevent John Potter from involving himself in the Leicester House

---

[44] B.L., Add. MS. 33002, ff. 411-12; Cobbett, *Parl. Hist.*, XIV, 268; B.L., Add. MS. 32724, ff. 280-1: Newcastle to the King, 10 May 1751; ff. 282-3: Newcastle to Bishop Drummond, 13 May 1751; Walpole, *Memoirs of George II*, II, 81-2; B.L., Add. MS. 35877, f. 174; Westminster Abbey Muniment Room, WAM 64581: Herring to Pearce, 1 Jan. 1755.

[45] B.L., Add. MS. 35877, f. 308; 33034, ff. 265-6, 259-60, 267-9, 314-6, 317.

[46] No division took place as the motion's supporters, seeing they were so few, 'gave it up without telling the House'. Walpole, *Memoirs of George II*, I, 219, 222, 223.

[47] For differing accounts of the events leading to the resignation of Hayter and Lord Harcourt, Governor to the Prince, see *ibid.*, pp. 197-9; James, Earl Waldegrave, *Memoirs from 1754 to 1758* (1821), pp. 36-7. The best modern account, of the resignation, of the allegations against Stone, Murray and Johnson, and of the bias of Walpole's account, is provided by Romney Sedgwick in his edition of *Letters from George III to Lord Bute, 1756-1766* (1939), pp. xxi-xxvii.

[48] This question was also given up without telling, its supporters numbering only nine in a House, which, according to the *Journals*, numbered 71. Cambridge U.L., MS. Add. 6851 (the Parliamentary Journal of Edward Harley, Third Earl of Oxford), II, ff. 79-80; *L.J.*, XXVI, 367-8. Clyve Jones and I are preparing an edition of Harley's Journal for publication.

opposition in the years immediately before his death. Although there is no evidence that he ever joined the parliamentary opposition to the ministry, he was prominent in supporting the candidature of the Prince of Wales for the Chancellorship of Cambridge University against the Duke of Newcastle, in defiance of the King's express wishes.[49]

The evidence of attendance and voting records has thus produced a rather inconclusive picture. On the one hand, it is inadequate to explain episcopal behaviour by the power of patronage, a simplistic assertion of the primacy of material self-interest. The bishops cannot be regarded as unquestioning ministerial voting fodder, even when religion and the church were not the subject of debate. On the other hand, Appendix 2 (below, pp. 159-63) makes it equally clear that they usually supported the administration – even Hayter and Maddox continued to be invited to the pre-sessional meetings of peers throughout Newcastle's tenure of the Treasury, although it is not known whether or not they attended.[50] This picture can be clarified only by a more detailed examination of the bishops' own perception of their role in the House of Lords in regard to both civil and religious affairs.

A general consensus existed that churchmen ought not to involve themselves in party politics. John Egerton reminded his clergy that it was their religious duty to preach obedience and 'to study to be quiet', but that it was 'improper . . . if not profane' to introduce politics into the pulpit, and destructive of the clerical character to 'interfere in political controversies, and busy themselves either in arraigning or defending the proceedings in the state'.[51] Even in Parliament the bishops believed that they had little part to play in discussions of civil measures. Archbishop Herring was not atypical in resolving to leave the care of his 'Politicks' to the Lord Chancellor.[52] This attitude was reinforced by more widespread assumptions about party, government and public duty. Condemnation of formed oppositions and dislike of opposition in general have often been portrayed as mere rhetoric in the mid-eighteenth century. But in Court circles participation in a formed opposition was still regarded as a sign of disloyalty.[53] Even when the existence of parties was recognized as a reality, however undesirable, their sphere of operation was severely

---

[49] B.L., Add. MS. 32711, f. 61: Bishop Gooch to Newcastle, 16 May 1747; *Memoirs of a Royal Chaplain*, p. 127.

[50] Hayter is known to have attended the meeting of 17 November 1760, the first of the new King's reign. B.L., Add. MS. 32995, ff. 242-5, 344-7; 32996, ff. 275-9; 32997, ff. 300-4; 32998, ff. 187-94, 327-34; 32999, ff. 80-7, 90-1, 341-8.

[51] Hertfordshire R.O., A.H. 1999 (Ashridge MSS.), ff. 26-30: charge to the clergy of Durham, 1778.

[52] B.L., Add. MS. 35598, f. 419: Herring to Hardwicke, 18 July 1749.

[53] A.S. Foord, *His Majesty's Opposition, 1714-1830* (Oxford, 1964), pp. 6-7; *Letters from George III to Lord Bute*, p. xvii.

restricted. As late as 1784, at the height of the struggle between Pitt and Fox, Paul Kelly has pointed out that 'straight party issues were exceptional . . . The greater part of the House of Commons public business lay outside the sphere of party politics as it was understood at the time', including importantly the raising of supplies.[54] This was still more the case in the House of Lords. The peerage's closer relation to the Throne, reinforced by a feeling of community of interest with the Crown forged in the trauma of the mid-seventeenth century, emphasized the duty it shared with the Commons, to assist in the carrying on of the King's business. This obligation weighed more heavily with the bishops who were appointed by the King himself. Thus, Thomas Secker denied that his opposition to the Spirituous Liquors Bill proceeded from a desire 'to distress the government', while Thomas Sherlock, speaking on the same occasion, protested that 'it was very unkind in the projectors of this Bill, to contrive such a scheme as should lay the members of both Houses under a necessity of opposing his majesty's supply, or of agreeing to a Bill which they could not but in their consciences condemn'.[55]

Several bishops recognized explicitly that their primary loyalty was to the King. After Herring had been persuaded that he would be of more use in opposing the '45 rebellion by remaining in Yorkshire, he still begged Hardwicke 'to excuse my attendance at the opening of Parliament to my Royal Master'.[56] Similarly, as Edmund Gibson explained to Newcastle, although he had 'discontinued a *personal* attendance upon his Majesty's affairs in Parliament' since his opposition to Walpole over the Quakers Tithe Bill in 1736, at the beginning of every session he made his proxy available to the ministry.[57] Because support of the King's government was normally synonymous with the support of his ministers, it is difficult to distinguish between loyalty to the King and to the administration. What was to one side dutiful attendance on public business, appeared to the other slavish dependence upon the ministry. But the episcopal behaviour over Fox's India Bill demonstrates that as late as 1784 the distinction was, to some extent at least, still a reality. William Markham, the Archbishop of York, was a Court bishop who was inclined to follow any intimation of the King's personal opinion. But the Archbishop of Canterbury, John Moore, had expressed his approval of the bill and was connected with the coalition through his

---

[54] P. Kelly, 'British Parliamentary Politics, 1784-1786', *Historical Journal*, XVII (1974), 739.
[55] Cobbett, *Parl. Hist.*, XII, 1298, 1236.
[56] B.L., Add. MS. 35598, f. 89: Herring to Hardwicke, 6 Oct. 1745.
[57] B.L., Add. MS. 32702, f. 25: Gibson to Newcastle, 24 Jan. 1744; H.L.R.O., Proxy Books.

brother-in-law, William Eden. Together with Markham and seven other bishops, however, Moore cast his vote, and that of the Bishop of London, whose proxy he held, against the ministry following a private audience with the King.[58]

These attitudes should not be accorded too much weight. The bench had been polarized between Whig and Tory during the first two decades of the eighteenth century, although it must be admitted that the events of these years were often later lamented and may be attributed to the centrality of religion, and the Church of England, in party ideology. Moreover, one of the points of this essay has been to demonstrate that even from the 1730s, by which time the bench was more or less exclusively Whig, bishops were not unquestioning supporters of government policy. None the less, this account of their perception of their parliamentary role, of their belief that it was their duty to support the King's government, does at least suggest that it is more important to explain their opposition to, than their support of, the ministry. Thus, in the 1760s it is not the bishops' desertion of their maker, Newcastle,[59] which is surprising, but the fact that so many of them were prepared at least occasionally to oppose the government. Only six new bishops were appointed between Newcastle's fall and the end of the session of 1768-9. It was, again, more common to find the majority of the bench supporting the ministry, but of the 31 who sat in the House of Lords during this time 21 can be shown to have voted against it on at least one occasion.[60]

During the 1760s, as during the 1740s and 1750s, the episcopate was uniformly Whig, yet in the new reign loyalties to patrons and to Whig principles did not reinforce the bishops' obligations to the Crown as certainly as they had done in earlier decades. Some, like John Hume, were inclined to follow the judgment of their patrons in the turbulent politics of the period. Personal loyalty was the most important consideration for him and, as he explained to Lord Lincoln, his political allegiance was determined by the answer to the question, 'Who as a publick Minister has conferrd most upon me, and has the first Right to

[58] J. Cannon, *The Fox-North Coalition. Crisis of the Constitution, 1782-4* (Cambridge, 1969), pp. 135, 137; *The Political Magazine*, V (1783), 404-5. Three episcopal proxies were also cast against the bill. Eight bishops (six in person and two by proxy) supported the ministry.

[59] H. Walpole, *Memoirs of the Reign of King George the Third*, ed. G.F. Russell Barker (4 vols., 1894), I, 134.

[60] W.C. Lowe, 'Bishops and Scottish Representative Peers, 1760-75', *Journal of British Studies*, XVIII (1978-9), 90.

demand my following him in publick Affairs'.[61] Philip Yonge was another bishop who felt strong ties of personal gratitude to Newcastle, but he was unwilling to become an unquestioning supporter of the 'Old Whig' opposition. Gratitude, he argued, could not be 'the only guide of publick conduct'. He was not prepared to support 'a random or ineffectual opposition', and thus refused to vote against the ministry over the Wilkes affair, preferring to abstain.[62] Others believed that constitutional issues were at stake during the decade. Archbishop Drummond claimed that he could 'never approve the system that seems to me to be established at present, and began by driving from the king's countenance the best persons that have supported his family upon Revolution principles'. He was as anxious as anyone among the 'Old Whigs' to 'undeceive my sovereign', yet his behaviour demonstrates clearly episcopal awareness of their duty to the Crown.[63] Even deeply held political principles did not enable the bishops to feel comfortable in opposition. If Drummond could not support men 'whose constitutional principles were at best suspicious', he 'believed it ungrateful and indecent actively to oppose the administration of a Prince to whom he personally owed the highest obligation'. Therefore, he stayed away from Parliament.[64] Archbishop Secker adopted a similar course of action. He supported the Rockingham ministry in 1765-6, and, although there is no evidence of his having voted with the opposition at other times between 1762 and 1768, he was often absent on days of divisions.[65] The same problem of conflicting loyalties had in fact been made apparent in the 1750s, during the brief interlude of the Pitt-Devonshire administration. Probably at some point between December 1756 and April 1757

---

[61] Nottingham U.L., Ne.C. 2961: Bishop Hume to Lincoln, 9 June 1767. On the resignation of the Rockingham ministry, Lord Lincoln intervened with Pitt to secure the bishopric of Salisbury for Hume, his former tutor. Lincoln had ceased to support his uncle, and when Hume left his proxy with the Duke of Newcastle, Lincoln regarded his behaviour as extreme ingratitude. But Hume went on in his letter to say, 'Surely when you did it, you could not do it by way of buying me off from my obligations to the Duke and Dutchess of Newcastle, or by way of purchasing my Vote in Parliament. Had this been the case, your Lordship would have plainly told me the Conditions, and th.. t I should for ever forfeit your Friendship, if I did not fulfil them. Had your Lordship hinted at this, I could not have accepted the Bishoprick.' See also Ne.C. 2960: Lincoln to William Pitt, n.d.; Ne.C. 2962: Lincoln to Hume, 15 June 1767.

[62] B.L., Add. MS. 32954, f. 152: Yonge to Newcastle, 22 Dec. 1763, quoted in Sykes, *Church and State*, p. 56.

[63] B.L., Add. MS. 32952, f. 370: Drummond to Newcastle, 16 Nov. 1763, quoted in Sykes, *Church and State*, p. 55.

[64] R. Drummond, *Sermons on Public Occasions and a Letter on Theological Study . . . To which are Prefixed Memoirs of his Life, by George Hay Drummond, A.M.* (Edinburgh, 1803), pp. xviii–xx.

[65] Lowe, 'Bishops and Scottish Representative Peers', p. 93.

Newcastle drew up a management list dividing the House of Lords into 'For' and 'Against', the former being those on whose support he believed he could depend if he attempted to bring down the government.[66] The situation was very different from that after his resignation in 1762, as it was clear in 1757 not only that he would return to power before long but also that he still had the confidence of George II. Thus it is not surprising to find 14 of the 23 bishops on the list classified as Newcastle's supporters. Those noted as 'Against', however, included not only some, like Hayter, who had become alienated from the duke, and others, like Newcome, whose patron, the Earl of Powis,[67] was a supporter of the new administration, but also figures like Keene and Pearce. The former was a Cambridge protégé of Newcastle who had been raised to the bishopric of Chester following his services as Vice-Chancellor of the University in the troubled years of 1750 and 1751;[68] the latter was closely connected with the Earl of Bath, listed as 'For', and was soon to be translated, on Newcastle's personal recommendation, to the bishopric of Rochester.[69] Both clearly believed that their first loyalty was to the King, and thus to the administration of the day – both deserted Newcastle for the Bute administration soon after his fall in 1762.[70]

The key, however, to understanding the behaviour of the bishops in Parliament, and the most important caveat to their portrayal as ministerial voting fodder, is their role, and their perception of themselves, not merely as lords of Parliament sharing the responsibilities of peers, but as the representatives and guardians of the church and clergy. Bishop Benson believed that this was the most important motive for their attendance. As he explained to Berkeley, 'it is so necessary for supporting the interest of the church, that the Bishops should be present in Parliament, that it is our duty I think to appear there, and if we take care to shew that it is not our private interest which brings us thither and rules us there, we may be able to do some good or at least hinder a good deal of mischief'.[71] Other bishops shared Benson's opinion that their first duty was to the church. When Edmund Gibson retired from public affairs in 1736, he promised Walpole his support, but warned him

> that if, on any future occasion, I see an attack made upon the Rights of
> Parochial Clergy in which the Court think fitt to take a part, I shall think my
> self obliged to concur with such of my Brethren as appear to be in the same

[66] B.L., Add. MS. 33034, ff. 214-15.

[67] For the connection between Newcome and Powis, see Exeter College, Oxford, Bray MSS.: Richard Blacow to Thomas Bray, 15 Feb. 1755.

[68] B.L., Add. MS. 32721, f. 54: Newcastle to Herring, 6 July 1750 [misdated June].

[69] 'The Life of Dr. Zachary Pearce', in *The Lives of Pocock, Pearce, Newton and Skelton*, I, 390-1, 401-2.

[70] B.L., Add. MS. 33000, ff. 239-40.

[71] B.L., Add. MS. 39311, f. 39: Benson to Berkeley, 7 Feb. 1738.

sentiments with me, in warning my clergy of their danger, and advising them to petition that they may be heard, before they are condemn'd.[72]

The same sentiment was expressed by Thomas Herring, although he was in general far more inclined to defer to the opinion of ministers in political matters. About the middle of the 1751 session it appeared likely that two bills would be brought into Parliament, for the relief of the Quakers and to fix a value for the tithe of hops. While approving of neither bill Herring was not strident in his opposition. None the less, he warned Newcastle that if 'the Clergy should take the alarm, as I cannot in that case separate myself fro[m] the Bench, so neither can the Bench withdraw themselves from the Clergy'.[73] In the absence of a sitting Convocation their responsibilities were all the greater. It is significant that debates concerning the church and religion witnessed both an increase in episcopal attendance – during the session of 1753 the bishops represented 18.6 per cent of those present; but for the three days of the second reading and committee stages of the Clandestine Marriage Bill, they formed 25.5 per cent of the House – and a greater readiness to voice their opinions.[74]

One of the reasons behind the sporadic opposition of the late 1730s and early 1740s appears to have been discontent with the religious policy of the Walpole administration. Bishop Smalbroke announced himself no friend to the administration 'on many accounts . . . but particularly that the Ministry does not favour the clergy and that the Papists have too much countenance'.[75] Secker was less violent in his objections to the ministry's policy, and recognized not only that many of its friends but also many of its enemies were 'vehement against' the clergy. This analysis was his justification for abandoning support of the ministry, and adopting instead a neutral position. He argued that the strength of the church did not lie 'in adhering to either party; as indeed I think it never can: but in the honest policy of acting uprightly between both and joyning with neither to do wrong'.[76] But the most striking evidence of the episcopate's role as guardians of the church, the clergy and religion is provided by its united opposition to the ministry on two occasions: the Spirituous Liquors Bill of 1743 and the Bill for Disarming the Scottish Highlands in 1748.

The Spirituous Liquors Act of 1743 (16 Geo. II, c. 8) repealed Sir Joseph Jekyll's Act of 1736, which had attempted to prevent the consumption of gin by imposing prohibitive duties on retail sales.

---

[72] St. Andrews U.L., MS. 5299 (Gibson Papers): Gibson to Walpole, n.d.

[73] B.L., Add. MS. 32724, ff. 161-2: Herring to Newcastle, 5 Mar. 1751.

[74] *L.J.*, XXVIII, 66-7, 77, 80; Kilvert, *Selections from the Unpublished Papers of Warburton*, p. 342.

[75] H.M.C., *Egmont Diary*, II, 342.

[76] B.L., Add. MS. 39311, f. 37: Secker to Berkeley, 29 June 1737.

Retailers had, however, largely ignored the act and had been supported
by popular opinion in so doing. During the 1743 debates both sides
agreed that Jekyll's act had failed, primarily because it was
unenforceable.[77] Carteret claimed that it was impossible to execute the
existing law 'but by a military force'.[78] The ministry's bill, therefore,
proposed to attack the problem in two ways. By a slightly increased tax
on consumption, thus raising the price of gin, the bill would reduce its
consumption and eradicate some of the worst evils of its abuse among the
poor. At the same time, by reducing the retailer's licence fee from £50 to
£1 there would be less incentive to evade the law, thus enabling the
justices to exercise some control over outlets, and, it was hoped,
encouraging licence-holders to enforce the law against illicit retailers. In
addition, the new duties would raise a substantial revenue for the
government.[79] These proposals, however, provoked fierce criticism
from the bishops. For Thomas Sherlock the bill was simply
incomprehensible; to 'prevent the excessive use of any thing, by
allowing it to be sold without restraint, is an expedient which the
wisdom of no former age ever discovered'.[80] Thomas Secker, however,
explained in detail the grounds of episcopal opposition. His objections
rested upon two points: that the liquors were pernicious; and that the bill
was not a sufficient restraint on their consumption. The first, that the
liquors were 'pernicious to the health, industry, and morals of the
people', was common to both sides. The drinking of gin was corrupting
the poor and thus, as Secker pointed out, endangering their chances of
salvation, since 'what is prejudicial to morals extends its consequences to
a world that shall never end'. It was the duty of a Christian legislature to
promote reformation. The main thrust of his argument, however, was
whether the bill was a sufficient remedy for a generally acknowledged
evil. 'And', he added, 'the question is not whether it be some, but
whether sufficient'. In his opinion it was not. The only remedy was to
put it out of the reach of the poor – 'nothing can stop this mischief, but
what will amount to a prohibition'. If present legislation was inadequate,
what was proposed was worse, since it would encourage the corruption
of the morals of the poor.[81] The bill was, therefore, immoral, and its
immorality was compounded by the manner in which the state was

---

[77] Cobbett, *Parl. Hist.*, XII, 1197, 1251; S. and Beatrice Webb, *The History of Liquor
Licensing in England Principally from 1700 to 1830* (1903), pp. 24–9.

[78] Cobbett, *Parl. Hist.*, XII, 1224.

[79] *Ibid.*, 1214–6, 1225–7; Webb, *Liquor Licensing*, pp. 29, 33.

[80] Cobbett, *Parl. Hist.*, XII, 1362.

[81] *Ibid.*, 1296–8. This speech is taken from Secker's own manuscript journal of
parliamentary proceedings. His notes of other speeches agree in broad outline with the
versions printed in Cobbett, *Parl. Hist.*, which were taken from the *London Magazine* for
October 1743.

taking advantage of 'vice' to 'increase the revenue'.[82]

The episcopate united against the bill and the ministry. A substantial majority of the bench agreed with Sherlock that it was 'the most unchristian Bill that was ever thought of by any government; and therefore I think it incumbent on me as a christian bishop, to give my testimony against it in the most open and express manner I can'.[83] On the second reading ten bishops[84] were present to vote against the bill, and seven episcopal proxies[85] were also cast against it. At the third reading 11 bishops voted against it in person, and a further six by proxy.[86] Of these 11, ten entered their protest against the passage of the bill, though without reasons.[87] In total 19 bishops opposed the bill at some point, and not one supported it. Of the remaining seven, Secker mentions four who did not attend the debates despite being in London – Willes of St. David's, Herring of Bangor, Hoadly of Winchester, and Gilbert of Llandaff.[88] Of the others, John Hough, Bishop of Worcester, had ceased attendance in Parliament some years before. Reynolds of Lincoln and Smalbroke of Lichfield, on the other hand, were both present in the House of Lords earlier and later in the session, so it can only be assumed that they had temporarily left London without depositing proxies.

The Spirituous Liquors Bill demonstrated the bishops' concern for the religion and morality of the nation. Their opposition to the Bill for Disarming the Highlands, on the other hand, was motivated by their concern for the effectiveness of the church, and for its rights and privileges as an independent society. The offensive part of the bill was a clause which prohibited all episcopal ministers in Scotland who had not received their orders from English or Irish bishops from officiating in

[82] B.L., Add. MS. 39311, f. 50: Benson to Berkeley, 23 Apr. 1743.

[83] Cobbett, *Parl. Hist.*, XII, 1236.

[84] Potter of Canterbury, Wilcocks of Rochester, Sherlock of Salisbury, Claggett of Exeter, Egerton of Hereford, Benson of Gloucester, Secker of Oxford, Maddox of Worcester, Gooch of Norwich, and Mawson of Chichester. Cobbett, *Parl. Hist.*, XII, 1300-1.

[85] Blackburne of York, Peploe of Chester, Clavering of Peterborough, Wynne of Bath and Wells, Chandler of Durham, Fleming of Carlisle, and Butts of Ely. H.L.R.O., Proxy Book, 1742. The bill was committed by 82 against 54, including proxies. Cobbett, *Parl. Hist.*, XII, 1367.

[86] Gibson of London and Butler of Bristol were present on this occasion, but Wilcocks, who held the proxy of Archbishop Blackburne, was absent. Butler had been present the previous day to vote against the bill in committee, but both Gibson and Wilcocks had been absent. Just before the second reading Gibson had withdrawn his proxy from Bishop Claggett, in the belief that he intended to vote for the bill. The bill was given a third reading by 59 against 38, including proxies. Cobbett, *Parl. Hist.*, XII, 1426, 1373-4, 1301; H.L.R.O., Proxy Book, 1742.

[87] *L.J.*, XXVI, 218. The bishop who did not enter his protest was Henry Egerton.

[88] Cobbett, *Parl. Hist.*, XII, 1426. Bishop Willes had been present on 22 February for the second reading, but had not stayed until the end of the debate. *Ibid.*, 1301.

any meeting-house. This clause was an amendment to a statute of 1746 (19 Geo. II, c. 38) which enacted that the orders of all episcopal ministers had to be registered by 1 September 1746, and that after that date only orders received from English or Irish bishops could be registered.

When it became known that the bishops intended to oppose this clause, the ministry was anxious to avoid the question of the validity of orders being debated.[89] But, contrary to the impression created by the contemporary report of the debate in the *London Magazine*,[90] this was not the reason for episcopal opposition. Thomas Secker, opening the debate, made his position on this issue perfectly clear. He asserted that deprivation did not destroy the episcopal character, but he did not regard the bill as an attempt by the civil power to legislate about the 'spiritual validity of orders'. Instead, it

appoints only, what shall or shall not be tolerated. Suppose the Orders given by Nonjuring Bishops ever so valid Theologically; the state may forbid mens officiating upon them, if the publick good requires it. And be they ever so much nullities, yet on the genuine principles of Toleration the state may and should suffer men to officiate upon them, if it do the publick no harm: just as other Sects are suffered; some with no orders, and some with Orders from we know not whom.[91]

The bishops' opposition to the clause was founded upon three arguments: that it was unjust; that it was impolitic; and that it was an effective denial of toleration to the episcopal church in Scotland. The clause was unjust because it applied even to those ministers who had obeyed the act of 1746 and registered their orders. It disqualified all who had obtained orders from Swedish or Danish bishops, or from nonjuring bishops, but who had later taken the oaths. In doing so it ignored the peculiar problems of the church in Scotland and the fact that earlier in the century English bishops had often refused to ordain Scottish

[89] B.L., Add. MS. 35598, f. 325: Herring to Hardwicke, 7 May 1748. Cf., Cobbett, *Parl. Hist.*, XIV, 279-80.

[90] Reprinted in *ibid.*, 269-315.

[91] Lambeth Palace Lib., MS. 1349, p. 166: Thomas Secker's speech during the committee on the Bill for Disarming the Highlands, 10 May 1748. The Lambeth Palace Library catalogue claims that this was Secker's speech at the third reading on 11 May, but internal evidence demonstrates conclusively that it was made the previous day. Thomas Birch's report of Secker's speech is accurate in its claim that he 'insinuated, that deprivation did not destroy the episcopal character' (Cobbett, *Parl. Hist.*, XIV, 270). But the report of the speech in *ibid.*, 269-76, taken from the *London Magazine*, bears little resemblance to Secker's manuscript. There is certainly no trace in the manuscript of the passage in which Secker is reported as claiming that the clause was 'an encroachment upon the Christian religion, as professed by the Church of England' (*ibid.*, 275-6). This discrepancy casts some doubt upon whether Sherlock is reported accurately later in the debate as describing it as an 'encroachment upon one of the most essential rights of the Church' (*ibid.*, 302).

candidates.[92] Sherlock regarded this as depriving those ministers who had registered their orders of their property, arguing that they had 'as good a right to their meeting-houses, and to exercise their function in those meeting-houses, as any man has to his estate'.[93] Because the bill was unjust, it was also impolitic. The episcopal clergy were distinguished 'by the purity of their religious doctrines, by their learning, by the decency of their behaviour, and chiefly by their sufferings'. They were precisely the sort of men whose support would strengthen the government in Scotland.[94] But they were being forced to become 'enemies to the Government for their bread; and the bitterer enemies, because they were not sufferd to be friends, when they would have been so'.[95]

Moreover, the clause amounted to a virtual declaration that 'no episcopal Church shall be so much as tolerated in Scotland'.[96] In fact, as Secker acknowledged, this was as much a consequence of the 1746 act as of the new clause.[97] The episcopal church in Scotland had been left as a body without a head. No one was legally entrusted with jurisdiction over those clergy who had been ordained by English and Irish bishops and who had taken the oaths to the government, nor was there anyone to perform the rite of confirmation.[98] Provision had indeed been made for the ordination of episcopal ministers, but it was hardly adequate. On the one hand, prospective candidates would have to undertake a long and expensive journey. On the other hand, English bishops were under canonical and other restrictions with respect to the granting of orders – they were not allowed to ordain a man without a title to an ecclesiastical living, nor without some credible testimony of his good life and conversation.[99] Even Archbishop Herring recognized that the clause would create great difficulties for the bishops, leaving them with the choice of failing to provide for the church in Scotland or of ordaining men about whom they knew nothing.[100]

These considerations combined to unite the bench against the clause. In the committee 20 bishops voted against it. These included Archbishop Herring, despite his distress at opposing the ministry. Before the committee stage of the bill he had discussed the matter with Butler,

[92] Lambeth Palace Lib., MS. 1349, pp. 165-6; Cobbett, *Parl. Hist.*, XIV, 300-1.

[93] Cobbett, *Parl. Hist.*, XIV, 301, 295.

[94] *Ibid.*, 296-7.

[95] Lambeth Palace Lib., MS. 1349, p. 158.

[96] Cobbett, *Parl. Hist.*, XIV, 303.

[97] Lambeth Palace Lib., MS. 1349, pp. 158, 161. Secker said of the 1746 Act that 'had I not been, as most of the Bishops were, in my Diocese, while it was depending I should probably have objected to it'.

[98] *Ibid.*, p. 158.

[99] Cobbett, *Parl. Hist.*, XIV, 303-4.

[100] B.L., Add. MS. 35598, ff. 325-8: Herring to Hardwicke, 7 May 1748.

Secker and Benson, and had been empowered to ask it of the ministry 'as the *common* and most *earnest* request of the whole Bench, that the Clause may be dropt'. In his letter to Hardwicke Herring added that nothing 'would oblige me or render me more happy than getting rid of the untoward Business in the way the Bishops desire'.[101] But his attempt to reach a compromise, by instituting an inquiry into the number of clergymen who would be affected by the legislation before it was enacted, was not taken up.[102] The six absent bishops were Chandler, Hoadly, Smalbroke, Peploe, Osbaldeston and Beauclerk. The first four were absent through age or illness, and the evidence suggests that Osbaldeston and Beauclerk had already returned to their dioceses. The former did not appear in the House of Lords after 11 February, the latter not after 6 April, and proxies were not admissable when the House was in committee. On this occasion the clause was rejected by 32 against 28. But the following day, 11 May, it was restored upon the report of the bill by 37 against 32, although on this occasion Archbishop Hutton and Bishops Sherlock and Willes were also absent.[103]

3

The basis of the account of the political behaviour of the mid-eighteenth-century episcopate provided by both opposition politicians and historians cannot be denied. Opposition of bishops to the ministry, though not unknown, was rare in the middle decades of the century. But to portray them as voting fodder, kept in subservience by the prospect of translation, is misleading. In the first place, their often unquestioning support was, above all, the expression of two assumptions: that civil affairs were not primarily their concern; and that, in common with the rest of the nation's political classes, they had a duty to assist in the King's government. There is, indeed, no doubt that bonds of loyalty and gratitude to patrons influenced their political behaviour, as did sincerely held political principles. But in the 1740s and 1750s, in contrast to the 1760s, such feelings tended to reinforce, rather than weaken, the episcopate's ties to the King's ministers. In the second place, bishops were churchmen, as well as members of the House of Lords, and they thus had another, arguably stronger duty, to protect and advance the cause of religion and the church. If the ministry was generally able to rely on their support in civil affairs, in debates touching on religion they jealously maintained their independence; the episcopate was united in defending the interests of religion and the church on both occasions

---

[101] *Ibid.*, ff. 330-1: Herring to Hardwicke, 8 May 1748.
[102] *Ibid.*, ff. 325-8: Herring to Hardwicke, 7 May 1748; Nottingham U.L., PWV/120/55: Thomas Herring to William Herring, 21 May 1748.
[103] Cobbett, *Parl. Hist.*, XIV, 272; *L.J.*, XXVII, 169-146.

during the 1740s on which it believed those interests were being threatened by the action of the government. In securing the support of the bishops for the ministry the success of Townshend, Walpole and, in particular, Newcastle and Pelham in keeping religion out of parliamentary debate and in restraining the excesses of their more anti-clerical supporters was as important as years of uninterrupted Whig control of the Crown's ecclesiastical patronage.

Appendix 1
Attendance of Bishops in the House of Lords, 1741-62[1]

	1741-46	1746-51	1751-56	1756-62	1741-62
F. Cornwallis		(77)	74	72	73
R. Trevor	(75)	75	66	43	62
S. Lisle	(71)	(50)			60
N. Claggett	57				57
J. Wilcocks	64	65	32		54
R. Terrick				(54)	54
M. Hutton	(79)	51	42	(34)	52
J. Ewer				(52)	52
C. Lyttelton				(51)	51
A. Ellys			(67)	(38)	51
M. Mawson	61	63	48	33	50
J. Green				(49)	49
P. Yonge				(48)	48
Z. Pearce		(60)	45	39	46
J. Johnson			(56)	38	45
R. Reynolds	(44)				44
S. Squire				(44)	44
E. Keene			(41)	41	41
W. Ashburnham			(57)	38	39
R. Osbaldeston		(46)	46	30	39

[1] The number of days on which each bishop was present in the House is expressed as a percentage of the days on which it was possible for him to attend; that is, those days on which he was eligible to sit in the House. Bishops are listed in order of the regularity of their attendance. Figures in brackets indicate that the bishop was not a member of the House of Lords for every session in that period. The figures have been calculated from the attendance lists printed in *L.J.*, XXVI-XXX.

	1741–46	1746–51	1751–56	1756–62	1741–62
J. Gilbert	58	49	45	(22)	38
J. Thomas[2]	(31)	49	34	35	38
H. Egerton	(37)				37
E. Willes	(50)	33	29	30	37
R. Drummond		(49)	35	28	35
M. Benson	41	30	(23)		35
I. Maddox	61	29	24	(14)	34
J. Conybeare		(61)	(22)		31
R. Newcome			(93)	19	30
J. Egerton				30	30
J. Butler	33	28	(12)		29
T. Gooch	51	19	(0)		29
T. Newton				(29)	29
T. Herring	26	44	17	(0)	28
W. Warburton				(28)	28
J. Thomas[3]		(45)	15	26	27
E. Cresset		(38)	(19)		27
T. Hayter		(49)	28	(15)	25
J. Potter	23	(27)			23
R. Smalbroke	32	12			23
T. Secker	22	13	17	32	22
J. Wynne	(15)				15
T. Sherlock	39	16	.7	(0)	14
G. Lavington		(21)	14	(8)	14
J. Hume				13	13
G. Fleming	12	(0)			10
J. Beauclerk	(28)	14	8	6	9
R. Butts	5	0			4
E. Chandler	6	(.3)			4
R. Clavering	4	(0)			3
S. Peploe	4	0	(0)		2
E. Gibson	1	(2)			1
L. Blackburne	(.7)				.7
B. Hoadly	1	0	0	(0)	.1
J. Hough	(0)				0
S. Weston	(0)				0

[2] Bishop of Lincoln and Salisbury.
[3] Bishop of Peterborough, Salisbury and Winchester.

Appendix 2

Behaviour of Bishops in the House of Lords: The Evidence of Parliamentary Lists[1]

	1	2	3	4	5	6	7	8	9	10	11	12	13	14	15	16	17	18	19	20	21	22	23	24	25	26	27	28	29	30	31	32	33	34	35
W. Ashburnham	–	–	–	–	–	–	–	–	–	–	–	–	–	–	–	–	–	P	P	(P)	–	–	P	P	P	P	P	P	(P)	P(	P(	–	P	(P)	P
J. Beauclerk	–	–	–	–	–	–	–	–	–	–	–	–	–	–	–	–	–	P	P	(P)	–	–	P	P	CQ	P	P	–	(P)	P	–	(P)	P	P	P
M. Benson	PD?/C	C	C	C	–	–	–	–	–	P	C	–	–	–	–	–	–	–	–	–	–	–	–	–	–	–	–	–	–	–	–	–	–	–	–
L. Blackburne	P	P	P	–	–	–	–	–	A	–	C	–	–	–	–	–	–	–	–	–	–	–	–	–	–	–	–	–	–	–	–	–	–	–	–
J. Butler	P	–	–	–	–	–	–	–	–	–	–	–	–	–	–	–	–	–	–	–	–	–	–	–	–	–	–	–	–	–	–	–	–	–	–
R. Butts	P	P	P	C	C	–	–	–	Ap	–	–	–	P	–	–	–	–	–	–	–	–	–	–	–	–	–	–	–	–	–	–	–	–	–	–
E. Chandler	P	P	P	C	C	–	–	–	–	–	–	–	–	–	–	–	–	–	–	–	–	–	–	–	–	–	–	–	–	–	–	–	–	–	–
N. Claggett	PD?	–	–	–	–	–	–	–	–	–	–	–	–	–	–	–	–	P	P	P	–	–	P	P	P	P	P	P	P	P	–	P	P	P	P
R. Clavering	–	–	–	–	–	–	–	–	–	–	–	–	–	–	–	–	–	P	(P)	P	–	–	P	(P)	P	P	P	P	P	(P)	P(	–	P	P	P
J. Conybeare	–	–	–	–	–	–	–	A	–	C	–	–	P	–	–	–	–	P	(P)	P	–	–	P	P	P	P	P	P	P	P	–	P	P	P	–
F. Cornwallis	D?/C	C	C	C	–	–	–	–	–	–	–	–	–	–	–	–	–	–	–	–	–	–	C	P	P	P	P	P	(P)	P	–	P	P	P	P
E. Cresset	–	–	–	–	–	–	–	–	–	–	C	–	–	–	–	–	–	–	P	P	–	–	C	P	P	P	P	P	P	P	–	P	P	P	P
R. Drummond	–	–	–	–	–	–	–	–	–	–	–	–	–	–	–	–	–	–	–	–	–	–	C	P	P	P	P	P	P	P	–	P	P	P	–
H. Egerton	P	P	P	C	–	–	–	–	Ap	C	–	–	–	–	–	C	–	P	P	P	–	–	P	P	A	C	C	C	(P)	(P)	P	P	(P)	(P)	P
J. Egerton	P	P	P	C	–	–	–	–	–	P	C	–	–	–	–	–	–	P	(P)	P	–	–	P	P	C	C	C	C	(P)	(P)	P	P	P	P	P
A. Ellys	–	–	–	–	–	–	–	–	A	–	C	–	–	–	–	C	–	P	P	P	–	–	P	P	A	C	C	C	–	(P)	(P)	(P)	–	–	–
J. Ewer	–	–	–	–	–	–	–	–	–	–	–	–	–	–	–	–	–	–	–	–	–	–	–	P	P	P	P	P	P	P	P	(P)	(P)	(P)	P
G. Fleming	P	P	P	–	–	–	–	–	–	–	–	–	–	–	–	–	–	P	P	P	–	–	P	P	P	P	P	P	P	P	P	–	P	P	P
E. Gibson	P	P	P	C	–	–	–	Ap	–	C	–	–	–	–	–	–	–	–	–	–	–	–	–	–	–	–	–	–	–	–	–	–	–	–	–
J. Gilbert	P	P	P	C	–	–	–	–	P	C	–	–	–	–	–	–	–	P	P	P	–	–	P	P	P	P	P	P	P	P	–	P	P	P	P
T. Gooch	P	P	P	C	–	–	–	–	A	C	–	–	–	–	–	–	–	–	–	–	–	–	–	–	–	–	–	–	–	–	–	–	–	–	–
J. Green	–	–	–	–	–	–	–	–	–	–	–	–	–	–	–	–	–	–	–	–	–	–	–	–	A	C	C	C	–	–	–	–	–	–	–
T. Hayter	P	P	P	–	–	–	–	–	–	P	C	–	–	–	C	–	P	P	P	–	–	C	C	P	P	P	P	P	(P)	(P)	–	P	(P)	P	P
T. Herring	P	P	P	–	–	–	–	–	A	–	C	–	–	–	–	–	P	(P)	(P)	P	–	–	C	P	P	P	P	P	–	(P)	–	(P)	P	P	P
B. Hoadly	P	–	–	–	–	–	–	–	–	–	–	–	–	–	–	–	–	–	P	–	–	–	–	P	–	–	–	–	(P)	(P)	(P)	(P)	P	P	P
J. Hough	–	–	–	–	–	–	–	–	–	–	–	–	–	–	–	–	–	–	–	–	–	–	P	P	P	P	P	P	P	P	P	P	P	P	P
J. Hume	–	–	–	–	–	–	–	–	–	–	–	–	–	–	–	–	–	P	P	–	–	–	C	C	P	–	P	–	–	–	–	–	C	–	–
M. Hutton	–	–	–	–	–	–	P	C	–	P	C	–	–	–	–	–	–	–	–	–	–	–	–	–	–	–	–	–	–	–	–	–	–	–	–

[1] All known division and management lists for this period have been used in the compilation of this table. See *A Register of Parliamentary Lists 1660–1761*, ed. D. Hayton and C. Jones (Leicester, 1979). I am grateful to Clyve Jones for allowing me to use his annotated copy of the *Register*.

	1	2	3	4	5	6	7	8	9	10	11	12	13	14	15	16	17	18	19	20	21	22	23	24	25	26	27	28	29	30	31	32	33	34	35
J. Johnson	—	—	—	—	—	—	—	—	—	—	—	—	—	—	—	—	—	P	P	P	—	—	P	P	P	P	P	P	PQ	—	—	P	P	P	P
E. Keene	—	—	—	—	—	—	—	—	A?	P	C	—	—	—	—	—	—	P	P	P	—	—	QC	P	A	P	P	P	P	(P)	—	P	P	P	P
G. Lavington	—	—	—	—	—	—	—	—	A	—	C	—	—	—	—	—	—	P	(P)	(P)	—	—	P	(P)	A	P	P	P	P	(P)	(P)	(P)	—	(P)	—
S. Lisle	—	—	—	—	—	—	—	—	—	—	—	—	—	—	—	—	—	—	—	—	—	—	—	—	—	—	—	—	—	—	—	—	—	—	—
C. Lyttelton	—	P	P	C	C	C	—	—	—	—	C	—	—	—	—	C	C	—	(P)	(P)	—	—	C	(P)	CQ	C	C	—	(P)	—	—	(P)	—	(P)	—
I. Maddox	P	P	P	C	C	—	—	—	—	P	C	—	—	—	—	C	C	P	P	P	—	—	C	(P)	A	P	C	—	P	P	—	P	—	P	—
M. Mawson	P	P	P	C	C	—	—	—	—	P	C	—	—	—	—	C	C	—	—	—	—	—	—	—	—	—	—	—	—	—	—	—	—	—	—
R. Newcome	—	—	—	—	—	—	—	—	—	—	—	—	—	—	—	—	—	—	—	—	—	—	—	—	—	—	—	—	—	—	—	—	—	—	—
T. Newton	—	—	—	—	—	—	—	—	A	A	C	—	—	—	—	—	—	—	(P)	—	—	—	—	(P)	A	—	P	P	P	(P)	—	(P)	P	(P)	—
R. Osbaldeston	—	—	—	—	—	—	—	—	A	P	C	—	—	—	—	—	—	—	(P)	(P)	—	—	QC	(P)	P	P	—	P	(P)	(P)	—	P	P	(P)	P
Z. Pearce	PD	—	—	—	—	—	—	—	—	—	—	—	—	—	—	—	—	P	P	P	—	—	QC	P	A	P	P	—	P	P	—	P	P	P	P
S. Peploe	P	P	—	C	—	—	—	—	—	—	C	—	—	—	—	—	—	—	—	—	—	—	—	—	—	—	—	—	—	—	—	—	—	—	—
J. Potter	C	C	P	—	—	—	—	—	—	—	—	—	—	—	—	—	—	—	—	—	—	—	—	—	—	—	—	—	—	—	—	—	—	—	—
R. Reynolds	PD?	P	P	C	C	—	—	—	A	—	C	—	—	—	—	—	—	P	(P)	(P)	—	—	P	(P)	—	P	P	P	P	(P)	—	(P)	—	P	P
T. Secker	P	P	P	C	C	—	—	—	Ap	—	C	—	P	—	—	—	—	P	P	P	—	—	P	—	—	P	P	P	P	P	—	P	P	P	P
T. Sherlock	C	C	—	C	—	—	—	—	A	—	—	—	—	—	—	—	—	P	—	—	—	—	—	—	CQ	—	—	—	—	—	—	—	—	—	—
R. Smalbroke	C	—	—	—	—	—	—	—	—	—	—	—	—	—	—	—	—	—	—	—	—	—	—	—	—	—	—	—	—	—	—	—	—	—	—
S. Squire	—	—	—	—	—	—	—	—	—	—	—	—	—	—	—	—	—	—	—	—	—	—	—	—	—	—	—	—	—	—	—	—	—	—	—
R. Terrick	—	—	—	—	—	—	—	—	A	P	C	—	—	—	—	—	—	P	P	P*	—	—	C	P	P	P	P	P	P	P	—	P	P	P	P
J. Thomas[2]	—	—	—	—	—	—	—	—	—	P	C	—	—	—	—	—	—	P	P	P	—	—	C	P	P	P	P	P	P	P	—	P	P	P	P
J. Thomas[3]	—	—	—	—	—	—	—	—	—	P	C	—	—	—	—	—	—	P	P	P	—	—	C	P	P	P	P	P	P	P	—	P	P	P	P
R. Trevor	—	—	—	—	—	—	—	—	—	P	C	—	—	—	—	—	—	—	—	—	—	—	—	—	P	P	—	P	P	(P)	—	P	P	P	—
W. Warburton	—	—	—	—	—	—	—	—	—	—	—	—	—	—	—	—	—	—	—	—	—	—	—	—	—	—	—	—	—	—	—	—	—	—	—
S. Weston	P	—	—	—	—	—	—	—	—	—	—	—	—	—	—	—	—	P	P	P	—	—	C	P	P	P	P	—	P	—	—	P	P	P	P
J. Wilcocks	—	P	P	C	C	—	—	—	A	P	C	—	—	—	—	—	—	P	P	(P)	—	—	C	(P)	A	P	—	—	(P)	(P)	—	—	—	—	—
E. Willes	—	—	—	—	—	—	—	—	—	—	—	—	—	—	—	—	—	P	P	P	—	—	C	(P)	A?P	A?P	P	—	(P)	(P)	—	P	P	(P)	P
J. Wynne	PD?	P	P	—	—	—	—	—	—	A	A	—	—	—	—	—	—	—	—	—	—	—	—	—	—	—	—	—	—	—	—	—	—	—	—
P. Yonge	—	—	—	—	—	—	—	—	—	—	—	—	—	—	—	—	—	P	P	—	—	—	C	—	—	P	—	—	P	P	—	P	P	P	P

[2] Bishop of Lincoln and Salisbury.

[3] Bishop of Peterborough, Salisbury and Winchester.

Sources for Appendix 2

(1) *Mid-Jan. 1742.* Forecast of support and opposition. B.L., Add. MS. 33002, ff. 400-1.
      P   = for
      C   = against
      D   = doubtful
      ?   = crossed off the list

(2) *19 Jan. 1742.* Those voting for and against a motion to appoint a date for the committee of the whole House on the state of the nation. B.L., Add. MS. 33034, f. 71.
      P   = against (i.e., supporting the ministry)
      C   = for

(3) *1 Feb. 1743.* Those voting for and against an address against the Hanoverian troops. *A List of the Members of Parliament who Voted For and Against Taking the Hanoverian Troops into British Pay* (1743).
      P   = against the address
      C   = for the address (i.e., against the ministry)

(4) *22 Feb. 1743.* Bishops voting against the second reading of the Spirituous Liquors Bill. Cobbett, *Parl. Hist.*, XII, 1300-1.
      C   = against

(5) *16 Apr. 1744.* Nine lords who voted against the reversal of judgment in the case of *Le Neve* v. *Norris.* Cambridge U.L., MS. Add. 6851, II, f. 79.
      C   = those in favour of reversal

(6) *2 May 1746.* Twenty-six lords who voted for an address against carrying on the war in Flanders. Cambridge U.L., MS. Add. 6851, II, ff. 108-9. No bishops opposed the ministry on this division.

(7) *24 May 1747.* Sixteen lords against the committal of the Heritable Jurisdictions Bill. Cambridge U.L., MS. Add. 6851, II, ff. 118-19. No bishops opposed the ministry on this division.

(8) *1747.* List of lords and commons in opposition. Bodl., MS. D.D. Dashwood D1/3/13. No bishops appear on this list.

(9) *1748.* Fifty-five lords absent (management list for the Buckingham Assizes Bill?). B.L., Add. MS. 33002, f. 411.
      A   = absent
      Ap = absent with proxy
      ?   = crossed off the list

(10) *23 Mar. 1748.* Those for and against committing the Buckingham Assizes Bill. B.L., Add. MS. 33002, ff. 411-12.
      P   = for
      C   = against
      A   = absent

(11) *10 May 1748.* Thirty-two lords who voted against the clause relating to episcopal orders during the Committee of the Whole House on the Bill for Disarming the Scottish Highlands. Cobbett, *Parl. Hist.*, XIV , 272.
      C   = against

(12) *15 Mar. 1749.* Sixteen lords who voted for the clause on the second reading of the Mutiny Bill, that no punishment shall be inflicted by a court martial relating to life or limb. Cambridge, U.L., MS. Add. 6851, II, ff. 130-1. No bishops opposed the ministry on this division.

(13) *20 Mar. 1750.* List of 28 lords who met at Newcastle House. B.L., Add. MS. 32994, f. 272.
      P   = present

(14) *10 May 1751.* Lists of minorities against the Regency Bill. H. Walpole, *Memoirs of*

George II, ed. J. Brooke (3 vols., New Haven, 1985), I, 78-9, 82.

(15) *17 Mar. '1752.* Twelve lords voting against the committal of the Forfeitures (Scotland) Bill. B.L., Add. MS. 32994, f. 295. No bishops opposed the ministry.

(16) *22 Mar. 1753.* Lords in favour of the Duke of Bedford's motion for papers relating to accusations of Jacobitism against Murray, Stone and Johnson. Walpole, *Memoirs of George II*, I, 223.

    C = for the motion (i.e., against the ministry)

(17) *3 Mar. 1754.* Lords in favour of the second reading of the Clandestine Marriages Bill. B.L., Add. MS. 35877, f. 174.

    C = for (i.e., against the ministry)

(18) *30 May 1754.* Lords summoned to the ministry's pre-sessional meeting. B.L., Add. MS. 32995, ff. 242-5.

    P = those on the list

(19) *13 Nov. 1754.* Lords summoned to the ministry's pre-sessional meeting. B.L., Add. MS. 32995, ff. 344-7.

    P = those on the list

    (P) = those on the list, but noted as being out of town

(20) *12 Nov. 1755.* Lords summoned to the ministry's pre-sessional meeting. B.L., Add. MS. 32996, ff. 275-9.

    P = those on the list

    (P) = those on the list, but noted as being out of town

    P★ = those on the list and noted as 'expected'

(21) *10 Dec. 1755.* Those voting for (i.e., against the ministry) on a motion for a vote of censure, relative to the treaties with Russia and Hesse-Cassel. H.M.C., *Hastings, MSS.*, III, 113. No bishops opposed the ministry on this division.

(22) *24 May 1756.* Those voting for the Militia Bill on its third reading and those who went away. B.L., Add. MS. 35877, f. 308.

    C = for (i.e., against the ministry)

(23) *Dec. 1756/Jan. 1757.* Analysis of the House of Lords. B.L., Add. MS. 33034, ff. 214-5.

    P = for (i.e., supporters of Newcastle)

    C = against

    Q = query (marked 'Q')

(24) *29 Nov. 1757.* Lords summoned to the ministry's pre-sessional meeting. B.L., Add. MS. 32997, ff. 300-1.

    P = those on the list

    (P) = those on the list, but noted as being out of town

(25) *9 May 1758.* Lists of lords present and absent (management list for the Habeas Corpus Bill). B.L., Add. MS. 33034, ff. 259-60, 265-6.

    P = for

    C = against

    Q = those with query by their names

    A = absent

(26) *24 May 1758.* List of lords 'for', 'against', 'absent' (management list for the Habeas Corpus Bill). B.L., Add. MS. 33034, ff. 267-9.

    P = for

    C = against

    A = absent

    ? = crossed off the list

(27) *31 May 1758.* List of lords 'for', 'against', 'doubtful', 'absent' (management list for the Habeas Corpus Bill). B.L., Add. MS. 33034, ff. 314-6.

    P = for

    C = against

(28) *2 June 1758*. List of lords for and against (management list (?) for the Habeas Corpus Bill). B.L., Add. MS. 33034, f. 317.

      P = for

      C = against

(29) *22 Nov. 1758*. Lords summoned to the ministry's pre-sessional meeting. B.L., Add. MS. 32998, ff. 187-94.

      P = those on the list

      (P) = those on the list, but noted as being out of town

      Q = those with query by their names

(30) *12 Nov. 1759*. Lords summoned to the ministry's pre-sessional meeting. B.L., Add. MS. 32998, ff. 327-34.

      P = those on the list

      (P) = those on the list, but noted as being out of town

(31) *15 May 1760*. Lords voting against the committal of the Commons Qualification Bill. B.L., Add. MS. 33034, f. 373. No bishops opposed the ministry on this division.

(32) *17 Nov. 1760*. Lords summoned to the ministry's pre-sessional meeting. B.L., Add. MS. 32999, ff. 80-7.

      P = those on the list

      (P) = those on the list, but noted as being out of town

(33) *17 Nov. 1760*. List of 81 lords who attended the ministry's pre-sessional meeting. B.L., Add. MS. 32999, ff. 90-1.

      P = present

(34) *5 Nov. 1761*. Lords summoned to the ministry's pre-sessional meeting. B.L., Add. MS. 32999, ff. 341-8.

      P = those on the list

      (P) = those on the list, but noted as being out of town

(35) *5 Feb. 1762*. Those voting for and against a resolution against carrying on the war in Germany. B.L., Add. MS. 33035, ff. 69-70.

      P = against (i.e. for the ministry)

Chapter 7

The House of Lords in the 1760s

Michael W. McCahill

1

Normally the eighteenth-century House of Lords was a bulwark of the Crown. At Westminster and in the country peers gave successive governments support, a support which, by strengthening those administrations, preserved the vitality of a constitution that accorded their lordships so great a measure of dignity. The nobility's opposition to the Americans' quest for independence, to the Whigs' drive to subordinate George III and to the growth of popular radicalism reinforced this allegiance. So too did their pursuit of offices or the ornaments of rank. For the most part these potentates left the detail of parliamentary business to their leaders; they attended the House of Lords only at major political contests or when business of personal or local interest came before the chamber. Usually they resolved grievances quietly with the appropriate minister or through agents in the House of Commons. Peers seemed determined to avoid disruptions in their own House.[1]

The regularity of its support led observers to dismiss the Lords as unimportant. 'Our miserable house', Chesterfield called it. According to Henry Fox it was the Commons which prevented the Crown from subverting the privileges of Parliament. Fifty years later, as he looked for support in the final campaign against Addington, Lord Melville rejected the notion that the Lords could effectively attack a government that continued to enjoy the King's support. Horace Walpole blamed the Lords' quiescence on the members themselves – 'a tame, subservient, incapable set of men, governed entirely by the Duke of Newcastle, and the two lawyers, Hardwicke and Mansfield.'[2] Later London radicals and the Rockingham Whigs assigned responsibility more narrowly to the

---

[1] M. McCahill, *Order and Equipoise. The Peerage and the House of Lords 1783-1806* (1978), *passim*.

[2] G. Harris, *The Life of Lord Chancellor Hardwicke* (3 vols., 1847), III, 52; J. Clark, *The Dynamics of Change. The Crisis of the 1750s and the English Party Systems* (Cambridge, 1982), p. 449; P.R.O., 30/58/5 (Dacres Adam MSS.): Melville to A. Hope, 5 Apr. 1804; A. Turberville, *The House of Lords in the XVIIIth Century* (Oxford, 1927), p. 300.

Scots, the bishops and the courtiers, a group whom David Large has transformed into 'the party of the Crown'. Large's work provided both Namierites and their opponents with a legitimate reason for ignoring the House of Lords. The upper chamber lacked the Commons' political weight because a consistent majority of its members, according to John Brooke, were mere 'creatures of the Crown', unwilling and unable to challenge the King or his ministers. This invariable servility ensured that the House of Lords could not undertake the sort of independent, critical activity that merited serious study.[3] Thus, the upper House has remained largely unexamined until quite recently.

These traditional views are faulty in two respects. The House of Lords did not invariably subordinate itself to the Crown, nor were its members naturally servile. Strong ministers such as Walpole, Henry Pelham, Lord North or the younger Pitt enjoyed large majorities in both chambers, in part because they attended so effectively to the needs of their supporters. Though these politicians insured stability at Westminster for much of the eighteenth century, there were interludes of instability – 1710-14, 1782-4, 1801-7 and, most importantly, during the 1760s. An examination of the House of Lords during this decade reveals not only that it too was thrown into a tumult by forces which disrupted the larger political world; in the midst of this disruption the House undertook action against the stated wishes of the Crown.

2

During the 1760s neither the House of Lords nor the 'party of the Crown' conformed to their prescribed patterns. Analysis of proxy lists and 22 divisions indicates that before 1768 a high proportion of peers opposed the King's government. The table below demonstrates that between 1762 and May 1765 the largest number of peers opposed the Crown at least once, and in 1766 and 1767 more than half the sitting members voted against the administrations of Rockingham or Grafton. One-third of those who broke with ministers between 1762 and 1767 were members of 'the party of the Crown'. It was not until the last two years of the decade that ministers began to impose more traditional standards of loyalty on their normal allies in the upper House.

[3] Cobbett, *Parl. Hist.*, XXIV, 210-1; D. Large, 'The Decline of the "Party of the Crown" and the Rise of Parties in the House of Lords, 1783-1837', *E.H.R.*, LXXVIII (1963), 669-95; J. Brooke, *King George III* (New York, 1972), p. 161; J. Cannon, *Aristocratic Century. The Peerage of Eighteenth-Century England* (Cambridge, 1984), pp. 94-104.

Voting Behaviour of Members of the House of Lords, 1762-1770[4]

	1762-May 1765	Dec 1765-June 1767	1768-1770
Government	69 (29.2%)	78 (35.9%)	106 (46.9%)
Opposition	106 (44.9%)	121 (55.8%)	70 (31.0%)
Doubtful	61 (25.8%)	18 (8.3%)	50 (22.1%)

However, to establish the Lords' independence on a firm basis, it is necessary to distinguish between various types of opposition. For example, during the decade 45 peers opposed only the Poor Law, introduced by a private member in 1765, and/or the repeal of the Stamp Act the next year. Each of these measures was objectionable to a number of peers, but a large portion of this group, attached to Lord Bute, voted against the proposals as a means of expressing their distaste for the incumbent ministers and their loyalty to the King. By March 1765 George III had resolved to rid himself of George Grenville and during the first weeks of February 1766 the King was widely assumed to oppose repeal. As we shall see there is no evidence to show that George plotted with peers to harass Grenville in the upper House, and Bute's allies continued to oppose repeal of the Stamp Act even after the monarch had publicly proclaimed his support for this step. Still, these peers could claim that in venturing into opposition they were acting according to the interests and needs of their sovereign. Rather than confirming the independence of their order, these limited forays into opposition would, for most historians, highlight their servility.

Another 15 were tentative oppositionists who voted only once against the stated position of ministers in whom the King clearly had confidence. Five supported the Duke of Bedford's motion in 1762 for an end to the war in Germany, a motion Bute took credit for defeating; another four in 1763 responded to the pressures of their neighbours and resisted an attempt to raise revenue by placing an excise on cider, thus joining the clamour that helped convince Bute that the time had come to retire. The same year three others refused to accept the ministerial argument that libel was sufficient cause to deprive John Wilkes of parliamentary immunity. In 1767 the Duke of Kingston and Lord Vernon joined in the first of those campaigns that threatened by late May to drive the Chatham administration from office. Eight of these peers also joined the Butes in harassing ministers in 1765 or 1766.

The true opposition group numbered about 120 peers. Ninety-seven opposed a series of administrations over the course of the decade. Most

---

[4] Those classified as government voted with administration at each division; the opposition category includes those who voted against the Crown in the specific period; doubtful contains those who failed to participate in divisions.

of these lords were followers of Newcastle or Rockingham, Grenville or the Duke of Bedford. Another 19 peers voted at least twice against the policies of Bute, the Duke of Grafton or Lord North while each enjoyed the support of George III. Opponents of the latter minister included nine men who entered the House after 1768 and during the 1770s actively supported Rockingham or Chatham in opposition.

Thus a majority of the active members of the House of Lords in the 1760s were oppositionists in the truest sense – they repeatedly resisted policies of ministers in whom George III had confidence. Among peers who voted more than twice during the 1760s, only 28 gave those votes consistently to the King's ministers; another 24 gave proxies or cast their one or two recorded votes for government. Even if we include Bute's associates as part of the Crown's phalanx, the latter includes only 97 peers (42.5 per cent of those who left any substantial evidence of political affiliation), a quarter of whom rarely participated in parliamentary affairs. Fifteen (6.5 per cent) voted against one measure proposed by a minister enjoying royal support. One hundred and sixteen (50.8 per cent) repeatedly opposed the Crown and its chosen politicians.

Personalities, competing views of politics and divergent war strategies tore apart the coalition that had achieved such success in the war against France. George III, the new, inexperienced monarch, guided by his equally raw and prejudiced mentor, the Earl of Bute, designed to break the political monopoly of Newcastle, the First Lord of the Treasury and leader of the 'Old Whig' corps that had dominated Westminster since the age of Walpole. Nor was William Pitt, the ministry's other principal pillar, any more congenial: George dismissed him as a 'snake in the grass' and objected to his aggressive war policy. For his part Pitt disdained his Whig colleagues and, after falling to convince them to undertake hostilities against Spain, he resigned in April 1761. Newcastle's resentment over Bute's influence with the King and the cabinet's refusal to continue subsidies to German allies led to his withdrawal in May 1762. Five months later George III dismissed Devonshire, his Lord Chamberlain, when the duke refused to attend a cabinet summoned to review the proposed peace with France. Newcastle called upon the 'Old Corps' to resign their posts in protest and join him in opposing Bute. The few Whig noblemen who sacrificed their jobs for principle and friendship formed the nucleus of the new opposition in the House of Lords.

Divisions within the government revealed themselves in the House on 5 February 1762 when the Lords rejected by 105 to 16 a resolution calling for an end to the war in Germany. The contest was remarkable because most of those in the minority were government supporters. The motion's author, the Duke of Bedford, shortly left for Paris to negotiate a peace treaty, and Bute's interventions were insufficient to prevent the defection of a number of friends and courtiers – Talbot, the Lord

Steward, Gower, the Master of the Great Wardrobe, a Scottish representative peer and two Lords of the Bedchamber. Despite these and other losses Bute boasted that the contest's outcome resulted from tactics he devised, a claim that only strained his already bad relations with Newcastle.[5] This seemingly minor skirmish is symptomatic of the problems ministers encountered in the House of Lords between 1762 and 1766; difficulties there were due as much to the disquiet of habitual supporters as to the exertions of a formed opposition.

For systematic opposition developed slowly in the House of Lords. Political observers expected Newcastle to mount a campaign there after he resigned, and Bute announced in November that the Lords would be the 'principal scene of action' when the peace preliminaries came before Parliament. In fact, the House adopted the preliminaries without a division, and Rigby told his master, Bedford, in January 1763 that 'I never saw the Parliament look so tame after the Christmas recess since I have been a Member as the present one does. This opposition has not a grain of Spirit to support Itself. Numbers and Abilities they are totally devoid of'.[6] Bute's political opponents suffered from a lack of unity and from poor organization. Pitt remained aloof from the 'Old Corps' whose leaders could neither gauge their strength accurately nor adjust to the practice of opposition which was, Hardwicke confessed, 'a kind of new trade to learn at a late hour'.[7]

Thus Bute's only crisis in the House of Lords came as a result of the government's own mismanagement. In February 1763 Sir Francis Dashwood, Chancellor of the Exchequer, introduced a revenue bill which placed duties on imported wine and an excise on cider. The last charge awakened old alarms about intrusive government and mobilized Whigs who were already disturbed by Bute's supposed onslaughts on established constitutional practices. Neither Dashwood in the Commons nor Bute in the Lords presented the government's case well, and the measure provoked an outcry in the cider producing areas of the west and southwest and in London where Pitt launched a press campaign against the insidious extension of the excise. In the Lords Pitt's canvass and the opposition of eight or nine 'cider lords' enabled Rockingham and other young Whigs to drag the 'Old Corps' into open opposition. Despite the Duke of Cumberland's scepticism and the indifference of some followers, 41 peers voted against the Cider Bill on 28 March to

---

[5] B.L., Add. MS. 33035, f. 75; *ibid.*, 32934, ff. 394-5. For a more generous assessment of Bute's role see K.W. Schweizer, 'The Bedford Motion and the House of Lords Debate 5 February 1762', *Parliamentary History*, V (1986), 107-11.

[6] H.M.C., *Lonsdale MSS.*, p. 131; Bedford Estates Office, Bedford MSS., 48, f. 30: Rigby to Bedford, 20 Jan. 1763.

[7] Sir Lewis Namier, *England in the Age of the American Revolution* (2nd edn., 1961), pp. 362-3; B.L., Add. MS. 32948, ff. 1-2.

form the largest minority in the House of Lords in almost 20 years.[8]

The campaign heartened the 'Old Corps' leadership and convinced them of the efficacy of opposition. They had recruited about 20 peers against the Cider Bill with little advance warning. Nine bishops, most connected to Newcastle, also voted against the measure. The Whigs' refusal to protest the bill's passage angered Pitt's followers, but the latter had no other possible allies. Thus, even the tremulous Hardwicke looked forward to another session and the rout of Lord Bute.[9] In fact, the minister resigned within a week of the bill's passage.

Both Horace Walpole and Newcastle are excessive in attributing Bute's withdrawal to the Lords' strong resistance to the Cider Bill.[10] The minister, who disliked political intrigue and was in bad health, had begun to plan his departure a month earlier. Nor is there any evidence that Bute was intimidated by his Whig opponents. However, the debate on 30 March highlighted the alienation of some of his own friends. Not only did many Tories oppose the bill; even colleagues in government remained silent that day. 'The ground I tread upon', he told a friend, 'is so hollow, that I am afraid, not only of falling myself, but of involving my royal master in my ruin. It is time for me to retire'.[11]

Neither the battle over the Cider Bill nor Bute's resignation seriously jeopardized the government's control of the House of Lords. Though the cider tax spawned an intense local opposition that was supported by at least ten peers, most of these men adhered to Grenville. In 1764 the 'Old Corps' leaders refused an invitation to coalesce with the measure's Tory opponents. Nor was Pitt an easy partner; Whig lords resented his high-handedness. In any case his patriotism precluded his association with any party, particularly so aristocratic a group as the 'Old Corps'. Thus, in November 1763 Lord Holland reported that except on the Wilkes issue Pitt was more violent against the opposition than against ministers.[12]

---

[8] For Pitt see P. Lawson, *George Grenville* (Oxford, 1984), pp. 147-9 and W. Lowe, 'Politics in the House of Lords, 1760-1775' (Emory, Ph.D., 1975), pp. 444-5, 451; B.L., Add. MS. 32947, ff. 313, 317-20, 327.

[9] Bishops voting against the cider tax included Chichester, Ely, Hereford, Lincoln, Lichfield, Norwich, Oxford, St. Asaph and Worcester (Cobbett, *Parl. Hist.*, XV, 1316). Hereford was pressured by local considerations against the bill (*Gentleman's Magazine*, XXXIII [1763], 255). The other eight were allies of Newcastle. Lowe, 'Politics in the House of Lords', pp. 450-1; B.L., Add. MS. 35422, ff. 230-1.

[10] *The Correspondence of William Pitt, Earl of Chatham*, ed. W. Taylor and J. Pringle (4 vols., 1838-40), II, 220-2; H. Walpole, *Memoirs of the Reign of King George III*, ed. G. Barker (4 vols., 1894), II, 201.

[11] *Letters to Henry Fox, Lord Holland*, ed. Earl of Ilchester (1915), p. 172; B.L., Add. MS. 51379, ff. 143-4; Lowe, 'Politics in the House of Lords', p. 454.

[12] For the continuing opposition to the cider tax see P. Woodland, 'Extra-Parliamentary Political Organization in the Making: Benjamin Heath and the Opposition to the 1763 Cider Excise', *Parliamentary History*, IV (1985), 115-36. J. Brewer, *Party Ideology and Popular Politics at the Accession of George III*, (Cambridge, 1976), p. 85; B.L., Add. MS. 32952, ff. 235-6; *ibid.*, 41416, ff. 118-9.

The Wilkes affair further strengthened the government's hold over the House of Lords. Under the patronage of Earl Temple, Grenville's brother, John Wilkes had in the *North Briton* campaigned on behalf of William Pitt while vilifying Bute. In the controversial No. 45 he not only criticized the peace treaty but may have libelled the King and his ministers. On these grounds Grenville and his colleagues moved by general warrant to arrest its printers who identified Wilkes as the author. Wilkes, a member of the House of Commons, was then arrested under the same warrant for seditious libel.

While the Commons pressed Grenville on the issue of general warrants and the legality of arresting a sitting M.P., his government encountered no problems during the discussions of the case in the upper House. In part ministers' success was the result of effective organization and tactical planning. They secured a good attendance for the opening of Parliament, and Sandwich's plan to condemn Wilkes as the author of the *Essay on Woman* left little room for his supporters. Not only were they surprised by this disingenuous ploy; the *Essay*'s notes purportedly authored by Warburton, Bishop of Gloucester, constituted a libel against a member of the House. Thus, Grafton disavowed libellers, and Temple's friend, Lord Lyttleton, denounced the notion that parliamentary privilege protected criminals; if it did, 'sedition would be spread from one end of the Kingdom to another'. But the main source of government's strength was the widespread noble hostility to Wilkes himself. Like Lord Ilchester, peers condemned the popular radical's 'insolence and impudence'. In the Commons 40 Tories opposed the legality of general warrants, but in the House of Lords none was prepared to deny that *North Briton* No. 45 was a libel which deprived its author of the privilege of Parliament, nor were there many independents ready to defend Wilkes.[13] While the main body of 'Old Corps' peers lamented Wilkes' arrest and the use of general warrants, they were unable to carry many of their colleagues. Hardwicke, the former Lord Chancellor, rejected the argument that parliamentay privilege protected Wilkes from prosecution, and most of Newcastle's bishops deserted their patron. Though opposed to a policy which had driven the King's best servants from his councils, Archbishop Drummond of York could not 'in this infamous affair of Mr. Wilks . . . concur in obstructing or parying the blow he so justly deserves. I neither think it for the Honor of any person, nor the good of the Cause of the Whigs to espouse such a Man and put ourselves so totally in the wrong in the eyes of the World'.[14]

---

[13] *The Yale Edition of Horace Walpole's Correspondence*, ed. W.S. Lewis, *et al.* (48 vols., New Haven, 1937-83), XXXVIII, 229-30; B.L., Add. MS. 51386, ff. 160-1, 172-4; Cobbett, *Parl. Hist.*, XV, 1365-71; B.L. Add, MS. 51421, f. 44; *ibid.*, 57810, ff. 60-1; Linda Colley, *In Defiance of Oligarchy. The Tory Party 1714-60* (Cambridge, 1985), p. 288.

[14] Harris, *Hardwicke*, III, 384-5; B.L., Add. MS. 32952, ff. 119-21, 370-1.

Thus in the one vote on the case in the Lords government carried its motion 114 to 35.

The administration position seemed equally strong at the outset of the 1765 session. Sandwich remarked in March that the 'opposition are so low that it scarcely deserves the name of a party'.[15] Yet during the session's final two months ministers endured a series of defeats and humiliations there that reflected their tenuous hold on the loyalties of men who had been government's supporters.

Trouble arose first from bishops who objected to the minor but controversial Ecclesiastical Estates Bill. The object of the measure was to facilitate the exchange of lands, as a result of which churches and colleges might trade remote or inconvenient portions of their domains for more suitable or conveniently located parcels. Critics of this apparently useful bill feared it would encourage the alienation of church lands; indeed, Bishop Yonge of Norwich told Newcastle that prelates had never had 'a greater reason to regret the Loss of your Grace's influence than at present'. Without a leading ministerial ally to abort the offensive measure, the episcopal bench had to act directly. Twenty-one bishops came to the House to oppose the bill, which was defeated 56 to 23. Ministers themselves were divided on the measure: Bedford and Suffolk supported its passage, but the Secretaries of State sided with the prelates. According to Yonge there was 'little appearance of party in the division; the much the greater part of Courtiers went below the Bar with the Duke of Bedford'.[16]

The bishops' defeat of the Ecclesiastical Estates Bill may have embarrassed those few ministers who worked for its passage; the growing discontent of Bute and his friends jeopardized the government's control of the House of Lords. From the ministry's outset Grenville and his colleagues were at pains to cut the King off from his old favourite. They deemed the separation as essential to their own survival and were thus alarmed by any sign of Bute's activity. When Lords Lichfield and Pomfret arrived drunk to disrupt Lord Halifax's pre-sessional meeting, Grenville remarked that 'this step appeared singular from two intimate friends of Lord Bute'. Several days later he berated the King about 'lukewarm friends . . . who profess'd attachment to his Majesty but at the same time thought themselves at liberty to oppose his measures and ministers'. The King listened to this lecture, Grenville reported, 'with a good deal of confusion and embarrassment'.[17]

---

[15] H.M.C., *Denbigh MSS.*, p. 194.
[16] B.L., Add. MS. 32966, ff. 71-2, 105.
[17] Henry E. Huntington Library, San Marino, California, (Stowe MSS.), Grenville Letterbook, St. 7(i): Grenville to Oxford, 1 Sept. 1763; *The Grenville Papers: Being the Correspondence of Richard Grenville, Earl Temple, K.G., and the Right Honourable George Grenville, Their Friends and Contemporaries*, ed. W. Smith (4 vols., 1852-3), III, 114-6.

The Lords' rough treatment of Thomas Gilbert's Poor Bill justified Grenville's apprehensions. After passing the Commons easily this private member's bill encountered widespread opposition in the upper House, where peers objected to the additional power it seemed to confer on government and to the introduction of the practice of electing poor commissioners. Inevitably Whig leaders, who shared some of these misgivings, took advantage of the storm the bill provoked. Rockingham and his friends rallied the 'Old Corps' against a measure warmly advocated by Bedford and his allies. Though the latter concerted with Grenville to secure support in the House, they could not beat back the measure's opponents. After carrying the second reading by three votes, Bedford and his friends lost a division in committee and only prevented outright defeat in the full House by a vote of 66 to 59.[18] Further consideration was postponed two weeks after which the bill was dropped.

The successful opposition to the Poor Bill attracted a diverse support. In all 63 peers voted against it in the full House: 23 were Whigs, three were Pittites. Twelve unattached peers joined to resist a measure that engendered considerable opposition from country gentlemen. But opposition was successful because 17 lords attached to the Court supported it on this occasion.[19] For this reason Horace Walpole proclaimed that 'all the world' regarded the campaign against the Poor Bill 'as a pitched battle between Lord Bute and Lord Holland on the one hand, and the Bedfords and Grenville on the other'.[20]

Nor did the episode mark the end of minister's problems in the upper chamber. On 29 April 1765 Bute and his followers joined the Whigs in voting against a government motion to postpone a bill allowing suits against peers and M.P.s. Ministers resisted this outgrowth of the Wilkes crusade but only carried the postponement 61 to 53. Bute himself voted

---

[18] B.L., Add. MS. 32966, ff. 71-2, 91-2; Sheffield City Library, Wentworth Woodhouse MSS. [hereafter cited as W.W.M.], (Rockingham Papers) R I-447: Newcastle to Rockingham, 26 Mar. 1765.

[19] Whigs (23): Abergavenny, Asburnham, Bessborough, Breadalbane, Cornwallis, Dartmouth, Grantham, Hardwicke, Monson, Newcastle, Portland, Rockingham, Scarbrough, Sondes, Spencer, Strafford, Walpole, Winchelsea and the Bishops of Chichester, Lichfield, Lincoln, Norwich and Worcester. Pittites (3): Bolton, Lyttleton and Temple. Independents (12): Courtenay, Dudley and Ward, Folkestone, Fortescue, Grosvenor, Milton, Poulett, Ravensworth, Sandys, Say and Sele, Shaftesbury and Wentworth. Court (17): Abercorn, Boston, Darlington, Denbigh, Egmont, Falmouth, Lichfield, Macclesfield, Montagu, Morton, Oxford, Peterborough, Pomfret, Roxburghe, Willoughby de Broke and the Bishops of Rochester and St. David's. Opposition included two supporters of Bedford (Trevor and Vere), Aylesbury, a Grenvillite, the Granby contingent including the Duke of Rutland and the Bishop of Llandaff, and that of Lord Holland: Holland, Ilchester and Leigh. Sheffield City Lib., W.W.M., R. 53-22; B.L., Add. MS. 32966, ff. 156-9.

[20] *Walpole Correspondence*, XXXVIII, 528-9.

in the minority, and ten days later his allies joined the Whigs to defeat the Marriage Bill, another of the measures pushed by Bedford.[21]

The motives which provoked Bute's opposition remain unclear. He and his friends must have resented Grenville's suspicion and Bedford's hostility; the measures they attacked were those the duke and his friends supported. But ministers were convinced that these peers acted in concert with the King who was by early April trying to find a more congenial government. The two did meet periodically, and George III was sufficiently aware of Bute's activities to challenge Sandwich's inclusion of the favourite on the list of the Poor Bill's opponents since Bute, his sovereign noted, did 'not attend the Bill'. For his part Bute certainly knew that the King was searching for another ministry, for George commissioned Lord Northumberland to serve as an emissary to Grenville's potential successors. Yet a student of the period rejects the notion there was a conspiracy between the two.[22] Bute himself told a friend that 'he had never advised a measure or recommended a person' since he resigned, and the King's reliance on his uncle, the Whig Duke of Cumberland, indicates he was in the process of jettisoning his old friend.[23] At most Bute and his friends knew that George shared their aversion to Grenville, but this knowledge was probably sufficient to spark their open hostility in the House of Lords. However much they may have disliked the Poor Bill, it is unlikely that these stalwarts of the Crown would have attacked it if Grenville had basked in royal favour.

The administration exacerbated a bad situation in the House of Lords by its inept handling of George III's Regency Bill. The official opposition did little to obstruct legislation necessitated by the King's recent illness. As the author of a similar bill in 1751, Newcastle could not oppose this one. Thus when the Pittite peers led by Lord Temple moved its rejection, 'Old Corps' peers abstained, went away or voted for the measure, thereby provoking Temple's petulant withdrawal. The next day the group did support an unsuccessful address to the King requesting that he name a regent, but most then left the House, many for the Newmarket races.[24]

[21] *The Correspondence of King George the Third from 1760 to December 1783 . . .*, ed. Sir John Fortescue (6 vols., 1927-8), I, 78-9; Walpole, *Memoirs*, II, 78-9; B.L., Add. MS. 32966, ff. 363-4.

[22] *Grenville Papers*, III, 125; D. Jarrett, 'The Regency Crisis of 1765', *E.H.R.*, LXXXV (1970), 282-316; but cf. J. Brooke, *King George III* (1972), pp. 110-14.

[23] *The Jenkinson Papers, 1760-66*, ed. N. Jucker (1949), p. 397.

[24] *Walpole Correspondence*, XXXVIII, 542-5; *Correspondence of George III*, I, 80-1; B.L., Add. MS. 32966, ff. 300-9. For the Regency Bill and attendant political manoeuvrings see Jarrett, 'Regency Crisis'; I. Christie, *Wars and Revolutions Britain, 1760-1815* (Cambridge, Mass., 1982), pp. 67-8; Brooke, *George III*, pp. 110-5; Lawson, *Grenville*, pp. 211-8.

Problems arose in the Lords because of the split between the King and his ministers. George III, who delayed naming his wife as regent in order to avoid a quarrel with his brother, the Duke of York, only stoked Grenville's suspicions by his reticence. The minister assumed Bute and his royal master were plotting to install the Princess Dowager, George's mother and Bute's good friend. Persistent probing in the House of Lords by the Duke of Richmond, a new recruit to the now decimated Whig opposition, heightened these tensions. His requests for a precise definition of the royal family's composition and the Queen's eligibility for the regent's role alarmed ministers who feared opposition would raise the issue of the princess. Thus, Sandwich and Halifax, the leader of the House, induced George to remove his mother from the bill, a decision Halifax announced to an astonished House on 4 May. Inevitably this insult to his mother provoked a royal change of heart; five days later a private member in the Commons moved to reinstate her. The government had to acquiesce, and on 13 May the Lords were called upon to rescind the amendment they adopted nine days earlier, a circumstance that provoked pointed comment from independent and opposition speakers. Ministers, Lord Hardwicke complained, had placed the House in a most anomalous position, 'first inducing them to leap over the stick one way, and then bringing them to jump over it the other'.[25]

In so far as Grenville and his colleagues encountered vigorous parliamentary opposition in 1765 they did so in the House of Lords. Nominal friends, not the official opposition, created the problems. It was Egmont, the King's friend, who raised the cry against the Poor Bill. Newcastle's cohort provided fewer than half the measure's opponents. Richmond, the new recruit acting on his own, raised the questions which led ministers to press George to remove his mother from the Regency Bill, and the bishops, then Bute's friends threatened or defeated legislation in which ministers had an active interest. These gestures did not bring down Grenville's government; the King performed that job. But they demonstrated that his ministry had lost effective control of the House of Lords. The fact that it was Bute's friends who transformed this bastion of support into a potential threat can only have reinforced the ministers' sense that the King and his favourite were conspiring against them. What else could provoke the Lords to such uncharacteristic behaviour?

In 1766 and 1767 the House of Lords occupied an even more central place in national political affairs and was, in fact, a principal cause for the instability that characterized those years. In February 1766 the peers adopted amendments hostile to the Rockingham administration's central

[25] Earl of Albemarle, *Memoirs of the Marquess of Rockingham and his Friends* (2 vols., 1852), I, 184; B.L., Add. MS. 51423, ff. 117-8.

legislative objective, repeal of the Stamp Act, thereby jeopardizing both the government and its policy. Throughout May and June 1767 a numerous opposition hammered the Chatham administration in the House, coming within four votes of victory on two occasions. A range of factors inspired the Lords' revolt: substantive disagreement on issues of policy, political ambition and a sense of the inadequacy of current ministerial arrangements. Though George III's curiously erratic behaviour complicated the Stamp Act's repeal, he did not consort with the measure's opponents. In fact, in 1766 and 1767 both ministries relied on the King to rally and sustain their meagre majorities. However, neither George III nor his politicians were able to reduce the King's friends to complete submissiveness.

The Stamp Act passed through both houses of Parliament in 1765 without opposition, for the political nation agreed with George Grenville that America should help maintain the army that protected it and that Parliament had a right to impose taxes for this purpose. Ministers knew the tax would provoke opposition but underestimated its force and extent; by December 1765 British authority in Massachusetts had disintegrated. The Rockinghams' decision to repeal was a pragmatic one. The act was apparently unenforceable, and the government was impressed by mercantile complaints that the Stamp Act had caused economic distress in America and Great Britain. On 19 January 1766 the cabinet resolved to introduce two bills, the first reaffirming Parliament's supremacy, the second repealing Grenville's duty.[26]

These bills consumed the attention of Parliament for almost two months. In the Lords a Committee of the Whole House began to examine documents and witnesses in late January. On the basis of the information gained in these sessions ministers formulated five resolutions for the consideration of the committee. The House adopted the first of these, upholding Parliament's right to tax and legislate, on 3 February by a vote of 125 to 5. However, on the 4 February Grenville's friend Lord Suffolk successfully amended the fourth resolution against the government's wishes; the vote was 63 to 60. Two days later ministers lost another division when Lord Weymouth carried a hostile amendment to the fifth resolution, 59 to 55.

The administration had anticipated these defeats. Two weeks earlier the Archbishop of Canterbury had urged Newcastle to act 'to strengthen the Hands of government, particularly in the House of Lords'. Reports of opposition among the King's friends in turn induced Rockingham to call upon George III to aid in shoring up the Bedchamber. But George

---

[26] P. Langford, *The First Rockingham Administration, 1765-6* (Oxford, 1973), pp. 109-29; P. Thomas, *British Politics and the Stamp Act Crisis* (Oxford, 1975), pp. 112-4, 150-3.

refused to force his friends to vote against their consciences. Thus, Rockingham, reporting the government's defeat in the Lords on 4 February, noted that it was 'the Fullest Proof of what Lord Rockingham has in duty been obliged to inform his Majesty was to be expected'.[27]

The defeats, though expected, precipitated speculation about the future of repeal and the politicians who sponsored it. Grenville's crony, Lord Hyde, pronounced the measure dead, and both courtiers and representatives of the colonies expected a change of ministers.[28] For the composition of the majority on the fourth was unusual: it included the King's brother, seven Scots, nine bishops and 11 officers of George III's Court.[29] Grafton pressed his colleagues to resign, but, bolstered by the King's promise to lobby his servants, ministers persisted.[30]

It was the House of Commons which retrieved repeal. On 7 February the government easily beat back an address moved by Grenville. The victory, as well as stimulating a rise in the stocks, mortified an expectant opposition. Lord George Sackville reported that 'the conversation is that the ministry may now stand their ground'.[31] Three days later the House of Lords adopted without debate resolutions it had earlier torn apart in committee.

For the next three weeks attention focussed on the Commons where both bills were introduced. The government used this lull to reinforce its position in the Lords. One manifestation of its success was the number of converts gained by early March from the opposition. The ministerial majority at the commitment of the bill repealing the Stamp Act on 11 March contained eight peers who had supported Lord Suffolk's amendment on 4 February: four other noblemen who had voted for that amendment were absent on the eleventh, and repeal's opponents only

[27] B.L., Add. MS. 32973, ff. 252, 330, 338-9; Albemarle, *Rockingham*, I, 292-3; *Correspondence of George III*, I, 256.

[28] B.L., Add. MS. 57814, ff. 100-1; Huntington Lib., Hastings MSS., Box 94: H. Stanley to Huntingdon, [4 Feb. 1766]; Thomas, *The Stamp Act Crisis*, p. 212.

[29] Scots: Abercorn, Argyll, Bute, Eglintoun, Loudoun, March and Morton. Bishops: Bangor, Bristol, Carlisle, Chester, Durham, Gloucester, Llandaff, London and Rochester (W. Lowe, who reconstructed a list for the 6 February division, claims Hereford and St. David's joined the opposition then: 'Politics in the House of Lords', pp. 973-4, 983-5. See also his 'Archbishop Secker, the Bench of Bishops and the Repeal of the Stamp Act', *Historical Mazazine of the Protestant Episcopal Church*, XLVI[1977], 435). Court: Ancaster, Boston, Buckinghamshire, Coventry, Denbigh, Harcourt, Lichfield, Orford, Oxford, Talbot and Willoughby de Broke. B.L., Add. MS. 33035, ff. 276-7; 33001, f. 91: 'Lords who are connected with the court who voted against the Question Recommend or Require'.

[30] 'A Narrative of the Changes in the Ministry, 1765-67', ed. M. Bateson, *Camden Miscellany* (Camden Soc., new ser., LIX, 1898), pp. 47-51; Albemarle, *Rockingham*, I, 303.

[31] Thomas, *The Stamp Act Crisis*, pp. 208-9.

enlisted one previous government supporter to their camp.[32] Not only did the Duke of Newcastle win converts as a result of his careful canvassing; he enlisted support from 36 peers who had not been present in February. Eleven of these appeared in person; 25 left their proxies in the hands of Newcastle's associates. Proxy voting, in fact, ensured the government majority. The losses in early February occurred in committee where peers could not exercise the special privilege of their House and cast votes on behalf of absent friends. On 11 March government's allies voted 32 proxies for the repeal bill's commitment. Grenville had hoped at the beginning of March that opposition might make trouble for repeal when the measure went into committee in the Lords, and Richmond looked forward to a close division on the issue.[33] In fact, its passage was now safe. Ministers carried its commitment by a vote of 105 to 71, and the opposition thereafter collapsed.

Grenville and the Duke of Bedford were natural leaders of the opposition to repeal. They were the authors of the Stamp Act. Each also had a sizeable following in the House of Lords – perhaps 25 in all.[34] A number of these noblemen were suspicious of the new minister and his inexperienced colleagues; they looked for Grenville's speedy return to power, not just because he was their leader but because many felt he was best equipped to govern Britain. The reversal of his imperial policy increased the urgency of making such a change. Not only was the Rockingham adminstration undoing the work of its predecessor; it was also undermining Britain's authority in America. No legislative assertion of parliamentary sovereignty, Bedford argued, could mitigate the 'disgrace of departing from the enforcing of the laws by constraint, and by open rebellion of the Colonists'.[35]

[32] Argyll, Cadogan, Exeter, Hardwicke, Northington, Willougby de Broke and the Bishops of Llandaff and London supported repeal. Boston, Courtenay, Morton and Shaftesbury, who earlier had opposed, did not vote on 11 March. New attenders were: Abergavenny, Delamer, Falmouth, Godolphin, Granville, Huntingdon, Richmond, Sussex, Thanet, Walpole and the Bishop of Bath and Wells. These figures are based on a comparison of division lists for 4 February and 11 March. B.L., Add. MS. 33035, ff. 276-7, 385-7.

[33] Huntington Lib. (Stowe MSS.), Grenville Letterbook, St. 7 (ii): Grenville to Halifax, 3 Mar. 1766; *Walpole Correspondence*, XLI, 9-11.

[34] On 14 Mar. 1766 Newcastle listed the following as belonging to the Bedford contingent: York, Bedford, Marlborough, Bridgwater, Pembroke, Suffolk, Sandwich, Essex, Coventry, Ferrers, Tankerville, Aylesford, Halifax, Waldegrave, Buckinghamshire, Gower, Guildford, Temple, Weymouth, Bolingbroke, Byron, Fortescue, Vere, Hyde, Mansfield, Lyttleton and the Bishops of Hereford, Chester, Bangor and Carlisle. York, Guildford, Mansfield, and the Bishops of Hereford and Chester did not normally act in opposition or with Bedford. B.L., Add. MS. 33001, ff. 161-2.

[35] *The Grenville Papers*, III, 68-9; Huntington Lib. (Stowe MSS.), Grenville Letterbook, St. 7(ii): Grenville to Hillsborough, 28 Feb. 1766; Lowe, 'Politics in the House of Lords', p. 554.

A portion of the King's friends comprised the other substantial block among the majority on 4 February. About 25 were associated with Lord Bute.[36] For these last the Rockingham administration represented no improvement over its predecessor. They resented the 'very Cruel Persecution' of Lord Bute and were offended and perplexed by the dismissal of his associates from office: 'the imprudent and impolitick Eviction of Power', Lord Harcourt grumbled, 'will by no means tend to Soften Matters, or to establish the Credit of the new Ministry in the Opinion of Mankind'. Like the Grenvilles Bute's friends doubted the durability of Rockingham's government. To spare the King the dilemma of another change, some resolved to support his new minister, but the government's faltering attempts at conciliation only heightened Bute's distaste for the administration. The earl had supported the Stamp Tax and was unprepared to 'sit tamely by and see our country, this great Empire crumble into pieces'. In the latter half of January he hosted dinners and meetings to arrange an opposition.[37] Many of the King's friends, even those who finally voted to repeal the Stamp Act, regarded the colonists as mutinous, but the largest portion who opposed the measure were also Bute's friends – Scottish representative peers or courtiers such as Denbigh, Lichfield and Talbot whom he had installed in their places.

The opposition also included a number of unattached peers. Some looked to politicians such as Grenville for occasional advice without being a part of their factions. Lord Wentworth, a self-proclaimed 'Country peer', deplored all unruly behaviour including that of the Americans. Others were convinced by superior opposition speakers, Lord Mansfield in particular. The Bishop of London came to the House looking for guidance: Mansfield provided it in the debate, and the bishop voted in opposition.[38]

The passage of the bill to repeal the Stamp Act was not merely the consequence of improved ministerial organization. Political considerations produced important allies. Though Pitt's small contingent disliked the Declaratory Bill, they also recognized that their opposition would jeopardize the Stamp Act's repeal. Thus they supported the government, as did Bute's former ally, Lord Holland, who detested Bedford and George Grenville and would not facilitate

---

[36] Newcastle's estimate of 41 on 14 March 1766 was too high (B.L., Add. MS. 33001, ff. 161-2), but because this group was short-lived a more accurate ennumeration is difficult.

[37] B.L., Add. MS. 38202, ff. 336-7; *ibid.*, 51423, ff. 207-8; *ibid.*, 38205, ff. 10; Langford, *The First Rockingham Administration*, pp. 170-1; *Grenville Papers*, III, 107-8; Walpole, *Memoirs*, II, 182-3.

[38] Warwickshire R.O. (Denbigh MSS.), CR 2017/243, ff. 36-7: Wentworth to Denbigh, 1 June 1767; B.L., Add. MS. 32973, f. 347.

their return to power by opposing Rockingham.[39] Indeed, the ministry managed to retain the support of a substantial portion of the Crown's traditional allies in the Lords. Eight bishops, two Scots and seven household peers opposed Suffolk's amendment in the committee on 4 February; five weeks later the group increased to include a dozen courtiers, six representative peers and 18 prelates, a total that exceeded the opposition's following among these groups.[40]

While some of these last peers were politically connected to a powerful ally of the Rockingham administration, a variety of other factors also induced them to support the Stamp Act's repeal. The measure was a money bill which the Lords could not amend; nor did the upper House often reject money bills passed by the Commons. In this instance ministers convincingly argued that the Lords' rejection of a conciliatory measure already passed by the lower House would leave the King helpless in combatting American agitation.[41] The Declaratory Bill made it easier for peers who wished to uphold parliamentary sovereignty to swallow repeal, particularly as a number were alarmed by the clamour the issue provoked. A few abstained from the battle because they could not see a clear line amidst the conflicting arguments, but many rallied to government as a means of restoring order in America and quiet at home. Lord Spencer was concerned by the colonies' 'distracted State'; he was even more upset that 'though this confusion was certainly occasioned by the inconsideration of the late Ministry, it will be made use of by them, now opposers, as a means to overthrow the present'. Likewise Lord Bathurst, who feared that partisan rivalries had prevented a good solution to the American question, hoped at least that a substantial majority for repeal would put 'an End to this troublesome affair'.[42] Finally, public clamour against the Stamp Act probably assisted ministers. Effective lobbying by merchants and commercial towns was a

---

[39] This is not to diminish the importance of improved organization for Frank O'Gorman attributes the government's defeats in February to its sloppy recruitment of support. *The Rise of Party in England* (1975), pp. 149-50; B.L., Add. MS. 51379, ff. 179-82; Thomas, *The Stamp Act Crisis*, p. 202.

[40] Courtiers supporting repeal in February included Ashburnham, Edgecumbe, Holdernesse, Manchester, Masham, Pomfret and Scarbrough; at least four were political appointments, arranged by ministers. Scots: Dunmore and Marchmont. Bishops: Chichester, Exeter, Lincoln, Lichfield, Oxford, St. David's, Worcester and York. By March the following had joined the government: Court: Bruce, Cadogan, Falmouth, Huntingdon and Willoughby de Broke; Scots: Argyll, Breadalbane, Hyndford and Stormont; Bishops: Bath, Ely, Llandaff, London, Norwich, Peterborough, St. Asaph, Salisbury and Winchester. B.L., Add. MS. 33035, ff. 276-7, 385-7.

[41] B.L., Add. MS. 32974, ff. 17-8, 153; *Selections from the Family Papers Preserved at Caldwell, In Two Parts*, ed. W. Mure (Maitland Club, XXI, 3 vols., Glasgow, 1854), II, 75-6.

[42] B.L., Add. MS. 57826, f. 55; B.L., Spencer MSS. (uncatalogued), F115: Spencer to Sir W. Hamilton, 25 Dec. 1765; Lowe, 'Politics in the House of Lords', pp. 570, 584.

decisive factor in carrying the measure through the Commons; the impact of this agitation on the Lords was certainly less significant. Nevertheless ministers pressed merchants and Americans to present appropriate statements to the upper chamber, and mercantile influence probably induced peers such as the Earl of Huntingdon to vote for the measure's commitment. George Grenville's pressure on noble allies to exert themselves against the merchants' efforts testifies to the importance he attached to their lobbying.[43]

A revolt supported by so many of his courtiers naturally raised questions about the King's attitude towards repeal and its authors. On several occasions he went out of his way to proclaim his preference for modifying rather than repealing the Stamp Act; in authorizing Lord Strange to report this preference on 10 February, he was contradicting his minister's public assertions. Indeed, he seemed throughout the crisis to condone his courtiers' opposition. In an extraordinary letter to Bute on 10 January 1766 he indicated that if the King's friends differed from 'Ministers where they think their honour and conscience requires it, that I not only think it right, but am of opinion it is their duty to act so'. Consistent with this view he refused repeated ministerial requests to punish office holders who opposed repeal.[44]

Yet George III remained loyal to his ministers if not to their policies. In his 10 January letter he admonished Bute not to bring down Rockingham and proclaimed his determination to support the government. He rebuffed Lord Harcourt when that associate of Bute intimated on 30 January that publication of royal sentiments on repeal would forestall its passage. When in February the Duke of York pressed him to meet Bedford as a means of securing modification of the Stamp Act rather than its repeal, the King again refused, citing the constitutional impropriety of such an encounter. George also took more positive steps on behalf of his ministers. In the last two weeks of January he solicited support among his friends, and after the 4 February debacle he promised Newcastle that he would do so again.[45]

Moreover, his refusal to dismiss recalcitrant courtiers was not a tactic he devised specially to harass Rockingham. Though annoyed by their wayward conduct, George III had endured his friends' forays into opposition since 1762. Several times that year he criticized office holders who spoke or voted against ministers, but neither then, in 1763 during

---

[43] 'Charles Garth', ed. J. Barnwell, *The South Carolina Historical and Genealogical Magazine*, XXVI (1923), 87-8; H.M.C., *Dartmouth MSS.*, II, 32-3; H.M.C., *Hastings MSS.*, III, 146; Huntington Lib. (Stowe MSS.), Grenville Letterbook, St. 7 (ii): Grenville to Botetourt, 2 Nov. 1765.

[44] *Letters from George III to Lord Bute, 1765-66*, ed. R. Sedgwick (1939), pp. 242-5.

[45] *Grenville Papers*, III, 353, 369-74; *Correspondence of George III*, I, 243-4; 'Narrative of the Changes of Ministry', pp. 49-50.

deliberations on the Cider Bill nor in 1765 did he dismiss peers for opposing ministers' projects. Indeed he told Lord Suffolk in July 1765 essentially what he told Bute six months later; that he was prepared to tolerate his friends opposing government when conscience dictated. This unusual position was consistent with the King's early political views. He did not expect his friends to chain themselves to his ministers, nor did he feel bound himself to support all the measures of politicians he wished to continue in office.[46]

Initially ministers were shocked and angered by George III's refusal to press his friends. The Strange episode renewed their jitters. Even after the King issued his clarification, stating his preference for modification but his willingness to countenance repeal if the former was impossible, some of the government's friends remained convinced he would desert them. Not so Newcastle who told Rockingham on 23 February 'upon the Whole, I think the Closest is as well as could be expected. I am afraid all we can expect, is a chearful Acquiesence in Repeal, without any Assistance in carrying it through'.[47] Newcastle's assessment, as well as being correct, indicates that the government had accommodated itself to George's peculiar stance.

In the end the King's behaviour was unsettling because it was so contradictory. There can be no doubt that George III did initially encourage Bute's friends to resist the Stamp Act's repeal: though the King had tolerated his courtiers' opposition to important government policies in the past, he had never so openly condoned such action as he did in his 10 January letter to Bute. With this letter he undermined ministers whom he told Bute he was determined to support. George twice refused to conspire with Bute's allies against the government, but he also refused to admonish friends whose opposition came close to driving the administration from office in early February. Thereafter his influence on the proceedings diminished; Dr. Langford is correct in asserting that the King's various statements to Strange neutralized his impact on Parliament. Some noblemen regarded George's clarification as an indication of his support for repeal, but many remained confused on the King's position;[48] in the end his friends divided fairly evenly for and against the repeal bill's commitment. Those who initially may have

---

[46] *Letters of George III to Bute*, p. 198. O'Gorman claims that George III not unjustly refused to punish his servants for acting according to their political beliefs and that Rockingham exaggerated the degree of the King's support for repeal after the 6 February defeat; he also finds George's conduct with Strange 'inexplicable'. *The Rise of Party*, pp. 163-7.

[47] B.L., Add. MS. 32974, f. 69.

[48] Langford, *The First Rockingham Administration*, p. 168; *Letters of David Hume*, ed. J. Greig (Oxford, 1932), p. 20; *Caldwell Papers*, II, pt. 2, 72-3.

assumed that the monarch opposed repeal persisted in their resistance even after he declared on behalf of his ministers' policy. Others who had hung back in February attended in March to support Rockingham. As we have seen, various considerations dictated these actions; even among his close associates the King's views were only one of the elements that shaped the Lords' conduct on the matter.

The restoration of political stability in the House of Lords began with the formation of the Chatham administration in July 1766. Unike his immediate predecessors, Grafton, the government's effective leader, enjoyed the confidence of George III who consequently exerted his influence on behalf of ministers when they encountered difficulties in the House. For his new administration was initially weak there, a factor which possibly influenced Pitt in his decision to accept the earldom of Chatham.[49] More certainly, his weaknesses in the Lords led Chatham to reach out to Bute and his friends, the first step in the restoration of a solid government majority in the upper chamber.

A desire for more durable government and an appetite for office and honours lured Bute's friends into the new ministry's camp. Bute was aware that some of his associates were hostile to union; they disliked Chatham's demagoguery, abhorred Lord Chancellor Camden because he had earlier released Wilkes and doubted that this new, suspect minister could last. This is why Bute gave his support. His object was 'to prevent these too frequent revolutions, that gradually weaken every bond of the State; and will if not prevented end in anarchy ruin and Confusion'. Others of his allies shared the longing for order, and Chatham's bestowal of offices, even dukedoms on Bute's noble allies made him all the more congenial as a minister. By the end of the year the union seemed secure.[50]

Strong opposition to the new government developed more slowly because its potential foes remained disunited. Until October when Chatham dismissed their friend, Lord Edgecumbe, from a minor office, the Rockinghams maintained an uneasy alliance with the new administration. Nor were Grenville, Bedford and Rockingham natural allies. Friends of the latter worried that the only fruit of their opposition might be Grenville's restoration to the Treasury. While the three leaders agreed on the malignancy of Bute's secret influence, they differed on America. Moreover, all sides attached importance to consistency; Rockingham argued that the public strength of his party derived from its commitment to principle. The prospect of compromise unnerved Whigs

[49] Turberville, *The House of Lords in the XVIIIth Century*, p. 330.
[50] B.L., Add. MS. 38205, ff. 95-6, 112; *Chatham Correspondence*, III, 253-4; Huntington Lib., Loudoun MSS., Box 45: Bute to Loudoun, 28 Oct. 1766; *The Correspondence of John, Fourth Duke of Bedford*, ed. Lord John Russell (3 vols., 1842-6), III, 360.

who were prepared to forsake office to preserve their honour.[51] In this environment campaigns in the House of Lords were poorly concerted and weakly contested. When, at the session's outset, Grenville challenged the legality of the government's embargo on the exportation of corn, the Whigs largely ignored the battle: some even supported the government, and others felt that Grenville was making an unnecessary fuss on a minor point.[52]

The eventual union of opposition parties was a pragmatic one, occasioned by the ministry's serious deficiencies and opposition's potential strength in the House of Lords. By early 1767 Chatham had retreated to his sick bed, leaving a divided government directionless: Charles Townshend's open opposition to his leader's East Indian inquiry and his unilateral announcement of new American taxes are the most notorious examples of the resulting disarray. On 27 February Grenville and William Dowdeswell, Rockingham's friend, orchestrated a successful attack on the land tax in the House of Commons, and by mid-March Newcastle's surveys revealed that the opposition groups there were a formidable force.[53] An apparent opposition fiasco reinforced this point. On 10 April the Duke of Bedford moved that the Privy Council review a controversial act of the Massachusetts Assembly, pardoning and in some cases indemnifying those who had participated in riots against the Stamp Act. The motion lost 63 to 36, in part because Rockingham, who was uninformed of Bedford's intentions, voted with the government while Newcastle and a larger group of Whigs abstained. In spite of the Whigs' apparent disarray, the episode highlighted a united opposition's potential strength in the upper House. Lord Hardwicke estimated that the three groups, had they acted in concert, would have come within two or three votes of defeating the administration, and Newcastle told Bedford shortly after that he believed the combined opposition had a 'Majority or very near it' in the Lords.[54]

This incident transformed the opposition. Immediately haphazard action gave way to careful planning, suspicion to frequent consultation. Armed with his most recent surveys of the House, Newcastle cultivated, recruited and badgered: his allies did the same. By 16 May the Duke estimated the opposition strength at 73 – 43 Rockinghams, 17 Bedfords

---

[51] *Bedford Correspondence*, III, 373; Sheffield City Lib., W.W.M., RI-756, 764: Newcastle to Rockingham, 23 Feb. 1767, Manchester to Rockingham, 15 Mar. 1767; B.L., Add. MS. 32979, f. 89; *ibid.*, 32980, f. 297; *Grenville Papers*, IV, 4-6; *The Correspondence of Edmund Burke*, ed. T. Copeland, *et al.* (9 vols., Cambridge, 1958-70), I, 284-5, 290-1.

[52] P. Lawson, 'Parliament, the Constitution and Corn: The Embargo Crisis of 1766', *Parliamentary History*, V (1986), 27-30; B.L., Add. MS. 32978, ff. 208-9, 225.

[53] B.L., Add. MS. 33001, ff. 379-81.

[54] *Ibid.*, 32981, ff. 125-6, 157; 35361, ff. 265-6; *Grenville Papers*, IV, 223-4.

and 13 Grenvilles. Though the Court contingent numbered 105, 20 doubtful peers gave the opposition a basis for hope.[55]

In May 1767 the Rockinghams and their allies mounted a campaign whose object was to topple the Chatham administration. A motion for papers relating to the Massachusetts Indemnity Bill, introduced by Bedford's friend, Lord Gower, lost by 52 to 43 (71 to 49 with proxies) on 6 May, in part because several opposition peers voted with the government.[56] Two weeks later Grafton, challenged by a numerous opposition, acceded to the Duke of Richmond's request for Quebec papers, and on 22 May the House rejected by six votes the first of two questions regarding the legality of the Massachusetts Indemnity Act which Gower moved to refer to the judges. The high point of the opposition's attack came on 26 May when they lost two questions by votes of 65 to 62. According to Lord Denbigh 'every Lord who could crawl, nay even be carried was by both sides brought into the House . . .' Grafton shared this assessment of his narrow escape and worried that his opponents continued to gain strength; in ten days they had recruited ten supporters.[57]

In fact the opposition had reached its peak. On 2 June the Duke of Richmond introduced two motions on Quebec: the first carried unanimously, but Grafton beat back the second 73 to 61 in what was heralded as a decisive victory.[58] Though the government still had to carry its controversial Dividend Bill against a strong opposition in the Lords, it was never again in danger there. Ministerial divisions remained acute, and opposition politicians were energetic and careful in orchestrating their attack on the India bills. Still their strength declined to 52 on 17 June when the House rejected Richmond's motion for a conference with the Commons. For eight days they contested the bill limiting the size of the East India Company's dividend, but their supporters refused to remain so late in London. Once again Grafton was in control.

It was not just the lateness of the session which blunted the opposition's onslaught. The Dividend Bill had powerful opponents in the House: Rockingham and Grenville regarded these attempts at regulating the Company's dividend as another arbitrary exercise of governmental authority, a stand which noble proprietors of the East

---

[55] Sheffield City Lib., W.W.M., R I-786: 'List of Peers, 16 May, 1767'.

[56] B.L., Add. MS. 32981, f. 325.

[57] Warwickshire R.O., CR 2017/243, ff. 35-6: Denbigh to Wentworth, 28 May 1767; *Chatham Correspondence*, III, 258; *Correspondence of George III*, I, 476.

[58] B.L., Add. MS. 38205, ff. 174-5; West Suffolk R.O., Grafton Papers, 423/778: Walpole to Grafton, 4 June 1767; Walpole, *Memoirs*, III, 40; *Correspondence of George III*, I, 484.

India Company supported.[59] But the company was unpopular in the House. Denbigh, a country peer, dismissed opposition for doing the work of 'stock jobbing Proprietors'. Several Whigs refused to attend the Dividend Bill, and others who had opposed Grafton on the Massachusetts Indemnity Act supported him on this issue.[60] In both instances the opposition failed to attract substantial independent support; Newcastle had identified 15 of these peers to cultivate in late May but gained only six for the 2 June division. On the other hand the independent Lord Radnor engaged Lords Castlehaven and Romney for the Court, two peers who had not attended the House in years.[61] The opposition effort to drive Grafton from office failed because of an inability to recruit and retain support beyond the coalition groups.

Both Burke and Newcastle acknowledged Grafton's energetic direction of his forces as a cause for the government's survival.[62] But Grafton, as well as misjuding his opponents, had begun to falter after the strong opposition showing on 26 May. It was the King who rallied the duke and helped him gain new support. For the first time since 1763 George III worked closely with a minister who faced challenges in the House of Lords.[63] Even his intervention was insufficient to rein in the episcopal bench, 12 of whose members supported the opposition in May and June.[64] But whereas 13 courtiers opposed repeal in February 1766, only four Bedchamber peers voted against the King's government during the 1767 crisis. Likewise Bute's adherence influenced the conduct of the 16 Scots, only two of whom voted in opposition.[65]

The House of Lords provided the principal parliamentary challenge to

[59] O'Gorman, *Rise of Party*, pp. 198-9; Lucy Sutherland, *The East India Company in Eighteenth-Century Politics* (Oxford, 1962), pp. 175-6. For a list of East India Proprietors in 1763, see *Additional Grenville Papers, 1763-1765*, ed. J. Tomlinson (Manchester, 1962), pp. 96-9.

[60] Warwickshire R.O., CR 2017/243, ff. 35-6: Denbigh to Wentworth, 28 May 1767; B.L., Add. MS. 32982, f. 342. P. Lawson argues there was strong hostility to the Company in both Houses. 'Parliament and the East India Inquiry, 1767', *Parliamentary History*, I (1982), 99-114.

[61] Lowe, 'Politics in the House of Lords', pp. 654-5; *Correspondence of George III*, I, 483.

[62] 'Narrative of Changes in the Ministry', p. 102; *Burke Correspondence*, I, 313; O'Gorman, *Rise of Party*, p. 205.

[63] *Chatham Correspondence*, III, 260-2; Brooke, *George III*, p. 140-1.

[64] Bishops in opposition included: Bangor, Bristol, Carlisle, Durham, Ely, Exeter, Gloucester, Lincoln, Norwich, Oxford, Salisbury and Worcester (B.L., Add. MS. 32981, f. 112; 33036, ff. 451-4; 33037, ff. 19-20, 53-4, 77-8, 111-12, 149-50, 155-6). On 22 May Walpole attributed the opposition of seven prelates to the Crown's 'permitting great lords to nominate to bishopricks: the reverend fathers sometimes having at least gratitude, or further expectations, if they have no patriotism'. *Memoirs*, III, 34.

[65] Four lords of the Bedchamber opposed: Buckinghamshire, Coventry, Eglintoun (also a representative peer) and Manchester. The recalcitrant Scots were Abercorn and Breadalbane (see B.L., Add. MSS. cited in note 64 above).

Chatham's administration in its first year. In was, Burke claimed, 'more adverse to administration than the Commons', and the King believed that Grenville, Bedford and the Rockinghams were joined together there with 'an intention to storm my Closet', a fear shared by Grafton and a number of King's friends.[66] Opposition may have been less sanguine about the Lords' ability to drive a minister from office: Newcastle hoped only that a victory would 'give great Satisfaction to the nation, and a good preparation for a new Parliament'. Still, Grafton contemplated resignation in late May, and though he eventually survived the ordeal, its lesson was clear: government could not continue without an accession of support. Thus, by the end of June he was preparing to negotiate with his opponents, a tactic they correctly ascribed to his recent difficulties in the Lords.[67]

3

The political instability that characterized the House of Lords for much of the 1760s derived initially from George III's rout of the 'Old Corps'. The immediate consequence of the new King's blunderings was the factionalization of political life at Westminster, a process that was accelerated and embittered by the foibles and personal rivalries of leading politicians.[68] By 1765 the House contained at least five political groups with a combined support of almost 100 peers. Though some lords were only loosely bound to a party or faction, each group had a solid core of support: the loyalty of Newcastle's bishops or of Grenville's followers, who endured a distasteful opposition in hopes of returning their leader to the Treasury, testify to the reality of that cohesion.[69] It is also clear from the preceding narrative that bonds which united peers to their leaders also engendered rivalries and emnities. Bute's friends resented Bedford, Grenville and Rockingham for their campaign against the earl's secret influence. For their part Rockingham's allies distrusted Grenville, and

---

[66] *Burke Correspondence*, I, 313; cf. Thomas, *The Stamp Act Crisis*, pp. 310, 321, 330; O'Gorman, *Rise of Party*, p. 205; *Correspondence of George III*, I, 480; *Chatham Correspondence*, III, 257-9; Warwickshire R.O., CR 2017/243, ff. 35-6: Denbigh to Wentworth, 28 May 1767.

[67] B.L., Add. MS. 32982, ff. 95-6, 99-100; 32983, ff. 55-8, 76. Grafton hoped that negotiations might 'disunite Parties, freshly so loosely united, in that some one among them may find it for their interest as well as Credit to fall in honorably with the Present Administration. If resentment comes in aid, on account of too little Consideration shewn to some, or too much Power grasped at by another, this Event may still be the more likely' (Northamptonshire R.O., Henley [Watford] MSS.: Grafton to Northington, 16 July 1767).

[68] Brewer, *Party Ideology and Popular Politics*, p. 135.

[69] W. Lowe, 'Bishops and Scottish Representative Peers in the House of Lords, 1760-1775', *Journal of British Studies*, XVIII (1978), 93-4; Lawson, *Grenville*, p. 287-9.

neither of those leaders was able to work with Pitt before 1768. But personal and factional rivalries were not the only factors that disrupted the Lords.

Specific controversial measures and more deep-seated cleavages prevented the House of Lords from maintaining its role as a bulwark of the Crown. With their extensive territorial interests peers were bound to advance the interests of their localities even when those brought them into conflict with the Court; loyalty to the King and Bute did not prevent nine Tory 'cider lords' from opposing Dashwood's bill. Gilbert's Poor Bill outraged a number of country gentlemen just as Bedford's ecclesiastical legislation annoyed the episcopal bench in 1765. Opposition politicians exploited these occasions as a means of embarrassing their enemies and building new support. The persistence of such issues aggravated existing tensions and weakened both Bute and Grenville in the House. But only two problems, America and the role of the monarch, divided peers for much of the decade.

Even on America there was substantial agreement. Benjamin Franklin noted after a visit to the House in 1767 that almost all lords decried the colonists' unruly behaviour and upheld Parliament's right to legislate for the colonies.[70] However, the crisis that accompanied the Stamp Act's repeal exhibited sharp divisions over the line to take to counteract discontent. A year later the persistence of these divisions delayed the formation of an opposition and limited the scope of its attack even after its leaders temporarily put aside their differences.

The conduct of George III and Lord Bute created even more disagreement. Deeply suspicious of the favourite's machinations, Grenville and Bedford challenged the propriety of individuals advising the monarch outside of the properly constituted channels. By 1767 the Rockinghams went even further to condemn the executive's intrusion on individual and corporate liberties; already they envisaged a strong, cohesive party as the check to an autocratic executive. For their part the King's friends by 1766 blamed corrupt factions for the succession of weak governments that prevented the smooth functioning of national business. In their eyes the King empowered his ministers, and the duty of the peers was to unite behind the Crown.[71] Thus despite his personal reservations Bute rallied to Chatham as a means of restoring order. The King's friends saved Grafton in 1767; though they lamented his hesitant response to national agitation in 1768 and 1769, they steadfastly supported his administration and policies.

The prevalence of faction, of personal rivalry and contentious issues did not eliminate the importance of patronage as a determinant of peers'

---

[70] *The Papers of Benjamin Franklin*, ed. L. Labaree (24 vols., New Haven, Conn., 1959-84), XIV, 108-9.
[71] O'Gorman, *Rise of Party*, pp. 210-11, 219; *Walpole Correspondence*, XXXVIII, 329.

conduct. Following Newcastle's resignation the Earl of Powis switched his allegiance to Bute in order to sustain his electoral interest in Shropshire. The needs of a large family and an aversion to faction induced the Earl of Hertford to desert his friends and accept the Paris embassy in 1764, just as the prospect of a peerage led Lorne to break with Bedford in 1767.[72] Certainly Chatham and Grafton relied on favours to construct a safe majority in the upper House. But the restoration of order there depended ultimately on the consolidation of factions and the prominence of issues that rekindled peers' traditional attachment to the Crown. Patronage shaped the conduct of individuals, not of the peerage as a whole.

A decisive step in this consolidation occurred in January 1768 when the Bedfords coalesced with government. Some within a group that was notorious for its cupidity had pressed for union earlier. Struggles between Grenville, Bedford and Rockingham during the negotiations Grafton initiated in July and again at the session's opening in November convinced that duke and his allies that opposition was not the path to office. In consequence Bedford entered into discussions which eventually gained for government about 15 supporters in the House of Lords, including Lords Gower, Sandwich and Weymouth, three of the chamber's most active debaters.[73] According to the Duke of Atholl the accession of the Bedfords, by adding 'great Strength to the Present Adminstration' would 'secure their Stability for we have had too many changes of Late'.[74] Grafton enjoyed a clear preponderance in the upper House for the remaining duration of his administration not only because of this union but also because of a more fundamental regrouping of noble opinion.

The Crown's reassertion of control over its traditional allies was a crucial step. George III, who had tolerated independence in his household since 1762, expressed to Grafton in April 1767 his 'surprise and indignation at the indecency of Some Men about My Person appearing in the Minority where they cannot plead conscience'. More importantly he acted on his displeasure. Two of the culprits lost their positions in November, and by 1770 the King refused even to tolerate

---

[72] Namier, *The Structure of Politics*, pp. 235-98; *Walpole Correspondence*, XXXVIII, 329-31; P.R.O., 30/8/48 (Chatham MSS.), f. 189: Lorne to Chatham, Monday.

[73] West Suffolk R.O., 423/779a: Walpole to Grafton, Monday morning; *The Autobiography and Political Correspondence of Augustus Henry, 3rd Duke of Grafton K.G.*, ed. Sir William Anson (1898), pp. 171-2, 183; *Grenville Papers*, IV, 236; Lowe, 'Politics in the House of Lords', pp. 686-7. According to Newcastle the Bedford party in the Lords included in 1767 the Bishop of Bangor, Bedford, Bridgwater, Bolingbroke, Eglintoun, Essex, Gower, Halifax, Marlborough, Pembroke, Powis, Sandwich, Scarsdale, Waldegrave and Weymouth (Sheffield City Lib., W.W.M., R I-789).

[74] Lowe, 'Politics in the House of Lords', p. 688; Warwickshire R.O., CR 2017/243, f. 102: H. Wilmot to Denbigh, 22 Dec. 1767.

hesitant adherence. Faced with the union of Chatham and the Rockinghams and the desertion of Lord Chancellor Camden, George informed Grafton that 'a little firmness and the making examples of those that have trimmed' would 'restore due subordination'. Manchester, a Rockinghamite, and Coventry, a relatively independent peer, resigned from the Bedchamber within a week of the session's first debate, and the King dismissed the Groom of the Stole, Lord Huntingdon, after the latter ignored three summonses to Parliament.[75] For the remainder of his active reign George's courtiers were generally docile. The few who ventured into opposition either resigned their posts or faced dismissal.

It was Bute, not George III or his ministers, who secured the adherence of the Scottish representative peers. Though 11 of them opposed government at one or more divisions before 1768, these peers remained detached from English politics. For much of the decade Bute exercised the strongest influence over them. He induced six to oppose repeal of the Stamp Act, and his decision to support Chatham undoubtedly swayed his colleagues. English ministers were less adept at managing the Scots. In 1768 Grafton succeeded in dropping Lord Breadalbane from the government list at the peerage election on account of his connection with Rockingham, but Lord Eglintoun, a more active opponent, received ministerial backing at that contest, probably because of his ties with Bedford and his seniority within the Scottish nobility. More notably, North's selection of Lord Dysart, an Englishman with a Scottish title but without Scottish property, to fill a vacancy in 1770 precipitated a Scots rebellion against ministerial manipulation of peerage contests. The proponents of 'free elections', who stressed their loyalty to the administration, did not begin to make a significant impact until the 1780s. The campaign they launched in 1770 is however important both as an expression of the Scottish nobility's determination to prevent the English from degrading their order and of their willingness to begin to move into the orbit of English politics. Eventually these broader political connections disrupted the group's traditional, though not invariable attachment to the Crown.[76]

The most dramatic change occurred on the episcopal bench. Prior to 1768 successive ministers failed to create a strong phalanx there, and the majority of attending prelates routinely supported oppositions at

[75] *Correspondence of George III*, I, 468-9; Sheffield City Lib., W.W.M., RI-1246: Manchester to Rockingham, 6 Nov. 1767; Lowe, 'Politics in the House of Lords', p. 742-3; *Chatham Correspondence*, III, 394; Huntington Lib., Hastings MSS., Box 95: Hemington to Huntingdon, 21 Jan. 1770; Walpole, *Memoirs*, IV, 30-1.

[76] *The Harcourt Papers*, ed. E. Harcourt (14 vols., Oxford, 1880-1905), III, 103-4; Lowe, 'Bishops and Representative Peers', pp. 104-5; M. McCahill, 'The Scottish Peerage and the House of Lords in the Late Eighteenth Century', *Scottish Historical Review*, LI (1972), 179-82.

divisions. By the early 1770s only two or three were regularly voting against North's government. There are several reasons for the change. Most of the bishops who ventured into opposition did so in the wake of lay patrons. Newcastle's death and the government's union first with the Bedfords and subsequently with Grenville's followers gained it at least eight episcopal adherents. Less important was the elevation of Cornwallis to the primacy. His predecessor, Secker, another of Newcastle's protégés, eschewed parliamentary politics rather than choose between his patron and incumbent ministers. Government supporters expected that a new archbishop would 'keep the Bench in better order than it hitherto has been'.[77] At the very least Cornwallis did set an example of active loyalty, and the lure of rich commendams and translations exercised its traditional influence: Grafton, for example, lured Newton of Bristol from Grenville in 1768 by holding out the prospect of St. Paul's deanery. Finally, the Crown benefited from the prelates' mortality. Four bishops died in 1768-9, ten between 1768-75. Grafton, North and George III consequently had the opportunity to reshape the bench. New bishops like their predecessors proved loyal to their patrons.[78]

The consolidation of the 'party of the Crown' also reflects the emergence of a more concerted and forceful leadership in the House of Lords. By 1767 George III put aside his favourites and emissaries and acted directly on behalf of his ministers; his determination that spring sustained Grafton and reinforced his government's strength in the upper chamber. Thereafter George III was fairly active in the management of the Lords; he recruited support and speakers, took a lead in shaping the character of the bench and reined in his courtiers.[79] The lesson of Huntingdon's dismissal was especially powerful. For ministerial leadership became more forceful as well. The union with the Bedfords secured for government several strong speakers, and a strengthened Grafton was able now to discipline recalcitrant followers. Not only did government marshal its forces with regular letters; the ministerial message was unequivocal. Sandwich, in summoning the Earl of Denbigh to the opening of the 1770-1 session, noted that 'any friend to Government must be more injudicious than your Countryman Lord Huntingdon, if he gives offense by absenting himself or being lukewarm upon that occasion'. Not surprisingly peers were increasingly careful to

[77] Lowe, 'Bishops and Representative Peers', pp. 95-6; Warwickshire R.O., CR 2017/243, f. 167: Denbigh to R. Stonehewer, 13 Aug. 1768, Stonehewer to Denbigh, 20 Aug. 1768; N. Sykes, *Church and State in England in the XVIIIth Century* (Hampden, Conn., 1962), p. 65.

[78] West Suffolk R.O., 423/344: Bishop of Bristol to Grafton, 3 Aug. 1768.

[79] J. Brooke, *The Chatham Administration, 1766-1768* (1956), pp. 150-2; West Suffolk R.O., 423/498, 540: George III to Grafton, 23 May 1770, 8 Jan. 1770.

make excuses to the leader of the House if they were unable to attend.[80]

Finally the principal issues of the day – Wilkes, popular agitation and America – reinforced most peers' attachment to the Crown. After a four year absence Wilkes returned to London in 1768 to seek re-election to the Commons and protection from his creditors. He was duly returned for Middlesex. A stringent sentence for past crimes precipitated riots, then shooting. In the face of tumult the House of Commons removed him and subsequently awarded the Middlesex seat to Wilkes' unsuccessful electoral opponent, Henry Luttrell.

Though Wilkes generated broad popular support, that support did not extend into the House of Lords. Some Whigs acknowledged that Wilkes was a friend to liberty, but their leaders refused to raise his business in the House while rioting continued. A year later Rockingham and Grenville resisted the metropolitan counties' radical petitions; those which they and their friends inspired were more narrowly framed to press the rights of the House of Commons.[81] In January 1770 Lord Chatham returned to the House to take up Wilkes' cause, a move that resulted in the resignation of his crony, Lord Chancellor Camden. Chatham, for once communicative, worked closely and not ineffectively with the Rockinghams. Briefly, opposition seemed threatening. Two Lords of the Bedchamber resigned their places; Earl Stanhope, long exiled in Geneva, returned to support Chatham's campaign; the Duke of Northumberland, a courtier, also transferred his support to Chatham whom he acknowledged as the only politician capable of rescuing England from its confusion.[82] The session was a combative one: opposition pressed the House to divide 18 times, most often on matters relating to Wilkes, but it never seriously threatened North's new government.

For popular agitation bound peers more closely to authority. They might complain of ministers' tentative response to riot and the petitioning, but the sin of hesitation paled in comparison to the opposition's flirtation with radicals. For peers viewed the confrontation in apocalyptic terms. Parliamentary deliberations on the City's Remonstrance in 1770 would, according to Lord Jersey, 'determine almost everything of real weight in this kingdom'; two years earlier the same peer, having witnessed the West End's craven pandering to the mob and Wilkes' 'insufferable insolence' confessed he 'was never so

---

[80] West Suffolk R.O., 423/897, 970: Grafton to Tankerville, 10, 15 Nov. 1769; Warwickshire R.O., CR 2017/243, f. 268: Sandwich to Denbigh, 14 Oct. 1770; Huntington Lib., Loudoun MSS., Box 37: Sandwich to Loudoun, 25 Nov. 1772.

[81] R. Hoffman, *The Marquis: A Study of Lord Rockingham, 1730-1782* (New York, 1973), pp. 218-31; Huntington Lib. (Stowe MSS.), Grenville Letterbooks, St. 7 (ii): Grenville to Buckinghamshire, 16 Aug. 1769, Grenville to R. Whately, 11 Oct. 1769.

[82] *London Chronicle*, 3-8 May 1770; *Burke Correspondence*, II, 91.

ashamed of my country in my life'. At a major debate in the House on 2 February 1770 the Earl of Egmont called the petitioning movement 'treasonable', and Lord Marchmont suggested that government would be justified in calling in foreign assistance if the opposition continued to challenge the Commons' right to unseat Wilkes.[83] Nor did peers manifest their concern exclusively in their rhetoric. A number actively opposed petitioners in their counties. They also attended in great numbers throughout the 1770 session and sat through interminable sessions in a crowded, stiflingly hot chamber. In a few instances the impact of popular agitation was even more dramatic. The Grenvillite Earl of Suffolk, who disliked opposition politics, took no part in deliberations relating to Wilkes after 1768 and joined North at Grenville's death as did the minister's step-brother, Lord Dartmouth. Formerly an ally of Rockingham, Dartmouth considered Wilkes to be a 'desperate incendiary', was alarmed by the 'madness of the mob about him', and lamented that his former colleagues could 'give sanction to the violence of any turbulent individual, however great, or association of individuals, however numerous'.[84]

Despite American resistance to the Townshend Duties, the House of Lords rarely discussed colonial issues between 1768 and 1770. In December 1768 Hillsborough, Secretary of State for the Colonies, introduced resolutions condemning Massachusetts for its resistance to the duties; the peers adopted them without dissent, thereby demonstrating, according to George III, 'that the House of Lords mean steadily to support the Superiority of the Mother Country over her Colonys'.[85] Such assertions failed to impress the Americans whose opposition remained steadfast. Instead in April 1770 the House quietly repealed all the duties save that on tea; when the Duke of Richmond moved to investigate the causes of Britain's failure a month later, only 26 peers supported his resolutions. The great body of peers still upheld the principle established by the Declaratory Act of 1766; they were not yet prepared to question ministers who acted to uphold that legislation.

For the Bedfords and Grenvilles America posed special problems. A number of these peers were uncomfortable in the role of opposition; the fact that the Grenville's Pittite partners had rejected the Declaratory Act while the Rockinghams would at least accommodate the colonists

[83] B.L., Spencer MSS., F84: Jersey to Lady Spencer, 13 Mar. 1770; *ibid.*, F83: Villiers to Lady Spencer, Thursday morning; *Chatham Correspondence*, III, 418; B.L., Add. MS. 35609, f. 146.

[84] B.L., Add. MS. 35609, f. 141; Huntington Lib., (Stowe MSS.), Grenville Letterbooks, St. 7 (ii): Greville to T. Pitt, 22 Oct. 1769; Warwickshire R.O., CR 2017/243, ff. 217, 237: Denbigh to J. Dyson, 3 July, 8 Nov. 1769; Lawson, *Grenville*, p. 289; B. Bargar, *Lord Dartmouth and the American Revolution* (Columbia, S.C., 1965), pp. 48-9, 52.

[85] West Suffolk R.O., 423/531: George III to Grafton, 15 Dec. 1768.

increased their discomfort. For both groups believed in coercion. Bishop Newton of Bristol had attacked repeal as 'the sacrifice of the honour and authority of Great Britain', and as the cause of 'all the subsequent troubles in America', and Lord Trevor, who followed Bedford into the government camp in 1768, looked anxiously that year for signs that the administration would curtail the Americans' insolence. Newton transferred his support to Grafton after receiving the deanery of St. Paul's. Lords Buckinghamshire and Hyde, who shared Trevor's views on America, waited until after Grenville's death to support North.[86]

Active royal support, the reunion of politicians, effective management of ministerial forces and the prominence of issues which reinforced peers' attachment to government together account for the restoration of the House of Lords to its traditional role. In 1758 Horace Walpole bemoaned the Lords' subservience to Newcastle and the lawyers; ten years later Whig leaders lamented their inability to enlist noble support for their crusades, and radicals berated peers for their servility.[87] Yet despite the restoration of ministerial preponderance, the new order in the House of Lords differed from that which existed before George III's accession. The leadership included fewer Whig grandees and more seasoned administrators or ambassadors such as Sandwich, Rochford or Stormont. By 1770 Tories ceased to exist as a distinct group in the House; a few remained unattached, but most had been absorbed either through the Court or the Bedford and Grenville factions into the ranks of government supporters.[88] Once again opposition was small, numbering about 40 peers at the end of 1770. It remained as it had been a coalition, dominated now by the Rockingham Whigs who worked in partnership with about ten relatively independent peers and about half a dozen Chathamites.

Brewer, O'Gorman and others have convincingly established the Rockinghams' distinctiveness and modernity. Unlike other political groups, the party had an encompassing ideology which Rockingham presented in speeches to the House even prior to the publication of Burke's *Thoughts on the Cause of the Present Discontents*. The Whigs' clear sense of mission made them exclusive; Burke's letters to Rockingham in 1768-9 reiterate his distaste for negotiation and amalgamation.[89]

---

[86] B.L., Add. MS. 38206, ff. 308-9; Turberville, *House of Lords in the XVIIIth Century*, p. 427; B.L. Add. MS. 57823, f. 185; Lawson, *Grenville*, pp. 289-93.

[87] Albemarle, *Rockingham*, II, pp. 91-2; *The Letters of Junius*, ed. J. Cannon (Oxford, 1978), p. 491.

[88] B.L., Add. MS. 38206, ff. 201-2; Colley, *In Defiance of Oligarchy*, pp. 288, 291; I. Christie, 'Party Politics in the Age of Lord North's Administration', *Parliamentary History*, VI (1987), 47-68.

[89] Brewer, *Party Ideology*, pp. 77-95; O'Gorman, *Rise of Party*, pp. 191-4, 210-2, 219; Cobbett, *Parl. Hist.*, XVI, 741-5; *Burke Correspondence*, II, 100-1.

Inevitably this opposition lacked the numerical strength of the coalitions of the mid-1760s, but the group was durable, and it began to make an impact beyond the House. Protests, prepared in conjunction with Chatham's friends and colleagues in the Commons, became by 1770 a principal means of publicizing its positions to the nation.[90]

Within the House the party had limited appeal. Lord Milton, who 'lamented the mischief and disunion the Kingdom received from the weakness and fluction of Government', told Lord John Cavendish that 'the only remedy for these evils, must arise from a body of men, who could unite faithfully and honestly to act together, and adhere to eachother'. He was exceptional.[91] A number of peers and their friends had rejoiced at Rockingham's failure to form a government in 1767. The Yorkes, more intent on office than most Whig families, were by 1768 wearied of 'an opposition so narrowed, so reduced as it has been by late events, and pointed at no object . . .' If Lord Hardwicke and his brother dismissed Whig efforts as futile, others saw them as pernicious. During the early weeks of 1770 Lord Jersey complained of the Whigs' 'very violent' protests, prayed that 'the malicious and factious attempts of opponents may not succeed', and later rejoiced when they differed as much among themselves as they did with the majority. At the same time Northington, the former Chancellor, deplored the conduct of men such as Chatham or Camden who seemed to be contending for the 'Country's Destruction at the Price of Honor, Gratitude and Decency'. To such men party was not a guarantor of liberty but a factious, often corrupt force whose existence was sufficient to justify their own adherence to the Crown. Stable government derived from the steady attachment of men of great property.[92]

4

The 1760s constitute an important episode in the history of the House of Lords because for much of the decade ministers could not take its support for granted. Even groups which traditionally subordinated themselves to the Crown at various times challenged administrations or their policies. In 1765 they may have done so with the King's blessing though there is no evidence to tie George III directly to Bute and his allies. A year later the King's refusal to press repeal of the Stamp Act on his household encouraged their initial resistance even though George reiterated his

[90] W. Lowe, 'The House of Lords, Party and Public Opinion: Opposition Use of the Protest, 1760-82', *Albion*, XI (1979), 143-56.

[91] B.L., Add. MS. 32990, f. 7.

[92] *Ibid.*, 35622, ff. 175-6; B.L., Spencer MSS., F84: Jersey to Lady Spencer, 23 Jan., 1, 9, 22 Feb. 1770; Northamptonshire R.O., Henley (Watford) MSS., Envelope E: Northington to Bishop Shipley (no date). Cf. Brewer, *Party Ideology*, pp. 55-7.

resolve not to conspire against Rockingham. However, many of those same peers persisted in the opposition even after their sovereign espoused the policy of repealing the Stamp Act, just as a body of noblemen acted contrary to their monarch's wishes in 1763 and 1767, thereby weakening ministers in whom he had confidence. Clearly the King was not the master of the upper chamber, nor was the 'party of the Crown' a reliable force at the disposal of all ministers. During the middle years of the decade politicians encountered more difficulties in the Lords than in the Commons, in part because of the discontent of a portion of that group.

If the Lords' unruly behaviour during the 1760s was not characteristic of its eighteenth-century demeanor, neither was it without parallel. Local considerations or those of a particular group provoked peers to rebel against ministerial policies throughout the century. In 1713 discontented Scots not only moved for a dissolution of the Union but, with the Whigs, almost defeated the government's Malt Tax, a measure that seemed to place a particularly heavy burden on Scotland. Twenty-three years later the bishops enraged the King and his chief minister by defeating a bill designed to reduce judicial costs for those Quakers who were sued for payment of tithes. Tory noblemen from the cider counties opposed Dashwood's tax in 1763, just as many Scots nobles supported resolutions defining eligibility for the representative peerage which the Pitt government opposed in 1787.[93] The King could also ignite an opposition against his ministers. Though it is impossible to define precisely his links to Bute in 1765, his intervention in 1783 enabled an already strong force in the House of Lords to defeat the India Bill. But in 1804 as in 1766-7 the Lords harassed ministers whom the monarch professed to support not on local issues but on those of broad national import; in so doing they severely threatened Rockingham and Grafton and later helped to drive Henry Addington from office.[94]

All three of these ministers were victims of a factionalization that tore apart a once dominant government phalanx in the Lords. By the mid-1760s this balkanization of national politics impinged even on the 'party of the Crown': among the friends of Bedford, Bute, Grenville or Newcastle were courtiers, bishops and Scots who followed their leaders into opposition partly out of personal loyalty and partly because they disliked incumbent ministers and their policies. Likewise in 1804 a number of King's friends joined Pitt and Grenville in attacking Henry

[93] G. Holmes and C. Jones, 'Trade, the Scots and the Parliamentary Crisis of 1713', *Parliamentary History*, I (1982), 47-78; Turberville, *House of Lords in the XVIIIth Century*, pp. 214-6; G.M. Ditchfield, 'The Scottish Representative Peers and Parliamentary Politics, 1787-93', *Scottish Historical Review*, LX (1981), 14-31.

[94] M. McCahill, 'The House of Lords and the Collapse of Henry Addington's Administration', *Parliamentary History*, VI (1987), 69-94.

Addington because they believed the former was better able to prosecute the war than the incumbent minister. The result in both instances was an unruly House, for, as Bute admonished in 1767, frequent changes of government 'gradually weaken every bond of State'.

It is important then to reassess the factors that shaped the political character of the House of Lords. Traditionally students of the upper chamber have stressed two – patronage and the monarch. Of course place or its prospects sustained and invigorated the allegiance of peers, most of whom proclaimed as their central political duty the maintenance of the King's government; it is also true that during the 1760s a number of lords persisted in opposition to the Crown even when such conduct jeopardized their places. George III also had a profound impact on the House, though in ways more varied than most would appreciate: towards the end of the decade he played a pivotal role in creating an unassailable administration majority there, but his manoeuvrings at the outset of his reign and in 1765-6 spawned divisions that made the House of Lords difficult to manage. Indeed, the experience of these years as well as pointing out the limits of royal authority or the impact of patronage also highlights the special importance of an additional factor – political cohesion – as a determinant of the chamber's behaviour.

A quiescent House of Lords was not an eighteenth-century inevitability. Rather it reflected the existence of a strong minister who enjoyed broad political support and the firm backing of the monarch. Neither Walpole nor Henry Pelham nor North nor Pitt the Younger faced serious challenges in the House of Lords. On the other hand relatively weak ministries including those headed by George Grenville, Rockingham, Chatham, Charles Fox and Lord North, or Henry Addington ran into real trouble there. Though most peers were inclined to support the King's ministers, many were also bound by personal allegiance to the monarch or, more frequently, to one of his leading politicians. Of course, these connections were not inviolable: Newcastle and George III spent much of the 1760s lamenting perfidy and ingratitude. But the decade is remarkable because so many peers followed a Newcastle, a Bute, a Grenville or a Bedford into opposition. Nor are the 1760s without parallel since a similar process occurred in the early nineteenth century. Peers were disinclined to break with governments on matters of policy unless they sensed royal disapproval or unless the politicians themselves were badly divided. Just as royal disenchantment justified placemen voting against an offensive ministerial effort, so the presence of important political leaders in opposition facilitated and sanctioned peers' own criticisms. In these circumstances noblemen who normally vilified opposition ventured to express their discontent.

In short, the loyalty of the peerage and, more notably, of the 'party of the Crown' depended on the unity of leading politicians as well as on the good offices of the monarch. Without that unity administrations could not count on the absolute reliability of the upper chamber, even when they enjoyed the monarch's support and controlled the dispersal of patronage. The 1760s is an important decade in the history of the eighteenth-century House precisely because of its instability. The succession of weak ministries, each existing to some degree as a repudiation of its predecessors, inevitably engendered political rivalries and enmities that disrupted the House of Lords and made it increasingly difficult to manage. An examination of its conduct under such conditions is crucial to the identification of those forces which shaped its behaviour during the longer, more stable and, therefore more characteristic periods of the eighteenth-century.

Chapter 8

The House of Lords in the Age of the American Revolution★

G.M. Ditchfield

1

During the 1980s there has been a revival of academic engagement with some of the more traditional and durable features of the eighteenth-century British political system – monarchy, aristocracy, prelacy. In keeping with this welcome development, the present essay seeks to analyse and relate to broader developments the pattern of politics in the House of Lords at what is widely seen as a time of internal as well as imperial crisis.[1] Its justification arises from the current state of the literature on the subject: it may be valuable to reinforce the survey of A.S. Turberville (whose volume on this period was published in 1927) and to fill what remains something of a gap between the detailed studies of M.W. McCahill and W. Lowe for the 1760s and early 1770s and those of McCahill and D. Large for the post-1783 period.[2] Such a relatively narrow concentration is, of course, exposed to the risk of isolating one decade and of exaggerating what might have been unrepresentative tendencies. Accordingly the essay will recognize that the period 1770-83 is best understood in a longer term historical context, one which suggests a substantial measure of continuity before 1770 and a limited but

★ I wish to thank Olive, Countess Fitzwilliam's Wentworth Settlement Trustees and the Director, Sheffield City Libraries for permission to consult and quote from material in the Wentworth Woodhouse Muniments and His Grace the Duke of Grafton for permission to consult and quote from the Grafton MSS. at Bury St. Edmunds and West Suffolk Record Office. Transcripts from Crown copyright records in the Public Record Office appear by permission of the Controller of Her Majesty's Stationery Office. I am grateful to Professor Ian R. Christie, Dr. J.C.D. Clark, and Sir John Sainty for helpful comments on an earlier draft of this essay.

[1] Notably by Sir Herbert Butterfield, *George III, Lord North and the People, 1779-1780* (1949).

[2] A.S. Turberville, *The House of Lords in the XVIII Century* (Oxford 1927); M.W. McCahill, 'The House of Lords in the 1760s', above, pp. 165-98; W.C. Lowe, 'Bishops and Scottish Representative Peers in the House of Lords, 1760-1775', *Journal of British Studies*, XVIII (1978), 86-106; M.W. McCahill, *Order and Equipoise: The Peerage and the House of Lords 1783-1806* (1978): D. Large, 'The Decline of "the Party of the Crown" and the Rise of Parties in the House of Lords, 1783-1837', *E.H.R.*, LXXVII (1963), 669-95.

significant measure of change after 1783.

Such a longer term perspective offers a safeguard against regarding the age of the American Revolution as unique or even unusual in the history of the House of Lords. The impact of the war of American Independence upon the Lords was undoubtedly considerable, but it did not alter the fundamental axioms which underpinned the upper chamber's existence. Parliamentary politics remained essentially a part-time occupation. As Table 1 indicates, the Lords rarely sat for 100 days in the year, a figure very similar to that under Queen Anne; there was no major change in the level of attendance; the meetings of the House of Lords were still largely occupied with local and private business. This essay will contend that what emerges primarily from a study of the Lords in the age of the American Revolution is less a new political order than the partial re-appearance of an older and more familiar configuration. Two ministries – those of North and Shelburne – were indeed laid low by the American issue, but their downfall was not caused by the House of Lords, although in Shelburne's case the voting of the peers over the peace treaties was very close. Much of the public business of the Lords directly or indirectly concerned America, but much other public business – the Falklands dispute, Royal Marriage Act, Civil List, religious controversy – was not American inspired. Perhaps the most immediate effect of the American war upon the House of Lords as an institution was its promotion of public scrutiny in the realm of finance: the consequent pursuit of economy under Pitt led to extra peerage creations as alternative sources of political rewards became scarcer. Hence the membership of the House of Lords was rapidly enlarged after 1783, although its social composition was not really altered.

The most thorough contemporary account of the early eighteenth century House of Lords is to be found in the London diaries of William Nicolson, Bishop of Carlisle. They cover the years 1702 to 1718.[3] It is true that in the subsequent half century the influence of the Lords vis-à-vis the House of Commons had declined; that the intense party conflict of Whig and Tory had subsided; that the Lords' proceedings were far more widely reported; and that the nature both of public business (with the increasing emphasis on America and other imperial themes) and of private business (with the growing number of enclosure, bridge, canal and turnpike bills) had changed. But there was much in the proceedings of the House of Lords in the 1770s that Nicolson would have recognized. In the intervening years there had been no major innovations in procedure; Cabinet offices were still almost completely monopolised by peers; Lords' debates were still dominated by 20 or 30 regular speakers;

---

[3] *The London Diaries of William Nicolson, Bishop of Carlisle, 1702-1718*, ed. C. Jones and G. Holmes (Oxford, 1985).

Table 1

Membership and Attendance in the House of Lords, 1762-1783.[4]

Dates of Session	Total No. of peers entitled to attend at start of session	No. of days on which House of Lords was sitting	No. of daily attendances of 75 or over	Average daily attendance (All members of House of Lords)	Average daily attendance (Bishops)	No. of Divisions	No. of Protests
25 Nov. 1762-19 Apr. 1763	206	60	7	48.88	9.70	3	2
15 Nov. 1763-19 Apr. 1764	207	80	19	57.03	11.19	2	1
10 Jan. -25 May 1765	206	82	24	60.77	10.20	11	–
17 Dec. 1765- 6 June 1766	206	79	26	60.96	8.53	8	2
11 Nov. 1766- 2 July 1767	208	107	24	54.94	8.62	16	2
24 Nov. 1767-10 Mar. 1768	209	49	5	42.37	6.98	1	1
10 May -21 June 1768	210	11	1	33.00	4.27	–	–
8 Nov. 1768- 9 May 1769	210	84	22	49.99	6.36	5	1
9 Jan. -19 May 1770	214	71	21	57.58	9.20	21	4
13 Nov. 1770- 8 May 1771	211	84	14	46.20	7.29	17	5
21 Jan. - 9 June 1772	209	78	8	36.96	6.47	10	2
26 Nov. 1772- 1 July 1773	207	106	1	25.88	4.05	17	3
13 Jan. -22 June 1774	206	93	5	34.78	5.16	14	2
29 Nov. 1774-26 May 1775	203	88	11	46.22	7.36	20	7
26 Oct. 1775-23 May 1776	203	108	17	40.88	6.71	15	3
31 Oct. 1776- 6 June 1777	211	87	5	29.51	5.29	13	4
20 Nov. 1777- 3 June 1778	212	87	24	52.57	8.15	35	4
26 Nov. 1778- 3 July 1779	211	121	32	49.46	7.13	36	7
25 Nov. 1779- 8 July 1780	210	95	14	36.12	5.96	18	3
31 Oct. 1780-18 July 1781	217	97	4	33.88	5.69	15	4
27 Nov. 1781-11 July 1782	216	99	14	44.86	6.38	20	3
5 Dec. 1782-16 July 1783	222	93	5	34.84	6.17	11	3

[4] This table has been compiled from *L.J.*, G.E.C., *Complete Peerage*, J.C. Sainty and D. Dewar, *Divisions in the House of Lords: An Analytical List, 1685-1857* (House of Lords Record Office Occasional Publications, No. 2, 1976), and *The Royal Kalendar; or Complete and Correct Annual Register for England, Scotland, Ireland and America.*

the size of membership was much the same; the defence of the Church of England still assumed a high priority; and the physical appearance of the chamber itself had not altered. The episcopal diarist of the Augustan age would not have been a complete stranger in the House of Lords of Chatham and Grafton.

Private business formed the majority of items in any day's proceedings. The private bill was an essential means whereby peers acquired a role in the promotion of estate, canal, turnpike and other projects designed to facilitate the agricultural and sometimes the industrial interests not only of themselves, but also of the regions to which they belonged. The industrial patronage of the aristocracy has been explored by Dr. McCahill.[5] Conducted in a way which tended to preserve, rather than challenge, existing asumptions as to property relationships, it kept members of the House of Lords in contact with, and indeed leaders in, contemporary economic and social developments. Industrial patronage, however, remained a subsidiary concern in the 1770s. The enclosure bill was rapidly becoming the most familiar type of private legislation. A sizeable increase in the number of enclosure bills can be traced to the mid 1760s and, under the combined pressure of poor harvests and high food prices on the one hand, and the prospect of high financial returns on the other, to 1771-4 and 1776-9. In 1772 the annual number of enclosure bills totalled 70 for the first time; in 1777 it reached 99, a figure not exceeded until 1802. Altogether, 763 enclosure bills reached Parliament between 1770-83 inclusive, compared with 625 between 1719 and 1769.[6] Although the House of Commons had virtually appropriated the initiation of enclosure bills (only nine began in the Lords between 1753 and 1774), Sheila Lambert has shown that such bills were subjected to rigorous and detailed scrutiny by committees of the House of Lords. In 1780 the Commons failed to sustain a claim that, on account of their financial nature, enclosure bills could not be amended in the Lords, and the process of amendment in the upper chamber continued – on grounds which were not solely technical but which allowed access to a variety of local representations.[7]

As the highest court of appeal, moreover, the House of Lords retained considerable political authority. On several occasions in this period the Lords displayed an independence of the lower courts by upholding appeals against their judgments. The two most significant were the

[5] M.W. McCahill, 'Peers, Patronage and the Industrial Revolution, 1760-1810', *Journal of British Studies*, XVI (1976), 84-107; I.R. Christie, *Stress and Stability in late Eighteenth Century Britain* (Oxford, 1984), pp., 67-9.

[6] 'Select Committee on Agricultural Distress', Appendix 16, *British Parliamentary Papers*, 1836, vol. VIII, pt. 2, p. 501.

[7] Sheila Lambert, *Bills and Acts. Legislative Procedure in Eighteenth Century England* (Cambridge, 1971), pp. 136-143.

decision, in the famous 'literary property' case of 1774, that, at common law, authors did not hold a perpetual copyright of their works after publication, and the determination (reversing a verdict of the Court of Common Pleas) in 1783 that general resignation bonds delivered by clergy to ecclesiastical patrons were illegal.[8] Several appeals were pressed to a division, in which all members of the House of Lords, irrespective of the state of their legal knowledge, and of the advice of the judges, were entitled to vote. This practice was controversial. On 11 May 1778 four opposition lords voted (unavailingly) in favour of John Horne's appeal on a writ of error against a verdict in the Court of King's Bench which had condemned him to fining and imprisonment on a libel charge. They incurred much criticism for 'having presumed to rise in opposition to the opinion of the twelve judges', but were stoutly defended by Dr. Johnson. 'The peers are judges themselves', he declared, 'and supposing them really to be of a different opinion, they might from duty be in opposition to the judges, who were there only to be consulted'. Boswell agreed.[9] Appeals still occupied a good deal of the Lords' daily work. One such suit, the Douglas case of 1769 became one of the causes célèbres of the century. Peers, moreover, were entitled to trial before the House of Lords, a right exercised by Lord Byron (on a murder charge) in 1765 and by the Duchess of Kingston (accused of bigamy) in 1776. The latter case was considered by the Lords in Westminster Hall on five separate days and produced the highest attendances of the whole period. The great impeachments of Hastings and Melville were still to come.

Private business and appellate jurisdiction enhanced the role of the Lords individually and collectively both as lobbyists and as the objects of lobbyists. In this way the peers served a vital, if sometimes unofficial, representative purpose. Herein lay much of their real influence. Over appeals they exercised an authority quite independent of the House of Commons; as members of a legislative chamber they were accessible, however indirectly, to influence from below. Finally they claimed a right of personal audience with the Crown. Lord Temple's exploitation of this unique entitlement over the India Bill of 1783 was the most spectacular, but far from the only, instance of its use.[10] The influence of the House of Lords can be appreciated fully only if it is recognized that several of its most important functions were peculiar to itself, yet involved it in harmonious relationships with other elements in the constitution and in society.

[8] Cobbett, *Parl. Hist.* XVII, 953-1003; XXIII, 876-94.

[9] J. Boswell, *The Life of Samuel Johnson, LLD*, ed. G.B. Hill, revised by L.F. Powell, (6 vols., Oxford, 1934-50), III, 345-6. Horne's appeal was rejected by 20 votes to 4.

[10] See for example Abingdon's speech of 8 Apr. 1778 in J. Almon, *Parliamentary Register* (82 vols., 1775-1804) [cited hereafter as *Parl. Reg.*], X, 402; and *The Correspondence of King George III*, ed. Sir John Fortescue (6 vols., 1927-8), IV, no. 2529.

As well as the great set-piece debates, the years 1770 to 1783 witnessed three of the most dramatic incidents in the entire history of the House of Lords – the collapse of Chatham, the siege of the chamber by the Gordon rioters and the fall of the Fox-North coalition following a well-publicised Lords' division. The Lords could boast peers of great debating ability and experience: Chatham, Shelburne, Richmond; the great lawyers, Mansfield, Camden and (from 1778) Thurlow; men of outstanding military and naval reputations – Ligonier, Hawke, Cathcart, Bolton; career diplomats such as Rochford and Stormont; and men with direct military and administrative experience of America, such as Amherst and Dunmore (though no nabobs).[11] Despite the illiberal manner in which peerages had been conferred upon commoners in the previous half century, several leading figures in the Lords had acquired their political reputations in the lower House – Chatham, Temple, Holland, Mansfield, Loughborough, although many of the other leading debaters – Townshend, Grafton, Portland, Gower, Manchester – had inherited their titles at too early an age for the full development of a Commons career.

At the same time there was a considerable and probably increasing public interest in the House of Lords, and in Parliament as a whole. There was pressure for the publication of the debates of both Houses. Newspaper proprietors and editors clearly believed, perhaps correctly, that their readers were eager to study parliamentary reports. During the early 1770s, however, the fulfilment of this public interest in Lords' debates was subjected to two important but temporary limitations. Firstly, the controversy over parliamentary reporting which arose from that ramification of the Wilkite affair known as the Printers' Case in 1771 meant that only sparse accounts of some Lords debates of the early 1770s have survived.[12] Secondly, the House of Lords displayed an obsession with 'strangers' which led to the exclusion from the chamber not only of the public but of M.P.s as well. When Gower insisted that the House be cleared during the Falklands debate of 10 December 1770 he employed the disingenuous argument that a public audience might include Spanish 'spies', and that the revelation of military and diplomatic detail could endanger national security. For several years Lords and Commons maintained a frigid hostility and a policy of mutual exclusion over this matter, while Sandwich in October 1776 and February 1778 refused on similar grounds to divulge to the Lords information as to the disposition

[11] Even Robert Clive 'had to be content with his Irish peerage' which excluded him from 'the inner circle of the English [sic] House of Lords': P. Lawson and J. Philips, ' "Our Execrable Banditti". Perceptions of Nabobs in Mid-Eighteenth Century Britain', *Albion*, XVI (1984), 228.

[12] See P.D.G. Thomas, 'John Wilkes and the Freedom of the Press (1771)', *B.I.H.R.* XXXIII (1960), 86-98.

of the fleet.[13] Repeated proposals for the construction of a gallery in the Lords, solely for M.P.s or for the public at large, were defeated. Although Carl Moritz observed in 1782 that Lords debates were 'conducted with more ceremony and decorum' than those of the Commons, he did not actually attend them. Lord Le Despenser contended in 1779 that a gallery would 'only become a laughing receptacle for ladies'.[14]

A much wider press coverage of Lords debates began in the session of 1774-5, when the feud with the Commons ended and the outcome of the Printers' Case made it more difficult to suppress the reporting of parliamentary proceedings. The Lords allowed greater access to M.P.s and relaxed the standing order which had excluded strangers from admission below the bar of the House. Referring to Chatham's bill on 1 February 1775 for the pacification of America, Horace Walpole declared that 'the newspapers . . . are now very accurate in recounting debates'.[15] Reporters joined the spectators below the bar and made semi-surreptitious notes.[16] Several Americans attended on 20 January 1775 for Chatham's motion for the withdrawal of British troops from Boston; the American loyalist Samuel Curwen was 'without difficulty admitted' on 24 November 1775 and numerous subsequent occasions; on 25 March 1777 the House was 'greatly crouded below the Bar with Members of the Lower House, and with Strangers, who were politely admitted' for the Lords' debate on the Annuity Bill.[17] Admission could be facilitated by connections with the peerage. Benjamin Franklin was conducted to the House on 1 February 1775 by Lord Stanhope and given a favoured position 'leaning on the bar'.[18] Large crowds gathered for public spectacles such as the trial of the Duchess of Kingston: 'You may think of America, if you please, but we think and talk but of one Subject, the solemn comedy that is acting in Westminster Hall', wrote Horace

[13] Turberville , *Lords in XVIII Century*, pp. 16-18; *General Evening Post*, 31 Oct.-2 Nov. 1776; Cobbett, *Parl. Hist.*, XIX, 668.

[14] C.P. Moritz, *Journeys of a German in England in 1782*, translated and edited by R. Nettell (1965), p. 54; *St. James's Chronicle*, 10-12 June 1779. A gallery had existed briefly in the House of Lords between 1704-11 and 1737-40, but had been dismantled on each occasion; see H.M. Colvin, *The History of the King's Works* (6 vols., 1963-82), V (1660-1782), 391-2.

[15] *Horace Walpole's Correspondence*, ed. W.S. Lewis (48 vols., New Haven, 1937-83), XXII, 235.

[16] See, e.g. *Morning Chronicle and Public Advertiser*, 10 Feb. 1778; *Public Advertiser*, 8 Dec. 1778; *St. James's Chronicle*, 29-31 Mar. 1781.

[17] Turberville, *Lords in XVIII Century*, pp. 358-9; *The Journal of Samuel Curwen, Loyalist*, ed. A. Oliver (2 vols., Cambridge, Mass., 1972), I, 87; *Public Advertiser*, 25 Mar. 1777.

[18] *The Papers of Benjamin Franklin*, ed. W.B. Willcox (25 vols. to date, New Haven, 1959-86), XXI, 581. *Pace* the editor (p. xxxix), Franklin was not 'in the gallery'; no such gallery existed in 1775.

Walpole on 17 April 1776.[19] The element of spectacle was also present in the debates on America in the later 1770s, with frequent press references to crowds, and the brief spate of published Lords division lists in 1775. When on 30 May 1777 it was known that Chatham would come to the Lords to move a motion for peace with America, 'all the Passages leading to the House of Lords were filled with a prodigious concourse of people'. The following January a false rumour of Chatham's presence had a similar effect.[20]

After 1774 there were only sporadic attempts to curb press reporting in the Lords. Although the House pursued William Parker of the *General Advertiser* in 1779-80, there was nothing on the scale of Gower's earlier attempt (1770) to arraign the *Middlesex Journal* for breach of privilege after it had published an opposition protest. Both Houses of Parliament were wary of making martyrs of printers. 'If you should be sentenced to the pillory, your fortune is made', asserts Henry Davis in Smollett's *Humphry Clinker*, 'C——— S——— has been threatened several times by the House of L———; but it came to nothing'.[21] Whatever the theory, public access to Lords' proceedings was not difficult in practice. At times spectators below the bar so far forgot themselves as to participate; on 26 November 1778 Shelburne's attack on the ministry in the debate on the King's speech ended with 'two or three of the Auditors very indecently beating their Canes upon the floor by way of Applause', and the House being cleared as a result.[22] None of this would have astonished Bishop Nicolson, in whose time the business of the Lords had occasionally been disturbed by strangers.[23] He would have been less familiar with the lengthy reports of Lords debates which by the late 1770s were appearing regularly in the London and provincial newspapers and in the periodical press. The reliability of such reports must, of course, remain problematical: the *Morning Chronicle and London Advertiser* in 1778 admitted that it provided 'rather the substance than the circumstance' of what occurred.[24] Professor Thomas has shown how press accounts of particular debates often derive from a single source, and that newspapers plagiarised each other: his conclusion that 'the value of newspaper reports is . . . limited to names and general arguments', though applied

---

[19] *Walpole Correspondence*, XXIV, 191.
[20] *Public Advertiser*, 31 May 1777; *London Evening Post*, 20-21 Jan. 1778.
[21] T. Smollett, *The Expedition of Humphry Clinker*, ed. A. Ross (Harmondsworth, 1971). C——— S——— is usually interpreted as Charles Say, printer of the *Gazetteer*, who was fined £100 for a libel on Lord Hertford in 1764.
[22] *St. James's Chronicle*, 26-28 Nov. 1778; *L.J.*, XXXV, 523.
[23] *London Diaries of William Nicolson*, pp. 84-6.
[24] *Morning Chronicle and London Advertiser*, 10 Feb. 1778.

to the Commons, might reasonably be extended to the Lords, especially before 1774–75.[25]

2

As with much which is performed effectively, North's management of the House of Lords before and during the American War is frequently taken for granted. That his administration took much trouble over this task is easily demonstrated: less widely accepted is the possibility that it faced a real problem. One may concede that the voting outcome in the Lords was genuinely unpredictable only when it was known that the ministry lacked the full confidence of the Crown, as with the first Rockingham administration and the Fox–North coalition, or when the normal ministerial adherents in the Lords were seriously divided, as under Grafton in 1767. Lord Chedworth even believed that the India Bill would easily pass in the Lords before he became aware of George III's active opposition to it.[26] The House of Lords could undoubtedly show independence of a Commons majority which did not have the support of the Crown, as with the Dissenters bills of 1772–3 and the India Bill ten years later. But the Lords showed much less independence of a Commons majority which had, and was known to have, the support of the Crown. Ironically, when a ministry which enjoyed the confidence of the Crown came nearest in this period to defeat in the Lords over a central issue of policy, with the passage of Shelburne's peace preliminaries by the dramatically narrow margin of 13 on 17 February 1783, the Commons had rejected the same proposals the previous day. North's ministry did not succumb in the upper chamber even when it had lost its majority in the Commons: 'I am sure this is not the *Lords*' doing – though it is marvellous in our eyes', quipped Walpole three days after North resigned.[27]

Yet the House of Lords could never be treated dismissively. It was dangerous to offend the susceptibilities of its members over rank, privilege and precedence. The House could be sensitive over its institutional rights, procedures and standing orders. In 1782 Thurlow advised Rockingham to ensure that the King's address recommending economy be directed to both Houses, not just to the Commons, since

You know the House of Lords has never given up Their Pretense to act in the

---

[25] P.D.G. Thomas, 'The Beginning of Parliamentary Reporting in Newspapers, 1768-1774', *E.H.R.*, LXXIV (1959), 623-36. It should not be assumed that the reporting controversy only concerned the Commons.

[26] *Letters from the late Lord Chedworth to the Rev. Thomas Crompton; Written in the period from Jan. 1780 to May 1795* (1828), p. 30.

[27] *Walpole Correspondence*, XXIX, 208.

manner of granting, applying or disposing of publick money. At the same time they have looked on very patiently, while all that business was in fact transacted by the House of Commons.[28]

The latter diagnosis was somewhat premature. The House of Lords rejected Economical Reform legislation in 1780 and was still capable of pursuing disagreements with the Commons to the extent of a joint conference of the two Houses. It did so with its insistence on an amendment to the Contractors Bill of 1782, before finally yielding the point.[29] Even North's ministry did not find the Lords to be invariably pliant. In November 1775 it was obliged to abandon its Military Indemnity Bill in the Lords, while in June 1779 the Lords deleted from the Militia Bill the clauses which would have permitted the augmentation of that body by means of a ballot.[30] In the latter case the Lords' amendments were accepted by the Commons even though some M.P.s argued that it was a money bill and hence not amenable to Lords' amendment.[31] The opposition groups in the Lords showed their ability to sting over such episodes as the Royal Marriage Act, Chatham's speeches on America and what George III called their 'very wicked' protest over the Spanish Manifesto in June 1779.[32] Regular opposition speakers included well-informed peers with ministerial, legal, military and naval experience, as well as independent-minded figures such as Richmond and Radnor, whom it could be awkward and time-consuming to offend. There was always the possibility that the House of Lords might be the stage for the revelation of scandal which could damage Crown and ministry, as when George III and North feared that Lord Grosvenor would seek to prosecute the King's brother, the Duke of Cumberland, for criminal conversation with his wife.[33] If Lowe and McCahill have perhaps exaggerated the restiveness of the House of Lords, they were certainly reacting quite understandably against a generalised depiction of servility which was in danger of hardening into an orthodoxy.[34] In view of Lowe's work on the 1760s, which showed that several ministries at times virtually lost their command of the upper chamber, the question as to how the ministry obtained and retained

[28] Sheffield City Library, Wentworth Woodhouse Muniments (cited hereafter as W.W.M.), Rockingham Papers R 1-2079: Thurlow to Rockingham, 15 May 1782.

[29] Turberville, *Lords in XVIII Century*, pp. 401-2. There were four such conferences during North's ministry.

[30] Cobbett, *Parl. Hist.*, XVIII, 1027-8; Bodl., North Papers, MS. d.25, f. 79: Brownlow North to the Earl of Guilford, 27 Nov. 1775.

[31] J.R. Western, *The English Militia in the Eighteenth Century. The Story of a Political Issue, 1660-1802* (1965), pp. 210-215.

[32] *Correspondence of George III*, II, nos. 1024, 1025A; III, nos. 1692, 2006; IV. no. 2667.

[33] S. Ayling, *George the Third* (1972), pp. 211-2.

[34] See especially J. Cannon, *The Fox-North Coalition: Crisis of the Constitution, 1782-4* (Cambridge, 1969), p. 125; and J. Brooke, *King George III* (1972), p. 252.

majorities in the House of Lords between 1770 and 1782 becomes a real one. Certainly the King and Lord North tried hard to avoid alienating individual peers or groups within the House. 'I desire I may hear no more of Irish Marquises, I feel for the English Earls and do not choose to digust them', wrote George III in 1776; six years later he warned 'if some attention is [not] shewn to the House of Lords by proper communication before offices usually held in that House are filled up, I fear my Service will not be benefited by such inattention'. As Stormont acknowledged in 1780, royal solicitude for the interests of the Lords was of 'essential advantage' to the ministry.[35]

One manifestation of that attention was the influence which a ministry exercised over the composition of the Lords, although it was an influence which fell far short of overall control. Ministers did not purge the episcopal bench of the appointees of earlier administrations, nor could they determine the political loyalties of those who entered the Lords by inheritance. Moreover the large-scale expansion of the peerage which is associated with the Younger Pitt had not yet begun. It is true that in 1776 seven new baronies were conferred, while there were two baronies for elder sons of Scottish peers and four promotions within the British peerage.[36] McCahill indeed sees these creations as the start of the period of enlargement,[37] although it should be remembered that there had been a greater number of new peerages in 1761-2, that there were no more creations in the 1770s than in the 1760s, and that the membership of the House of Lords was slightly smaller in November 1779 than in January 1770. Strictly speaking, 1776 is no more the starting point of the subsequent enlargement than 1761-2. However it was the largest block creation of new peers since 1711-12 and it was followed by a further group of six in 1780. The purpose was hardly to strengthen the ministry's majority in the Lords, even in 1778-80, when opposition numbers began to grow. The explanation lies in the need for intellectual reinforcement (as with Thurlow in 1778), the wish to reward such distinguished individuals as Amherst and Hawke, and the need to gratify, at least in part, the cravings of peerage-seekers. Not all the new elevations were designed to aid the ministry: North regretted Brudenell's peerage as likely to 'make him and me ridiculous'.[38] Although royal refusal to grant peerages could damage a ministry, as the Coalition discovered, the truth was that peerage creations were not really

[35] *Correspondence of George III*, III, no. 1837; V, nos. 3131, 3518.

[36] If one includes the barony conferred on Elizabeth, Duchess of Argyll, ten British baronies were created on one day, 20 May 1776: G.E.C., *Complete Peerage*, V, 536.

[37] M.W. McCahill, 'Peerage Creations and the Changing Character of the British Nobility, 1750-1850', *E.H.R.*, XCVI (1981), 259.

[38] *Parliamentary Papers of John Robinson, 1774-1784*, ed. W.T. Laprade. (Camden Soc. 3rd ser. XXXIII, 1922), p. 35.

necessary to maintain North's command of the House of Lords.

One explanation frequently offered for the ministerial majority in the Lords is the high proportion of peers who held office or some other favour from government. A combination of cabinet, and other ministerial office-holders, members of the royal household, naval and military commanders, the great law officers, holders of local office, notably lords lieutenant, and recipients of pensions, could hardly fail between them to deliver a bloc vote.[39] Certainly there were peers who believe that they had a right to charity from the Crown. In the declining years of North's administration several ministers and ex-ministers, among them Rochford, Bathurst and Sandwich, pleaded with the King for financial relief: 'Earls have generally had from £600 to £800', recalled George III in 1781.[40] These were rewards for past services; other pensions, such as that requested by Falkland, were non-political, Namier's 'aristocratic dole', and Dr. Johnson was not alone in his belief that the peerage should be protected against the extremes of poverty, lest its independence be totally forfeited.[41]

The precise composition of the ministerial majority in vital divisions is not easily discovered, since most surviving Lords' lists from the 1770s are of the minority only. But the majority grouping can at times be reconstructed from the *Lords Journals* and in the Appendix (below, pp. 237-39) an attempt is made to provide a full voting list for the division on the Address of 25 November 1779, a major confrontation at the start of a new session, which produced an attendance of 129. Among the 82 lords who voted in person with the ministry on that day it is not surprising to find (in addition to 15 bishops and nine Scottish representative peers) many leading figures of government, with other office-holders, such as Cadogan (Master of the Mint), Northington (a Teller of the Exchequer) and Pelham (Surveyor-General of the Customs of London). The household peers, led by Northumberland (Master of the Horse) and Hertford (Lord Chamberlain), together with 14 other household officers (including eight Lords of the Bedchamber) are well represented. There were 14 Lords Lieutenant and at least four recipients of pensions (Essex, Montfort, Scarsdale, Macclesfield).[42] Of the 82, only 13 held no office or favour of any kind. There is no reason to suppose that this was a markedly untypical division.

Evidence such as this fuelled contemporary allegations that the House

[39] See J. Cannon, *Aristocratic Century. The Peerage of Eighteenth Century England* (Cambridge, 1984), pp. 94-99.

[40] *Correspondence of George III*, V, nos. 3570, 3591, 3431-2.

[41] *Ibid.*, V, no. 3283; Boswell, *Johnson*, V, 101-2.

[42] Of the nine Scottish representative peers, seven also held some kind of office. G.E.C. *Complete Peerage* has been used for office holders; see also the survey of pension holders in J. Norris, *Shelburne and Reform* (1963), pp. 186-195.

of Lords was 'bought', and dominated by a 'dead majority'.[43] In the 1770s the opposition press occasionally printed its own catalogue of ministerial peers with their offices, to try to show that the majority was 'dead and rotten' and the minority 'sound and free'.[44] But several qualifications to these suggestions of a 'bought' house must be registered. In the first place, Court and other appointments often reflected a pre-existing loyalty on the part of the peers concerned, and were not necessarily the cause of that loyalty. Secondly, household offices in particular were becoming more openly political after 1782: George III lamented the changes in personnel imposed by the second Rockingham ministry and as a result, at least some of these appointments could be made by an administration not favoured by the Crown.[45] Thirdly, office-holding was not necessarily a guarantee of attendance or regular pro-government voting in the Lords: it was not even a guarantee of political attachment to the current ministry. Camden in 1770 and Grafton in 1775 behaved with remarkable disloyalty to the administrations of which they were members until they had virtually to be driven from office. Several household lords rebelled: Jersey voted against government in 1775 but was not dismissed from the Bedchamber until two years later, North regarded the political conduct of Talbot (Lord Steward) as 'pernicious . . . to the weight and credit of government', while Pembroke and Carmarthen opposed North in 1779–80, resigned from the household and were dismissed from their Lord Lieutenancies.[46]

Moreover the regular minority in the Lords during the 1770s contained a significant number of appointees whose offices were studiously omitted in opposition publications. In 1774 Debrett's *History, Debates and Proceedings* duly listed the peers who had usually voted with the ministry during the previous session, along with their offices.[47] It also listed 47 opposition peers, but failed to add that they mustered 12 Privy Councillors, seven Lords Lieutenant, such placemen as Sondes (Joint Auditor of Imprest, Mint and Coinage), Manchester (Collector of Subsidies in the Port of London) and Scarbrough (Deputy Earl Marshal), together with local office-holders such as Archer (Recorder of Coventry), Camden (Recorder of Bath), Spencer (High Steward of St. Albans), an admiral (Bolton), two Irish governors (Devonshire and

---

[43] See, e.g., *London Evening Post*, 28–31 Jan. 1775; *Walpole Correspondence*, XXXV, 588.

[44] *London Evening Post*, 28–31 Jan. 1775.

[45] *Correspondence of George III*, V, nos. 3593, 3596; Large, 'Party of the Crown', p. 685.

[46] *Correspondence of George III*, III, no. 2096; V, no. 3128; Turberville, *Lords in XVIII Century*, p. 387.

[47] J. Debrett, *History, Debates and Proceedings of both Houses of Parliament, 1743-1774* (7 vols., 1792), [cited hereafter as Debrett, *Debates*], VII, 16–18.

Leinster) and two Army officers (Romney and Effingham). The *London Evening Post* printed a division list over the Contractors Bill on 14 April 1780 which purported to show that only three of the 38 British peers who helped to form the majority vote of 60 were independent of government influence, while giving no indication of the favours enjoyed by the minority of 41. In fact the minority contained two bishops, seven Lords Lieutenant, Percy (a general), Radnor (Recorder of Salisbury) as well as several of the minority of 1774, including Sondes, Bolton, Manchester, Camden and Devonshire. The minority of 41 on the vote on the Address of 25 November 1779 (see Appendix) included 19 who held some kind of office, excluding Privy Councillors. It would not be difficult to find examples of prominent opposition peers who held office: Shelburne was a general, Temple a Teller of the Exchequer, Rockingham a Lord Lieutenant.[48] Lord Lieutenancies indeed reflected a peer's local eminence (and the difficulty of running a county without him). Under pressure of war George III vowed in 1781 that he would appoint no new Lords Lieutenant 'whose sentiments are not cordial with government'.[49] But except for Pembroke and Carmarthen, this policy was not made retrospective. 'The Head of the Derby family is the proper person to fill the office of Lord Lieutenant of the County of Lancaster', the King declared in 1776, but when Derby went into opposition two years later, no steps were taken to remove him. Few opposition peers incurred more royal indignation than Richmond, Lord Lieutenant of Sussex. Yet for all George III's complaints as to his unsuitability and disloyalty in that capacity, he was not dismissed.[50]

A fourth qualification concerns the necessity of identifying, rallying and organising in the ministerial interest these supposedly 'natural' supporters of government. This task fell to the government leader or manager in the House of Lords and Sir John Sainty has indicated that by the early years of George III's reign it was normally undertaken by the senior of the two Secretaries of State. The picture is clarified by the fact that every occupant of these posts during North's ministry sat in the Lords and the role of leader was exercised, with varying degrees of effectiveness, successively by Weymouth, Rochford, Suffolk, Weymouth (again) and Stormont. The duties of the leader included the provision of reports to the King on proceedings in the Lords, although other ministers, especially Sandwich on matters of naval administration, reported directly to George III when issues concerning their own departments appeared before the upper chamber.[51] He was responsible

[48] Professor Cannon accepts at least some of these reservations: *Aristocratic Century*, p. 99.

[49] *Correspondence of George III*, V, no. 3435.

[50] *Ibid.*, III, no. 1827; IV, nos. 2737, 2756.

[51] *Ibid.*, IV, nos. 2616-7, 2666; J.C. Sainty, 'The Origin of the Leadership of the House of Lords', *B.I.H.R.*, XLVII (1974), 53-73.

for the preparation of business. Since peers dominated both the large 'formal' cabinet and the inner circle of 'efficient' ministers, it was important that they be well informed in advance of Lords' debates. Hence the 'formal' cabinet was regularly summoned to St. James's to hear the King's speech, while the 'inner cabinet' was similarly kept informed as to ministerial policy as a whole.[52] Grafton as Lord Privy Seal between 1771-75 was summoned to cabinet meetings when matters of significance were due for debate in the Lords, despite his reluctance to attend.[53] Equally important was the organization of pre-sessional meetings of ministerial lords, usually about 60 to 70 in number, for the reading of the King's speech. The evidence from the 1770s is incomplete, but it is clear that Rochford summoned the pre-sessional meeting at his own house in January 1772.[54] However, the meeting which immediately preceded the next session in November 1772 was held at the house of the Earl of Suffolk, Northern (and, at that time, junior) Secretary.[55] Clearly Suffolk acted for Rochford on this, and possibly other occasions before taking over the leadership of the Lords on Rochford's resignation in November 1775.[56] In November 1779 the meeting took place at the house of the newly appointed Stormont and 53 lords attended, while some 220-230 M.P.s were present at the parallel gathering at the Cockpit of government supporters in the Commons.[57] Stormont's successor as leader in the Lords was Shelburne, who arranged the pre-sessional meeting, attended by 62 peers, in December 1782.[58]

It was also necessary to recruit peers to move and second the Address of thanks in reply to the King's speech. The ministerial side needed an able exposition of its case at the outset of a new session, and the Lords debate on the Address assumed an added importance from 1774-75, when the opposition shed some of its previous ineffectiveness. In November 1774 George III was anxious that the Address be moved by 'a Peer of some degree of Weight', such as Hillsborough, 'as it must naturally contain strong assurances of supporting the Authority of the Mother Country over its Colonies'.[59] By the latter 1770s, however,

---

[52] See P.R.O., S.P. 37/11, f. 264 (end of session, May 1776); 37/13, f. 249 (Nov. 1779); 37/14, f. 335 (Oct. 1780); Stormont's 'Note to the Cabinet', 23 Oct. 1780, 37/14, f. 332.

[53] P. Durrant, 'A Political Life of Augustus Henry Fitzroy, Third Duke of Grafton (1735-1811)' (Manchester Ph.D., 1978), p. 318. There is no evidence that Grafton actually attended cabinet meetings between 1771-5.

[54] P.R.O., S.P. 37/9, ff. 9-12: list of lords who were summoned to, and who attended, the meeting at Rochford's house, 20 Jan. 1772.

[55] *Ibid.*, ff. 313-4: list of lords summoned, 25 Nov. 1772; Sainty, 'Leadership of the Lords', p. 70.

[56] See *Correspondence of George III*, III, nos. 1413, 1428, 1849, 1866.

[57] *Ibid.*, IV, nos. 2846, 2851.

[58] *Ibid.*, IV, no. 4008.

[59] *Ibid.*, III, no. 1555.

moving and seconding the Address had become a less desirable office, the execution of which could incur the sardonic comments of opposition newspapers. It was reported that Buccleuch had declined an invitation to do so in 1778, while the following year Stormont had to approach four peers before finding willing candidates in Grantham and Chesterfield.[60] He encountered no less difficulty in 1780 and in renewing his application to a reluctant Brownlow had to assure him that 'The Seconder of an Address is at Liberty to extend or contract his Speeches [as] he thinks fit; and this Introduction has generally been considered as the best way of taking an active Part in Parliament'.[61]

This endeavour was reinforced by efforts to secure the actual attendance of government supporters on particular days and thus turn potential into actual support. A small batch of whips and circulars in the names of successive leaders, although apparently only random survivals, indicates how seriously this was taken.[62] They were supplemented by appeals from the leader and his closest colleagues to individual peers for their presence and votes, together with briefings on specific issues.[63] Dartmouth requested the attendance of Denbigh and 'some few peers' on 7 December 1775 to discuss the petition of Congress immediately before that business was to be considered by the Lords.[64] Finally, if the attendance of individual supporters were not obtained, their proxy votes (though a second best in view of their unavailability in committees or appeals) could be garnered. Here the ministry's success was convincing to the point of supererogation. In the 13 sessions from January 1770 to July 1782 proxies were used in 71 (28.29 per cent) of the 251 divisions but affected the result in only three.[65] In the 50 divisions of major political import, where proxies were called, and where there was a definite clash between government and opposition, those proxies ran at an average of 7 to 1 in favour of administration. On no occasion of this sort did the ministry need proxies to win the vote; they served instead to enhance its existing majority. It is not surprising that Richmond complained that

---

[60] *London Evening Post*, 23–25 Nov., 1779; *St. James's Chronicle*, 24–26 Nov. 1778; P.R.O., S.P. 37/13, ff. 236–240.

[61] P.R.O., S.P. 37/14, f. 334; see also *ibid.*, ff. 329, 331, 333, for Stormont's draft letters to Ailesbury, Aylesford and Westmorland in Oct. 1780.

[62] E.g. *Calendar of Home Office Papers of the Reign of George III, 1770-1772* (1881), p. 464; *Calendar of Home Office Papers of the Reign of George III, 1773-1775* (1899), p. 215; P.R.O., S.P. 37/10, f. 253; S.P. 37/27, ff. 50–1; S.P. 37/14, f. 270.

[63] Among many other examples see H.M.C., *Denbigh MSS.*, p. 297; Bodl., North Papers, MS. d.16, f. 59: Rochford to Guilford, 30 Oct. 1775; *Calendar of Home Office Papers, 1773-1775*, p. 259.

[64] H.M.C., *Denbigh MSS.*, p. 298. See also P.R.O., S.P. 37/13, f. 140: Stormont to Chesterfield, 19 Nov. 1779 (draft).

[65] Sainty and Dewar, *Divisions in the Lords*, microfiche 4. All three of the divisions concerned took place over private bills.

proxies were 'a most useful engine to all Administrations', when 'the Judgement of those present by a great Majority may be over-ruled by the Proxies of foreign Ambassadors and Governors at Petersburg and at Virginia'.[66] For the 1770s at least, the allegation that proxies overturned the verdict of those present was incorrect, but they certainly divided on average in a higher pro-ministerial ratio than the votes cast in person. Few ministries in the eighteenth century exploited proxy voting more thoroughly than that of North. Full use was made of the proxies of diplomats and serving officers who were peers, and the leading lords in cabinet were regular proxy holders. In the 50 relevant divisions, the average proxy vote for the ministry was 18.6, for the opposition 2.6. It is perhaps worth adding that in the 31 major political divisions under Walpole in which proxies were called, the average proxy vote for the ministry was also 18.6, but that for the opposition was 15.1, a pro-ministerial ratio of only 1.2 to 1.[67]

One's overall impression is that firm leadership largely accounts for the contrast between the lack of solid governmental control in the mid 1760s and the command of the Lords enjoyed by North's ministry.[68] Rochford was at least adequate, Suffolk energetic and Stormont efficient if prickly. It is true that there were complaints as to Weymouth's 'inattention to business and silence in the House' as his second term as leader witnessed the gradual secession of himself and his fellow-Bedfordites from the ministry.[69] But his term was too brief to be of serious consequence and there are signs that Stormont had effectively taken over his duties some weeks before his resignation.[70]

Two other relevant factors may be added. The ministry did not face

[66] Alison Olson, *The Radical Duke. The Career and Correspondence of Charles Lennox, Third Duke of Richmond* (Oxford, 1961), p. 134. The Ambassador to St. Petersburg was Cathcart, the Governor of Virginia was Dunmore; both were also Scottish representative peers who regularly left their proxies with ministers.

[67] H.L.R.O., Proxy books, 1770–82, show that the proxies of Harcourt, Cathcart, Stormont (to 1778), Dunmore, Grantham, Cornwallis and others were regularly lodged with ministers. It is odd that Cannon (*Aristocratic Century* p. 95) should observe that 'the use of proxies meant that ministers must always be on guard against ambushes'. Far from threatening ministers, proxies improved their majorities and they were most vulnerable to ambushes on those occasions (in committee) when proxies were not available.

[68] Cannon (*Aristocratic Century*, p. 102) recognizes what could be achieved by 'resolute management', while only by implication acknowledging the chaos which could result from its absence. But North's command of the Lords cannot be explained by a growing number of placemen. Professor Cannon's own figures (p. 96) for those peers with 'a specific interest in supporting the administration' are 'about ninety' in 1752, 'more than ninety' in 1769 and 'about eighty six' in 1777 and do not substantiate his claim that the 'party of the crown increased considerably in strength as the century progressed'.

[69] H.M.C., *Abergavenny MSS.*, p. 25; see also *Correspondence of George III*, IV, nos. 2791 and 2820.

[70] *Correspondence of George III*, IV, nos. 2822 and 2846.

serious challenge in Lords' committees. By the early eighteenth century there had emerged a regular chairman of Committees of the Whole House. In the early 1770s, as before, this office was held by peers who loyally supported the ministry – Wentworth, Boston and Scarsdale; their two predecessors in the 1760s had been 'poor lords' in receipt of pensions. By the time of Scardale's appointment (1775) an annual allowance of £1500 from secret service funds was attached to the chairmanship. Scarsdale in fact chaired well over half of the meetings of the Committee of the Whole House for the sessions 1774-5 to 1782-3 inclusive. So firmly a ministerial figure did he appear that on 2 February 1778 Richmond took the highly unusual step of moving (unsuccessfully) that a prominent opposition lord, the Duke of Portland, should replace Scarsdale as chairman of the committee on the state of the nation to consider the conduct of the American war.[71] On 25 November 1779 all seven lords named by Sainty as the most frequent chairmen of Committees of the Whole House during the 1779-80 session voted with the ministry in the division on the Address.[72] As far as select committees were concerned, the main difficulty in managing the Lords was the search for peers willing to serve and attend, not the prospect of opposition, and in any case on most private bills the issues were not of a directly confrontational sort, but involved a maze of private currents and interests.

In addition, the ministerial majority contained a number of personal and family groupings. North's success at the outset in absorbing other factions in the Commons was more than matched in the Lords. By the end of 1771 former Grenvillites (notably Suffolk and Aylesford) and Bedfordites (Gower, Weymouth, Carlisle) were firmly incorporated into the ministry, as was Grafton. North himself was not without personal allies in the Lords: Horace Walpole was less than accurate in asserting that he had 'neither connexions with the nobility nor popularity with the country'.[73] In fact, North's father (Guilford), uncle (Halifax), step-brother (Dartmouth) and half-brother (Bishop, successively of Lichfield, Worcester and Winchester) were all members of the House of Lords for at least part of the 1770s. They were reinforced by individual ministers – Hillsborough, Rochford, Stormont, Thurlow – who regarded themselves primarily as the King's servants, without obligation to any group. The great lawyers on the governmental side, especially Mansfield and Thurlow, commanded enormous respect in debate, as even their opponents grudgingly conceded: 'Mon Chancelier is a clever

---

[71] J.C. Sainty, *The Origin of the Office of Chairman of Committees in the House of Lords* (H.L.R.O. Memorandum No. 52, 1974), pp. 1-2; Cobbett, *Parl. Hist.*, XIX, 651-3. Richmond's motion was defeated by 58 votes to 33.

[72] See Appendix I and Sainty, *Chairman of Committees*, p. 29.

[73] Quoted in Turberville, *Lords in XVIII Century*, p. 345.

fellow, but his wings must be clipped, or La Chambre Haute had better be shut up', wrote Pembroke in 1781.[74] When the *Public Advertiser* in March 1778 opined that the ministry consisted of 'the Buteites, the Kingites, the Bedfordites and the Northites', it was seeking to illustrate their disunity, yet in a crude and over-simplified way, it came close to describing the essentially composite, heterogeneous nature of the ministerial majority in the House of Lords.[75] That majority might be described as the 'party of the Crown' delineated by Large, together with personal groupings attached to the ministry by office, and individual peers whose suspicion of the allegedly factional and disloyal connotations of opposition far exceeded such reservations as they might have entertained towards the current administration. What one does not detect among North's supporters, however, is any sense of a 'Tory party' either as a survival from the pre-1760 period or as the fore-runners of the Tory party in a fully fledged Whig-Tory two-party system of the sort recognizable in the 1830s.

What, then, bound ministerial supporters in the Lords together? One may cite a common feeling of loyalty and duty to the monarchy and, in some cases, of outraged patriotism in the face of rebellion in America. North's ministry stood for imperial unity in a manner which transcended party and which commanded considerable support in the Lords, as well as in the Commons and in the country.[76] To that may be added a shared Anglicanism at a time when religious issues were explicit (Dissenters' bills) or implicit (America, Ireland, reform) in political debate. In terms of ecclesiastical allegiance the House of Lords was even more uniform than the Commons. Bishops formed another section of the ministerial majority in the Lords. Admittedly their average daily attendance did not match the high level achieved under Anne;[77] this figure was reached only twice in the 1760s and never in the 1770s. The average daily episcopal attendance between 1770-82 was only 6.45. So meagre a turnout did not escape contemporary attention and has led Professor Lowe to warn against any over-estimation of the bishops as a 'pro-ministerial force'.[78] However, high episcopal attendances were less necessary in the 1770s

[74] *Pembroke Papers, 1780-1794. Letters and Diaries of Henry, Tenth Earl of Pembroke and his Circle*, ed. Lord Herbert (1950), p. 90. See also F. Kilvert, *Memoirs of the Life and Writings of Richard Hurd* (1860), p. 255, and McCahill, *Order and Equipoise*, pp. 113-19.

[75] *Public Advertiser*, 20 Mar. 1778.

[76] See *Correspondence of George III*, III, no. 2077; I. R. Christie and B. W. Labaree, *Empire or Independence 1760-1776*. (New York, 1976), pp. 191-3. Dr. Langford observes 'Many of the leaders of the North regime were of sound Whiggish family for at least two generations': 'Old Whigs, Old Tories and the American Revolution', *Journal of Imperial and Commonwealth History*, VIII (1980), 121.

[77] *London Diaries of William Nicolson*, p. 29.

[78] Bodl., North Papers, MSS. d.25, f.54; d.26, f.54: Brownlow North to Guilford, 31 Oct. and 11 Nov. 1775; Lowe, 'Bishops and Scottish Representative Peers', pp. 89-90.

than in Anne's reign because of the much wider gap between the voting numbers of government and opposition: absences did not necessarily amount to disaffection. Furthermore, episcopal attendance for major divisions was always very much higher than the sessional average. From 1775-81 inclusive, for instance, 15 bishops on average were present for the debate on the Address. On 25 November 1779 eighteen were present, with 15 voting with the ministry to form 18.29 per cent of the ministerial vote. Episcopal support for North's administration was intellectual as well as numerical. During the American war the ministry faced only two, or at most three, episcopal critics. Otherwise, with varying degrees of enthusiasm, bishops, including most surviving appointees of Newcastle, supported the policy of coercion towards America. None quite matched the ardour of Butler (Oxford), but he was far from untypical: the American rebels were also foes of episcopalianism.[79] Despite their reputation for silence, bishops were capable of powerful, if occasional, interventions on American issues: thus Archbishop Cornwallis stoutly opposed the repeal of the Quebec Act in 1775, Porteus in his first Lords speech on 9 March 1778 defended North's peace commission, while eight days later Lowth upheld the ministry's American policy in the debate on the King's message respecting the Franco-American Treaty.[80] In November 1775 Brownlow North even reported that he had received the proxy of the habitual absentee Beauclerk (Hereford) as 'a Testimony of a very friendly disposition towards my Brother'.[81] Above all, the bench stood for theological orthodoxy in an age when the political nation was becoming conscious of a Socinian challenge to the doctrine of the Trinity and of a connection between some of the leading protagonists of that 'heresy' and the parliamentary opposition. Partly for this reason 25 bishops voted against the Dissenters' Relief Bill of 1772 and almost as many the following year.[82] When urging the claims of Dr. Balguy to be elevated to the bench George III cited his effective writings against the Feathers Tavern petition, and favoured the advancement of Porteus in 1776 on the grounds that he would prove 'an ample match in any debate in the House of Lords' for Hinchliffe (Peterborough), who was emerging as an ally of opposition.[83]

Lowe has indicated a surprisingly high level of 'episcopal opposition'

---

[79] See John Butler's pamphlets, published under the pseudonym 'Vindex', and William Markham, *A Sermon preached before the Society for the Propagation of the Gospel in Foreign Parts* (1777).

[80] Cobbett, *Parl. Hist.*, XVIII, 671; XIX, 866-7 and 922-3.

[81] Bodl. North Papers, MS. d.26, f.25: Brownlow North to Guilford, 11 Nov. 1775.

[82] See G. M. Ditchfield, 'The Subscription Issue in British Parliamentary Politics, 1772-79', *Parliamentary History*, VII (1988), 45-80.

[83] *Correspondence of George III*, V, no. 3371; III, no. 1939; V, no. 3368.

to successive administrations in the 1760s. Yet one must distinguish between the antagonism of bishops to a ministry (Rockingham, 1765-6) which did *not* command the full confidence of the Crown or suffered deep internal divisions (Chatham/Grafton 1766-68) and their voting against a ministry (Bute 1762-3) which did enjoy that confidence. To oppose Bute over the Cider Tax was emphatically different from opposing Rockingham's American policy, where the King's views were until the last moment uncertain and where many royal friends including Bute himself, were hostile. Of the nine bishops who voted against the Cider Tax in 1763, only one (Beauclerk) was among the eight who voted against the repeal of the Stamp Act three years later.[84] At least two separate groups of bishops must be identified here and the 'opposition' of each could not take place simultaneously. Even in the 1760s there was no solid phalanx of bishops in long term opposition.

If one removes hostility of bishops to a ministry not fully backed by the Crown, or with obvious internal rifts, then not much is left of 'episcopal opposition'. One would expect desertions amongst traditional adherents of administration during a succession of brief ministries, each appointing its own (practically irremovable) bishops, and when at least some bishops remained faithful to a particular leader who might rapidly return to office. 'Episcopal opposition' was far less likely under the type of long, stable ministry headed by North, fully backed by the King and making its own episcopal appointments. The bishops who had opposed before 1770 were not reinforced: they either died or became isolated. Ewer and Keppel, for instance, had voted against North in the session of 1770, yet Ewer was succeeded at Bangor by the loyal Moore in 1774 and Keppel at Exeter three years later by John Ross, the client and former tutor of Weymouth, North's Secretary of State.[85] By the late 1770s only Hinchliffe, Shipley (St. Asaph) and, very rarely, Law (Carlisle) were left. All three were appointed before 1770 and not one was translated thereafter. During the 1770s a far more representative episcopal figure was Richard Hurd, scholar, courtier and close personal friend of George III, who loyally backed North and regarded the Lords' opposition as 'faction'.[86] Only after the fall of North, particularly under the brief Rockingham and Coalition ministries, did other bishops oppose government. Porteus, for instance, spoke against the Contractors Bill in 1782, and, in highly unusual circumstances, bishops divided 12-8 and 11-8 against the Coalition in the two crucial divisions on the India Bill.[87]

[84] For the relevant minority lists see Debrett, *Debates*, IV, 139-140, 374-5.

[85] Ewer had already been provoked by the anti-episcopalianism of the American colonists to support the coercive policy; see Lowe, 'Bishops and Scottish Representative Peers', pp. 96, 106.

[86] Kilvert, *Memoirs of Hurd*, p. 128.

[87] Cobbett, *Parl. Hist.*, XXII, 1372; Debrett, *Parl. Reg.*, 2nd series, XIV, 107-8.

Under North, however, episcopal reliability was the rule and it compared well not only with the 1760s but with the ministry of Walpole after its breach with Gibson over the Quakers Tithe Bill,[88] and with the Whig ministries of 1714-23, which faced the powerful animosity of Atterbury and his allies.

Reliability was even more characteristic of the Scottish representative peers. In parliamentary terms the period 1770-82 (and especially after 1774) was for them an oasis of political tranquility, a hiatus, as it were, between the restiveness of the 1760s detected by Lowe and the greater assertiveness of the 1780s portrayed by McCahill. The earlier restiveness, however, should not be exaggerated, and in voting against the repeal of the Stamp Act by eight votes to six in March 1766 the Scottish lords behaved in a quite untypical way.[89] They hardly ever opposed under North, and even if their attendance was low (though not disproportionately so in comparison with the whole House) they provided the ministry with the negative advantage of absence of opposition. Actual voting deviations among the representative peers under North were minimal. Atholl endorsed the second reading of the Dissenters' bill of 1773 and Stair opposed the ministry's American policy towards the end of the 1774 session.[90] Otherwise no representative peer voted with opposition in the surviving division lists of 1770-82 except in the highly unusual case of the Militia Bill on 30 June 1779 when there was a Bedfordite-led revolt of some of the ministry's usual supporters. Not surprisingly, the Scots feature prominently in ministerial lists for the House of Lords.[91] Their turnout for debates on the Address invariably exceeded their average daily attendance; nine were present, and all voted with the ministry, on 25 November 1779.[92] In 1774 Debrett's *History, Debates and Proceedings* listed all 16 as 'usually supporting the Court'.[93] One of their number, Stormont, became Secretary of State and leader of the Lords (the only Scottish representative peer to serve in the latter capacity) between 1779-82, while Marchmont, Galloway and Abercorn regularly chaired Committees of the Whole House. During the 1770s the ministry could rely on more loyalty (and less trouble) from the 16 than could Pitt between 1783 and 1793.[94]

[88] C. Jones, 'The House of Lords and the Growth of Parliamentary Stability, 1701- 1742', *Britain in the First Age of Party, 1680-1750. Essays presented to Geoffrey Holmes*, ed. C. Jones (1987), pp. 93-5.

[89] Lowe, 'Bishops and Scottish Representative Peers', p. 101 n. 64.

[90] Cobbett, *Parl. Hist.*, XVII, 790; Debrett, *Debates*, VII, 18.

[91] P.R.O., S.P., 37/9, ff. 9-12 (Jan. 1772), ff. 313-4 (Nov. 1772); S.P. 37/13, ff. 266-7 (Nov. 1779).

[92] See Appendix (below, pp. 237-39).

[93] Debrett, *Debates*, VII, 17.

[94] Sainty, *Chairman of Committees*, pp. 29-30; M.W. McCahill, 'The Scottish Peerage and the House of Lords in the Late Eighteenth Century', *Scottish Historical Review*, LI (1972), 172-96.

How is this phenomenon explained? Care was taken to avoid offending the Scottish peerage. George III protested in 1775 that to award the Thistle to an Irish peer would 'give the Noblemen of Scotland real cause of displeasure', and efforts were made not to dispose incautiously of offices normally held by Scottish peers or turn away those who applied for favours.[95] Such pains were necessary, since the Scottish peers could be extremely concerned for their dignity. Nothing made this clearer than the elections to the representative peerage and the role of the Westminster administration in their management. The Secretary of State who acted as leader of the Lords was responsible for the King's list, the regular device whereby the ministry indicated its own preference in peerage elections. In November 1774 the starkness of Suffolk's circular letter caused great offence at Holyrood and provoked lengthy complaints at the blatancy of ministerial interference. Yet in the event all the governmental candidates were elected, with only scanty support for their opponents. In 1780 the matter was handled far more tactfully and all the ministerial nominees were returned unopposed.[96] The rare Scottish peers who opposed were quietly dropped: Stair, who had been sponsored by the ministry in December 1770 was not even a candidate in 1774. Although its origins belong to the late 1760s, the growth of an 'independent' peers' movement, pledged to resist such involvement, really acquired substance only after 1782. In the 1770s even the few 'independent' peers (Breadalbane in 1774 and Eglintoun in 1776) who secured election to the 16 did so in alliance with ministerial influence and not in contention with it.[97]

Nor were the Scottish representative peers alienated by the outbreak or conduct of the American war. No section of the House of Lords accepted the validity of that struggle more completely than they did. There was a Scottish stake in North America, and Saratoga was followed by a flurry of military recruiting in Scotland which the Scottish aristocracy encouraged; loyalty and integration with England mattered far more to them than secession or rebellion. Apart from Stair, no Scottish peer voted against the coercive legislation of 1774; none joined the opposition in the divisions on America in 1775. Nor did they succour the campaign for Economical Reform; on 14 April 1780, 11 voted against the Contractors' Bill and none in its favour.[98] Behind this adherence to the ministry lay a comparative absence of Scottish issues, and especially of issues which involved the privileges of the Scottish peerage, from parliamentary politics. During the 1780s, on the other hand, the

---

[95] *Correspondence of George III*, III, no. 1647; V, nos. 3517–8, 3290.
[96] H.M.C., *Dartmouth MSS.*, V, 369–70; W. Robertson, *Proceedings Relating to the Peerage of Scotland, from January 16, 1707 to April 29, 1788* (Edinburgh, 1790), pp. 377–89.
[97] McCahill, 'Scottish Peerage', p. 182 n.2.
[98] *London Evening Post*, 20–22 Apr. 1780.

Hamilton decision of 1782, which allowed Scottish peers with post-Union British titles to sit in the House of Lords, brought a multiplicity of such issues to the very centre of the stage.[99] The unity of the Scottish representative peers in the 1770s, moreover, did not survive the Fox-North coalition. After its fall, many Northite peers went into opposition to Pitt; among them was Stormont, who took a leading part in asserting the 'independence' of the representative peerage in defiance of Pitt and Dundas. Overall the presence of the representative peers was useful but not totally indispensable to North; one retains the impression that had a higher attendance been necessary for the survival of the administration, it would have been forthcoming.

3

In view of the considerable research recently devoted to late eighteenth-century opposition and the growth of 'party', it is perhaps rather surprising that relatively little of it has concerned the House of Lords. During the period 1770-83 a study of opposition in the Lords presents an intriguing and at times revealing story.

Outwardly the pattern of opposition between 1770 and the fall of North was fairly consistent. There were two main groups, the Rockinghamites with some 25-35 adherents in the Lords, and the supporters of Chatham (led from 1778 by Shelburne) who numbered about six. But there were also individual peers in opposition who maintained a cool distance between themselves and the principal groups even when they voted together. Grafton acted independently of the Rockinghamites after he left the ministry in 1775 and, although working in co-operation with them, did not join their withdrawal from Parliament in 1776-7. His relations with the Chathamites, and especially with Shelburne, were somewhat warmer, but generally he remained aloof and pursued his own course. Abingdon, too, though loosely associated with the Rockinghamites, maintained a separate line: in Professor Christie's words he was 'near to the independents'.[100] The same was true of Rutland in the late 1770s. Other peers who have been regarded as Rockinghamites could equally be described as independents who followed no 'party' line – Bristol, Bolton, Derby – but whose opposition to North brought them into sometimes uneasy contact with the Rockinghamites.

Though not completely lacking in colour, the tenor of opposition and of debates in the Lords tended usually, if not quite always, to be rather more sedate than in the Commons. But opposition in the Lords required

---

[99] G.M. Ditchfield, 'The Scottish Representative Peers and Parliamentary Politics', *Scottish Historical Review*, LX (1981), 14-31.

[100] I.R. Christie, *The End of North's Ministry, 1780-82* (1958), p. 223.

more fortitude – allegiances were more predictable, there was less of a 'floating vote' and the onus was firmly upon the opposition to take the initiative. Partly for this reason the early eighteenth-century practice of lengthy pauses between speeches in debate seems to have continued into the 1770s. On 5 March 1778 Suffolk allowed a considerable silence to elapse, rather than put the ministerial case immediately, as he waited 'till some objections were first pointed out at the other side'.[101] But opposition efforts in the upper House were not necessarily wasted: there was a forum for the expression of opinion and the presentation of a case in debate, in protests, and in the press. There were always hopes of exploiting divisions in the ministry, as with the Militia Bill of 1779, when North's colleagues were visibly disunited. There was the possibility of surprising the ministry by the divulging of confidential information acquired from authoritative sources. In February–March 1778 Grafton, primed from Paris by Thomas Walpole, not only provided Fox with evidence of the Franco-American treaty for use in the Commons, but revealed that evidence in the Lords, to the discomfiture of Weymouth.[102] This coup shook ministerial nerves and led North, not for the last time, to seek an accommodation with sections of the opposition.

There were sharp differences between the numerical and perhaps the intellectual fortunes of opposition in the early and the late 1770s. The years 1770–75 saw the opposition decline in numbers and suffer losses of personnel to the ministry. This contributed to, as well as reflected, its ineffectiveness and the disappointment of its hopes in 1769–70 when the Middlesex election petitions enabled it to launch a united onslaught against Grafton's administration. But it was the secession of Camden and Granby, the death of Yorke and the demoralization of Grafton himself, not defeats in the Lords, which eroded that ministry; as late as 9 January 1770 it won a victory on the Address by 89 to 36. Even after Grafton resigned, the ministry, though shorn of its remaining Chathamite elements, re-grouped under North, retained the confidence of both Houses as well as of the King, and absorbed the Grenvillite section of the old 'united opposition'.[103] North's opponents failed to make much impact over the Falklands crisis, Royal Marriage Bill or East India Regulating Bill, and between 1770–74 impressed contemporaries only by their weakness. For four successive sessions, 1770–71 to 1774 inclusive, there was no division on the Address. In January 1772 the Address was

---

[101] *London Diaries of William Nicolson*, pp. 96–7; *London Evening Post*, 5–7 March. 1778; Cobbett, *Parl. Hist.*, XIX, 839.

[102] Cobbett, *Parl. Hist.*, XIX, 769, 834–6; *Autobiography and Political Correspondence of Augustus Henry, Third Duke of Grafton, K.G.*, ed. Sir William Anson (1898), pp. 298–300.

[103] H.M.C., *Townshend MSS.*, p. 407: P. Lawson, *George Grenville: A Political Life* (Oxford, 1984), pp. 291–3.

not even debated, 'a circumstance scarce ever remembered', though one repeated in January 1774 when George III hoped that the unanimity of the House of Lords would impress the rebellious Bostonians.[104] All the time the ministry was gaining support from opposition. The former Rockinghamite Lord Dartmouth accepted office as American Secretary in 1772, providing an affirmative answer to Richmond's plaintive 'Is not this man gone?' the previous year.[105] The Yorke family was successfully courted by North; the 2nd Earl of Hardwicke, whose father had been Lord Chancellor and a leading Court Whig under the Pelhams, went over to the ministry, while his brother, James Yorke, rapidly mounted the ladder of episcopal promotion from St. David's (1774) to Gloucester (1779) to Ely (1781). Nor did the reappearance of American legislation in 1774 give the opposition any comfort: despite the return of Chatham and a flurry of activity in 1774-5 there was little resistance in the Lords to the Quebec Act or the coercive measures against Massachusetts in the aftermath of the Boston Tea Party.[106] Twice (in November 1772 and again four years later) the Rockinghamite section of the opposition staged a ragged secession from Parliament. North's ministry enjoyed the full confidence of the Crown, of most of the former factions of the 1760s and of a solid section of mercantile opinion. In the mid-1770s, his financial policies seemed at their most successful. Opposition was as attenuated in the Lords as in the Commons.

America might have presented the opposition in both Houses with more opportunities. Yet here too North enjoyed the confidence of the Commons, with few interruptions, until the aftermath of Yorktown. Compared with the late 1760s, mercantile opposition had declined markedly by 1774-5. If the war of American Independence in the end vindicated the Rockingham group and gave retrospective justification to what Dr. O'Gorman calls its 'noble' but 'vain' pleas for conciliation,[107] in the short term it presented the group with severe problems. Opposition needed to avoid the charge of sympathizing with rebels and behaving in an unpatriotic manner, a charge all the more damaging with the rallying to the ministry and the substantial military recruitment which followed the French entry into the war.[108] The American issue, moreover, illuminated the divided nature of the opposition in both Houses, but

[104] *Calendar of Home Office Papers, 1770-72*, p. 422; Debrett, *Debates*, VII, 2; H.M.C., *Dartmouth MSS.*, IV, 500.

[105] Sheffield City Lib., W.W.M., R.1-1352: Richmond to Rockingham, 22-23 Jan. 1771.

[106] F. O'Gorman, *The Rise of Party in England. The Rockingham Whigs, 1760-82*, (1975), p. 312.

[107] F. O'Gorman, *The Emergence of the British Two-Party System, 1760-1832* (1982), p. 11.

[108] See, e.g., P. Marshall, 'Manchester and the American Revolution', *Bulletin of the John Rylands University Library of Manchester*, LXII (1979-80), 168-86.

most spectacularly so in the Lords. The Rockingham and Chatham groups differed bitterly over the Declaratory Act of 1766 and over American Independence: in the latter case, indeed, there was a three-way split, with the Rockinghams in favour, Chathamites hostile and Grafton vacillating.[109] After Saratoga it was to the Chathamite rather than the Rockinghamite, section of opposition that the King and North turned for succour. In the most dramatic conflict of all, on 7 April 1778, the antagonists were not government and opposition but Richmond and Chatham, and the differences were not healed by the latter's death. America also served to remind contemporaries that Rockingham's claim that his party articulated the sole voice of true and traditional Whiggery lacked plausibility. The truth was that several 'Whig' viewpoints on America existed and Rockingham's was only one of them. In asserting that the objective of the American war was the enforcement not of the rights of the King but the supremacy of Parliament, North could reasonably claim to be adopting a Whig position. Critics of the war were not the only Whigs. On 30 May 1777, when opposing Chatham's motion to end hostilities in America, Archbishop Markham of York declared that 'a government founded in law is entitled to demand and exact obedience'. To Grafton's allegation that he had spoken against the Revolution of 1688 he replied 'The noble duke is a Whig, but I say he knows not what Whiggism is'.[110]

Nevertheless, as the American conflict developed from 1775 there was a slow improvement in the strength of opposition in the Lords. While most ministerial adherents remained loyal, the opposition succeeded in reversing its losses of the early 1770s and in achieving some recruitment between 1775 and 1782. Its most prosperous years were 1777-80, as reflected in the increased Lords attendances in the sessions of 1777-8 and 1778-9, and the high minority figures for 1779-80. Of the defections from the ministry, the most important was that of Grafton, who came increasingly to doubt the wisdom of the policy of coercion and, after Lexington, to say so openly. On 26 October 1775 he spoke against the ministry in the debate on the Address and was deprived of the Privy Seal. But though a prestigious figure, he took with him into the minority on that day only four lords – Lyttelton, Jersey, Ferrers and his episcopal protégé Hinchliffe, all of whom had featured in pro-ministerial lists in the early 1770s.[111] Of these, only Grafton and Hinchliffe remained in permanent opposition until 1782. They were joined by Radnor, who subsequently despatched his proxy to Grafton, declaring that 'the very

[109] Durrant, 'Duke of Grafton', pp. 348-51.

[110] Cobbett, *Parl. Hist.*, XIX, 327, and Langford, 'Old Whigs, Old Tories', pp. 110-111.

[111] Cobbett, *Parl. Hist.*, XVIII, 726; Grafton, *Autobiography*, pp. 270-75; Durrant, 'Duke of Grafton', pp. 327-32.

critical State we are so unfortunately reduced to . . . and the Plan resolved on for prosecuting a War, which whatever is the Issue, must be fatal to the true Interest of this Country, will no longer suffer me to remain neutar'.[112]

Other than Grafton, however, ministers who resigned did not subsequently vote in the minority. Weymouth, in resigning as Secretary of State (South) over the Falklands in December 1770, and Hillsborough, in resigning as American Secretary over the Vandalia affair in August 1772, continued to support the general policy of the ministry, took a particularly hard line over the colonies and had little in common with opposition views on America. Weymouth indeed returned to his former office in November 1775 in the general reshuffle caused by Grafton's departure; Hillsborough, too, rejoined the ministry, succeeding Weymouth himself when the latter resigned for a second time in November 1779. On that occasion, it was the Bedford group, led by Gower, which, after months of dissidence, seceded from the ministry. Their reasons, however, apart from their own ambitions, hinged on North's lack of direction, and they did not co-operate with the opposition.

Other government supporters, however, did defect, as the American war took an unfavourable and expensive turn. On 8 April 1778 Hinchliffe reported to Grafton that Lord Egremont had 'for the first time' appeared in the minority on an American question, and Egremont certainly voted regularly with opposition in the divisions covered by the surviving lists of 1779-80. He was reinforced by Derby, Pembroke, Carmarthen and Effingham; the latter resigned his army commission in 1776, although an earlier dissatisfaction with the progress of his military career might have been as strong an influence as disagreement with North's American policy.[113] In addition, the opposition had a stroke of good fortune in 1779 on the death of Suffolk, than whom, according to North, there was 'nobody more steady, and resolute, and active, and more fit to lead the business of the Crown in the House of Lords'; when Suffolk's posthumous son died in August, his uncle Thomas Howard M.P. succeeded as 14th Earl and promptly continued in the Lords the opposition to the ministry which he had pursued in the Commons.[114] Clearly the opposition found their best opportunities when the high costs of the war, and alleged corruption resulting therefrom, were under scrutiny. On 7 December 1779 the minority numbered 36 (against 77) on

[112] Bury St. Edmunds and West Suffolk R.O., Grafton MSS., 423/56: Radnor to Grafton, 4 Nov. 1775.
[113] West Suffolk R.O., Grafton MSS., 423/733: Hinchliffe to Grafton, 8 Apr. 1778; *Correspondence of George III*, IV, no, 1469; Cannon, *Aristocratic Century*, p. 99 and n. 14.
[114] *Correspondence of George III*, IV, no. 2191. Thomas Howard had remained in opposition when most other Grenvillites had joined North's ministry in 1771.

Richmond's motion for reform of the Civil List. 'I never saw so *good a Day* in the House of Lords since I sat there', wrote Rockingham five days later.[115] Rutland agreed: 'Though our numbers were small, yet appearances were strongly in our favour', he claimed, noting that three 'new votes', those of Paget, Saye and Sele and Townshend, had been gained.[116] In the division on the Address, 25 November 1779, the minority vote reached 41. Early in 1780 Economical Reform and attacks on the conduct of the war gave the opposition its highest voting figures in the Lords under North: 55 (against 101) on Shelburne's motion for a reform of public expenditure on 8 February; 41 (against 60) in favour of the Contractors' Bill on 14 April; 51 (against 92) on coastal defence on 25 April. There was some falling away in 1780-1 in the aftermath of the Gordon Riots (which led Richmond to exclaim 'I mean to go no more to London this year and probably never to Parliament again'),[117] British victories in the southern colonies and a temporary revival in North's fortunes. Early in 1782, after Yorktown, the Lords were more obsessed with the Sackville peerage than with the removal of North. When on 6 March Chandos introduced a motion critical of the American disaster, opposition mustered only 37 votes and the ministerial total of 72 was not catastrophically lower than usual. However, the fall of North in March and the advent of the Shelburne administration in July precipitated a realignment in the Lords as in the Commons. With most of North's friends hostile to Shelburne, the reinforced opposition achieved a vote of 59 against the peace preliminaries on 17 February 1783. The Fox-North coalition faced comparatively few tests in the Lords until December 1783 but the opposition votes against the India Bill (87 on 15 December, 95 two days later) were in no way comparable with those before February 1783 because of the royal intervention.

Under the North ministry, high minority voting figures in the Lords were very much the exception. The usual experience for the opposition was a sense of frustration, difficulty in securing the attendance of supporters and sometimes bitter internal recriminations. Significantly the opposition's greatest success of the 1770s did not occur in the British Parliament at all. In 1773 the Rockinghamites led a campaign to secure the defeat of proposals for a tax on absentee Irish landlords, an imposition which, they feared, would have fallen disproportionately upon themselves. By co-ordinating a memorial against the tax, Rockingham and his friends undermined the ministry's confidence in the scheme and contributed to its rejection in the Irish House of

---

[115] Sheffield City Lib., W.W.M., R1-1869: Rockingham to Stephen Croft, 12 Dec. 1779.
[116] H.M.C., *Rutland MSS.*, III, 22-3.
[117] Sheffield City Lib., W.W.M., R1-1900: Richmond to Rockingham, 12 June 1780.

Commons.[118]

The main task of opposition groups in the Lords, however, was more mundane – the preservation of identity and the prevention of desertions. Unless that were achieved, the longer term aims – to resist unacceptable policies, to embarrass the ministry and exploit its miscalculations, to win over the support of the uncommitted, to seek to form a new administration or derive some benefit therefrom – would remain unrealised. Survival as much as recruitment was the objective. Such a priority is reflected in opposition methods, which concentrated essentially upon the identifying, informing and securing the attendance of its own supporters. This required organization, little of which was forthcoming from the Chathamite peers, a small cluster of individuals whose whole ethos was anti-party. Such oppositional organization as existed in the Lords was provided by the Rockingham group. Its strength, however, should not be exaggerated. O'Gorman's mild verdict is that the organization was characterised by 'personal informality and intermittent enthusiasm'.[119] The pre-sessional meeting, so familiar an aspect of ministerial preparations, was arranged only irregularly by the main opposition group. There were no such meetings in 1773, 1776, 1777 or 1778. Otherwise the evidence is sketchy. Richmond hosted a series of dinners for Rockinghamites of both Houses early in 1771, and a party whip to colleagues in the Lords on the Shoreham Disfranchisement Bill survives for May of that year.[120] From November 1775 the group consistently divided against, and sometimes proposed an amendment to, the Address of Thanks, with the intention of projecting a show of strength at the start of the session and followed the vote with a published protest. This required co-ordination between spokesmen in each House and the authorship of Burke has been detected in the protests.[121]

The Rockinghamites were far more effective in mobilising for a single campaign or for a specific occasion than in sustaining an effective presence throughout an entire parliamentary session. They could organize meetings at short notice when a seemingly promising target offered itself. Thus on 15 March 1778 meetings of Rockinghamite supporters decided to pursue motions in both Houses for the withdrawal of all British troops from America, and the Lords' version was duly moved by Richmond on 23 March.[122] On this occasion the initiative

[118] O'Gorman, *Rise of Party*, pp. 302-7.
[119] F. O'Gorman, 'Party in the Later Eighteenth Century', *The Whig Ascendancy. Colloquies on Hanoverian England*, ed. J. Cannon, (1981), p. 83.
[120] Olson, *Duke of Richmond*, p. 33; *The Correspondence of Edmund Burke*, ed. T.W. Copeland, *et. al.* (9 vols., Cambridge and Chicago, 1958-70), II, 197; Sheffield City Lib. W.W.M., R1-1376: circular to 'the Whig lords', 6 May 1771.
[121] O'Gorman, 'Party in the Later Eighteenth Century', p. 83.
[122] O'Gorman, *Rise of Party*, p. 372.

merely succeeded in emphasizing the divided nature of the opposition and the hostile Chathamite response led directly to the dramatic events of 7 April. However, over the Indemnity Bill (1775) and the inquiry into the management of Greenwich Hospital, there was rather more success.[123] Rockingham himself helped to secure good attendances for the debates on the Spanish Manifesto and the Militia Bill in June 1779.[124] But relatively favourable performances such as these owed more to the impact of military defeat and the demoralization of the ministry than to Rockinghamite whipping.[125] Nor did proxy votes bring much aid to the opposition. It is true that the Rockinghamites made sporadic efforts to ensure that the proxies of absent colleagues were registered, but, as we have seen, proxies ran in a strongly pro–ministerial direction throughout the 1770s. A skilful opposition would always seek to exploit opportunities in Committee, where proxies were unavailable, which explains why it was not unusual for oppositions to demand a Committee on the State of the Nation. Between 1778-80, moreover, as opposition attendances increased somewhat, proxies were less necessary. But as far as the Rockinghamites were concerned, the deposition of a proxy was as likely to represent disillusionment and a sense of the futility of personal attendance, as efficient organization.[126]

The Lords, like the Commons, opposition was sometimes in a position to stimulate, or join in uneasy alliance with, extra-parliamentary movements. Indeed, peers were often well-placed, through Lord Lieutenancies and other forms of territorial influence, to involve themselves with freeholder and gentry opinion via the county meeting, or even with City protest. But the quest for extra-parliamentary popularity was always problematical for a parliamentary opposition. There was the danger of lack of support, with the consequent charge that there was no public demand behind the issue concerned. Richmond complained in 1775 that absence of outside pressure weakened parliamentary effectiveness in attacking the Prohibition of Trade Bill; 'You may tell the merchants that you cannot get an attendance of Lords unless they will take a more detailed part, and firmly stand by them in their general System of Politics'.[127] There was the danger that a popular movement might develop a spontaneity of its own, rejecting aristocratic leadership and taking an unacceptably radical

---

[123] Olson, *Duke of Richmond*, p. 169 n. 3. The opposition secured a vote of 39 (against 88) for the removal of Sandwich on 23 Apr. 1779.

[124] H.M.C., *Rutland MSS.*, III, 17; West Suffolk R.O., Grafton MSS., 423/72: Rockingham to Grafton, 22 June 1779; Sheffield City Lib., W.W.M., R1-1835: Grafton to Rockingham, 23 June 1779.

[125] O'Gorman, *Rise of Party*, p. 365.

[126] See, for instance, Sheffield City Lib., W.W.M., R1-1430, R1-1980: Manchester to Rockingham, 12 June 1773, Portland to Rockingham, 30 Jan. 1782.

[127] Olson, *Duke of Richmond*, p. 169.

direction. This, to some extent, underlay relations between the Rockinghamites and the County Association movement of 1779-80. Despite the personal involvement of several Rockinghamite peers, that relationship ended in division and recrimination, leaving the Rockinghamites in the Lords (as elsewhere) little better placed than before the agitation began.

The particular devices available to opposition require slightly more detailed consideration. Firstly there was the division of the House. The number of divisions per session rose from the rather low levels of the late 1760s to 21 in 1770-1, fell back slightly in the mid–1770s and rose again sharply in 1777-8 and 1778-9. In the latter session there were 36 divisions, a figure previously exceeded in only four sessions since 1688. As opposition hopes rose after Saratoga, divisions were called more frequently. They were intended to underline the opposition's sense of purpose; even if there were little or no hope of winning the vote, a point was still to be made, with the opportunity to deny that the House was unanimous, to publish a minority list in the press and possibly issue a protest, all of which might be expected to hearten supporters beyond the House of Lords. The danger for opposition in the calling of divisions lay in the possibility of a humiliatingly low vote, which would merely indicate weakness. Opposition secured votes of only 25-30 over American legislation in 1774. It could also prove difficult to carry all the opposition groups together as a united body. Hence divisions were usually most effective when aimed in a generally critical way against government, rather than called to endorse a positive proposal. By the end of the decade it was easy to denounce the ministry's incompetence and attribute its survival to the most sinister causes. '*All* the *Opposition* were *united* in opinion, that the weight of the power and influence of the Crown had been the Means of the Ruin of this Country', wrote Rockingham of the division on the Civil List of 7 December 1779 when the opposition had mustered 36 votes.[128] This, however, was exceptional, and the number of Lords divisions sank back to 15 in the last full session (1780-1) of North's ministry.

Secondly, a protest could set out in the Journals and possibly in the press a reasoned minority case after an unsuccessful division. It could be co-ordinated with outside propaganda, such as an Address from the City of London, as part of a wider campaign.[129] Individuals and groups in opposition contributed to a slight increase in the number of protests from 1770 (Table 2): there were seven in 1774-5 and seven in 1778-9, with 54 altogether in the sessions of 1770-1 to 1782-3 inclusive. Most, as might be expected, were inspired by American legislation and the conduct of

---

[128] Sheffield City Lib., W.W.M., R1-1869: Rockingham to Stephen Croft, 12 Dec. 1779.
[129] See, e.g. Olson, *Duke of Richmond*, p. 137.

the war, and protests could certainly find their mark.[130] But this was not
the whole story, and some protests were the sole work of individual
peers, with no other support. Two of the seven protests in the session of
1774-5, for example, had nothing to do with America or with any group:
they were personal objections on the part of Radnor to the Manchester
Playhouse Bill.[131] Like divisions, protests were of limited value to
opposition. They, too, could illuminate weakness and discord. In
December 1775 a protest against the second reading of the bill to prohibit
trade with the American colonies won only eight signatures, while in
May 1774 the Chathamite lords refused to sign a Rockinghamite protest
against the Massachusetts Justice Bill.[132] The names missing from
protests are often as significant as those appended thereto, especially
when two opposition groups co-existed on uneasy terms. There was the
danger that the value of protests could be diminished by over-use; if
employed too often, Camden warned Rockingham, protests 'will
become a very feeble weapon'.[133] Moreover protests drawn up with an
eye to a wider public were anything but new. Lowe claims that 'the
accession of George III marked a general quickening in the frequency
with which they were employed', while Dr. O'Gorman writes of them
as an 'apparently infrequent practice', before *c.* 1770.[134] In fact, Lords'
protests were not a Rockinghamite innovation, and there were far more
protests under William III and Anne than in the 1770s. They reached a
peak in the early 1720s when Tory peers mounted a vehement rearguard
action against the Whig ministry's prosecution of suspected Jacobites.
The total number of protests in the 1770s was 41, yet two sessions, (1721-
2 and 1722-3) in the time of Francis Atterbury had produced no fewer
than 59. In each of the five successive decades 1690-1740 there were more
Lords' protests than in the 1770s. Nor was there a significant qualitative
change under George III; Cowper and Atterbury, too, had aimed at
public opinion, and, indeed, the Tory protests under George I provoked
so much irritation that the Whig majority in the Lords at times insisted
on their deletion from the Journals, a fate which the protests of the 1770s
escaped.

Overall it seems reasonable to suppose that the numbers of divisions
and protests serve as some kind of index as to the existence of divisive
issues, the intensity of opposition, and willingness to pursue that

---

[130] E.g., *Correspondence of George III*, IV, no. 2674.

[131] *L.J.*, XXXIV, 429, 448.

[132] *Ibid.*, p. 536; Sheffield City Lib., W.W.M., R1-1490: Richmond to Rockingham,
18 May 1774.

[133] Sheffield City Lib., W.W.M., R1-1616a: Camden to Rockingham, 28 Oct. 1775.

[134] W.C. Lowe, 'The House of Lords, Party and Public Opinion: Opposition Use of
the Protest, 1760-1782', *Albion*, XI (1979), 143-56; O'Gorman, 'Party in the Later
Eighteenth Century' p. 83.

Table 2
Divisions and Protests in the House of Lords.[135]
Averages by Decade, 1690-1799

Dates	No. of Sessions	No. of Divisions	Average no. of Divisions for decade	No. of Sessions	No. of Protests	Average no. of Protests for decade
1685 Jan. 1689-Jan. 1690	1	9	9.00	1	5	5.00
Mar. 1690-May 1699	2	72	36.00	2	20	10.00
Nov. 1699-Apr. 1709	10	217	21.70	10	72	7.20
Nov. 1709-Apr. 1719	10	192	19.20	10	78	7.80
Nov. 1719-May 1729	10	190	19.00	10	58	5.80
Jan. 1730-June 1739	12	143	11.92	10	96	9.60
Nov. 1739-June 1749	10	162	16.20	10	54	5.40
Nov. 1749-June 1759	10	69	6.90	10	33	3.30
Nov. 1759-May 1769	11	30	2.73	11	8	0.72
Jan. 1770-July 1779	11	49	4.45	11	10	0.91
Nov. 1779-Aug. 1789	10	198	19.80	10	41	4.10
Jan. 1790-July 1799	11	151	13.73	11	22	2.00
	10	144	14.40	10	56	5.60

135   This table was compiled from material in *L.J.* and Sainty and Dewar, *Divisions in the House of Lords*.

opposition to considerable parliamentary lengths. It is noteworthy that the lowest point for both was the 1750s and early 1760s – Namier's decades – with only 61 divisions and 14 protests between 1746 and 1765. The evidence of divisions and protests, and the pressures which gave rise to them, suggest not a new, radical departure nor an innovative or particularly dynamic Lords opposition in the 1770s, but a partial, incomplete return to the conditions of the earlier eighteenth century. Walpole faced a more formidable opposition in the House of Lords than did North.[136] There was nothing new about complaints against royal influence, in demands for Place Bills or in appeals to a wider public. But this in itself is not conclusive evidence of the existence of a party system; many divisions and protests were not occasioned by anything resembling party considerations. In the 1770s the struggle was not between Whig and Tory parties but between government and opposition, in which each side was a loose confederation of individuals and groups. The pattern of protests in the 1770s gives at least some reinforcement to Turberville's characterization of opposition in the Lords as 'more personal than organic'.[137]

4

It has been suggested that the influence of the House of Lords in this period had 'declined' to a point at which the upper chamber had 'hardly any major role' to perform.[138] Unfortunately such a view implies a certain disdain towards the highly necessary task of examining the House of Lords as a working institution. Moreover it was a view presumably not shared by those who relentlessly pursued applications for peerages and sought membership of the Lords; by those who devoted much time to resurrecting claims to dormant peerages; by the Scottish peers whose ambitions had rested not only upon British peerages but upon the right to sit in the upper House and who were rewarded after 1782; by the great lawyers such as Thurlow and Wedderburn who, in their political prime, demanded peerages with obsessional fervour. Nor was this view shared by successive administrations, which took care to maintain a series of effective spokesmen in the Lords, nor, necessarily, by leading politicians themselves, who, as McCahill shows, were able 'to go to the Lords without jeopardising their political careers'.[139] As late as the heyday of Lord Liverpool, and even as late as Lord Salisbury, it was perfectly possible for a Prime Minister to operate effectively from the House of Lords. Some of Professor Cannon's literary flourishes to the effect that

---

[136] See Jones, 'House of Lords and the Growth of Parliamentary Stability', pp. 101-5.
[137] Turberville, *Lords in XVIII Century*, pp. 345-6.
[138] Cannon, *Aristocratic Century*, p. 125.
[139] McCahill, 'Peerage Creations', p. 271.

the House of Lords was 'more picturesque than important' and that its members were 'firemen in a town without fires' might thus be received with caution.[140] The Dissenters' bills of 1772-3 illustrate quite effectively the defensive role of the Lords. Nor were those bills a totally isolated instance of its application. As George III told North at the height of the Printer's Case:

> It is highly necessary that this strange and lawless method of publishing Debates in the Papers must be put a stop to; but is not the House of Lords as a Court of Record the best Court to bring such miscreants before, as it can fine as well as imprison; and as the Lords have broader shoulders to support any schism that this salutary measure may occasion in the minds of the vulgar.[141]

The House of Lords featured in the schemes of the parliamentary reformers of the 1770s and 1780s, although for much of the time they were content to give higher priority to criticisms of aristocratic and other landed influence in the House of Commons than to attacks on the House of Lords per se.[142] For a few radicals the Lords were indeed a target: the young Sylas Neville and his Dissenting friends were fond of denouncing aristocracy, while *The Patricians* attacked the hereditary principle as well as the performances of individual peers.[143] Yet when the House of Lords was most strongly attacked, as, for instance by Junius over the Middlesex Election Petitions,[144] it was because it agreed, rather than disagreed, with the Commons. In condemning the 'hereditary legislators' for their rejection of Chatham's conciliation proposals of February 1775, Franklin had to add, 'But this was a hasty reflection; for the *elected* House of Commons is no better' – having passed coercive legislation by large majorities.[145] This harmony with the Commons over matters so controversial no doubt helps to explain the survival and widespread acceptance of the House of Lords, for in such circumstances, as Professor Cannon observes, 'Aristocracy was not perceived separately but as a part . . . danger came when aristocracy could be perceived separately and when men could conceive that aristocratic privileges might be abolished without society at once falling into dissolution and ruin'.[146] Yet even when the Lords differed from the Commons it could

---

[140] Cannon, *Aristocratic Century*, pp. 95, 125. A reviewer justly commented 'perhaps there were more fires than are allowed for': J.C.D. Clark, in *E.H.R.*, CI. (1986), 181. See also Jones, 'House of Lords and the Growth of Parliamentary Stability,' p. 86.

[141] *Correspondence of George III*, II, no. 913.

[142] E.g., J. Burgh, *Political Disquisitions* (3 vols., 1774-5), I, 54-5.

[143] *The Diary of Sylas Neville, 1767-88*, ed. B. Cozens-Hardy (Oxford, 1950), pp. 17-19; *The Patricians. Or a Candid Examination into the Merits of the Principal Speakers of the House of Lords* (1773).

[144] *The Letters of Junius*, ed. J. Cannon, (1978), pp. 196-7.

[145] *Papers of Benjamin Franklin*, XXI, 582.

[146] Cannon, *Aristocratic Century*, p. 170.

often claim to be closer to public opinion; the outcome of the crisis of 1783-4 suggests that by any measurable standard the rejection of the India bill received public endorsement.

In this period the most significant disagreement between the two Houses occurred over the Dissenters' bills of 1772-3. Religious debate began, if only in a small way, to polarize attitudes towards the House of Lords in the 1770s. Radical Dissenters thereafter drew a sharp distinction between the passage of their bills in the elected chamber and the defeat in its unelected counterpart.[147] Unitarians in particular developed a hostility to the House of Lords, and its bishops, as a result of the events of 1772-3, events which added yet more fuel to the Dissenting opposition to episcopacy in North America.[148] Moreover the attacks on episcopacy from both sides of the Atlantic undoubtedly strengthened the enmity of bishops in the Lords to the Dissenters' bills. This religious issue helped to promote the idea that the House of Lords possessed a separate and less defensible role than the Commons, and while this attitude was confined to a relatively small number of heterodox Dissenters, they were an articulate group with much influence upon the subsequent development of British radicalism.[149]

Yet although some radicals disliked the peerage and many Dissenters criticized the role of the Lords in 1772-3, all this was outweighed by the manner in which the same religious question helped the House of Lords to re-emerge as a champion of the orthodox Anglican majority. It was the Dissenters bills that led Johnson to proclaim in 1773: 'We know the House of Peers have made noble stands, when the House of Commons durst not. The last two years of a parliament they dare not contradict the populace'.[150] Probably he was too pessimistic, from his own point of view, as to the disposition of the 'populace'. From the spring of 1776, when the London press was filled with subscription lists of those anxious to alleviate 'the Distresses of the Clergy of the Church of England in North America',[151] to the outpouring of 'Church and King' sentiment in the 1790s, there is overwhelming evidence that the House of Lords was

---

[147] Among many other examples see A. Kippis, *A Vindication of the Protestant Dissenting Ministers* (2nd edn., 1773), pp. 52-5; and W. Belsham, *History of Great Britain, from the Revolution 1688, to the Conclusion of the Treaty of Amiens, 1802* (12 vols., 1805), VIII, 379-80.

[148] See J.M. Sosin, 'The Proposal in the Pre-Revolutionary Decade for Establishing Anglican Bishops in the Colonies', *Journal of Ecclesiastical History*, XIII (1962), 76-84; Dr. Williams's Library, London, Lindsey Correspondence: Theophilus Lindsey to William Turner, 2 June 1772.

[149] See J.C.D. Clark, *English Society 1688-1832. Ideology, Social Structure and Political Practice during the Ancien Regime*, (Cambridge, 1985), Chapter 5.

[150] Boswell, *Life*, V, 101-2.

[151] *Public Advertiser*, March and April 1776, *passim*. Similar lists may be found in *London Evening Post*, and other newspapers of these months.

in alignment with, not a target for, the forces of popular Anglicanism. As Langford has demonstrated for the 'country gentlemen and the broader body of provincial opinion', this process was facilitated by the American war and the contemporaneous religious issue.[152] When the mob threatened the House of Lords in 1780 it was to resist, not demand, religious liberalization. Perhaps in a wider sense the most important role enjoyed by the Lords lay in its contribution to the stability of the Hanoverian regime by helping to attach to it those – notably the High Church Tories of the earlier eighteenth century – whose previous alienation had been a major source of political instability. Their reconciliation after 1760 was a politically unifying factor and one which may at least in part be ascribed to the House of Lords.

[152] Langford, 'Old Whigs, Old Tories', p. 127.

Appendix

Division in the House of Lords, 25 November 1779

The division was on the question 'That words stand part' on the Address of Thanks in reply to the King's Speech at the opening of the session. The voting was *Contents* 90 (including 8 proxies), *Not Contents* 41. The tellers were Chesterfield (*Contents*) and Effingham (*Not Contents*).[153]

The Minority

There is a list of the minority of 41 lords, together with the names of six lords who 'went away', and the statement 'L. Weymouth absent', in P.R.O., State Papers (Domestic) 37/13, f. 258. The *London Evening Post* of 27–30 Nov. 1779 prints a similar, though not quite identical, list of the minority which omits Cumberland, adds Lyttelton, and does not include those who 'went away' or any mention of Weymouth.

For these purposes the P.R.O. list, which includes Cumberland in the minority and states that Lyttelton 'went away', will be used; newspaper accounts of eighteenth century parliamentary divisions tend to be among the least reliable of the versions which may be available. In this case the differences are only marginal.

The Majority

The total number of peers named as present in *L.J.*, XXXVI, 3–4, on 25 Nov. 1779 is 129. All those in the minority lists cited above, and the six lords who 'went away' before the division, are named as present in *L.J.*; according to *L.J.*, moreover, the P.R.O. list is correct in stating that Lord Weymouth was absent.

If one subtracts 47 (41 + 6) from 129, the remainder is 82, exactly the total of the lords who voted in person in the majority. It follows that the 82 lords listed as present in *L.J.* on 25 Nov. 1779 who are *not* in the minority list or among those who 'went away' comprise the entire group of personal voters in the majority.

The proxy votes in the majority can be identified from the Proxy Book for the session 1779–80 in the House of Lords Record Office. Eight proxies had been registered on or before the day of the division. As the number of proxy votes on the ministerial side was also eight, and as all eight holders of these proxy voters were present (and, as is argued above, voted) on that day, it is safe to assume that they all duly cast the proxy votes which had been entrusted to them. The final touch of authenticity is provided by the absence of the proxy voters themselves.

[153] See *L.J.*, XXXVI, 5, and Sainty and Dewar, *Divisions in the House of Lords*, microfiche 4.

Square brackets indicate editorial insertions. S = Scottish Representative Peer; I = Irish title. In the cases of Shelburne and Bessborough the Irish and British titles are given; it was by virtue of the latter, of course, that they were members of the House of Lords.

'Minority 25 Nov. 1779': P.R.O., S.P. 37/13, f. 258.

D. of Cumberland
    [Prince Henry Frederick]
    Manchester [4th Duke]
    Portland [3rd Duke]
    Bolton [6th Duke]
    Grafton [3rd Duke]
    Richmond [3rd Duke]
    Rutland [4th Duke]
    Devon[shire] [5th Duke]
M. of Rockingham [2nd Marquess]
E. of Coventry [6th Earl]
    Effingham [3rd Earl]
    Ferrers [6th Earl]
    Derby [12th Earl]
    Stamford [5th Earl]
    Scarbrough [4th Earl]
    Abingdon [4th Earl]
    Chatham [2nd Earl]
    Tankerville [4th Earl]
    Radnor [2nd Earl]
    Temple [3rd Earl]
    Spencer [1st Earl]
    Cholmondeley [4th Earl]
    Egremont [3rd Earl]
    Harcourt [2nd Earl]
    Fitzwilliam [2nd Earl]
    Jersey [4th Earl]

    Suffolk [14th Earl]
V. Hereford [12th Viscount]
    Courtenay [2nd Viscount]
L. Abergavenny [17th Baron]
    Craven [6th Baron]
    Camden [1st Baron]
    Beaulieu [1st Baron]
    Shelburne [2nd Earl (I):
      Baron Wycombe (GB)]
    Foley [2nd Baron]
    Bessborough [2nd Earl (I):
      Baron Ponsonby (GB)]
    King [6th Baron]
    St. John [13th Baron]
B. of St. Asaph [Jonathan Shipley]
    Peterborough [John Hinchliffe]
    Carlisle [Edmund Law]

went away

D. of Gloucester [Prince William Henry]
E. Sussex [3rd Earl]
    Plymouth [5th Earl]
    Hardwicke [2nd Earl]
L. Lyttelton [2nd Baron]
    Sondes [1st Baron]

L. Weymouth absent.

The Majority of 82 lords in the division on the Address, 25 Nov. 1779; compiled from presence list in *L.J.* XXXVI, 3-4.

[The names are arranged, according to rank, and within rank, in the order in which they appear in *L.J.*]

Beaufort [5th Duke]
Marlborough [4th Duke]
Queensberry [4th Duke(S)]
Ancaster & Kesteven [5th Duke]
Chandos [3rd Duke]
Dorset [3rd Duke]
Bridgwater [3rd Duke]
Northumberland [1st Duke]
Lothian [5th Marquess(S)]
Bathurst [2nd Earl]

Dartmouth [2nd Earl]
Talbot [1st Earl]
Hertford [1st Earl]
Huntingdon [10th Earl]
Denbigh [6th Earl]
Peterborough & Monmouth [5th Earl]
Chesterfield [5th Earl]
Sandwich [4th Earl]
Essex [4th Earl]
Carlisle [5th Earl]

Gainsborough [6th Earl]

Rochford [4th Earl]

Cassilis [10th Earl(S)]

Abercorn [8th Earl(S)]

Galloway [7th Earl(S)]

Loudoun [4th Earl(S)]

Dalhousie [8th Earl(S)]

Marchmont [3rd Earl(S)]

Oxford [4th Earl]

Aylesford [4th Earl]

Macclesfield [3rd Earl]

Pomfret [2nd Earl]

Ashburnham [2nd Earl]

Brooke [2nd Earl]

Powis [2nd Earl]

De La Warr [3rd Earl]

Northington [2nd Earl]

Hillsborough [1st Earl]

Ailesbury [1st Earl]

Clarendon [1st Earl]

Mansfield [1st Earl]

Montague [7th Viscount]

Say & Sele [6th Viscount]

Townshend [4th Viscount]

Stormont [7th Viscount(S)]

Falmouth [2nd Viscount]

Wentworth [2nd Viscount]

Dudley & Ward [2nd Viscount]

Hampden [1st Viscount]

Thurlow [1st Baron]

Le Despencer [11th Baron]

Willoughby [De] Br[oke] [14th Baron]

Paget [10th Baron]

Osborne [Baron]

Onslow [4th Baron]

Cadogan [3rd Baron]

Montfort [2nd Baron]

Edgecumbe [3rd Baron]

Sandys [2nd Baron]

Grantham [2nd Baron]

Scarsdale [1st Baron]

Boston [2nd Baron]

Pelham [2nd Baron]

Amherst [1st Baron]

Brownlow [1st Baron]

Rivers [1st Baron]

Harrowby [1st Baron]

[*Archbishops*]

   Canterbury [Frederick Cornwallis]

   York [William Markham]

[*Bishops*]

   London [Robert Lowth]

   Ely [Edmund Keene]

   Chichester [Sir William Ashburnham]

   Llandaff [Shute Barrington]

   Worcester [Brownlow North]

   Rochester [John Thomas]

   Lichfield & Coventry [Richard Hurd]

   Bangor [John Moore]

   Chester [Beilby Porteus]

   Oxford [John Butler]

   Exeter [John Ross]

   Lincoln [Thomas Thurlow]

   St. David's [John Warren]

Proxy voters in the majority.

[The proxy voters are listed in the order in which they appear in the Proxy Book for 1779–80. The holder of each proxy is added in square brackets.]

Ker [2nd Earl]   [Proxy held by Ailesbury]

Rosebery [3rd Earl(S)]   [Proxy held by Loudoun]

Newcastle [2nd Duke]   [Proxy held by Stormont]

Somerset [9th Duke]   [Proxy held by Hertford]

Bishop of Norwich   [Proxy held by Beilby Porteus, Bishop of Chester]
  [Philip Yonge]

Exeter [9th Earl]   [Proxy held by Sandwich]

Guilford [1st Earl]   [Proxy held by Dartmouth]

Breadalbane [3rd Earl(S)]   [Proxy held by Clarendon]

Index